Stress, Coping, and Relationships
in Adolescence

RESEARCH MONOGRAPHS IN ADOLESCENCE
Nancy L. Galambos/Nancy A. Busch-Rossnagel, Editors

Cohen/Cohen • Life Values and Adolescent Mental Health

Côté • Adolescent Storm and Stress: An Evaluation
of the Mead–Freeman Controversy

Seiffge-Krenke • Stress, Coping, and Relationships
in Adolescence

Stress, Coping, and Relationships in Adolescence

Inge Seiffge-Krenke
University of Bonn, Germany

LEA LAWRENCE ERLBAUM ASSOCIATES, PUBLISHERS
1995   Mahwah, New Jersey   Hove, UK

Lawrence Erlbaum Associates, Inc., Publishers
10 Industrial Avenue
Mahwah, New Jersey 07430

Library of Congress Cataloging-in-Publication Data

Seiffge-Krenke, Inge.
    Stress, coping, and relationships in adolescence / Inge Seiffge-
Krenke.
        p.   cm. — (Research monographs in adolescence)
    Includes bibliographical references and indexes.
    ISBN 0-8058-1235-0 (alk. paper)
    1. Stress in adolescence. 2. Adjustment (Psychology) in
adolescence. 3. Interpersonal relations in adolescence. I. Title.
II. Series.
    BF724.3.S86S45 1995
    155.5′18—dc20   95-19661
                                                           CIP

Books published by Lawrence Erlbaum Associates are printed on acid-free
paper, and their bindings are chosen for strength and durability.

Printed in the United States of America
10 9 8 7 6 5 4 3 2 1

To Dirk, David, and Moritz

Contents

Preface

The passing from childhood to adolescence and from adolescence to adulthood have both been considered developmental transitions (Cornell & Furman, 1984). According to Antonovsky (1981), individuals tend to become more vulnerable during periods of biological, social, and psychological transition. In this book, developmental aspects of dealing with normative stressors are investigated. Of special relevance is the manner of coping with these demands and the functions that close relationships may fulfill in this context. Current research on adolescent development differs from earlier research in important aspects. First, the quantity has dramatically increased, as evidenced by increased numbers of journal articles, new journals, and edited volumes on adolescence accompanied by the foundation of new professional societies and an increasing number of researchers concerning themselves with this area (Petersen, 1988). Second, important changes in adolescent theory and research are obvious. There has been a shift from stage-oriented approaches, which focus on the aspect of turmoil, to process-oriented approaches, which stress the ability of the adolescents to function well (Keating, 1987). Cross-sectional and longitudinal studies on large representative samples are becoming more common. Development in many areas is now conceptualized as involving continuous, progressive changes rather than a transformation from one stage to another. The rosy picture of increasingly positive development over adolescence even seems to be true when we analyze adolescents living under divergent economic, political, and social conditions. Although it is hard to objectively compare the stress adolescents had in previous generations, the data of Offer and his coworkers (see e.g., Offer, Ostrov, & Howard, 1989) do not indicate that the 1980s were more stressful for teenagers than were previous decades. Fend (1988), in comparing representative surveys in West Germany from 1956 to 1980, came to the same conclusions. How can we explain this basic competence in coping and what are the mechanisms and processes that lead to a positive outcome? What precisely is the function of close relationships to parents and friends in this process? And what can be said about those adolescents who are unable to cope with stressors during the transition period?

The idea for this book originated in 1984, during my first studies on stress and coping. Dissatisfied with research on adolescent coping, which reflected so little of the everyday experiences of adolescents, I became interested in the appraisal of everyday events, the analysis of coping strategies, and the influence of internal and social resources on the coping process. In the process, it occurred to me that social support is too narrow a construct for examining the influence of close relationships on stress and coping. This crucial developmental perspective, including changes in perceived stressors, in the ways of coping with these demands, and in relationships with significant others was later supplemented by the clinical perspective, which is dealt with in a separate volume.

This book sets out to explore the activities, thoughts, and feelings of adolescents when dealing with naturally occurring stressors. I begin with a literature review in chapter 1, where the major shortcomings and limitations of coping research that set the starting point for our own research are discussed. Chapter 2 looks at our own project and provides an outline of the seven studies detailed in this book. Based on a model of stress, coping, and outcome, the main research questions and research methods are briefly discussed. Then, an overview of the seven studies is given to answer these questions. Although the seven studies presented were carried out in Germany, comparison with cross-cultural results enabled us to apply the findings to a more general context.

In the next three chapters, aspects of everyday events in the lives of adolescents and the manner in which young people tackle them are considered. In chapter 3, the process of coping with these minor events is analyzed, whereas in chapter 4 the emphasis shifts to the consideration of event parameters that may influence adolescents' coping behavior. In chapter 5, the focus is on presenting instruments that, based on the first two studies, were developed to allow the assessment of minor stressors and coping style on larger and more representative samples. Furthermore, the important distinction between functional and dysfunctional coping styles is discussed. The findings demonstrate the great competence of adolescents in dealing with minor stressors while at the same time highlighting the differential nature of functional coping according to age, gender, and socioeconomic status. Furthermore, we see how the context or situation influences how one copes.

Based on these results, chapter 6 addresses the question of important internal resources for functional coping such as self-concept and personality type. The coping–defense debate is reappraised in light of our data. Chapter 7 looks at adolescents in the context of the family situation. More specifically, family characteristics that contribute to functional or dysfunctional coping behavior are discussed. The long-term consequences of perceived family climate on stress perception and coping style are then analyzed. In chapter 8, another social resource, friends and peers, is considered. This chapter looks at the types of friendships formed by adolescents and the purposes they serve. Do close friends serve as coping models? In what ways do close friends offer support and coping assistance? By analyzing adolescent diaries and investigating diarists, the role of the diary as a possible coping aid is also explored.

In chapter 9, issues relating to adolescents' health are brought into focus. Important variables throughout this book such as stressors and internal and social resources are brought together to address the question of stress-buffering. Two different models were tested, the interaction model and the main effect model. Finally, chapter 10 provides an overall review and summary of all seven studies presented in the previous chapters and discusses what conclusions can be drawn. It may provide guidance for those working and living with adolescents.

ACKNOWLEDGMENTS

In this volume, studies on normal samples are presented. Since the 1980s, 2,176 German adolescents, ages 12–19, took part in the cross-sectional and longitudinal studies described in this book. Furthermore, about 1,200 adolescents were investigated in Israel, Finland, and the United States. I express my gratitude to all these adolescents together with their parents. I also thank several of my postgraduate students and assistants, who contributed to different parts of the studies: Ralph Drewes, Gerlinde Aland, Anette Ries, Gaby Sautner, Gerlinde Dravoy, Merja Luwe, Annette Boeger, Carina Schmidt, and Frank Kollmar. Several of my projects in the field of stress, coping, and relationship have been supplemented by grants. The Coping Process Study has been supported by the Deutsche Forschungsgemeinschaft (No. 408 1/3), as has been the Event Exploration Study (No. 408 2/3) and the Survey Study (No. 408 3/3). In addition, parts of the Diary Study have been granted by the Deutsche Forschungsgemeinschaft (No. 408 3/1). The longitudinal study on stress perception and coping style related to perceived family climate is part of an ongoing research project on Coping with Illness funded through a grant by the Bundesministerium für Forschung und Technologie (No. 0706567).

Over the years, many colleagues in the field of developmental psychology have assisted me by providing valuable comments and criticism related to my work. I have profited greatly by discussing aspects of family relations with Catherine Cooper and Harold Grotevant and topics of friends and friendships with Brett Laursen. As well, I wish to acknowledge with gratitude the contributions made by Bruce Compas and Stuart Hauser toward developing my ideas on coping with stress in an individual and family perspective. Some of the studies discussed in this book were conducted in close collaboration with Shmuel Shulman from

Tel-Aviv University, whose support has been admirable over all these years. I am also grateful to Anne Petersen, who not only pioneered the first U.S. test of the CASQ, but also encouraged me to write this book and helped me to establish initial contact with Lawrence Erlbaum Associates. Nancy Busch-Rossnagel and Nancy Galambos, as series editors, have provided substantial editorial assistance, and through their kind encouragement, made it a pleasure to work on this book. Special thanks are due to Cornelia Daub-Metz, who patiently deciphered and typed the various drafts of the manuscript. For her extraordinarily efficient and conscientious secretarial assistance I am very grateful. Annekatrin Ott and Nicole Aengenheister worked through the final version and helped in preparing the references; Roland Röhrig prepared the figures. My thanks also to Christina Hottner and Linda Lewis, who competently assisted me in preparing the translation of the present work.

Inge Seiffge-Krenke

Adolescent Coping:
Pointing to a Research Deficit

In accordance with Petersen and Spiga (1982), *adolescence* is defined here as a period of transition characterized by accelerated processes of change in cognitive, social, and psychological functioning, accompanied by marked physical restructuring. As research on adolescent development shows (cf. Douvan & Adelson, 1966; Offer & Offer, 1975), successful adaptation in adolescence rather than crisis should be given more prominence in research. This is supported by the fact that continuous focusing on and solving of developmental problems seems to be the rule, whereas failure in the coping process is comparatively rare (e.g., Coleman, 1978). Recently, Bosma and Jackson (1990) suggested that adolescence can profitably be seen as a period of successful coping, and of productive adaptation. The adolescent is confronted with many different changes and is able to adapt to these changes in a constructive fashion, and in a way that results in developmental advance. Considering the large variety of tasks and problems encountered, adolescence is characterized by impressively effective coping in the majority of young people, a fact that has been widely neglected.

Lazarus (Lazarus & Launier, 1978) defined *coping* as "efforts . . . to manage (i.e., master, reduce, minimize) environmental and internal demands and conflicts which tax or exceed a person's resources" (p. 288) and this shows that coping is a hypothetical construct that is sufficiently complex to take into account both person-specific and situation-specific aspects. In Lazarus' research, stressors and social resources are also two important concepts. In the approach here, I go beyond the concepts of social resources and social support, and look more generally at relationships, which may contribute indirectly to coping. Because all three constructs (stress, coping, and relationships) cover a broad range of meanings (S. Cohen & Wills, 1985; Elliot & Eisdorfer, 1982; Lazarus & Folkman, 1991) and are

1

not independent of each other, this chapter begins by analyzing more thoroughly research using *adolescent coping* as its key concept. The significance of coping behavior is evident in resiliency research showing that it is coping that makes the difference in both the adaptational outcome (Garmezy, 1983; Werner & Smith, 1982) and in research on symptomatology, illustrating that the most reliable predictor for mental health is not so much a lack of symptoms, but the competence with which age-specific developmental tasks are handled (Achenbach & Edelbrock, 1987; Compas, Davis, Forsythe, & Wagner, 1987).

In adult research, a tradition in coping has long been established (Lazarus & Folkman, 1991). In recent years, more interest has been shown in questions of coping behavior in adolescence, reflected by an increasing number of conferences and publications on this subject. Two different phases in research on adolescent coping are clearly apparent and are dealt with later on. Furthermore, approaches differ in Anglo-American and European studies. In the following, I sum up and comment on research on adolescent coping.

HISTORICAL DEVELOPMENT AND THEORETICAL CONCEPTS IN COPING RESEARCH

Before delineating research trends in adolescent coping, some introductory remarks on conceptualization and research trends in adult studies should be given. Since the publication of Lazarus' (1966) book, *Psychological Stress and the Coping Process*, coping appears more and more often as an independent key word in the subject index of *Psychological Abstracts* (before, relevant publications on this topic could only be found under headings like "adaptation," "mastery," or "competence"). A review of the number of publications on coping since its introduction by Lazarus (1966) shows that, following a dramatic increase in research activity in the mid-1970s, interest in coping behavior has remained consistently high (see Seiffge-Krenke, 1986). In 1984, for example, the *Journal of Personality and Social Psychology* devoted an entire issue to coping in adults, and an equivalent volume summing up adolescent coping was published in the *Journal of Adolescence* in 1993, illustrating again a certain delay in research including adolescents.

As the term *coping* can include all types of observable reactions to a particular event, Pearlin and Schooler's (1978) criticism regarding the "bewildering richness of coping relevant behavior" (p. 4) seems to be justified. The coping concept as used in this book, however, is based on the definition by Lazarus, which seems to have met the highest consensus. As stated already, Lazarus, Averill, and Opton (1974) defined coping as "problem solving efforts made by an individual when the demands he faces are highly relevant to his welfare . . . and where these demands tax his adaptive resources" (p. 15). This view of coping takes into account situational elements and classifies different reactions to potentially stressful or challenging stimuli. There are other approaches that emphasize the functionality and effectiveness of coping (cf. Pearlin & Schooler, 1978; Rodin, 1980). These authors postulate certain person–environment changes to be a result of the coping process and this is reflected in their definitions of coping. Lazarus focused primarily on the cognitive, information-processing aspects of coping, and shares with Haan (1977) and Meichenbaum, Henshaw, and Himel (1982) a view of coping as problem-solving behavior. However, even among those authors who regard coping as problem-solving behavior, there exist major differences. This is a result of different orientations and research traditions, and a result of independent approaches. This can be shown by comparing the work of Haan and Lazarus.

Both Lazarus et al. (1974) and Haan (1977) stressed the role of cognitive functions in coping with critical events. According to Lazarus' theory, three interconnected cognitive discrimination and evaluation processes are necessary for successful problem solving: primary appraisal, secondary appraisal, and reappraisal. Whereas Lazarus emphasized cognitive evaluation processes in coping, Haan distinguished between successful coping, and processes of defense or fragmentation. As Haan explained, coping processes are goal-directed, flexible, and allow an appropriate expression of affect. Defense processes, on the other hand, are rigid and inappropriate to reality, including distortion of affect. These two processes differ only quantitatively with respect to the criteria of affect expression, reality orientation, and goal directedness; fragmentation, on the other hand, represents a switch into pathology: The reactions are automatic, ritualized, and irrational. Lazarus' and Haan's approaches to coping also differ with regard to the dynamics and stability attributed to the construct. Whereas Haan (1977) emphasized trait components, Lazarus stressed situational specifity. In his process-oriented model of coping, trait aspects are secondary and situations and actualization possibilities very much in the foreground. Sources of coping are to be found both in the person (problem-solving abilities, attitudes) and in the environment (financial resources, social support). Both determine the way coping is realized in a particular situation. In his classification of coping processes, Lazarus distinguished between the mode (e.g., action, inhibition of action, information seeking) and the function of coping (e.g., problem-oriented vs. palliative). Coping processes are the result of transactional relationships between situational and personality variables (Lazarus & Launier, 1978; Roskies & Lazarus, 1980): "Stress occurs neither in the person nor in the situation, although it is dependent upon both. It arises much more from the way in which the person evaluates the adaptive relationship" (Lazarus, 1981, p. 204). Lazarus chose the concept of transaction for this relationship because it emphasizes the reciprocal influence of personality and situational characteristics. Thus, it is not a one-sided, linear model, but a bidirectional model that takes into account the effects of the coping behavior itself on the person and the situation.

To sum up, the construct of coping has proved somewhat hard to pin down. A number of different definitions of coping exist, in part due to the fact that different aspects of the construct have been focused on, for example, the coping process, personal characteristics, person–environment interaction, or the effects of coping (Krohne, 1990). In addition to theoretical and conceptual problems, methodological problems arise (Panzarine, 1985). For example, how might the effect of situational components be distinguished from personal ones? Also, the determination of relevant situation parameters is crucial (Lazarus & Folkman, 1991). Further methodological problems may arise from the complicated temporal conditions of the individual parameters (Folkman & Lazarus, 1985). The confounding of coping with outcome is a problem outlined impressively by Lazarus and Folkman (1991), when efficacy is implied by coping and inefficacy by defense. The focus of research has undergone some change, too. Historically, the differentiation of various coping modalities (e.g., instrumental or palliative coping, cf. Lazarus & Launier, 1978) and the coping–defense debate (cf. Haan, 1974, 1977) was followed in the late 1970s by a shift in research trends, from a trait-oriented approach (Haan, 1974; Vaillant, 1977) to a transactional perspective (Lazarus et al., 1974). In this context it should be considered that coping research originally derived from animal experimentation and ego-psychoanalysis, and that both have influenced coping theory and measurement. Therefore, traditional models of coping tend to emphasize cognitive traits or styles, which results in speaking of people who are *repressors* or *sensitizers* or people who are *deniers* or *copers*. But trait conceptualizations and measures of coping underestimate the complexity and variability of actual coping efforts, and this has led to the development of models attempting to integrate aspects of both the person and the environment. Furthermore, the concept of stressors in this research has been refined. In the 1980s, a change from the analysis of critical events to the investigation of both mildly stressful, normative events (Kanner, Coyne, Schaefer, & Lazarus, 1981) and long-term, chronic stressors has taken place (Lazarus & Folkman, 1991).

To conclude, many of the theoretical conceptualizations and operationalizations arose from research on adults. Despite the impressive amount of research activity, coping research has not yet been able to provide satisfactory solutions to some conceptual and methodological problems.

RESEARCH TRENDS IN ADOLESCENT COPING: THE FIRST PHASE (1967–1985)

Coping research on adolescents has not yet reached a comparable degree of differentiation. Due to the small amount of research activity, it has been limited to certain specific questions and approaches (cf. Seiffge-Krenke, 1986). Two phases can be clearly differentiated in research on adolescent coping: (a) a clinically oriented approach until the mid-1980s, and (b) a more developmentally oriented approach since about 1985. In these phases, different sampling and research methods have been used. In the following, the history and background of coping research on adolescents are described together with a summary of the more important results in this area. Possible reasons for the quantitative and qualitative differences between coping research in adults and adolescents are examined and an explanation is given for the differing approaches in Europe and the Anglophonic countries in early coping research. Since the later 1980s, both research trends are converging.

Upon analyzing the publications on coping that appeared between 1967 and 1984, it becomes apparent that over a period of nearly 20 years only about 7% of the publications are devoted to studies on adolescents, whereas 42% deal with adults and 17% with children. College students make up for a further 24% of the subjects, and in 10% of the studies age was not specified (see Fig. 1.1).

Regarding content, research on adults and adolescents has followed a similar path. A large number of studies in both age groups investigated coping with critical life events (31% of the studies on adults and 22% on adolescents) and coping with more everyday stressors (21% of the studies on adults and 11% on adolescents). In the literature, coping with illness apparently entails coping with a critical life event, but it appears to be a strong and homogeneous research question. Accordingly, we have categorized coping with serious illness separately. As one would expect, more research has been carried out on adults coping with a very serious, chronic illness than on adolescents (35% on adults vs. 24% on adolescents). Theoretical and methodological problems received very little attention in adolescent research; only 6% of the studies on adolescent coping are concerned with this question and consequently no new models have been presented in this early phase of coping research.

Adding up the percentages of the three topics "everyday stressors," "physical illness," and "critical life events," it is shown in Fig. 1.2 that a general category "coping with stress" takes up more room in the literature than any other question

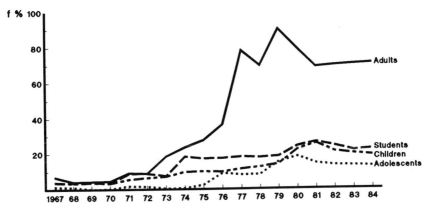

FIG. 1.1. Relative proportion of publications on the subject "coping" from 1967 to 1984, differentiated according to age groups (Source: *Psychological Abstracts*).

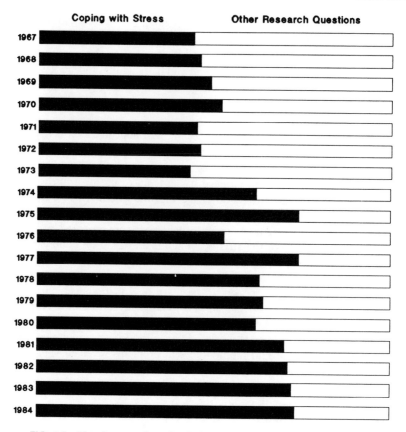

FIG. 1.2. Classification of articles dealing with adolescents under the subject heading "coping," subdivided into "coping with stress" and "other research questions" (Source: *Psychological Abstracts*).

of coping behavior, such as operationalization or methodology, developmental aspects, and so on.

As can be seen in Fig. 1.2, in 1984 two thirds of all publications on coping in adolescence were concerned with major and minor stress. The most important results of both research areas are discussed here.

Coping With Critical Life Events

Since 1975, a great deal of attention has been directed toward critical life events in research on coping in adolescence. A comparison with studies on adults reveals similar developments and proportions of research activity—with a certain time lag in the research peaks (1973 for adults, 1975 for adolescents). However, one must take into account that of the 265 studies concerning coping with critical

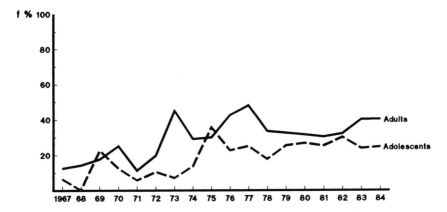

FIG. 1.3. Comparison of research activities on critical life events in adolescents and adults between 1967 and 1984 (Source: *Psychological Abstracts*).

life events between 1967 and 1984 only 20% (49 studies) were carried out on adolescents (see Fig. 1.3).

For a long time, the number of articles concerning clinical or epidemiological aspects of critical life events (cf. B. S. Dohrenwend & Dohrenwend, 1974, 1981) was disproportionately large. Critical life events had been used as an organizing principle to explain changes over the total life span, and increasing attention had been paid to social, financial, and psychological resources for coping with critical life events (Kahn & Antonucci, 1980; Nuckolls, 1972). An analysis of the literature on adolescent coping with critical life events shows that the problems in life event research on adults, particularly those from the earlier, epidemiologically oriented phase, are even stronger here. Studies on critical life events in adolescence, published between 1967 and 1984, were almost exclusively clinically oriented and can be roughly grouped into three categories: (a) studies on critical life events in the stricter sense compared to studies with adults; (b) studies on very serious, traumatic events; and (c) studies on the relationship between a critical life event and subsequent psychological disorder or physical illness.

In one third of the studies on adolescents, critical life events in the sense of Holmes and Rahe (1967) were analyzed. These studies investigated how adolescents coped with the divorce of their parents (M. Steinberg, 1974; Young, 1980), with the end of schooling (Weinberger & Reuter, 1980), or with unplanned pregnancy (e.g., Coletta, Hadler, & Gregg, 1981). Adolescents from broken homes and those faced with unexpected motherhood or fatherhood have been studied most intensively, considering also the effects of age, gender (Hendricks, 1980; Parks, 1977), and social support (Coletta et al., 1981). Unplanned pregnancy at an early age, for example, entails the following profound changes: Most adolescents leave school, give up their friends, and live in conditions of financial hardship. When a critical life event occurs at a time that differs substantially from the formal or informal age norms, it entails the risk of losing social support (Brim & Ryff,

1980). One can therefore expect that because of the deviation from the age norm, pregnancy will affect a 14-year-old girl more strongly than a 24-year-old woman who has already fulfilled at least some of her developmental tasks.

Possibly because of the very threatening nature of critical life events, studies on adolescents were often combined with a crisis intervention program. In fact, the supplementary offer of crisis intervention seems to be specific to studies on adolescents. Weinberger and Reuter (1980), for example, accompanied a school class during their last year of school and helped preparing them to leave home, friends, and family and to anticipate a new life phase. Young (1980) set up a predivorce workshop for young people that included the integration and gradual coping with the divorce event over a period of several weeks, up to the final court date.

As in research on adults, the relation between critical life events and the occurrence of psychological illness has been investigated on adolescents. The question of interest is whether there is an association between critical life events and the occurrence of psychosomatic disorder (Zlatich, Kenny, Sila, & Huang, 1982), anxiety attacks (Dzegede, Pike, & Hackworth, 1981), attempted suicide (Isherwood, Adam, & Hornblow, 1982), or depression (Chatterjee, Mukherjee, & Nandi, 1981; Finlay-Jones & Brown, 1981). In these large epidemiological studies, several thousand subjects from different age groups were examined. The results for adolescents were similar to those of the younger and older subjects. For example, Andrews' (1981) extensive longitudinal study of 1,500 subjects, including adolescents, found that individuals who were symptom-free at the beginning of the study did indeed undergo critical life events about 3 months prior to the occurrence of certain symptoms. As in studies on adults, however, the problem of causal interpretation remains.

About half of the publications between 1967 and 1984 on adolescent coping with critical life events are concerned with unusually stressful events such as kidnapping (Terr, 1979), rape (McCombie, 1976), temporary imprisonment (R. Johnson, 1978), homosexual abuse (R. Johnson, 1978), murder of family members or school friends (Meyers & Pitt, 1976; Morawetz, 1982; Petti & Wells, 1980), and traumatic accidents (Bulman & Wortman, 1977). Because of their low level of controllability and extremely harmful effects, all the events studied pose a particularly noxious threat to the development of these young people. Early occurrence of the events, lack of compensatory resources, and unavoidable finality are characteristic features. They seem to clash with other age-typical developmental tasks. Rape endangers the separation from home, the attainment of spatial independence, and the testing of sexuality just as it is beginning (McCombie, 1976). Cancer in a parent causes the adolescent to undergo overt role changes (e.g., increased responsibility for household tasks and siblings), but also leads to a subtle restructuring wherein the adolescent becomes the new partner of the remaining, healthy parent (Wellisch, 1979). Even the death of a sibling usually entails an increase in duties and responsibilities, sometimes resulting in a stabilization of the parents at the expense of the adolescent's own chance to mourn (Morawetz, 1982). A traumatic event, like the one described by Terr (1979, 1983) in *Children of Chowchilla*, where an entire school class was kidnapped, arouses regressive needs and fear of parental loss, thus hindering autonomy and separation.

Events that have been investigated under the topic *critical life events* are therefore primarily those that result in loss or damage as described by Lazarus (1966). In half of the studies, the event was so severe that the term *trauma* would be more appropriate. Analyses of how these events are dealt with focus on defense processes and symptom formation, rather than on successful coping. Global effects, often rated by people other than the affected (e.g., Hendricks, 1980; Morawetz, 1982; Parks, 1977), have been used as a measure of coping. Very few studies distinguished between strategies chosen by the young people during the different coping phases (e.g., hours, days, or months after the event). Often, the various offers of social support were not analyzed.

Terr's (1979) study deserves particular attention because of the homogeneity of the event. Twenty-six children and adolescents were kidnapped in their school bus and freed after 46 hours. Terr was able to differentiate between short- and long-term consequences of the event and analyzed the coping process over different phases. Her work, like that by McCombie (1976), shows that the time impact, or the phase of coping one chooses to study, respectively, is critically important. The phase of increased defense and simultaneous reduction in anxiety that immediately follows an acute shock and anxiety reaction, is often mistakenly interpreted as successful coping (e.g., Bulman & Wortman, 1977). In the third phase, coping efforts are renewed. This takes into account positive and negative aspects, which together with one's own participation seem to be more adequate criteria for successful coping. These studies also make clear that the most effective interventions are those that immediately follow the event.

Coping With Serious Physical Illness

The way adolescents deal with serious physical disease is the most frequently studied question on coping in adolescence. Compared with adults, however, the absolute number of studies on adolescents is fairly small (61 as opposed to 290, as of 1984). The comparatively small number of adolescents affected by a serious illness suggests that this event is to be regarded as a non-normative event. Despite the large amount of space this question takes up in studies on adolescents, only some of the most important results are considered here because the majority of the studies are single-case analyses or reports on very small groups. This is partly due to the low incidence of these kinds of illnesses, but it also reflects the clinical orientation of most authors. Often, the illnesses studied are those with a very low risk of contagion and a high mortality rate as no treatment is yet available. These include heart disease (e.g., J. Mehler, 1979), hormonal diseases (e.g.,

Drotar, Owens, & Gotthold, 1980), cancer (e.g., Earle, 1979; Kikuchi, 1977), sickle-cell anemia (e.g., LePontois, 1975), and Huntington's disease (e.g., Elash, 1977). On the other hand, coping with frequently occurring, less severe physical and mental handicaps (Anderson, 1979; Lynch & Arndt, 1973) play a smaller role. Serious physical illness requires the person affected to cope not only with chronicity and the accelerated breakdown of physical and mental abilities, but also with death. All the studies show the extraordinary extent to which adolescents feel threatened by the physical changes that accompany the disease. This is very pronounced in a study by Earle (1979), who analyzed the reactions of adolescents with bone cancer to amputation. Often, the increasing loss of control was experienced as significantly more threatening than the actual mortality rate (Stoddard, 1982). Several authors carried out very precise process analyses beginning at the time the patient was first informed about the disease, often up to the death of the adolescent. Thus, the different coping modalities used by the adolescents, including support measures provided by their social network, were impressively documented. One very important factor appears to be the information about the disease; at different stages of the disease the young people asked for information in very different ways (Mehler, 1979). Because the young people are dependent on others for a long period of time, they often develop highly aggressive attachments to the caregiver, in most cases the mother (LePontois, 1975). As helpful and supportive as the family network may be for the young person, the parents' unlimited care does represent a major problem to them, because the increased drive for separation that is specific to this phase is delayed or even made impossible. Also, studies on less seriously ill adolescents show that they often feel "over-mothered" even in relatively healthy phases (e.g., Ritchie, 1981) and that parents find it difficult to overlook the illness or handicap and to permit the young person to develop independence (Minde, 1978). Because regular school attendance is not possible and contacts with peers are limited, adolescents afflicted with a serious illness often end up in a situation that is in many respects deficient. Rapid status changes in their peer groups as a result of the illness are a source of concern (Easson, 1970), and the adolescents also worry about the increased physical degeneration. Male adolescents find it particularly difficult to cope with impairments to their strength and physical abilities (Hofmann & Becker, 1979), whereas female adolescents suffer more from changes that make them outwardly less attractive (Weinberg, 1968).

The severity of the studied disorders makes it obvious why it is mainly the sick person's defense behavior that is analyzed. This includes the previously mentioned modalities of information regulation. Furthermore, in extreme cases, the severity of the illness is denied. Hofmann and Becker (1979) reported that the denial of particularly severe physical impairment, but also of the approaching death, may be shared by the parents. Especially frequent is intellectualization that, according to Blos (1967), is the preferred defense mechanism of adolescents in general. Although cognitive coping with the illness appears to be successful, the adolescents remain retarded in emotional coping and infantile behaviors reoccur. Projective coping, a mechanism used equally by the ill adolescents and their parents, permits tensions to be loaded onto people outside the family (e.g., nursing personnel, see Earle, 1979). It was in this context that Rutter, Graham, Chadwick, and Yule (1976) pointed out the compensatory benefits of a relationship with the psychologically more stable parent. In his summary of studies on adolescents with severe chronic illness, Geist (1979) concluded that psychological intervention is successful only when it is carried out during the initial stage of the illness, because this is when the appropriate switches can be made for coping behavior.

Coping With Minor Stressors

Since about 1980 a noticeable trend can be observed in adult coping research away from the analysis of very stressful events to the analysis of everyday stress situations operationalized in Lazarus' concept of everyday hassles as "irritating, frustrating, distressing demands that in some degree characterize everyday transactions" (Kanner et al., 1981, p. 9). Although adolescent research shows that it is not so much the major crises, but rather the minor everyday conflicts between adolescents and their parents that are most significant and preoccupy the adolescents (Coleman, George, & Holt, 1977; Montemayor, 1986), we were able to find only a few studies on adolescent coping with minor stressors in Anglophonic studies published before 1984. As shown in Fig. 1.4, since 1975 there have been significantly fewer studies on coping with less stressful factors than on coping with critical life events or coping with severe physical impairments.

The average percentage of studies between 1967 and 1984 on coping with minor stressors (11%) amounts to exactly half of the research activity devoted

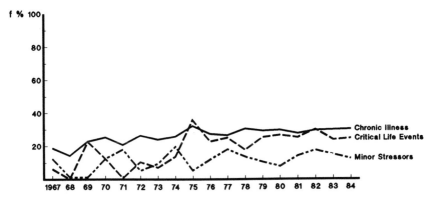

FIG. 1.4.   Percentage of studies investigating minor stressors compared with studies on critical life events or chronic illness in adolescence (Source: *Psychological Abstracts*).

to the analysis of adolescents' coping with critical life events over the same period of time. These studies focus on tasks and difficulties confronting the adolescent that do not pose a serious threat to him or her. Most of these studies are concerned with aspects of coping behavior at school or at work. They include investigations of the effects of school structure reorganization on the classroom climate (e.g., Schilhab, 1977), on the students' well-being (Vandewiele, 1980), and on their tendency to turn to other occupations in class (see activities listed under the category "goofing off" in the work by Everhart, 1982), as well as analyses of differences between adolescents with effective and ineffective coping strategies in performance situations (e.g., Dweck & Wortman, 1982; Jacks & Keller, 1978). Coping with the threat of unemployment was studied by Fleming and Lavercombe (1982). Such studies, most of which were carried out in Great Britain, reveal that about one third of those questioned had been confronted with this problem at some stage, and that the time the problem began, possibly directly after leaving school, and the duration of unemployment, had a clear influence on the choice of coping strategies. An early onset and a long period of unemployment led to lasting passivity in the young people.

The influence of social support by parents, friends, and institutions has also been studied in this regard. Generally, the relationship to parents (Sharma, Sarawathi, & Gir, 1981), teachers (Carducci, 1980), or authority figures (Hauser & Shapiro, 1976) plays a more important role than contacts with peers, so that apparently only a certain segment of the social support system has been assessed. Interestingly, several studies can be found on coping with family-related stress (e.g., the studies by Moffatt, 1975; Moos & Billings, 1982; Rouse, Waller, & Ewing, 1973; Sachs, 1977, on adolescents in families with alcoholics), but there are scarcely any on coping with age-typical problems in peer groups (Newman & Newman, 1975). Not only are studies on coping with minor stressors under-represented in the Anglophonic literature, but also both their content and methodology need improvement. The term *coping* used in most of the studies can hardly be distinguished from more general constructs such as *behavior* or *development*. Operational definitions are hardly given and coping is often globally assessed on the basis of evaluations by teachers or parents, or on the basis of ratings by the researcher. The actual process of coping has remained largely neglected, details about strategies are not given, and information is missing on antecedent or consequent conditions.

Training Programs

Earlier in this section we noted that two thirds of all studies on coping in adolescence are concerned with coping with highly stressful events, and that interest in this area has gradually increased over the years. Despite the methodological problems that doubtless exist, particularly the sampling problems limit the representativeness and generalizability of the results obtained. The studies just cited throw some doubt on the validity of the construct of coping. Similar reservations arise when one examines the articles under the heading "coping" that deal with training programs, offers of therapy to young people, or reports on the success of these measures.

In his review of training programs in the coping literature, Meichenbaum (1977) concluded that there are five characteristics that distinguish coping skills training from other types of therapeutic intervention. These characteristics are as follows:

1. The patient learns how important his or her own thoughts and feelings are in the definition of a stressful situation; an attempt is made to identify negative self-perceptions.
2. The patient learns to give up negative self-related thoughts and negative self-related behaviors.
3. Specific skills training is given in problem-solving abilities.
4. In addition, training is given for certain psychological variables that are assumed to affect coping behavior. These include self-assurance, positive self-evaluation, attention focusing, and relaxation.
5. When possible, training in real-life situations is provided.

Only rather loose approximations to these five characteristics can be detected in most of the training and therapy programs analyzed for this review. Instead, we find an eclectic collection of different training methods that may affect coping directly or indirectly, for example: story telling (Abrams, 1977), model learning (Schell, 1976), verbal instructions (Malless, 1978), the use of media (Elias, 1983), or consideration of the social support system (Carducci, 1980). The aims of the programs are also heterogeneous: for example, to improve social competence (Briedis, 1978), to strengthen emotional control (Elias, 1983), to increase frustration tolerance (Sobel, 1979), or the decision-making ability (Temoshok, Riess, Rubin, & Leahy, 1978). If one applies the criteria described by Meichenbaum (1977), only two of the studies satisfy these requirements, the work by Murgatroyd (1982), who distinguished between coping behavior and coping resources within a crisis counseling situation, and that by Gottlieb (1975), who analyzed the benefits of the social support systems under preventive aspects. Because of this limited number of adequate studies, I do not present a more detailed portrait of so-called "training programs."

Age and Gender Differences in Coping Behavior

Almost half of all the studies in the category "other research questions" (see Fig. 1.2) are concerned with the problems of prevention, training, and treatment, described briefly in the last section. The remainder of the studies examine the relationship between coping and development, successful coping and defense, or the influence of certain variables such as age, gender, social class, ethnic origin, and personality characteristics on coping behavior. It is worth noting that neither the conceptual nor the methodological approach applied with adolescents differs from that used in research on adults, so that these results can for the most part be regarded as replications of the studies on adults. Developmental questions play a subordinate role.

Gender differences in the use of coping strategies by male and female adolescents have been observed in several studies. They indicated that female adolescents show a greater willingness to resort to social contacts when coping with problems (e.g., Anastasi, 1975; Holbrook, 1978; Moriarty & Toussieng, 1976), whereas males are more likely to play down the stressful nature of a problem situation (Rauste-von Wright, von Wright, Frankenhaeuser, 1981). As far as age-related differences are concerned, our knowledge until the mid-1980s can be described as sketchy. As a rule, adolescents form a small subgroup within a research sample with a broad age range, rather than being differentiated according to age. The study by Pearlin and Schooler (1978), for example, analyzed 18- to 64-year-olds. The authors found that with increasing age there was a decreasing willingness to accept help or conditions for help. Other authors found associations between increasing age and increased primitivization and rigidification of coping abilities (e.g., Gutman, 1970), a finding that is probably related to the shift toward higher ages in the samples. However, in his study on 20- to 90-year-olds, McCrae (1982) was not able to find any differences in coping behavior between younger and older subjects whether the events be threatening, stressful, or stimulating. Different strategies being chosen by the two age groups was a function of perceived stress rather than of the subject's age. Significant differences in coping behavior do exist, however, between adolescents belonging to different ethnic groups (e.g., Mar'i & Levi, 1979). Dispositional prerequisites for effective coping behavior have been studied by several authors. Similar to results from research on adults, correlations have been found between effective coping behavior and a positive self-concept, or between ineffective coping strategies and greater dispositional anxiety (e.g., Houston, 1977) or lower frustration tolerance (Malaviya, 1977). The locus-of-control concept has gradually assumed a special role in coping research on adolescents, as it has in research on adults. Gatz, Tyler, and Pargament (1978) and Tyler (1978) found that among young people with active coping styles, a large number chose realistic goals and attributed the effect to themselves.

Coping and Development

Five longitudinal studies published in the 1970s attempted to clarify the process of adaptation in adolescence and to establish a relation between this developmental stage and other phases of human development. Their approaches are very different themselves and the studies cover a long period of time (up to 30 years). The Youth in Transition Study (Bachman, O'Malley, & Johnson, 1978) investigated stability and changes in more than 2,000 male adolescents from 87 high schools. The first data were collected in 1966 when the boys were in the 10th grade; the last assessments were made in 1970 and 1974, 1 to 5 years following the end of school. Primarily in middle and late adolescence (15- to 23-year-olds), there was a surprising amount of stability in developmental events. Relationships between academic success, family background, and future aspects were still valid in predicting vocational aspirations 5 years after leaving school.

The study by Kelly (1979) was also mainly concerned with the question of academic and vocational adjustment. The Opinions of Youth Project investigated high school students' adaptation to their school environment. Again, only male adolescents were studied. The first assessments were carried out in 1966 and continued until 1979. More than 30 different researchers participated in giving tests, questionnaires, and interviews and performing observational studies. Kelly began by analyzing preferences in the coping styles of adolescents who came from different social milieu. Observed differences in social exploration then led Kelly to select 20 high, 20 low, and 20 moderate "explorers" from different school communities for a longitudinal study. Self-concept, attitudes, and activities of the young people, along with their perception of school, were continuously recorded over a period of 10 years. Of particular interest are the interactions reported by Kelly between coping style and environmental variables.

Vaillant's (1977) Grant Study focused on changes in defense processes that he classified into three categories: immature, neurotic, and mature. Male adolescents were first examined in 1930 and again 30 years later, when the original group was about 50 years old. Compared to their scores in adulthood, the adolescents' scores in immature defense forms were twice as high. Interestingly, one group of adolescents who had originally been classified as particularly mature, and who had been compared to Moriarty and Toussieng's (1976) "censors," made no further gains in adulthood. Moriarty and Toussieng's study is the best known of the five. In particular, their typological classification into sensors and censors aroused much interest. The authors identified four different coping styles in adolescents that are variations of these two types. Two groups were described as censors, the obedient traditionalists and ideological conservatives. This type of coping limits sensory experience and rejects information that does not conform to traditional values. The sensors contained two other groups, the cautious changers and the passionate revitalists. What they have in common is their desire for new experience and an especially great tolerance for deviant information. Sensors comprised 72% of the sample, with more females belonging to this group. Sensors and censors differed in their attempts to cope with the transition from childhood to adulthood: Censors tend to reject peer conformity and are oriented toward their parents' values that they also regard as being binding for society. Sensors, on the other hand, try to work out the best possibility in commitment to others by choosing alternative methods. The authors feel that the sensors are the better, more effective copers because of their attempts to consider different viewpoints. However, with a sample size of 54, the database is too small to draw extensive conclusions. This is the only one of the studies described so far that includes female adolescents. Moriarty and Toussieng (1975, 1976), like Haan (1977), based their interpretations of coping in adolescence partly on psychoanalytic or neoanalytic theories.

The distinction between "coping" and "defending" played a major role in Haan's (1974) interpretation of changes she observed in her 20-year study of 97 subjects. The 48 males and 49 females were a subsample of the Oakland Growth Study. They were interviewed in 1937, when they were 16 years old, and in 1969, when they were 47 years old. In addition, personality traits and coping and defense behavior were assessed with the help of the Q-sort techniques. Using this method, the adolescents were divided into copers and defenders and followed up longitudinally. Copers were characterized by high achievement motivation, high value ratings of intellectual demands, broad interests, and verbal fluency. They had well-balanced relationships with their parents and other young people. Defenders had a particularly defensive, negativistic personality structure, were more philosophically oriented and sympathetic in their dealings with other people. Haan observed an extensive reorganization in coping behavior over the following years, but the basic differences between active copers and people who frequently used defense processes remained.

Clearly, these five longitudinal studies differ greatly, both with regard to methodology and to content. Cross-sectional studies on large groups of, for the most part, male adolescents on questions concerning general adaptation (and often academic and vocational adaptation) contrast with longitudinal studies on small groups of both genders in which projective tests and interviews were used and the distinction between effective coping and defense behavior played an important role. The studies took place over a long period of time, without adequate control of interim events. Because of cohort differences that are known to exist even between birth cohorts who are close together, problems of interpretation may arise.

RESEARCH TRENDS IN ADOLESCENT COPING:
THE SECOND PHASE (1985–PRESENT)

To summarize what has been outlined so far, since 1966 substantial contributions have been made to coping research on adult subjects. Coping behavior of adolescents on the other hand has been studied in only about 7% of all publications. Studies dealing with this question also differ qualitatively from studies on adults. We have to stress that studies in the first phase of coping research on adolescents were carried out almost exclusively in the United States and Great Britain;

almost no interest was shown in this field by European developmental psychology. But also in Anglo-American research a change in perspective is apparent since 1985, which has led to a more refined and more complex assessment of coping including different types of stressors. Most research from the second phase in coping research is detailed throughout this book. Here, I point to a further change as compared to early coping research: the emerging of a European perspective. In the last few years one can observe an increase in the study of adolescent coping in Europe that is reflected in special conferences and monographs on the subject (Bosma & Jackson, 1990; Oerter, 1985; Olbrich & Todt, 1984; Rutter, 1992; Seiffge-Krenke, 1986, 1990b, 1993a). The stressors studied (e.g., hassles, developmental tasks, and minor events) emphasize the mildly stressful, more normative nature of the events studied, imply frequent occurrence, and thus offer a better chance to study successful development. Methodologies include intensive assessments of small groups of young people under natural conditions as well as longitudinal, partly prospective studies on representatively selected large groups of young people. There has also been a noticeable attempt to operationalize both events and coping more precisely, guided by theories.

The developmental task is the main construct used by the Munich Research Group under the direction of Oerter. This construct allows one to study interactions between the individual and his or her environment, because developmental norms and current ability have an interdependent relationship (Oerter, 1977). Discrepancies between developmental norms and abilities or changes in the norms themselves are regarded as the cause for developmental dynamics (Oerter, 1978). In a study of 14- to 18-year-olds, the significance of certain developmental tasks and subsequent coping were analyzed. Semistructured interviews revealed that adolescents are indeed capable of coping with tasks typical for their age (see Oerter, 1985).

Fend and coworkers investigated a similar segment of coping behavior. Based on the concept of developmental tasks (for which they drew up a precise list of indices) everyday problem situations were analyzed with regard to their latent problem structure, and appraisal aspects were derived (cf. Lazarus & Launier, 1978). The underlying idea is that stressors are effective only to the extent to which they are subjectively evaluated. In distinguishing between subjective and objective stressors in school and home environments, it was found that objective risk factors are much less important than subjectively experienced stress. Fend and Helmke (1981) found stress syndromes in 10% to 20% of all the children studied. On the basis of their comprehensive longitudinal studies on 1,500 subjects in which coping behavior was analyzed over 3 successive years. Fend and Schroer (1989) could show that the parent–child relationship is more important than peer relationships, but that both types of relationship are necessary for successful coping with developmental tasks.

The research group of Bosma and Jackson (1990) focused on the relation between self-concept and coping, thus adding an important facet to under-

standing the contribution of internal resources. In this same volume, stress resistance and coping with difficult school situations are discussed by Tyszkowa
(1993). This study, carried out in Poland, presents a comprehensive list of school
situations that young people perceive to be difficult. Tyszkowa described the
type of coping strategies they evoke and the effectiveness of these coping styles.
The results indicate clear developmental progress in the ways adolescents cope
with stressful school situations. A relatively high self-esteem seems to be crucial
in this process. Furthermore, Jackson and Rodriguez-Tomé (1993) presented the
results of a French study of sources of anxiety experienced by normal adolescents
and how they cope with situations that they perceive as threatening. In the
evolution of fear from childhood to adolescence, a clear transition from phobias
to anticipatory anxiety was found. In Switzerland, Herzog (1987) determined
type, cause, emotional component, and relational context of problems and the
attempts to solve them in analyzing letters seeking advice from a youth magazine.
The work of Honess and Edwards (1990) links existing research to the European
studies examining major life events. The authors investigate how poorly qualified
school leavers accommodate to the social and physical changes of adolescence
in a situation where employment prospects are poor. Youth unemployment has,
from the very beginning of coping research, been a very prominent issue in
British studies. Jerusalem (1992) tried to predict coping preferences by individual
and cultural differences in coping resources between German and Turkish youths.
In the European research, only some clinical samples were investigated. Reinhard
(1986, 1989) and Seiffge-Krenke (1990b) analyzed the relative importance of
coping and defense among adolescent psychiatric patients.

Other research focuses more strongly on the failure of coping processes, but
still remain within the realm of normal coping forms. One important question
addressed by the research project led by Hurrelmann (1990) was the assessment
of the adolescents' status passage. Because of its wide-ranging consequences for
the adolescent's personal career, the economic area was examined particularly
thoroughly. A second area of the research program analyzed the "intervention
potential" of adolescents' social environment that is responsible for coping. The
aim of a further study by Lösel (1983) was to define subgroups of adolescents
who are able to cope with stressful or exciting life conditions with varying success
and for whom person–environment relationships are stable. Although it is not
difficult to recognize the construct of invulnerability here, the Bielefeld approaches are clearly developmentally oriented despite their preventative claims
(Lösel & Bliesener, 1990).

Our own approach, which is described in detail in this book, is concerned
with coping with minor and major events. It focuses on the everyday events
that confront adolescents and analyzes the process of coping as well as the
situation-specific choice of coping strategies. Relationships with significant others, as investigated in these studies, is regarded as an important contribution,
which goes beyond social support. Furthermore, cross-cultural studies presented

validate the results won on stress, coping, and relationship. Although the cross-sectional and longitudinal studies detailed in this book were mainly carried out on normal adolescents, several clinical samples were included in order to provide a more comprehensive picture of the developmental processes involved. The research on clinical samples, however, are detailed in a second volume (see Seiffge-Krenke, 1995). For my own research, the contributions of Bruce Compas and Stuart Hauser were most relevant, both of whom are representatives of the changing perspective in Anglo-American coping research since 1985.

The main impetus came from the research group around Bruce Compas. Compas (1987a, 1987b) reviewed Anglo-American research on coping with stress in childhood and adolescence and emphasized the developmental perspective. Also, a new method for the assessment of major and minor events was developed. The Adolescent Perceived Events scale (APES; see Compas et al., 1987) reflects chronic daily stressors in the life of adolescents and is clearly age-related in event sampling. The hypothesis that negative daily events mediate the relationship between major negative events and symptomatology could be confirmed using a three-wave panel design. This led to the formulation of an integrative model of psychosocial stress (Wagner, Compas, & Howell, 1988). A major finding in this study was that daily events were even more strongly associated with psychological symptoms than major events. The relationship between stress, coping, and symptomatology was pursued in several studies on nonconspicuous adolescent samples, partially including parental stressors and symptomatology, too (Compas, Howell, Phares, Williams, & Giunta, 1989; Phares, Compas, & Howell, 1989). Further contributions of the Vermont research group are concerned with the ways adolescents perceive the cause of an event (Compas, Forsythe, & Wagner, 1988), or more generally the interaction between cognitive appraisal of stressful situations and subsequent coping (Compas & Phares, 1986). Conceptually, and with respect to research methods and the critical analysis of methodological problems (e.g., Slavin & Compas, 1989), Compas and coworkers contributed much to the reduction of theoretical and methodological deficits that characterized the earlier phase of coping research.

Further important contributions came from the research group around Hauser. They took social support to be a crucial mediating variable and added the perspective of family coping to individual coping, the latter having been most prominent in previous research. Their newly developed measure, the Family Coping Coding System (FCCS) was constructed to identify and study familial responses to stressful situations (Hauser, 1991). In earlier studies, the Boston research group examined adolescent defense processes and adaptive strength aspects of individual coping (Beardslee et al., 1986). Their interest then developed to include the concept of *transactions* formulated initially by Lazarus et al. (1974). This new method allowed the investigation of the influence of the family on adolescent coping styles. This technique was demonstrated on families with adolescents suffering from diabetes, and led to the distinction between constraining and enabling interactions in the family (Hauser, DiPlacido, Jacobson, Willett, & Cole, 1993). This conceptualization demonstrates the strong developmental orientation in this research group. The emphasis on adolescent autonomy and ego progression, embedded in a family context, is also stressed by Hauser (1991). A recent study on normal and psychiatric adolescent patients and their parents impressively shows how the family is influenced by adolescent development (Hauser, Borman, Jacobson, Powers, & Noam, 1991). Parental ego development was related to the variability of adolescent coping strategies.

Both researchers are representatives of a reorientation in research of adolescent coping. This reorientation is characterized by paying more attention to conceptual and methodological problems, and by an even balance between research on minor and major events. Several other authors reported on newly developed coping measures such as the Adolescent Coping Orientation for Problem Experiences (Bird & Harris, 1990), the Coping Response Inventory developed by Moos et al. (1990), or on new methods for quantifying stress (e.g., the APES by Compas et al., 1987). For the first time, stressors and social resources have been included in measurement (see Life Stressor and Social Resources Inventory by Daniels & Moos, 1990). Theoretical work includes, for example, the discussion of adolescent coping and vulnerability within a developmental framework (Eisen, 1986), the application of the transactional model of stress and coping for adolescents (Garcia, 1987), or the implication of cognitive psychology in coping behavior among youths (Giddan & Whitner, 1989). Lammert (1988) developed a model for coping with stress in adolescence that involves (a) the interaction between individual and environment; (b) the flow between regression and growth, vulnerabilities and competencies; and (c) the interactive effects of psychological, social, and physical factors. It is a feature of the second phase of coping research that the scope of the term *stressor* also includes minor events, such as school or family stress (e.g., Daniels & Moos, 1990; Stark, Spirito, Williams, & Guevremont, 1989; Stern & Zevon, 1990; Tolor & Fehon, 1987), everyday hassles (e.g., Kanner, Feldman, Weinberger, & Ford, 1987), everyday stressors (Kliewer, 1991), and normative transitions such as school transition (Schinke, Schilling, & Snow, 1987). Coping with developmental tasks as another normative demand has been analyzed, too (Palmonari, Pombeni, & Kirchler, 1990; Patterson & McCubbin, 1987).

In these studies on quite large samples of normal adolescents, age and gender differences in coping styles are discussed (e.g., Blanchard-Fields & Irion, 1987). Although most studies clearly focus on normative demands and normative samples, the clinical perspective is frequently included, for example when investigating gender differences in coping strategies and symptomatology (e.g., Kurdek, 1987). A typical example of this is the study by Kanner et al. (1987) on uplifts, hassles, and adaptational outcome in early adolescence. Their results indicate that both hassles and uplift patterns vary as a function of gender and that in general major hassles were associated with negative outcome such as anxiety, depression, and distress. Another example may be found in Glyshaw, Cohen, and Towbes (1989), who conducted cross-sectional, longitudinal, and prospective analyses of the relationship between life stress, coping, and distress in adolescence. They found that problem-solving ability was negatively related to depression. In investigations including representative samples, a broad range of giftedness is conspicuous ranging from highly or poorly gifted adolescents (Gregory & Stevens-Long, 1986; Wayment & Zetlin, 1989) with a flowing transition to clinical populations. For example, a study by Smith, Smoll, and Ptacek (1990) focused on social support and coping skills in adolescents with sports injuries. Only athletes low in both coping skills and social support exhibited a significant stress–injury relation and in the vulnerable subgroup, negative major life events accounted for up to 30% of the injury variance.

Other studies investigated coping skills in connection with problem behavior. Baer, Garmezy, McLaughlin, Pokorny, and Wernick (1987) reported more alcohol abuse among adolescents who reported more life events, more daily hassles, and more conflict in the family. A stress-buffering effect of low family conflict on life events could not be substantiated for extent of alcohol abuse. Other authors have analyzed the different cognitive and behavioral strategies employed in high-risk situations by adolescent drinkers and nondrinkers (Brown, Stetson, & Beatty, 1989) or investigated stress and coping in relationship to substance abuse (Labouvie, 1986; Wills, 1986). A further example of the transition between normal and clinical samples is the study by Woodward and Frank (1988) on coping with loneliness in nonreferred youths. As mentioned already, within these normative approaches, family stressors and perceived family climate was an important aspect (Stern & Zevon, 1990).

This focus is also identifiable in two further core research questions since 1985. Coping with critical life events or major events continued to be frequently investigated in research, but contemporary approaches differ substantially from earlier research. Studies on traumatic events (such as kidnapping, rape, or murder) that formed a substantial proportion of earlier life event research are missing. In contrast, major events in the classic sense of critical life events (Johnson, 1986) were investigated, including larger groups as well. Here again, we notice a broadening of the scope of events such that minor stressors in the everyday life of the adolescent are included as well as major events. Again, the importance of the family is stressed and coping with major events is seen as a process of adaptation in the whole family. Bird and Harris (1990), for example, investigated coping with parental divorce, but analyzed perceived family strain among adolescents, too. Teenage pregnancies (Codega, Pasley, & Kreutzer, 1990; Panzarine, 1986), parental unemployment (Marotz-Baden & Colvin, 1989), and traumatic injuries of their offspring (Slater & Rubenstein, 1987) are further areas of research, where social support is stressed and individual and family coping with the event are investigated.

As in the research focusing on minor events, the relationship between major stressors and symptomatology gains attention. Besides Compas and coworkers, some other authors have taken up this perspective. Armistead et al. (1990), for example, analyzed coping with parental divorce and found that only avoidance coping, which was used less often, was related to internalization and externalization syndromes. However, it should be pointed out that research on clinically referred adolescents is rather exceptional, whereas in general, high-risk adolescents not yet referred to counseling or psychotherapy, constitute the main samples. Among those researchers investigating clinical samples, patients with internalizing syndromes were preferred. These studies tried to examine, for example, cognitive processes and coping efforts leading to depression and suicide (Baron & Labrecque, 1988; Cole, 1989; Spirito, Overholser, & Stark, 1989). The latter group found that social withdrawal was a particularly maladaptive coping strategy and increased the likelihood of attempted suicide.

In the second phase of coping research on adolescents, coping with severe illness is no longer a major focus. In addition, a change from incurable disease to chronic illnesses with low mortality and appropriate treatment is apparent. Besides the work of Hauser, several other researchers focus on diabetes. Delamater, Kurtz, Bubb, and White (1987), for example, analyzed stress and coping in relation to the metabolic control of adolescent diabetics and found more wishful thinking and avoidance, but also a higher frequency of stressful events in groups with poor metabolic control. A comparable study, including perceived family climate, was undertaken by Hanson, Cigrang, Harris, and Carle (1989). Other authors have investigated adolescent patients suffering from coronary heart disease (Keltikangas-Jarvinen & Jokinen, 1989) or cystic fibrosis (Patton, Ventura, & Savedra, 1986). But coping with acute disease and short-term hospitalization has also been dealt with (Stevens, 1989), including family variables (Stevens, 1988). As already noted in research dealing with coping with minor and major stressors, family coping processes became more and more prominent (see e.g., Donovan, 1988). Moreover, the implications for health professionals dealing with ill adolescents has emerged as a new perspective (Eiser, 1989; McCune, 1988) in that not only the adolescent's coping behavior in medical situations is noted, but also the reaction of the medical staff. Another index of change in coping research is the decrease in publications on training. This demonstrates the sharpened awareness in researchers regarding the numerous conceptual and methodological problems they face, especially a possible confounding of coping with outcome.

CONCLUDING REMARKS

At the beginning of this chapter I claimed that in order to analyze stress, coping, and relationships, I would begin with an outline of research activity using adolescent coping as a key concept. I noted that even in research on adults, understanding the nature and process of coping confronts researchers with some challenging problems. Coping research on adolescents, however, entails some additional problems that cannot be fully appreciated without reference to the history of adolescent research in general. Clearly, adolescence is a developmental stage that has experienced a particularly discontinuous research history. Research interest has waxed and waned—there was, for instance, an almost 30-year pause in research in Germany (Hetzer, 1982)—and there have been noticeable shifts in theories and research methods, resulting in a heterogeneous collection of research findings. Although work on this developmental phase has intensified since the mid-1980s, probably as a result of pressure from public and political sources, the volume of research still lags far behind that in child psychology. Indistinctness in concepts and theories and heterogeneity in subject matter can also be observed in parallel to the waxing interest in adolescent research. A clinical perspective was long sustained and it was apparently more difficult to apply developmentally related thought to this age group than to other stages of the life span.

Research in the field of adolescent coping is in many ways paradigmatic for this trend: Research activity in this field was very sparse until the mid-1980s. Early research in Great Britain and the United States was mainly clinically oriented and, as a result, had taken little notice of new directions in adult coping research, nor had it attempted to connect with the other fields of adolescent research that confirm that, for the majority of adolescents, there is almost continuous adaptation (e.g., Bachman et al., 1978; Offer, 1984; Offer, Ostrov, & Howard, 1989). This research branch is thus a good example of what Grinder (1982) described as "isolationism in adolescent research" (p. 223).

Moreover, when compared with studies carried out on adults during the same period, early studies on adolescent coping reveal several qualitative differences. The prototypical approach has remained clinical. Usually, small, homogeneous groups of adolescents were studied after they had experienced a very stressful, critical, or even traumatic event. Compared to studies on coping with critical life events in adulthood, the events studied on adolescents have a low incidence, a particularly low level of controllability, are clearly damaging, and have an unavoidable finality. Too little thought has been given to how the occurrence of these extremely stressful events hinders, delays, or makes it impossible to cope with age-typical developmental tasks. Because of these factors, most studies assess defensive rather than coping aspects. Some studies apply the naive label of *successful coping*, although the absence of emotions such as anger, sadness, and dependency in individuals when facing very stressful events makes one wonder whether defense mechanisms such as denial or intellectualization are at work. Few studies investigate the entire process of coping and distinguish between short- and long-term consequences of events. They do, however, provide information that allows us to view successful coping in a new light. According to these results, intervention should take place immediately after an event has occurred. Typical developmental questions such as aspects of age-related change play a negligible role, especially compared to the clinical orientation. Only a few studies can be found that focus on this important aspect, and most of these databases are more than 30 years old and therefore suffer from problems with validity. Conceptual and methodological issues were barely mentioned in publications on adolescent coping until the mid-1980s. To some extent this is due to an uncritical adoption of adult standards, and to ignoring salient age dependencies, which again underlines the fact that a developmental perspective has not been taken up. From this point of view, training programs have to be regarded as particularly problematic. On this basis, research on questions of adolescent coping until 1984 permit hardly any statements to be made about the coping behavior of "normal" adolescents in more everyday problem situations like those with which the majority of adolescents are faced in the transition period. Bearing in mind the limited range of validity and the selective parameters of the events studied up to this time, however, this work deserves credit for distinguishing short- and long-term consequences of very stressful events for each phase of the coping process and for exploring the importance of social support systems. However, due to the limited range of stressors and a restricted definition of relationships with significant others (to provide instrumental or emotional support) changes in internal and social resources that might be expected during adolescent years have been overlooked.

Since 1985, a second phase of coping research can be distinguished in the United States, which is clearly developmentally oriented. This provides the starting point for a broader definition of an event, for the development of more refined research methods, and for the analysis of factors that mediate the impact of stressors. Going beyond individual patterns and investigating how families as a unit cope with stress has thrown additional light on developmental interrelationships. The characteristics of this second phase of coping research on adolescents are accordingly, studies conducted using large representative samples with a broad range, including adolescents at risk; a more refined and systematic assessment of stressors and coping processes; a simultaneous assessment of major and minor events, taking into consideration their interdependency; smooth transitions between developmental and clinical research questions; an emphasis on the role of social support in coping; and combining individual and family coping approaches. Particular attention is given to the relationship between developmental and clinical research questions. Although the number of clinically referred subjects was small, virtually all studies focus on minor events in examining the relationship between stress and symptomatology. To this end, the major limitations of the early phase of coping research were largely overcome and in consequence, a fuller appreciation of adaptational processes has developed.

Differences between research cohorts in the United States and Europe are also interesting and deserve further consideration. In addition to pointing out a dividing line between the generations (e.g., adolescent research compared to adult research on coping), there are cross-cultural differences. In recent years more normative events in the lives of adolescents have been studied in Europe and new instruments were developed for assessing the coping process. Developmental questions played a major role, leading to cross-sectional and longitudinal studies on prevailingly normal samples. This fortunate development, however, has its roots in a cumulative deficit: Whereas U.S. adolescent research on coping in its first phase lagged behind new developments in adult research (as for example in the event-centered approach), European adolescent research first became aware of the construct when a reorientation in the direction of coping with normative events had already taken place. The longstanding, clinically oriented tradition in Anglo-American research has, with few exceptions, no counterpart in European research tradition.

Since 1985 the research trends in the United States and Europe converged more and more. The integration of major and minor stressors in a model of stress is a major contribution of the North American researchers. Compared with research on adults, new conceptual differentiations and methods seem to demonstrate an increasingly independent development. One core theme is the integration of developmental and clinical aspects in terms of developmental psychopathology (see Sroufe & Rutter, 1984). A further central aspect, the significance of relationships, however, has in my opinion been neglected in extant coping research, and therefore forms a main theme of this volume. This implies going beyond familial and including friendship relationships. In this volume, I emphasize normal development, a separate volume considers clinical samples to supplement the developmental perspective by clinical aspects of stress, coping, and relationships (see Seiffge-Krenke, 1995).

Conceptual Approach for Studying Stress, Coping, and Relationships in Adolescence

Research on the role of stress, coping, and relationships in adolescence has lagged behind similar research with adults. This is a result of several factors. Early research focused narrowly on clinical aspects; furthermore, a theoretical framework to guide research and adequate measures to assess stressors and coping in young people has been lacking. In recognizing these deficits, which were detailed in chapter 1, we were encouraged to develop a new approach in which the establishment of a theoretical framework, development of instruments, and an integration of a clinical and developmental perspective are important parts. Although results on clinical samples will be presented in a separate volume (see Seiffge-Krenke, 1995), in this volume I intend to focus on normative samples. Seven studies analyzing stress, coping, and relationships in normative samples involving more than 2,000 German adolescents, aged 12 to 19, are presented.

The theoretical model that has served as a guideline for my research is outlined in the following. The main research questions, designs, and methods based on this model are described, followed by a short overview of research procedures and instruments used. Finally, I present an overview of the seven studies presented in this book, together with a rationale of how these studies are connected.

DEVELOPMENTAL MODEL FOR ADOLESCENT COPING

The plan for the various studies was developed over a 10-year period. During this time, many other investigators played a vital role in developing the approach and furthering understanding. Concerning the theoretical framework of adolescent development, I greatly benefited from the work of John Coleman and Anne

Petersen. Since my first studies on stress and coping I have also drawn on the work of the Lazarus group (e.g., Lazarus & Folkman, 1984), in which cognitive appraisals of stressful events play a crucial role. In subsequent work, emotional factors became increasingly important in shaping my research perspective. The analysis of different types of stressors, also found in the work of Compas et al. (1987), made me look more closely at those parameters that define an event as stressful. Lazarus et al. (1974) already claimed that stress assessment could also be influenced by the internal resources of the individual, an aspect that was taken up in our studies on internal resources of coping behavior. The importance of social relationships in coping with stress is another perspective that I have addressed in recent years. Theoretical concepts arguing for the protective influence of close relationships (Sroufe & Fleeson, 1986) stimulated my work. Similarly, theoretical concepts of Grotevant and Cooper (1986) and Hauser et al. (1984) regarding the significance of family ties and parental models as well as theoretical approaches in analyzing friendship relationships (Buhrmester & Furman, 1987) were instrumental in setting the stage for my own work on stress, coping, and relationships. These perspectives have not yet been incorporated into a unified theoretical framework appropriate for the study of adolescent adaptation. For our model of stress, coping, and outcome, we selected coping as a key construct and incorporated a broad range of variables that one would expect (on theoretical and empirical grounds) to be associated with coping behavior and contribute to adaptive or problematic outcomes. This preliminary model, depicted in Fig. 2.1, is based on a set of variables that are complex, interrelated, and qualify the stress-outcome association. According to this model, stress has a determinant influence on adaptive and maladaptive outcomes. The adolescent's internal resources and the quality of relationships that enable the adolescent to meet the challenges facing him or her are additional elements of the model.

Thus, type of stressor, internal, and social resources are all important determinants of the coping response. However, not all coping efforts lead to positive outcome. I suggest that the manner in which an individual copes with stressors is not only influenced by his or her adjustment but also determines in part the internal and social resources and the relationships that will be available. Consequently, coping with stressors can be a sorting point and is therefore central in my approach. Some adolescents meet challenges well and may even be stimulated by them. They may emerge from an encounter with increased abilities and resources (e.g., more efficient coping styles and an improved self-image). Others may not be able to cope with these stressors in an adaptive manner and develop problem behavior. The model acknowledges the contributions of previous experiences with stress, coping, and relationships. In other words, the historical background of relationships and stress management procedures will influence current coping behavior. In addition, the model not only recognizes the moderating effects that relationships can have but also incorporates coping response as a factor influencing the outcome.

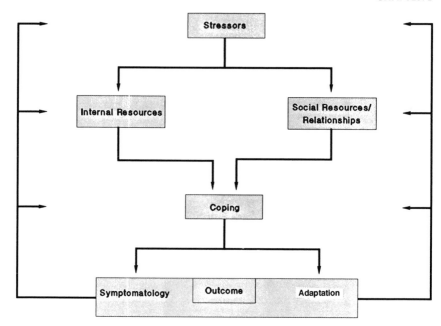

FIG. 2.1. Model of stress, coping, and outcome in adolescence.

The usefulness of a developmental approach is obvious. Adolescence is a developmental period in which the individual is confronted with a series of complex and interrelated changes and events that have to be mastered, while at the same time dramatic changes in relationships with parents and friends occur. Of special relevance, therefore, is the way adolescents cope with these stressors and their subsequent adaptation. We have, however, to consider that there is considerable controversy about several issues that are crucial to the formulation of a comprehensive theory of adolescent coping. There is much confusion about the definition of central constructs of stress and coping, the overall "stressfulness" of this developmental period, and the underlying mechanisms that contribute to adaptive coping. It is also unclear whether the changing relationships to parents and peers should be conceptualized as stressors and/or as buffers against stress in our model. Moreover, we need to know if there are age- and gender-specific variations in the interrelationship between the constructs that may require a differentiation in models for girls as compared to boys or early as compared to late adolescents.

To begin with, the field of stress and coping has been soundly and appropriately criticized for the failure to adequately define the concepts of *stress* (Compas & Phares, 1986) and *coping* (Seiffge-Krenke, 1993a). Our approach is essentially based on definitions provided by Lazarus that are, by and large, the most widely accepted. However, in Lazarus and Folkman's (1991) definition of *stress* as a "particular relationship between the person and the environment that is appraised by a person as taxing or exceeding his or her resources and endangering his or her well-being" (p. 19), an overlap in meaning between stress and adaptation is apparent. In addition, this definition implies that stress sometimes is the agent and sometimes the response. Among the numerous definitions of coping, again one of the clearest is offered by Lazarus et al. (1974), who have defined *coping* as "problem-solving efforts made by an individual when the demands he/she faces are highly relevant and tax his/her adaptive resources" (p. 29). In this conceptualization, no distinction is made between adaptive or maladaptive outcome. Nevertheless, the definitions of the Lazarus group reflect the interdependence of both constructs, which our model takes into account as well.

MAIN RESEARCH QUESTIONS AND ISSUES

In the following, the main research questions and issues that form the basis of my studies are briefly outlined. They exemplify the programmatical character of our approach and the expected relations between the constructs. I then return to our preliminary model in order to elaborate on the main constructs.

Clarifying Constructs and Developing Instruments

My first studies on stress and coping were motivated by a dissatisfaction with early research on adolescent coping, where the threatening nature of very stressful events was very much in the foreground. The complexity of the coping construct was thus limited to aspects of defense. It was unknown how representative and salient such events and the coping strategies they elicit are for the majority of adolescents. Apart from obvious problems of construct validity, I was interested in how the concepts of both stressors and coping could be refined. Few concepts in adolescent research have been as important, but at the same time as difficult to define, as *stress* and *coping*. Numerous definitions have emerged, some of which have been so broad or difficult to operationalize as to render them useless for scientific research (see for a critique, Lazarus, 1990). Unlike studies on adult coping, in which there has been a substantial effort to develop methods that focus on different types of stressors, adolescent research has continued to be dominated by questions important only for selective samples. The development of rigorous methods to assess stress and coping in adolescence did not begin until the middle of the 1980s. Thus, at the beginning, my goals were twofold: first, to develop clear definitions of both constructs (i.e., stress and coping), and second, to construct assessment techniques for identifying and quantifying their dimensions.

Type of Stressors

A crucial step in understanding the processes and effects of coping behavior entails the study of stressors that elicit coping. Isolated experiences such as critical life events obviously have dramatic effects on coping behavior. If we focus, however, on competence and mastery, we cannot solely concentrate on events that are restricted to selective samples or special periods of transitions. In other words, a sampling of relevant and frequent stressors from everyday life, which are representative and salient for the majority of adolescents, is necessary. Event sampling and a thorough description of stressors that require coping were therefore prerequisites for all further steps. I started by collecting a large number of events that were relevant for adolescents and experienced by the majority of them. This event sampling was following by an investigation of event parameters, such as frequency of occurrence, perceived stressfulness, and controllability. It is important to have a comparable set of dimensions according to which different types of stressors (i.e., major and minor, normative and nonnormative) can be evaluated. In identifying the types of stressors and describing their main characteristics, I hope to establish whether the transition to adulthood is perceived as particularly stressful, and if so, precisely which events or problems challenged adolescents most. Age and gender differences in perceived stressfulness of events also had to be explored.

Coping Process and Coping Structure

A comprehensive perspective on adolescent stress includes both the objective nature of an event or problem as well as its subjective appraisal. Following the conceptualization of Lazarus and Folkman (1984), neither objective nor subjective elements alone are sufficient to understand individual differences in the perception of stress. Given the variability of stressors, I had to examine the various ways adolescents cope with stressful events or situations. According to the model of Lazarus et al. (1974), cognitive appraisal and coping are closely intertwined in the dynamic transactions between person and environment. Since the very early stages of my research it has been my aim to examine coping from this perspective. Although I was aware that one cannot fully clarify all components of this model and its interrelationships, I was convinced that observing real-life transactions between the adolescent and his or her environment would furnish valuable information about the nature of adolescent coping.

The assessment of coping across different normative situations or events is another aspect that has been sadly neglected in adolescent coping research. In addition, types of coping strategies used by the adolescents and the functions of these strategies need to be examined. Given the variety of stressful events, can a considerable variability in coping across situations be expected? Wills (1986), for example, suggested that adolescents may display greater consistency in coping than adults. Thus, cross-situational consistency or variability has to be examined as well as individual differences in coping. A closely related research question concerns the effects of coping. Not all coping efforts have beneficial results. Although some coping responses may facilitate adjustment to stressors, others may increase the risk of maladaptation. In pursuing this line of thought, the developmental processes and differential effects of age and gender should be considered, too. Are adaptational coping styles, for example, more likely to be exhibited by more mature, older adolescents?

Internal Resources

A better understanding of how adolescents respond to perceived stress is promoted by analyzing individual characteristics of the adolescents, such as internal resources. Coping theories often refer to specific skills, aspects of self-concept, and personality variables in the search for those factors that constitute a "good coper" (Haan, 1974). In the research presented in this volume, I focus on self-concept and personality variables in order to determine the way they influence appraisal of an event or stressor, shape subsequent coping responses, and possibly buffer the effect of stress. The analysis of personality variables that contribute to coping is very much in the foreground, thus reflective of the great conceptual significance of personality variables in existing definitions and models of coping. As is well-known, Lazarus et al. (1974) referred to variables of the person and his or her environment as *unit*. Considering internal resources, one has to expect major changes due to development, especially with respect to self-concept, but this also applies to the complexity of cognitive appraisal and the flexibility in selection of appropriate coping responses. Once the manner in which internal resources determine the appraisal of stress and subsequent coping has been analyzed, the relative influence of situational and personal factors becomes relevant. Is the employment of a certain coping strategy more likely to be due to situational or personal factors, or is there a systematic interaction between them? In pursuing this line of thought we may even ask if there is empirical evidence for individuals who are outstandingly good copers regardless of the problem at hand. The results obtained here add to the important conceptual distinction between functional and dysfunctional coping styles.

Stress, Relationships, and Adjustment

At a later step of my research I also began to consider questions about the influence of family and friendship relationships on stress appraisal and subsequent coping. In recent years, the literature examining the relationship between social support, stress, and adjustment has increased, and the general findings have shown that family members and friends are a major source of support for adolescents (Daniels & Moos, 1990; Johnson, 1986; Werner & Smith, 1982). However, my interest went further than this. I wanted to know whether the social bond to parents and friends contributed to functional or dysfunctional coping styles and, if so, what were the processes and paths of influence. It was my impression that social support was far too narrow a construct to cover all these different and salient influences in adolescents' lives. I do not limit myself to support, because this means leaving out a variety of activities both on verbal and nonverbal levels such as communication patterns, availability of resources, solving problems together, accepting offers of help, observing how others appraise and cope with different demands, as well as the more general contextual factors in the family and among friends such as living conditions, time spent together, and shared activities. We have to broaden our research focus to include these divergent and interrelated aspects.

Family Context

There is good reason to believe that family interactions contribute to adolescent coping. Several aspects have to be considered here. Parents can either provide emotional, instrumental, or material support in helping to solve problems. In addition, their own way of tackling difficulties may serve as models for stress perception as well as for solving problems. Moreover, observing parental problem solving can guide the adolescent's behavior and help him or her to identify appropriate or inappropriate coping strategies. Not all of these features may occur on a visible level, nor can they be pinned down to concrete actions. It is likely that certain dimensions of family climate are relevant to the adolescent's appraisal of problems and also contribute to coping behavior, even if they do not directly address the question of stress management. To give an example, a family with a basically positive attitude toward the world acts flexibly and cooperatively, and will create a developmental context that facilitates coping with challenging or threatening events. The question may thus arise whether there is continuity in coping behavior across generations, that is, whether coping parents have coping offspring or whether defensive parents bring up defensive adolescents. By recognizing the family as a major context for development in adolescence, we may explore family indicators for possible changes in stress perception, which in turn may have consequences for adolescent coping. In particular, we have to look for those dimensions of family climate, which are related to adolescent stress perception and coping style over time.

The Contribution of Peers and Friends

Another important issue I have focused on in my research concerns the unique contributions of peers and friends to adolescent coping, a perspective that has been sadly neglected so far. Given the changing relationships with parents, friendships become more intense, enter into an increasing amount of daily activities, and pose new demands. Moreover, the changing quality of friendships (see Buhrmester & Furman, 1987; Hartup, 1989) provides the adolescent with the opportunity to engage in new activities, to fulfill new and different needs, and to exhibit new coping responses. The events perceived as exciting or threatening or problems discussed among close friends may differ fundamentally from the events and conflicts discussed and resolved with the help of parents. As in the family context, adolescents probably obtain much emotional support and coping assistance from friends. We may ask, however, whether the processes and pathways are similar to those experienced in the family. I would suggest that a need for being understood and cared for is basic to both types of close relationships. But the core processes operating among friends lie more in consensual validation and modeling on a nonverbal level, and the issues discussed between friends may be different from those raised with parents. Again, as on the family level, we expect that some coping processes take place beyond the verbal level and do not manifest themselves openly. It is our impression that processes of identification, modeling, and emotional support between friends operate secluded from the adult world and are accessible to the researcher only under certain conditions.

Social Support and Stress Buffering

According to the model of Lazarus et al. (1974), the belief that others can provide potential resources can modify the degree to which a certain situation is perceived as stressful. Several studies have demonstrated the stress-buffering effect of certain qualities of family interactions. In contrast, the possible stress-buffering effects of friendship and peer relations in adolescent symptomatology have not received much attention in research in the past. Despite a burgeoning literature on the significance and functions of adolescent friendship, comparatively few investigators have studied close friendships from a developmental psychopathology perspective. Therefore, we wish to ascertain whether close friendships serve as a stress buffer, and if these stress-buffering effects of close friends show a distinctive developmental pattern. Are parents or peers more efficient in buffering stress, and do the relative contributions of parent and peer relationships in buffering the effect of stressful events change across the adolescent years? According to Cohen and Wills (1985) we may distinguish between several models that attempt to explain how stress is buffered. We tested these different models to identify factors that moderate the impact of stressors.

OVERVIEW OF RESEARCH QUESTIONS
RELATED TO THE MODEL

Having outlined the major conceptual issues and research questions, the preliminary model presented in Fig. 2.1 is now complete.

In summary, the following interrelated questions are central to our approach: What types of stressors are salient for the vast majority of adolescents? How do adolescents cope with the special and complex demands that arise during this phase of development? How do age and gender differences shape coping behavior? How does the family influence and respond to coping? What do we know about the nature of close friendships in adolescence and how do they contribute to individual coping? How can we understand adolescents who are unable to meet the challenges during these years as well as those who are highly effective in dealing with the transition?

In my model, several aspects have to be considered when examining the way stress relates to coping and adaptation in adolescence that include (a) the specific nature of the stressor (e.g., type of stressor, event parameters such as frequency or controllability describing the stressor), (b) the individual appraisal of these event parameters and the availability of coping strategies, (c) internal resources such as personality structure or self-concept that may buffer the effects of stress, and (d) social resources such as support and coping assistance by parents and friends. Moreover, the quality of relationships with parents and friends may not only serve as a buffer against stress, but also as a model for functional or dysfunctional coping (i.e., an adaptive or maladaptive outcome). Coping is not only a central construct in my research, but is also an important mediating variable in the interface between stress and outcome. Coping is influenced by internal resources and external resources provided by relationships, and conversely, coping may affect relationships. I furthermore suggest that not all coping processes and mechanisms may function on a visible level, and that this is again especially true for coping with relationship stressors.

My model is placed in a developmental context; thus, developmental changes are taken into account in most of the variables analyzed. This implies a focus on normative development. However, it is likely that the same constructs are relevant in explaining maladaptation. As mentioned earlier, this volume is devoted to results on normative samples; the association between stress, coping, relationships, and symptomatology is detailed in a separate volume (see Seiffge-Krenke, 1995).

RESEARCH DESIGNS AND METHODS

My research methods were strongly guided by the revised model (see Fig. 2.2) that incorporates a host of interrelated research questions. My investigation must account for the multifactorial nature of coping, hence a variety of research methods have been selected to adequately focus on all relevant variables.

There are good reasons for employing more than one kind of measure, especially regarding aspects of validity of the constructs under scrutiny. There are several possible means for assessing stress, coping, and relationships, and by using different types of dependent variable measures, one can rule out method-specific sources of error (Carlsmith, Ellsworth, & Aronson, 1976). Some measures are better than others in their potential to provide more valuable sources of information about our variables (and lead to greater external validity). In addition, besides using different types of measures, systematic replication with at least some central measures may improve the validation process. Standardized assessment procedures in stress and coping help draw conclusions about the generality of a finding. Although different measures with varying approximation to reality may add to external validity, replications may increase construct validity.

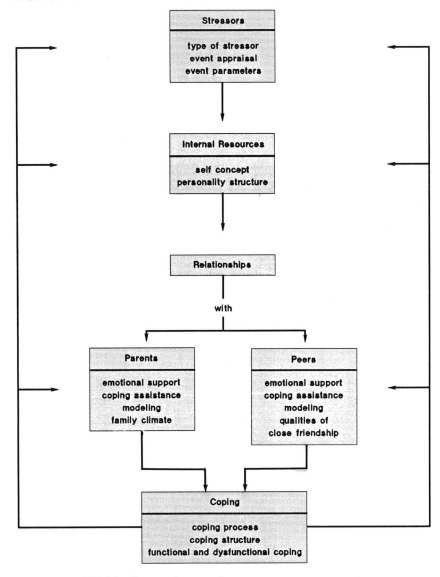

FIG. 2.2. Conceptual issues and major questions in our approach.

Research Methods

In summary, I chose a programmatic approach that is characterized by (a) assessing the same variable using different methods, (b) replication of some measures in different studies, (c) expanding standardized instruments by more open data gathering, and (d) using several informants. In this multivariate–multimethod approach, the adolescent, however, continues to represent the main source of information. My data collection technique aims to establish scientifically reliable findings while remaining oriented toward and appreciating the real lives of adolescents. The following research methods were applied to this end.

Standardized Questionnaires

For part of my procedures I was able to rely on standardized instruments. This applies particularly to procedures measuring parent and peer relationships, personality variables, and self-concept. For two central constructs of my research program, *stress* and *coping*, however, no appropriate procedures were available when the studies were launched. Therefore, at the very beginning I first had to sample relevant events and coping strategies and transform and standardize them by processes of careful selection, pretesting, and revision. In other words, I followed a "funnel approach" (i.e., I began with a very broad, unstructured sampling and progressively refined my standardized instruments). The Problem Questionnaire, which assesses minor events and everyday stressors, and the Coping-Across-Situations-Questionnaire (CASQ), which evaluates anticipatory coping were developed according to these procedures. These standardized questionnaires enabled me to collect information on a variety of questions using large samples and to examine the interrelationships of these variables, the individual differences, and the developmental change.

From a methodological point of view, the assurance of anonymity may increase the likelihood of an honest response. The participants may feel reasonably comfortable about a standardized form not only because the private nature of the issues involved but also because they are encouraged when a given answer represents his or her own thoughts and experiences well. These advantages are countered, however, by some disadvantages (Carlsmith et al., 1976). Needless to say, the use of straightforward questions does not automatically force experience into close categories. However, some participants may have difficulty in organizing their knowledge and experiences in a way that can be communicated through items. This is probably not just a question of age or cognitive level. Standardized questionnaires predetermine what can be communicated. Thus it was necessary to employ other techniques in order to get closer to the adolescents' inner worlds and social contexts.

Interviews

The great advantage of an interview over questionnaires is that an interviewer has a better chance of obtaining a serious and honest response. The interview also makes it possible to ensure that the participant understands the question and responds in the desired amount of depth and detail. This applies particularly to difficult and intimate questions (i.e., questions that require a high degree of self-reflection), but it applies also to processes the individual does not introspect about, which simply "happen." My experience has shown, for example, that coping with everyday events very often occurs automatically. The Coping Process Interview was developed to assess perceived stressors and coping strategies immediately after their occurrence. In this interview, the precise meaning of a question can be emphasized, the adolescent can be urged repeatedly to think carefully before answering, and the interviewer can repeat sections that are unclear. This makes the interview an almost perfect medium for deep analysis of the coping process. Consequently, this procedure is more time-consuming than a questionnaire, but it is time well spent. It not only helps the adolescents to understand the questions, but also helps us to understand the answers.

Written Open-Ended Questions

Whereas the Coping Process Interview was useful for pilot testing in areas about which little was known, a more closed form including written open-ended questions was also developed. In a way, this tool resembles the interview technique, but can be applied to larger samples. I employed them, for example, in order to analyze important events and coping strategies in the Event Exploration Interview. Generally, the technique of written questions was introduced at several times and in different samples throughout my work. For the most part, open-ended questions were presented, to which the respondents replied in writing. In some cases, questions with rating scales were provided. Written questions were used when I wanted to give the subject plenty of time to reflect on an issue and when I wanted to provide the adolescents with an opportunity to answer in their own way. Consequently, my analysis of the written questions required the development of categories and the scoring of responses, a procedure that is more work intensive than a questionnaire but at the same time provides more information about an area, the structuring of which is left to the adolescent.

Analysis of Documents

Document analysis is also based on the idea that data relevant to the situation of the individual may be acquired by analyzing information provided by other forms of communication (i.e., at the textual or nonverbal levels). I concentrated on adolescent diaries because diaries are a youth-specific form of expression and adolescents tend to be quite capable of reporting their experiences in a highly descriptive manner. From a scientific point of view, the fact that the entries are generated freely and in a self-motivated manner in such a private and intimate communicative situation represents a great advantage for the investigator. Such reflections may help validate other results obtained by employing standardized instruments, and the authenticity and credibility of other accounts are strengthened. Nevertheless, although the diaries contain authentic declarations of the authors, their subjective view of reality may not necessarily coincide with the objective events or the views of others. Furthermore, given the private and intimate nature of some of the revelations entered into diaries, it may be difficult to gain access to such documents. And finally, content analysis (see Holsti,

1969) may pose special problems and challenges. Despite these problems, the wealth of information and the insight into the day-to-day world of the adolescent to be obtained by examining such documents overrides these difficulties.

Research Designs

My multivariate–multimethod approach was realized in a combination of cross-sectional and longitudinal designs. Both differ with respect to questions they address, the number of variables used and the required workload. I believe that they complement each other in their findings.

Cross-Sectional Designs

The concern in my approach with development, on the one hand, and adaptation on the other, requires special consideration with regard to designs. I am very interested in individual differences in each of the variables under scrutiny. Before studying the determinants of developmental changes, we need to know more about which dimensions these variables have, and how they may be quantitatively defined. With a multivariate approach that examines relations between different variables, designs appropriate for larger samples are necessary prerequisites. Throughout all of my research, comparisons of individuals differing in age, gender, and socioeconomic status (SES) are important. In order to answer my primary question of how adolescents cope with stressors, I also included adolescents whose mental health statuses vary. Analyzing stress, coping, and relationships in a group of at-risk adolescents will provide insight into coping mechanisms that are studied later in clinical samples in detail (see Seiffge-Krenke, 1995).

Differences in coping styles for various categories of problems in different age groups is another example of the need to study individual differences. I believe that examining individual differences represents an acknowledgment of the various person- and situation-specific components involved in the coping process and does necessarily preclude embracing questions related to development. Cross-sectional studies only provide information about differences between age groups, they can be useful in the descriptive analysis of developmental changes, especially, if it is not exactly clear what the relation is between age and the variable in question. Given the few studies that deal with age and developmental changes in coping (see for a summary McCrae, 1982), we have to explore a "dark continent." The replication of the multivariate designs on new samples over a period of several years, as was characteristic for my approach, provides at least some control for age and cohort differences, one of the major drawbacks of cross-sectional designs (Wohlwill, 1977).

Longitudinal Designs

There are many reasons to believe that stressors and coping strategies may not remain stable throughout adolescence. Adolescents have to accomplish a great number of tasks in a relatively short period of time. According to the very influential focal theory of Coleman (1978), the adolescent masters the transition to adulthood by continuously taking on and coping with relevant developmental tasks. The focus on tasks that are perceived as salient, challenging, or threatening changes correspondingly during adolescent years. This theory also says something about unsuccessful mastering of tasks, by assuming that accumulation of events may overexert coping abilities and thus lead to dysfunction. Therefore, it is important to determine whether stressors remain constant across adolescence, and whether a change in coping strategies takes place. Furthermore, according to the Lazarus model (Lazarus et al., 1974), cognitive processes play an important role in understanding coping. One may therefore expect that the major cognitive developments in adolescence have an impact on coping. Change and stability in stressors and coping strategies and main developmental forces that contribute to these changes are thus important research issues. As mentioned already, there are also good reasons to expect that relationship patterns change throughout the adolescent years. Consequently, I have been interested in pursuing psychosocial development in the family and among friends. Several longitudinal studies were included to investigate the extent of stability and change in stress appraisal and coping, the coping process, and changes in internal and social resources. Accordingly, the time periods between data collection varied from brief intervals (2–6 weeks) to relatively long periods (1–3 years). In using these two designs, I tried to come to grips with the question of how developmental and differential elements may effectively be integrated into a coherent whole. Not all variables and not all methods are followed continuously in all studies, but the main body of research questions traverses through several measurement points. The methods employed are related to one another: Semi-structured interviews and open-ended, written questions formed the basis for the development of the standardized questionnaire procedures. The results thus obtained were validated by comparison with those furnished by the analysis of personal documents, in this case, diaries. Thus, the funnel approach (e.g., starting on a very broad, less structured level and progressing to a standardized instrument) was finally supplemented by very closely approaching the adolescents' worlds.

AN OVERVIEW OF THE STUDIES PRESENTED

Finally, I wish to present a brief overview of the seven studies forming the basis of my research approach and a short discussion of how they are related to one another.

Altogether, more than 2,000 adolescents took part in the seven studies. The studies can be grouped according to four main categories, specifically (a) studies with the focus on stress and coping, (b) studies analyzing internal resources, (c) studies with the focus on relationships, and (d) studies analyzing the stress buffer of relationships (see Fig. 2.3).

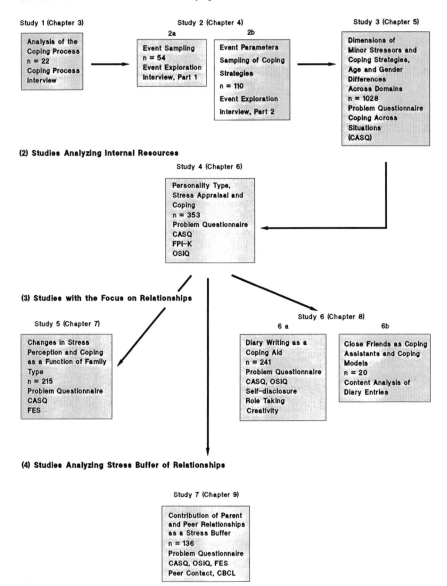

(1) Studies with the Focus on Stress and Coping

Study 1 (Chapter 3)

| Analysis of the Coping Process n = 22 Coping Process Interview |

2a

Study 2 (Chapter 4)

2b

| Event Sampling n = 54 Event Exploration Interview, Part 1 |

| Event Parameters Sampling of Coping Strategies n = 110 Event Exploration Interview, Part 2 |

Study 3 (Chapter 5)

| Dimensions of Minor Stressors and Coping Strategies, Age and Gender Differences Across Domains n = 1028 Problem Questionnaire Coping Across Situations (CASQ) |

(2) Studies Analyzing Internal Resources

Study 4 (Chapter 6)

| Personality Type, Stress Appraisal and Coping n = 353 Problem Questionnaire CASQ FPI-K OSIQ |

(3) Studies with the Focus on Relationships

Study 5 (Chapter 7)

| Changes in Stress Perception and Coping as a Function of Family Type n = 215 Problem Questionnaire CASQ FES |

Study 6 (Chapter 8)

6 a

| Diary Writing as a Coping Aid n = 241 Problem Questionnaire CASQ, OSIQ Self-disclosure Role Taking Creativity |

6b

| Close Friends as Coping Assistants and Coping Models n = 20 Content Analysis of Diary Entries |

(4) Studies Analyzing Stress Buffer of Relationships

Study 7 (Chapter 9)

| Contribution of Parent and Peer Relationships as a Stress Buffer n = 136 Problem Questionnaire CASQ, OSIQ, FES Peer Contact, CBCL |

FIG. 2.3. Overview of the studies presented in this volume.

40

Studies With the Focus on Stress and Coping

Altogether, three studies focus on stress and coping. The aim of the first two studies was to clarify concepts and gather basic information on stress and coping for developing standardized instruments. Sampling of different types of stressors, including major and minor events, and sampling of coping strategies were thus the main foci, introduced by a study that examined the coping process.

Study 1 (presented in chap. 3) involved a thorough analysis of the coping process. During a period of 6 weeks, a sample of 22 adolescents (11 males and 11 females) took part in the Coping Process Interview. They phoned immediately after an event had taken place and were asked about this event, their coping strategies, and their appraisals at different stages.

Study 2 (presented in chap. 4) consisted of two closely related studies. Initially, 54 adolescents (27 males and 27 females) took part in the Event Exploration Interview (Study 2a). They were asked to report any important events that had occurred during the previous 14 days. This prestudy provided 1,099 events, from which 10 universal events were selected (i.e., frequently occurring events in the sample across age and gender). These 10 universal events were presented to a new group of 110 adolescents who were comparable in all sample characteristics (age, gender, SES) with subjects from the prestudy. These 110 adolescents were asked in a written questionnaire to describe these events, to match them against several event parameters, to describe the coping strategies employed, and to indicate whether the intended effects were achieved (Study 2b).

Finally, based on the material gained in Studies 1 and 2, assessment procedures were developed and revised in order to investigate stress and coping. Because hardly any major events were named in both studies, these instruments focus on minor events or everyday stressors and coping strategies. Two instruments were developed, the Problem Questionnaire, which assesses perceived stressfulness of minor stressors in seven developmentally relevant fields, and the CASQ, which assesses coping strategies for eight problem areas stemming from these developmental fields. These instruments were then applied in all further studies.

In Study 3, the Survey Study, a large representative sample of 1,028 adolescents aged 12 to 19 (479 males and 549 females) was investigated, applying these standardized instruments. The main variables under scrutiny were age, gender, and SES influences on stress perception and coping style. In addition, event- or problem-specific use of coping strategies was analyzed. A conceptually important distinction between functional and dysfunctional coping styles was derived from this sample. From this cross-sectional study, a subsample of 94 was formed and followed up longitudinally over the course of 1 year. Stress and coping, using the standardized instruments, were assessed three times within this year. The occurrence of major events and changes within this time was registered. Study 3 is presented in chapter 5.

Studies With the Focus on Internal Resources

Study 4 (chap. 6) aimed at analyzing the relationship between stress, coping, and personality structure. A subsample of 353 adolescents taken from the survey study, consisting only of adolescents aged 15 to 19, was investigated. These adolescents additionally answered the FPI-K (Fahrenberg & Selg, 1970), a personality questionnaire. In this study, the analysis of personality variables associated with functional coping styles was a major issue. Self-concept as a further internal resource was also investigated and supplemented the results.

Studies With the Focus on Relationships

Although in the first studies attention was also paid to relationships, stressors, and coping strategies including social resources, I wanted to elucidate the various influences and pathways in other studies. In the following, the focus switched from stress, coping, and internal resources to relationships. Altogether, two studies were conducted to investigate the various aspects and contributions of relationships to stress management.

In Study 5 (chap. 7) a main issue was the relationship between family climate and coping behavior. In a sample of 215 adolescents aged 12 to 16 years, the FES (Moos & Moos, 1976), the Problem Questionnaire, and the CASQ were employed. In this study, relevant family characteristics that contribute to functional or dysfunctional coping were analyzed. Four different types of family climate were found that were related to stress perception and coping style. Adolescents stemming from different types of perceived family climate were then followed up longitudinally over 3 years to reveal stability and change in stress appraisal and coping, dependent on family climate, over time.

The main aim of Study 6 (presented in chap. 8) was to contribute to our understanding of processes of peer support, modeling, and intimacy between close friends. In Study 6, the Diary Study, two different samples of diarists were investigated. In Study 6a, a sample of 93 adolescent diarists aged 12 to 17 and their nonwriting control group ($n = 148$) was analyzed regarding their stress and coping pattern and were questioned about the function of diaries as a coping aid. In Study 6b, a sample of 20 diarists was analyzed who not only took part in an assessment of stress, coping, and internal resources, but additionally gave us their diaries for content analysis. A content analysis aimed to elucidate stress management and relationships as described in the diary entries.

Studies With the Focus on Stress Buffering and Adaptation

Finally, in Study 7, the relative contribution of parents and peers as a stress buffer was investigated in a sample of 136 adolescents, aged 13 to 17. The adolescents filled in various questionnaires to measure minor and major stress, internal resources and coping, and several instruments to measure parent and peer relationships. Symptomatology was assessed by parents' ratings (Child Behavior Checklist [CBCL], Achenbach & Edelbrock, 1987). Study 7 is presented in chapter 9.

This study is connected to a second volume (see Seiffge-Krenke, 1995), in which stress, coping, and relationships are analyzed from a clinical perspective by investigating adolescents at different stages of symptomatology, their parents, and health professionals. Because stressors do not necessarily lead to problematic outcome and the specificity of outcome is not clear anyway, in Study 7 non-referred adolescents served as a group through which the buffering effect of relationships and the relative contribution of minor and major events can be proven. Besides everyday stressors, critical life events were assessed. The results of these seven studies are then integrated in order to answer the main questions posed in this volume. In discussing the results of these seven studies I occasionally refer to several studies on cross-cultural samples that have been conducted more recently, using my methods and instruments. I hope that these studies may add to the validity and generality of my findings across cultures.

An Analysis of the Coping Process

Lazarus and Folkman (1991) pointed out that the coping process has three key features: the individual's action, the specific context (coping does not occur in a vacuum, thus it is responsive to contextual requirements), and how an individual's actions change as the stressful encounter unfolds. The authors characterize coping as a process of continuous appraisals and reappraisals of a shifting person–environment relationship. The reevaluation of what is happening (reappraisal) in turn influences subsequent coping efforts. The coping process is thus continuously mediated by cognitive reappraisals. The entire coping process may occur within a few moments or hours or may continue over weeks or even years. In my first study, I investigated the different stages of the coping process by analyzing adolescent coping with minor and major events over a period of 6 weeks. The theoretical framework for this descriptive and process-oriented study is based on the stress and coping model developed by Lazarus (Lazarus & Folkman, 1987; Lazarus & Launier, 1978).

THE STRESS AND COPING MODEL BY LAZARUS

As detailed in chapter 2, *stress* is understood by Lazarus and Launier (1978) to be created by any event in which an environmental or internal demand (or both) tax or exceed the adaptive resources of an individual. Lazarus defined *coping* as a process of managing these external or internal demands that tax or exceed the resources of a person (Lazarus & Launier, 1978), whereby two key features are emphasized, namely, the process and the description of coping in terms of relationships between the person and the environment. The concept of transaction was developed to describe how variables of person and environment are combined into new concepts (see Lazarus & Folkman, 1987). In this dynamic approach, "coping and stress are but the two faces of the same coin" (Roskies & Lazarus, 1980, p. 45). In developing a process-oriented model of stress and coping, both constructs are united and described by their interrelationships. Cognitive activities, termed *appraisal*, were found to play a prominent role in this approach. Appraisals consist of a "continuously changing set of judgments about the flow of events for the person's well-being" (Lazarus & Launier, 1978, p. 302). One of the major tenets of Lazarus' theory of stress and coping is that the way a person appraises an encounter determines how he or she will cope. Two kinds of appraisal, primary and secondary, are distinguished. They have different functions and deal with different information (see Lazarus & Folkman, 1987). Primary appraisal relates the event to its significance for the person's well-being and is thus concerned with the motivational relevance of what is happening while secondary appraisal relates the event to available coping resources and options.

Primary appraisal of stress are of three types: harm–loss, threat, and challenge. All three types involve some negative evaluations of one's present or future state of well-being with challenge providing the least negative and the most positive feeling tone. Harm–loss refers to damage already experienced, threat refers to harm or loss that has not yet occurred but is anticipated and challenge entails the potential for mastery and gain. Lazarus considered challenge as a stress appraisal, because a person must mobilize him or herself in order to cope with obstacles and to ensure a positive outcome. As outlined in Lazarus and Launier (1978), the distinction between threat and challenge is more a matter of positive or negative tone, that is, whether one emphasizes the potential harm or the potential gain. This distinction may be related to a person's beliefs and way of thinking, especially because some people "put a good face on things" even in the face of adversity. This illustrates why, in a given situation, one person may respond as if threatened, whereas another may feel challenged, and still another may find the situation irrelevant. In *secondary appraisal*, other aspects of the situation are evaluated (i.e., appraisal of the event is oriented toward what can be done). More specifically, evaluative judgments are made about whether any action can be taken to improve the troubled person–environmental relationships, and if so, which coping option may work. The word *secondary* does not mean that it necessarily follows primary appraisal in time or is less important. Secondary appraisal is a crucial supplement to primary appraisal because harm, threat, or challenge depend also on how much control we think we can exert over outcomes. Research has focused mainly on the extent to which situations can be changed or have to be accepted (Folkman, 1984; Folkman, Lazarus, Gruen, & DeLongis, 1986). The two forms of appraisal also influence each other. The knowledge that one can overcome a potential danger may make that danger less imperative; as well, the knowledge that one is in danger typically initiates a search for information about or evaluation of what can and cannot be done. The central reason why secondary appraisal has so much to do with primary appraisal of loss, threat, and challenge is to be found in the definition of stress itself. A situation or event is not a source of harm if the person can master it easily. It is thus a central assumption that the two forms of appraisal influence each other without necessarily showing a temporal ordering. Furthermore, there is an interplay between appraisal and coping. With respect to primary appraisal, when stakes are high there should be a mobilization of coping activity. But coping thoughts and actions also depend on secondary appraisal (i.e., whether anything can be done to alter the stressful relationship with the environment). Moreover, secondary appraisal is important in shaping the coping activities of the person under stress, as well as in shaping the primary appraisal process itself. The manner in which primary and secondary forms of appraisal influence each other and coping is best illustrated in the Berkeley Project Field Study (Folkman & Lazarus, 1980). One of the tenets of a process-centered conceptualization is that coping changes as an encounter unfolds. Folkman and Lazarus (1985) used a college examination to study changes in coping across time, asking the students to describe how they cope with the demands at the different stages of an exam. They found considerable flux in coping behavior, depending on the changing appraisal of the situation and on individual differences. One of the difficulties inherent in this cognitive approach to coping is that appraisal and coping are often interdependent and difficult to distinguish. An important class of coping consists of cognitive and intrapsychic strategies that were called *reappraisal* (Lazarus & Launier, 1978). Reappraisals point again to the feedback system that incorporates information from one's own reactions and from the environment. Such reappraisals as a result of feedback can be thought of as cognitive coping efforts clearly directed at managing the demands or the distress. As Lazarus and Folkman (1984) outlined, there is no simple way to differentiate an initial benign appraisal, for example, that there is no danger and no harm has occurred—from a cognitive coping strategy. Coping and appraisal are interdependent, because many coping strategies can have an appraisal function in that they shape the meaning of an event and, conversely, many forms of appraisal can have a coping function in that they help to regulate distress.

Consistent with the transactional perspective, coping alters the person–environment relationship. The different types of stress (e.g., harm–loss, threat, and challenge) are also relational concepts that transcend the separate set of person and environment variables with which they are comprised. Threat, for example, cannot be described in terms of person or environment alone, but must be defined by both. A person may feel threatened because the external demands seem very taxing and the resources available to manage them weak. Due to the dynamic relationship between appraisal and coping, the designation of appraisal or coping as an antecedent or a consequence depends solely on the point at which the ongoing transactions between the person and the environment are being observed (see Folkman, 1984). For instance, one can enter the appraisal–coping–reappraisal process at the appraisal phase, in which case appraisal is identified as an antecedent and coping as a consequence. On the other hand, if the process is entered at the coping phase, then coping is an antecedent variable that determines subsequent appraisals.

RESEARCH QUESTIONS

A major issue in this chapter is the analysis of the coping process according to the Lazarus model. The process involves change over time and across situations. In order to ensure that my first study was explicitly process-oriented, the following requirements had to be met: (a) coping must be examined within the context of a specific stressful encounter, (b) what adolescents actually do in dealing with the stressor must be described, and (c) multiple assessments must be made during the encounter in order to examine changes in coping over time as the encounter unfolds. An additional, important prerequisite for the study was that appraisal and coping should be recognized as including emotions, thoughts, and actions that have taken place or are occurring during a coping encounter. Lazarus and Launier (1978) claimed that laboratory experiments do not readily provide descriptive ecological information on the sources of stress response in the daily life of ordinary people and maintained that "these topics must be studied in the life setting where they occur" (p. 300). As Argyle, Furnham, and Graham (1981) pointed out, nearly all research has concentrated on symbolic presentation of events while neglecting actual situations that are difficult to assess. In seeking to understand coping or its antecedent and consequent correlates, there is no substitute for direct assessment of an individual's coping efforts and appraisals. I thus opted to observe adolescents in real-life situations as closely as possible by interviewing them shortly after an event had taken place. Through this "in-vivo" approach, I intended to tap a broad range of events, especially those related to everyday stressors. In the literature review (see chap. 1), I found that only 12% of studies on adolescent coping in the past have dealt with these salient and frequent stressors. I expected that within a limited amount of time (i.e., several weeks), several encounters would unfold, including minor and major stressors as they naturally occur in the lives of adolescents.

Stress, appraisal, and coping are obviously complex and interwoven processes. Nevertheless, I was prepared to analyze these processes according to the information provided by the adolescents in their verbal reports about their feelings, thoughts, and interpretations of what was happening to them. I began the analysis by identifying and assigning verbal material according to three conceptually distinct domains: event parameters (including the context in which an event had occurred), appraisals (including primary appraisal, secondary appraisal, and reappraisal), and coping strategies. My preferred method of obtaining such information was a semistructured interview with the adolescents conducted shortly after the event had taken place. The aim of such interviews was to glean as much information as possible from personal introspection and self-observation (see Lieberman, 1975). However, the results of the study show, for example, how various types of secondary appraisal feed back to primary appraisal (e.g., in shaping degree of threat) and how they shape the coping process. Although context analysis and primary and secondary appraisal as well as coping strategies were assessed at Time 1 (i.e., immediately after an event occurred), reappraisal (e.g., the feedback about the coping behavior) was assessed at Time 2, two days later. Unfortunately, repeated intraindividual observations are costly and time-consuming. As a consequence, the sample had to be small. In addition, the results of this process-oriented approach remain basically descriptive. It is intended to supplement it by research on stress and coping using larger samples and more standardized methods. This study (Study 1) thus represents the starting point from which I developed more refined methods to be applied in the following six studies. In using the in-vivo approach just detailed, I hoped to identify the types of stressors adolescents face in their everyday life and their ways of coping with these demands. This includes addressing the question of whether individual differences in coping style are displayed consistently across a variety of situations. A further question concerns whether adolescents who appraise an event in the same way exhibit concordance with others in coping responses. In summary, based on Lazarus' model on stress and coping, the interface of appraisal and coping was analyzed as well as the cross-situational consistency in coping behavior and concordance in coping between persons.

METHOD

Procedure

The following principles were considered to be essential in developing a procedure for assessing coping behavior: (a) subjective descriptions of the event and the individual's reactions to it must take place as soon as possible after the event begins, (b) in order to explore the process of dealing with the event, a standardized interview guide must be available that accommodates the variability of a report not only with respect to the answers of the adolescents but also to the questions posed by the interviewers, and (c) the content analysis of verbal material must be carefully carried out by several independent raters.

According to these considerations, the following procedure was selected: A group of adolescents was requested to come and speak with the study team should an event occur in their daily lives that particularly concerned them. Concerning the subjective definition of the event, we did not offer a definition of *event*, neither in respect to the degree of stress involved nor its structure. The adolescents were singularly requested to approach us in order to discuss "something that has happened which worries you." In order to ensure that we could discuss the event within the shortest time period following its onset, the adolescents were requested to call us immediately after the event took place and be willing to participate in an interview concerning the event shortly thereafter. It was very important for us to be able to make statements about the consistency or variability in the perception of events and the coping efforts related to them, thus we selected a time period of 6 weeks within which the interviews could take place. Within this time, the adolescents could, should an event occur that required coping, come and talk to us about it. Two days after participants came for an interview, we called them to evaluate the results of their coping behavior.

We presented our study in schools. From this preliminary sample of 6th graders ($n = 24$), 8th graders ($n = 26$), and 10th graders ($n = 21$), 65 adolescents volunteered to participate in the interviews. From this pool of interested individuals, we selected a subgroup 30, balanced in respect to the distributions of age and gender (i.e., 15 males, 15 females, 10 of each age group). We wrote to these individuals to provide them with information concerning the planned course of the study. In this written communication the adolescents were requested to contact us by phone as soon as an event should occur in their day-to-day lives. To this end, a telephone hotline service was maintained so that the adolescents could reach us daily from 9 a.m. to 9 p.m. and arrange a date for an interview. Great care was taken to ensure that each adolescent had the opportunity to speak with the same interviewer, should he or she come several times. The adolescents were also provided with precise instructions and a map indicating where we were located. The length of the study was limited to 6 weeks. The adolescents made quite different use of the possibility of participating in interviews, so that a group of 22 adolescents that came six times for interviews remained. Eight adolescents had to be excluded from the group because they came inconsistently (e.g., between three and five times).

Sample

During a period of 6 weeks, a sample of 22 adolescents (11 male and 11 female, 12 to 17 years) took part in our Coping Process Study. Eight adolescents were 12 to 13 years old (4 males and 4 females), eight adolescents were 14 to 15 years old (4 males and 4 females), and six adolescents were 16 to 17 years old (3 males and 3 females). They were pupils in the Grades 6, 8, and 10 of German high school. The participants phoned us immediately after an event had taken place and took part in several process-oriented interviews directly after the event occurred. Interviews with the adolescents were conducted by our research team (consisting of 4 males and 4 females). The interviews were postdoctoral research assistants and university professors aged 26 to 44 years.

The Coping Process Interview

In order to analyze the coping process, we developed an interview guide (see Table 1 in the appendix) for conducting a semistructured interview. As mentioned, we simply defined *event* as "something that has happened that worries you." The following eight areas were established that represented sequential phases of the adolescents' responses:

1. their framing and definition of the event,
2. their depiction of the context in which the event occurred,
3. questions about the causes of the event,
4. primary and secondary appraisal of the event,
5. coping response,
6. intended effect,
7. reappraisal of the event, and
8. the coping history in which the event was embedded.

Questions about reappraisal were posed separately in a telephone interview 2 days after the event occurred. The deep structure of the interview was supplemented by providing alternative formulations of questions that the interviewer could employ at his or her discretion in order to request additional information pertaining to the event, to establish the proper sequence of events as well as the relationships between them (see Goode & Hatt, 1966). The surface structure of the interview guide contained corresponding alternative questions that were grouped according to the respective aspect of the event, the appraisal, and the coping behavior. Both the selection of the corresponding questions and their sequence were oriented to the individual structure that the adolescent provided in the interview. The questions assisted the interviewers in ascertaining which relevant aspect of coping an adolescent was addressing during the interview and at which point the interviewer could obtain more detailed information about the particular coping process by appropriately posing additional questions. In the overview provided in Table 1 in the appendix, the deep and surface structures of the interview as they correspond to each other are presented. After completing the interview guide, an intensive training session with the interviewers took place. First, the sequence of questioning and answering in the course of the interview was simulated by role-plays. This involved a "tailoring" of the question–answer sequences and acquiring a thorough understanding of the deep structure of the interview, which was especially important for the interviewer. Finally, two trial interviews were conducted with adolescents. The results of the 2-week trial period revealed that the interview guide was an appropriate method for investigating the mechanisms of coping with events.

Following this training, which aimed at increasing the flexibility of the interview technique, the Coping Process Interviews were conducted over a period of 6 weeks. These process-oriented interviews were conducted immediately after an event occurred (i.e., not later than 1 hour after the event). The adolescents phoned us, came shortly thereafter to the department of psychology, and took part in the semistructured interview concerning the different stages of appraisal of the event and their subsequent coping. The mean length of the interview was 27 minutes with a range of 19 to 35 minutes. The interviewers were advised to be responsible for the same adolescents and to tailor the interview situation to him or her by alternative framing, repetitions, and follow-up questions, a procedure that is recognizable in the questions printed in Table 1 in the appendix. In addition, the interviewers were instructed to phone each adolescent they interviewed 2 days following the interview in order to inquire about reappraisal. The mean length of the telephone interview was 10 minutes with a range from 6 to 14 minutes. An example of the first and second interview, carried out with a 12-year-old female, Meike, is found in Table 2 in the appendix.

RESULTS

Overview of the Analysis

At the beginning, a thorough content analysis of the 72 Coping Process Interviews was carried out. Two independent raters categorized the material according to 39 main categories. Interrater reliability coefficients were determined using kappa. Then, frequencies in event structure and event parameters were analyzed for the whole sample; chi square tests were used to establish differences between males and females. In the next phase, the manner in which adolescents dealt with the events they reported was analyzed in accordance with Lazarus' model of coping. Thus, spontaneous reports of the adolescents concerning the coping process were considered to represent the adolescent's primary appraisal of the situation, and a subsequent, more detailed analysis of the individual intentions, goals, and aids employed toward coping as secondary appraisal. Coping behavior, including the feelings, thoughts, and actions related to mastering the event was determined. Finally, reappraisal (i.e., the thoughts about intended and accomplished goals, the quality of the change that occurred, and the like) was evaluated. Significant differences between males and females were again tested with chi square. The relationships between the different forms of appraisal and coping behavior based on 72 events were then determined by tetrachoric correlation coefficients.

Further analyses were conducted across situations and persons. Thirty-two thematically similar events were analyzed in respect to the different appraisals and coping. Concordance coefficients (Kendall's Tau) were calculated between the coping responses of those adolescents who had described a thematically similar event. Finally, changes in coping across time were analyzed by calculating concordance coefficients between the coping responses of 11 adolescents who contacted us four times. Two case studies presented here illustrate the coping process after the period of 4 weeks.

Content Analysis of the Coping Process Interview

In order to permit a more detailed analysis of coping process, the Coping Process Interviews were tape recorded and then transcribed verbatim. The content analysis performed on this material was oriented toward identifying two separate thematic categories, namely, description of the event structure and the description of the coping process, which as Lazarus and Launier (1978) suggested, include primary and secondary appraisal and reappraisal. The first step of the content analysis involved a component analysis as developed by Argyle et al. (1981), whereby the event structure is described according to such factors as "who is there, what is going on and where is it taking place" (p. 36). The next step involved coding aspects of primary and secondary appraisal, followed by an analysis of coping efforts, and finally of reappraisal. Whereas the component analysis, the analysis of primary and secondary appraisal, and the analysis of coping were carried out on the material assessed at Time 1, the analysis of reappraisal was conducted solely on material assessed at Time 2. Altogether, 39 categories were developed: (a) eight categories covering event parameters and event structure (familiarity, predictability, complexity, stressfulness, conflictiveness, contents, person named, context); (b) 17 categories covering the different forms of appraisal; primary appraisal (neutral, challenge, threat, and loss), secondary appraisal (ego-involvement, impact, preparedness, availability of resources, causal attribution, aims, expected success, controllability, perceived barriers, action planning), and reappraisal (interim changes, evaluation of own coping behavior, perceived stressfulness), and (c) 14 categories to describe coping behavior including affects (diffuse affect, positive affect, negative affect, and mixed feelings), cognitions (diffuse cognitions, denial, worrying/pessimism, realistic analysis, evaluation of own coping options, intentions to act, anticipatory reflection of consequences), and actions (starting of initiatives, problem avoidance, and ambivalent behavior). These 39 main categories were further differentiated into subcategories (e.g., negative affect: shock, stress, suspicion, envy, rivalry, anger, fear, embarrassment, disappointment, mourning). Two independent raters categorized the material. Considering the complexity of the material and the various main categories and subcategories, the coefficients measured by kappa (see Fleiss, 1971) can be regarded as sufficient. They amounted to $k = .83, p < .001$ for event structure, $k = .70, p < .001$ for the different forms of appraisal (primary appraisal, $k = .83$; secondary appraisal, $k = .59$; reappraisal, $k = .69$), and finally $k = .78, p < .001$ for coping.

Event Structure and Event Parameters

Our first objective was to analyze the descriptive characteristics of the event by means of the component analysis according to Argyle et al. (1981). This procedure involves identifying and categorizing the contents of the events described, including the number and types of persons involved and context in which the event happened. The analysis was supplemented by recording event parameters such as stressfulness, conflictiveness, complexity, and familiarity.

Rather unexpectedly, the adolescents named several events in their interviews. Altogether, 116 events were named, from which 72 events that the adolescents claimed to be reasons for eliciting contact with us and coming for interviews were selected. From these 72 spontaneously quoted events, only 6% represented major events or critical life events that happened unexpectedly during that time (e.g., "I watched a roofer fall down and die"). It was surprising that 74% of all events involved an interpersonal conflict (e.g., "I got an invitation for a party tonight, but my parents won't let me go"). Eight percent of the adolescents named a problem with themselves (e.g., "I am shocked about the weight I've put on"), and only 12% of events were "conflict-free" in that they were related to exclusively factual problems (e.g., "I lost my key"). The rate of reported interpersonal conflicts was higher for females than for males (81% and 69%, respectively). In describing this conflict, male adolescents mostly referred to the fields leisure time and school (41% and 31%, respectively); among female adolescents, the domains mostly concerned peers, parents, and identity/self-related problems (28%, 20%, and 20%, respectively). Male adolescents reported about three times more events from the area leisure time [$\chi^2(1, n = 22) = 7.9, p = .05$] and four times more events from the area school [$\chi^2(1, n = 22) = 8.2, p = .04$] than female adolescents. Due to this difference, the number of persons involved in the conflicts covaried (see Fig. 3.1), for example, the number of involved peers quoted by the girls was twice as large as the one stated by the boys (72% vs. 30%), whereas male adolescents indicated a higher number of involved adults such as trainers, teachers, and group leaders.

Events including parents were most frequently named by males and females of the youngest age group; the number decreased sharply with increasing age. Siblings were only mentioned by the youngest age group and only in association with the areas parents, peers, and school. In general, whereas male adolescents reported events involving three to four persons, or even larger groups, females rarely reported events involving more than two individuals.

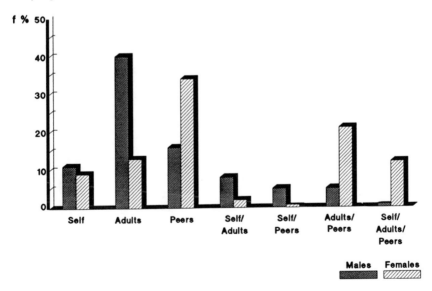

FIG. 3.1. Adult versus peer orientation in 72 spontaneously quoted events.

We may summarize the analysis of the structural components of the events at this point by stating that two thirds of all spontaneously reported events entailed an interpersonal conflict from different problem areas, including differing numbers of persons involved. Concerning event parameters, more females than males described the underlying conflict as being familiar $[\chi^2(1, n = 22) = 4.6, p = .06]$ and complex $[\chi^2(1, n = 22) = 5.1, p = .02]$. The perceived degree of stress was judged by 32% of the adolescents as low, by 59% as average, and by 9% as great. This indicates that the majority of the events discussed in the interviews were in fact only mildly stressful for the adolescents.

The Coping Process

In the next step, we analyzed the different appraisals of the events and subsequent coping processes according to the Lazarus model detailed earlier.

Primary Appraisal

According to Lazarus, primary appraisal entails a general evaluation about how significant or threatening an event is, and whether or not the event requires immediate action. We supplemented Lazarus' differentiation of stressfulness according to the properties of challenge, loss, or threat by adding the category "neutral," which, however, only accounted for 5% of all events mentioned.

Nearly two thirds of the adolescents described the events as more or less aversive (loss: 46%, threat: 27%, challenge: 32%). As can be seen in Figure 3.2, females described the events as threats four times more often than males $[\chi^2(1, n = 22) = 4.1, p = .05]$.

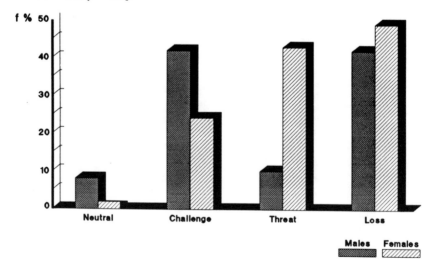

FIG. 3.2. Primary appraisal of 72 spontaneously quoted events.

Before the adolescents were encouraged to provide us with a more specific analysis of the situation in relation to their intentions and resources, their initial reactions to the event were documented. These reactions included irritation (50%), associations (41%), positive and negative affects (27% and 36%, respectively), shock and inability to act (32%), as well as thoughts of running away (14%).

Secondary Appraisal

The way people actually cope depends heavily on the resources available to them and on the constraints that inhibit the use of these resources in the context of a specific event. Secondary appraisal was therefore assessed by asking the adolescents to evaluate his or her coping options. Then the adolescents were requested to describe perceived barriers and possibilities of control, their ego-involvement, and their aims and resources. Nearly all adolescents (92%) described the event as highly relevant. Moreover, ego-involvement was described as high by 89% of the adolescents. Also, the expected consequences of the event were regarded as far-reaching by 72% of the adolescents. However, 79% of the adolescents reported a low possibility of control over the event (see Fig. 3.3) and 68% reported barriers preventing mastery of the event. External barriers such as control of the situation by others were more frequently named (68%) than internal barriers, such as personal disposition (32%).

Thus, adolescents perceived many barriers to solving the problem at hand. In particular, female adolescents reported higher expectations of failing to solve the conflict: 42% vs. 21% among male adolescents, $[\chi^2(1, n = 22) = 6.8, p = .001]$.

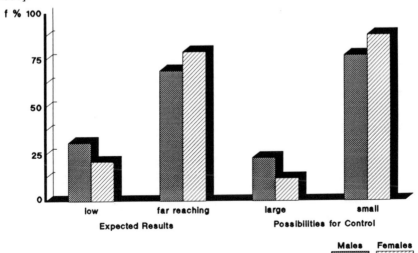

FIG. 3.3. Expected results and scope of action in 72 spontaneously quoted events.

The rather mixed judgment of possible success is related to the fact that the adolescents so often experienced a situation as being beyond their control. If, as illustrated in Fig. 3.3, the scope of action is restricted, and, at the same time, the events are regarded as significant and the expected consequences as far-reaching, then it becomes clear why adolescents regard the events as predominantly stressful. With respect to ego-involvement, controllability, perceived barriers, and causal attribution, no gender differences emerged. As mentioned earlier, however, females appraise the chances for success more pessimistically than males. Of the adolescents, 59% felt unprepared for the encounter with a particular event and 41% were prepared; 64% judged their skills and knowledge to be adequate for solving the problem and 36% to be not adequate. The anticipated consequences concerned situative factors (68%) and less often changes in interaction partners (18%) or in the adolescents themselves (14%), a finding that is consistent with their perception of predominantly external barriers and their causal attribution. The planning of action was carried out independently by 59% of the adolescents, 28% involved other individuals.

Coping

In the next step, we analyzed coping behavior. We measured coping by asking the adolescents what they thought, felt, or did in order to cope with events. There were 570 reports (40%) assigned to the dimension "affects," 565 (or 40%) to "cognitions," and 285 (or 20%) to "actions." The differentiation into subcategories revealed the following percentages: (a) affects (diffuse affects: 4%, negative affects: 24%, positive affects: 10%, and ambivalent feelings: 4%), (b) cognitions (diffuse cognitions: 6%, reflection and analysis: 16%, self-evaluation: 10%, reality testing: 5%, intention to act: 2%, and denial: 2%), and (c) actions (starting of initiatives: 11%, withdrawal: 7%, and ambivalent behavior: 2%).

Males and females did not differ with respect to the preference of a certain coping dimension. Cognitions were used increasingly with age by both genders, named by 24% of the 12- to 13-year-olds, 36% of the 14- to 15-year-olds, and 45% of the 16- to 17-year-olds, $[\chi^2(1, n = 22) = 8.0, p = .001]$.

Reappraisal

The last point, elucidated in the process-oriented interviews concerned tertiary appraisal or reappraisal. As a rule, we inquired about reappraisal 2 days after the first interview. In these second interviews, we found that after the coping process was over, the event usually lost its significance. This was especially true for male adolescents, whereas the females still experienced the event as persistent $[\chi^2(1, n = 22) = 8.9, p = .001]$, but less stressful $[\chi^2(2, n = 22) = 5.3, p = .05]$. On the whole, we found that for both genders, the intended goals could not be achieved (59% of all individuals). Failure was predominantly attributed to the situation (72%) and less to own efforts (22%) or coincidence (6%). In retrospect, most adolescents judged their coping behavior as positive, although girls did so slightly less frequently than boys (51% and 68%, respectively).

The Relationship Between Appraisals and Coping

Tetrachoric correlations between different forms of appraisal revealed substantial relationships. Table 3.1 illustrates that loss events are related to the first reaction of shock and anxiety as well as a low estimation of success in coping. It can be seen that events spontaneously described as challenging were perceived as rather confusing and surprising.

As expected, categories of appraisal and coping were related. High scores in cognitions are correlated with several categories of secondary appraisal, e.g., high impulse control ($r_{tet} = .36$, $p = .04$), precise goal intention ($r_{tet} = .38$, $p = .04$), and clearness of situation perception ($r_{tet} = .33$, $p = .08$). Adolescents with high scores in cognitions also had higher scores in attribution to internal conditions in others, i.e., they regarded the perceptions of others involved in the event as triggers for their own behavior ($r_{tet} = .48$, $p < .001$). Adolescents who frequently named affects as a coping strategy had high scores in the perception of an event as threatening ($r_{tet} = .36$, $p = .04$), unclear characterization of the situation ($r_{tet} = .31$, $p = .07$), and diffuse goals of coping ($r_{tet} = .32$, $p = .07$). Moreover, their scope of action was experienced as rather limited ($r_{tet} = .35$, $p = .05$). Similar conclusive results show the relationships between the primary and tertiary appraisal. Events initially perceived as challenging were judged positively in relation

TABLE 3.1

Relationship Between Primary Appraisal, the First Spontaneous Reactions, and Perceived Control and Expected Success in Mastering the Event (r_{tet}; $n = 22$)

	Primary Appraisal of Event as			
	Challenge	Threat	Loss	Neutral
First Reactions to Event				
Confusion	.30*			
Shock	−.46*	.55**	.65**	
Fear		.35*	.56**	
Associations	−.37*			
Surprise	.45**			
Secondary Appraisal				
Expected Success				
successful	.35*			
unsuccessful	−.46**		.55**	
Perceived Control				
external	−.58**		.42**	
internal	.67**	.31*	−.55**	

Note. Only significant correlations are reported: *$p < .05$. **$p < .01$.

TABLE 3.2
Relationships Between the Primary Appraisal and Reappraisal of Events
(r_{tet}; $n = 22$)

Reappraisal	Primary Appraisal			
	Challenge	Threat	Loss	Neutral
Intended Effect				
Improvement	.49**		−.43*	.47**
Worsening			.39*	
No change		.32*		
Attribution of Success or Failure				
Situation	.31*			−.40**
Chance	.32*		−.39*	
Ability				
Effort	.37*			
Final Evaluation				
positive	.42**		−.38*	
negative		.59**		
Significance of Event				
increased				
decreased		−.33*		.40**
Coping with Event				
completed	.56**	−.33	−.59**	.40**
not completed	−.58**	.41**	.43**	−.31*

Note. Only significant correlations are reported: *$p < .05$. **$p < .01$.

to the desired effects, whereas threatening events were later characterized as negative and the coping process as incomplete (see Table 3.2).

Coping Across Situations

The 72 spontaneously quoted events were grouped together thematically. Altogether, 10 thematic focal points could be identified. We selected five domains related to the coping process for a more detailed analysis. Thus, 32 events were consolidated according to five common underlying themes: (a) "betrayal": the adolescents felt betrayed or abandoned by another individual of the same gender; (b) "humiliation": the adolescents were ridiculed, embarrassed, insulted, or attacked by another individual of the same gender; (c) "autonomy": the adolescents resisted adhering to the rules and regulations imposed on them by parents; (d) "new friendship": the adolescents acquired a new friend of either gender or fell in love; and (e) "loss": a relationship between the adolescent and another individual of either gender was discontinued or the adolescent was separated from another. In addition, (f) "critical life events" reported by the adolescents were registered. Primary appraisal of the various events differed in that losses and critical life events were perceived as most stressful, whereas new friendship and, in part, autonomy were experienced as more challenging.

Secondary appraisal analysis revealed that perceived scope of action was extremely limited in loss and critical life events and greatest in new friendship. As can be seen in Fig. 3.4, perceived external barriers were extremely high in loss events.

The analysis of coping dimensions across events with common themes revealed an obvious shift in the relative proportion of affects, cognitions, and actions, illustrated in Fig. 3.5. It is worth mentioning that events that were experienced as very stressful (e.g., losses or critical life events) evoked many affects, and, at the same time, resulted in a suspension of actions. Conflict with parents, on the other hand, initiated many cognitions. When adolescents fell in love or met a new friend, affects, cognitions, and actions were more evenly balanced.

Concordance coefficients (Kendall's Tau) were calculated for those adolescents who had experienced events with the same theme. As can be seen in Table 3.3, high scores in concordance can be found in affects and cognitions, whereas the actions elicited by the events varied.

To give an example, when we selected those events that share the common theme, humiliation, the most frequently experienced affect was distrust, followed by anger and irritation, and in third place, fear and shame. For cognitions, unanimously high values were observed for anticipation of consequences and the analysis of motives of others and their manners of behaving. There were striking differences, however, in the manner in which adolescents reacted. Events with the common theme autonomy also showed high values for the affect (especially in anger and irritation), as well as for cognitions (including reflection, self-doubt, and realistic appraisal). Again, there were striking differences in the actions between the adolescents experiencing these events.

It is striking that the loss events were dealt with very heterogenously; this is possibly related to the type of loss in question. Two adolescents reported that their

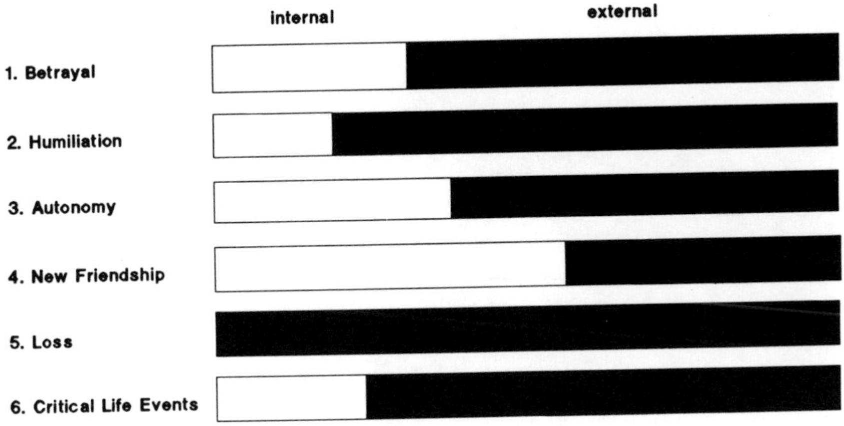

FIG. 3.4. Perceived barriers in thematically similar events.

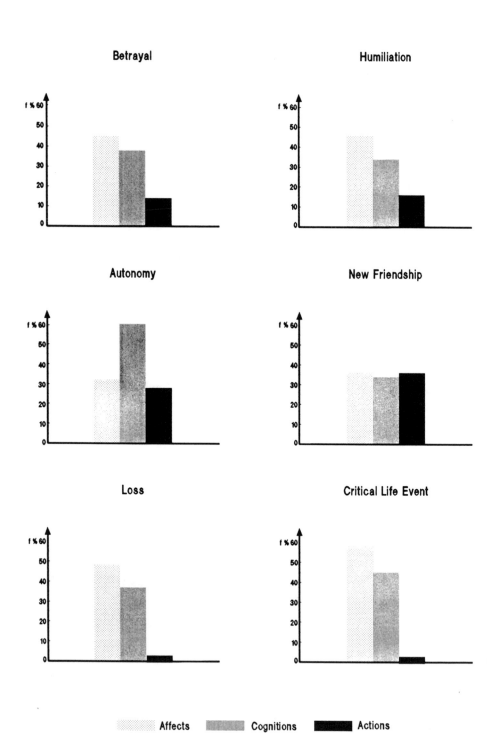

FIG. 3.5. Cognitions, emotions, and actions named in coping with thematically similar events.

TABLE 3.3

Concordance Coefficients (Kendall's Tau) in Coping Among Adolescents
Who Described Events That Were Thematically Similar (n = 22)

	n	Coping Dimensions		
		Affects $Tau_{(corr)}$	Cognitions $Tau_{(corr)}$	Actions $Tau_{(corr)}$
Betrayal	5	.70**	.47*	.35
Humiliation	4	.63*	.55*	.64**
Autonomy	6	.48*	.53*	.34
New friendship	5	.65**	.56*	.98**
Loss	5	.38	.42	.31
Critical life event	6	.26	.51*	.29

Note. *p < .05. **p < .01. ***p < .001.

heterosexual partners had left them, and two reported the loss of a same-gender friend; these losses are thus qualitatively quite different in nature. Surprisingly, critical life events elicited only concordant cognitions, whereas affects and actions differed greatly among the adolescents. Compared to other categories of events, those belonging to new friendship were dealt with in the most uniform way. The affects were, as to be expected, positive; overall the cognitions were related to self-appraisals, and the actions nearly completely concordant. The most frequently named type of action was the starting of initiatives.

Coping Across Time

In order to analyze coping across time, we analyzed the interviews of 11 adolescents (6 females, 5 males) who described how they coped with four events occurring within a time period of 4 consecutive weeks. Structural analysis of these 44 events revealed that the domains named did not differ across the four measurement points [$\chi^2(3, n = 22) = 17.1, p = .20$]. No differences existed in the number of persons involved [$\chi^2(3, n = 22) = 19.8, p = .25$] or the kind of interaction, e.g., peer- or adult-oriented interaction [$\chi^2(3, n = 22) = 17.7, p = .45$] across the four measurement times. The 44 events described by the adolescents were thus structurally similar. Concordance coefficients calculated separately for each adolescent across the four events demonstrated remarkably little conformity. Neither affects, nor cognitions, nor actions across time showed significantly high concordance (Kendall's Tau) between the values of 11 adolescents for the time points of measurement. A significant coefficient of concordance in actions ($Tau_{corr} = .90, p < .001$) was found in only one adolescent. A careful inspection of the data revealed that this adolescent had coped with all four events predominantly by withdrawal. The concordance coefficients calculated for each individual for all points of measurement, are conspicuously low, thus indicating that the adolescents reacted very differently to each event. Accordingly, the coping repertoire is not stable intraindividually, but varies depending on the event. By going beyond the structural traits of events and examining appraisal and coping in case studies, the reasons for this finding become apparent.

Case A

Annette, 12 years, described in her first event how she and her father had made plans for a trip to Hungary. The mother destroyed these plans by refusing to go with them and insisted on the annual holiday by the North Sea. Annette experienced the event as rather neutral because she was familiar with this problem, which had occurred previously in a similar way. She assessed her scope of action as fairly small and did not anticipate much success from her actions because she experienced control of events as being external.

A few days later, she reported another event that she encountered unexpectedly and by which she felt threatened. She was hardly prepared for this threat and found it difficult to develop coping strategies. In this case, her parents did not permit her to ride her bicycle far away from home anymore, which led to an extreme limitation of her spatial scope of movement. She regarded this as a threatening event with far-reaching consequences. She thought frequently about the reasons behind this parental ban, but at the same time, tried to act according to their wishes. When Annette attended the third interview, she reported that her boyfriend had left her surprisingly. She named affects such as shock and envy, she felt deserted and speculated about the causes of this separation. Regarding actions, she felt rather blocked. In the last interview, Annette had just received the results of a school test on which she performed poorly. Her ego-involvement in this event was much lower than in the third event that worried her considerably. On the contrary, she felt that receiving the bad grade challenged her to be more active at school and she expressed concrete plans of joining a study group in order to improve her school performance.

Figure 3.6 illustrates that the frequencies of the three coping dimensions vary strongly according to the event. The proportion of cognitions is much greater in the second event that was experienced as threatening, whereas the bad grade most obviously caused Annette to take action. The concordance between Annette's coping with the second event (belonging to the thematic area autonomy) and the reports of other adolescents in events of the same type is conspicuous (cf. Fig. 3.5). This applies also to Annette's third event, which belongs to the loss type of events.

Case B

The four events and the manner of coping with them are different for Jürgen, 17 years. In the first interview, Jürgen reported that his girlfriend had gone on a cruise with her family. He was worried that she might meet somebody and was afraid

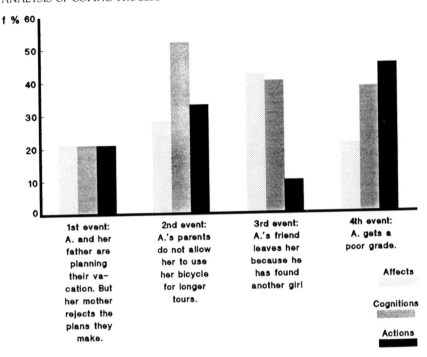

FIG. 3.6.   Coping across situations: Affects, cognitions, and actions related to coping efforts for four consecutive events reported by Annette, 12 years.

that she might leave him. Jürgen felt deserted and named specific affects such as jealousy and despair and was strongly involved in the event. He pondered a lot about it and wondered whether he himself might have contributed to his girlfriend making this decision (i.e., he attributed the result to himself and anticipated possible consequences for the future). He also felt emotionally blocked. Concordances existed between the descriptions of similar loss events reported by other adolescents (cf. Fig. 3.5).

One week later, Jürgen reported witnessing an accident involving two cars in front of a construction site. Although he was able to observe the whole event, the police ignored him as a witness. He felt that his self-worth had been hurt by this experience yet made several different attempts to start a conversation with the policemen and relate his observations. Because the accident occurred in front of a construction site belonging to his father, he concluded that the policemen tried to avoid him since his interests were not completely impartial.

Later on, Jürgen attended the third interview after his mother had reprimanded him for receiving a bad grade in school. He experienced the problem as being hardly threatening and rather familiar. He reflected only briefly about the most recent deterioration of his achievements at school but claimed to have embarked on a new learning schedule the same day. He felt comparatively well prepared for this event since he had experienced similar events many times before.

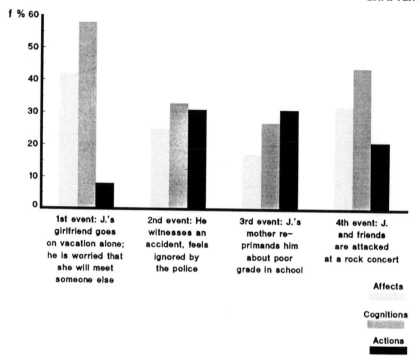

FIG. 3.7. Coping across situations: Affects, cognitions, and actions related to coping efforts in four consecutive events reported by Jürgen, 17 years.

In the fourth interview, Jürgen reported attending a rock concert with friends the night before where they were provoked and attacked by some other individuals. He reported surrendering completely to their violence. A great deal of time in the coping process was devoted to reflecting about the circumstances surrounding this surprising event, but in the long run, the causal attribution remained unclear to him. His actions were limited to avoidance behaviors.

Figure 3.7 illustrates the coping responses in four events reported by Jürgen. These examples show clearly why adolescents cope with events in such different ways, namely, appraisal aspects differ significantly although the events are structurally similar, which leads to differences in coping.

DISCUSSION

In our first study, we were interested in determining which phases of coping with events can be identified and whether changes in the coping process are associated with structural characteristics of the events. Several focused interviews were conducted with individuals belonging to a small group of 22 adolescents directly following the occurrence of an event. In these interviews, the adolescents described the process of various appraisals and their subsequent coping efforts. Two days following interviews concerning a given event, the feedback-process related to these coping strategies was analyzed again. The content analysis conducted on the 72 events (based on the component analysis by Argyle et al., 1981, and the coping model of Lazarus & Launier, 1978) revealed many interesting results. As was expected, major events occurred only rarely during the 6 weeks. It was surprising that more than two thirds of the minor events involved an interpersonal conflict; the domains this conflict was stemming from, however, differed for males and females. These differences in the content of events covaried with other event characteristics such as number and type of persons named as involved in the event. Compared to research on adults, the percentage of events involving an interpersonal conflict (74%) was even higher in our sample. Pearlin and Schooler (1978) reported that 60% of the events reported in their study on adult samples involved interpersonal problems. Females reported more identity and relationship events, whereas males reported more events related to school and leisure time. Also, the number of peers and friends involved in events described by females was twice as high as compared to males.

In analyzing the coping process, we found impressive evidence for the validity of the Lazarus model. Different stages of appraisal and coping could be exemplified and the importance of event parameters and appraisal for subsequent coping was demonstrated. The majority of the named events were assessed as being mildly stressful. This corresponded exactly to our intention of studying the manner in which adolescents cope with minor events or daily hassles as understood by Lazarus (see Kanner et al., 1981). Primary appraisal was usually followed by an initial reaction, in which confusion, first cognitive coping efforts, and impulses to act played a role. In secondary appraisal, very accurate estimates of the coping resources, the scope of action and the predictions about success were made. The prevailing negative appraisal of these minor events reported by the adolescents was somewhat surprising as were the numerous obstacles, barriers, and the limited changes brought about by coping.

The adolescents consistently attributed the limited effects of coping very much to external barriers and situational obstacles and less to their own efforts. As well, situative changes were named in the reappraisals. Research on the perception of social situations has in fact shown that individuals generally judge their behavior as being dependent on the situation, whereas the behavior of others is generally attributed to their personality (Nisbett, Caputo, Legant, & Marecek, 1973). Argyle et al. (1981) explained this phenomenon by noting that acting individuals and their observers focus their attention differently. Acting individuals do not observe their own behavior, they rather focus on situative stimuli that are significant for the planning of their actions.

Surprisingly, over one third of the coping strategies assigned to the category actions were characterized by the inability to act or by withdrawal. Actions were not frequent at all, and negative affects and cognitive processes of reflection and evaluation of the situation accounted for the greater proportion of the coping response. Apparently, this is related to primary appraisals in which most events are perceived as rather aversive as well as secondary appraisals in which the number of possible coping options are considered to be few due to the external barriers and limited scope of action. We do not believe that this result is youth-specific because Pervin (1976) observed very similar results in his analysis of open-ended answers to questions about person–situation interactions. In his study, affects emerged as an important basis for organization of situations. What was striking was the extent to which situations were described in terms of affects and less, for example, in terms of actions in his research. Our results also support Lazarus and Folkman's (1991) suggestion that situations appraised as showing the possibility for control and change were associated with more problem-focused coping (or actions, in our terms) than those that had to be accepted as they were. On the other hand, learning that one lacks control over the most significant aspects of a situation encourages the use of strategies to regulate emotions. Because of the specific event parameters exhibited, strategies for subduing emotions as well as reflections on possible solutions were more frequent in our study. Lazarus described these efforts to regulate emotions and explained: "It is often useful for a person to find ways of controlling the emotions, keeping it within bonds or reducing it where possible" (Lazarus & Launier, 1978, p. 315). Later on, he referred to the capacity of "inhibition of action" (p. 317) to conform with environmental or intrapsychic demands. This relationship becomes even clearer if one analyzes events that are similar in their thematic content and structural properties. Highly stressful events such as critical life events lead to a high amount of affects and mostly result in a blockade of action. More challenging events such as new friendship, on the other hand, lead to a high amount of activity.

We were able to demonstrate high concordance in the coping behaviors of adolescents experiencing an event that was thematically and structurally similar. However, adolescents might also react in a similar way to events with different parameters and behave in a similar manner in different situations. We therefore looked at individual courses of coping in analyzing the data of a subgroup of 11 adolescents who participated in four interviews within 4 weeks. Across all four measurements, the adolescents unanimously named events involving an interpersonal conflict. Thus, the degree of conflict reported in the first interview persisted throughout the whole interview sequence. However, every adolescent reported variable coping adapted to the different appraisals of these events.

From these results we may conclude that consistency in coping behavior requires thematic and structural similarities of events. Having experienced events with different thematic and structural properties, however, the adolescents adapt their coping behavior in accordance with these changing event characteristics. Thus, coping may be characterized as variable in that it is responsive to changing characteristics of the event, but may also be seen as consistent when different adolescents appraise an event as similar. Bem and Allen (1974) presented similar arguments along this line. They pointed out that one may only expect stable behavior across different situations when individuals are observed in situations that they themselves have perceived as being similar. At the same time, our findings confirm the strong dependency of coping on appraisal as outlined by Lazarus.

In our findings, not many age differences were found. Adolescents of different ages differed with respect to the domains to which the events belonged. Moreover, with increasing age, reflections about an event were reported much more frequently. Gender differences, however, were more striking. Females reported more events involving identity and relationship stressors than males, they felt more threatened by an event and were more pessimistic about the chances of solving underlying conflicts. An analysis of the reappraisal after the coping process revealed that female adolescents still reported a higher percentage of ongoing stress. For them, the underlying conflict was still virulent, although less stressful than in the primary appraisal. We may conclude that male adolescents are better able to separate themselves from a problem, regardless of whether it has been solved satisfactorily or not. Although the stressful encounter is over, it brings in its wake a new set of anticipatory processes. This is especially marked among the females. Being able to relax and shift attention away from one's own troubles offers a potential advantage in daily life.

It is, of course, not possible to rule out the possibility that our observations based on the conversations with the adolescents are not purely documents of what was actually done, felt or appraised, rather, they may also reflect the implicit theory our subjects hold about the coping processes as well as beliefs about how one should deal with events appropriately. This interpretation remains a logical possibility that cannot be dismissed when one is using self-report data. On the other hand, a number of interesting and consistent findings support the validity of our approach, especially with respect to the theoretical model of stress and coping introduced by Lazarus and Launier (1978). According to Lazarus, this process is best explained by a continuous unfolding or flow of events that have to be appraised. The way a person copes changes as an encounter unfolds, and consequently, different appraisals will occur. This conceptualization basically refers to the existence of transactions or various interdependencies between the constructs of different appraisals and coping. Indeed, the adolescents in our first study found it difficult to disentangle the flow of events and to describe the various appraisals and the coping process without skipping back and forth. From the 116 spontaneously named events we thus selected the 72 most salient events for the interview and adapted the sequence of the questions in the interview according to what they had already reported. Finally, we analyzed the material later on sequentially. Among the 72 events analyzed, differences in saliency and stressfulness were found, too. Conceptually, this reminds us of a distinction made by Lazarus and Folkman (1987) between "central hassles," which consist of important ongoing, sometimes troubling personal themes or conflicts and "peripheral hassles," which reflect vicissitudes of the moment such as accidents related to the weather or traffic jams. In a way, central hassles reflect personal problems, unsatisfied needs and expectations as well as deficits in coping skills, and they may be related to what Luborsky (1977) referred to as the core conflictual theme. Our grouping of events into those that are not only structurally similar, but also belonging to the same theme, follows these ideas. We would expect, in accordance with Lazarus and Folkman (1987), that these central hassles are more important for an individual's well-being than peripheral hassles. Our first study also raises issues concerning the accumulation of stressful events in the everyday lives of adolescents. During a period of 6 weeks, the adolescents were likely to experience seemingly contradictory states of mind and emotions concerning the events selected for analysis. Given that nearly all adolescents reported additional events at the beginning of the interview, and given that these events were mostly perceived as threatening, then adolescents have to manage a continuous flow of comparably stressful events. Thus, the widely used life-event approach is not an adequate measure of stress in adolescents' lives. It must be supplemented with measures of the more ordinary stressful experiences of daily living.

Our first study has provided many informative findings about the coping process and its course over time. In particular, the results on coping with thematically similar events are noteworthy, although given the limited data basis, only tentative conclusions are warranted. In the future, a cross-validation based on a larger sample would be appropriate and would offer us the possibility of conducting a more complex statistical analysis, as for example, is used in cross-sectional time series experiments (cf. Simonton, 1977). Nevertheless, even with this small sample of adolescents of various ages, it has been demonstrated that it is possible to isolate the different phases of the coping process and describe their interrelationships.

Assessment of Daily Stressors: Event Parameters and Coping

It may sound surprising, but at present we know less about the events that belong to the normal course of an adolescent's day and that may challenge him or her to cope than what we know about how adolescents master major crises such as death of a relative, affliction with cancer, or imprisonment. As explained in chapter 1, this may be due to the fact that adolescence, despite new conceptual orientations shared by many researchers, continues to be understood as a developmental period filled with crises. As a result, the role of minor events has rarely been examined. However, a consideration of such events may be an essential aspect in developing and applying comprehensive measures of stressful events for this age group.

In the study presented here (Study 2), everyday events in the lives of adolescents were under consideration once more. In particular, we wished to understand how such events are experienced and which effects their appraisals have on subsequent coping processes. In our event-centered approach, we aimed to address these questions by developing assessment methods that integrated both very common, everyday events as well as exceptionally stressful events. The sampling of these events, their descriptions according to selected event characteristics and subsequent coping were guided by the expert knowledge of the adolescents themselves.

PROPERTIES OF EVENTS
THAT MAKE THEM STRESSFUL

In recent years there has been widespread interest in the properties that make events stressful. In research on adults, most efforts have focused on aspects of life events such as their frequency, predictability, uncertainty, and control (see

69

Lazarus & Folkman, 1991, for a summary). In their research, Hultsch and Cornelius (1981) categorized different event parameters. Due to the nature of the specific events investigated and the different probabilities of event occurrence for both age groups, the results of such research can only be partly applied to adolescent events. Likewise, research on adolescent studies has mostly focused on highly stressful, non-normative events in selected samples. The study of Terr on the *Children of Chowchilla* (1979, 1983) represents a good example of how adolescents react when faced with extreme circumstances, and where preexisting knowledge has no relevance whatsoever. In this case, a group of children and adolescents were kidnapped from school and held hostage by their abductors for several days. At the beginning, the situation was highly ambiguous and uncontrollable. Only at the end of the episode did the adolescents begin to recognize the event as a kidnapping. Due to these event parameters, the adolescents had no opportunity to develop specific coping skills to deal with the situation, and the awareness of this coping deficit also increased the degree of threat perceived. Terr's report illustrates that passivity and shock prevail as long as the meaning of the event is unclear. Indeed, only after the children and adolescents realized they had been kidnapped, did some of them actively participate in an attempt to free themselves.

According to Lazarus and Folkman (1991), event predictability is an additionally important event parameter in that it allows anticipatory coping to take place. These authors argued that predictability of an event allows individuals to prepare themselves for it in some way, thereby reducing the aversiveness of the stressor. Although the likelihood of event occurrence undoubtedly influences appraisal, it has been shown that subjective probability estimates often differ from objective probabilities of occurrence (Goetz & McTyre, 1981). This mismatch is even more apparent with respect to adolescents. For example, knowledge about teenage pregnancies and car accidents does not essentially increase the use of contraceptives or reduce dangerous behavior such as driving under the influence of alcohol (Moore & Rosenthal, 1993; Morrison, 1985). Furthermore, it must be pointed out that predictability of an event is not uniform for all ages; especially major events occur with different probabilities among adolescents and adults. Chronic illness, for example, is experienced only by 10% of the adolescents, but is rather common in old age. These differences may result in a change of other event parameters (e.g., from non-normative to more normative) and consequently, in changes in anticipatory preparation and social support. If illness and death of relatives occur more frequently, as in late adulthood, we would expect more anticipatory coping as well as empathetic reactions from significant others. Consequently, the emergence of a critical life event such as serious illness during adolescence may have more dramatic consequences. Neugarten (1979) pointed out that people have a concept of a normal life cycle that includes expectations that certain events will occur at certain times. If an event occurs prematurely, this may have consequences for social support and can deprive the person of the chance to develop internal coping resources. Timing of the event is therefore another important event parameter.

A related event parameter is concerned with the interval during which an event is anticipated. Imminence refers to the time left before an event occurs. Here, corresponding to the timing of events in the life cycle, it is expected that an optimal amount of time helps in searching information and permits enlisting the support of significant others, thereby aiding in the preparation for coping (Lazarus & Folkman, 1991). From the studies of Mechanic (1962) we know that for students preparing for doctoral exams, there exists a curvilinear threat arousal pattern as the event grows more imminent. On the other hand, Hurrelmann and Engel (1989) were able to show that threat was highest when high school students feared not being advanced to the next grade, whereas when this actually happened it resulted in a reduction of stress as well as psychosomatic symptoms.

The differentiation of an event according to its various parameters shows to what extent they may influence appraisal and subsequent coping. It is important to note that there are some methodological problems that may impede attempts to characterize the events and their parameters accurately. For one, because most event parameters are assessed retrospectively, reports of the frequency of events and other parameters may differ or be distorted due to forgetting. Short-term threatening events are reported more reliably than long-term ones (Parry, Shapiro, & Davies, 1981). In addition, personal history and current mood may alter the extent to which an event is judged as threatening, unpredictable, uncertain, or imminent (Antonovsky, 1981). Finally, the accumulation of events may represent another methodological problem complicating the assessment of event parameters, especially in older age groups.

MEASURES OF ADOLESCENT STRESS

Similar to the assessment of event parameters, most measures of life stress in adolescents have been designed to resemble those applied to adults. More recently, several instruments have been developed that are suitable for younger age groups (Johnson, 1986). Due to the aforementioned methodological problems, the approach in gathering and selecting everyday events and the construction of an inventory of coping strategies for these events should be closely oriented to the concerned individual. As well, the adolescents should be permitted to generate and describe such events as freely and openly as possible. This approach is by no means self-evident. In the past, critical life events were often operationalized so that researchers requested adolescents to select their responses from fixed inventories of stressful events; other individuals, such as the parents, were asked about the frequency or stressfulness of the events (see Coddington, 1972; Garrison & McQuiston, 1989; Johnson, 1986). One exception can be found in the recent work on the development of the APES (Compas et al., 1987). This scale is based on minor and major events generated by adolescents. Open-ended lists of daily and major life events were obtained from a sample of more than 600 adolescents aged between 12 and 20 years. There were 213 nonredundant life events and daily stressors generated, which could be organized into three slightly different sets of items representing events of early, middle, and late adolescence. Three event parameters—desirability, impact, and causality—were found to be relevant. In studies employing other instruments it was established that the types of events generated were strongly dependent on the ages of individuals. Coddington (1972), for example, analyzed life events as a function of age and found an increased number of life stressors between the ages of 12 and 18 years, which consequently led to the construction of age-specific life event lists. The instrument developed by Compas and colleagues is, however, the only one that allows a combined assessment of minor and major stressors and that differentiates between different event parameters. Because stressors may vary depending on context and culture, event characteristics for the samples of German adolescents participating in our research had to be acquired independently.

RESEARCH QUESTIONS

The first study, presented in chapter 3, explored the coping process with different stressors. It was found that in the ordinary transactions in the lives of adolescents, it was not so much a major event, but a continuous series of irritating, frustrating, and distressing events that mattered most. In the second study, presented in this chapter, we wished to deepen our understanding of how such events are experienced and which effects their appraisal had on subsequent coping. We thus analyzed two elements of the coping process in more detail, namely, event parameters and coping strategies. First, we analyzed the event parameters of naturally occurring events, again with the focus on minor events. We expected that event parameters such as predictability, controllability, stressfulness, timing, and accumulation would not be confined to major events and would have important implications for coping. The second part of the analysis focused on coping strategies used in dealing with a selection of these minor events.

Accordingly, two consecutive studies are presented here. The main emphasis in Study 2a lies in the sampling of events and obtaining a precise description of these events according to several event parameters. From the results of Study 2a, we selected 10 "universal" events (i.e., events that were experienced most frequently by a great number of adolescents, regardless of age and gender). These universal events are analyzed in Study 2b in greater detail. Using a new sample of adolescents, the events are assessed according to various event parameters. In addition, each adolescent was requested to indicate how he or she dealt with each event.

One seldom has the opportunity to study samples of individuals who experienced an event under such controlled conditions as described earlier for the kidnapping episode studied by Terr (1979). Nevertheless, in obtaining universal events we aimed to identify those events that were important for the greatest number of adolescents possible. In order to avoid retrospective distortions, only events occurring within a range of a few days to 2 weeks before the interview should be investigated. Although with this procedure we could not exclude that the adolescents would report non-normative events (i.e., those occurring extremely seldom), it is still most probable that the adolescents would primarily report events typical for their ages (i.e., that a high correlation between certain named events and the age of the adolescents would exist). An additional event characteristic—predictability—is confounded with age. Finding universal events thus offers the advantage of being able to compare interindividual variability in event parameters such as predictability, controllability, and stressfulness, which in turn, may have an effect on coping behavior.

METHOD

Procedure

As mentioned already, two consecutive studies (Studies 2a and 2b) were conducted to assess everyday events and subsequent coping. The focus of Study 2a lay in event sampling and the generation of 10 universal events, whereas in Study 2b, event characteristics and coping strategies in dealing with these universal events were investigated. Several principles guided our research in both studies. First, the definition of *event* was intentionally left open. At best, an event was described as being some matter with which the adolescents were especially concerned (see Study 1 in chap. 3). Second, in order to reduce distortions in the adolescents' accounts due to retrospective reporting, the events to be described should not have taken place more than 2 weeks before the interview. Third, in order to encourage the adolescents to provide the freshest report possible, they were requested to call up the event in their memory as if it had just taken place. The Event Exploration Interview was used in both studies but was slightly altered in order to accommodate for the different aspects under scrutiny in the two studies. In Study 2a, the choice of events to be evaluated was left to the adolescents themselves. The adolescents were interviewed and their answers were documented. In Study 2b, the 10 universal events derived from Study 2a were presented to a new sample of adolescents in written form, and they rated the events according to the event characteristics provided and described the coping strategies on their own. The sample for both studies consisted of 164 adolescents. Three equally sized groups of adolescents were selected from students attending Grades 6, 9, and 11 in a German high school. The individuals in these groups were then randomly assigned to participate in Study 2a or Study 2b.

Study 2a

Sample

Data was obtained from 54 adolescents (27 males and 27 females), belonging to three age groups: 12-year-olds ($n = 18$), 15-year-olds ($n = 19$), and 17-year-olds ($n = 17$). We asked them to report important events that had occurred in the previous 2 weeks, to describe these events and to rate them according to several event parameters. Four postdoctoral research assistants, two males ($M = 27$ years) and two females ($M = 25$ years), interviewed the adolescents with the help of the Event Exploration Interview, Part 1: Event Sampling. The interviewer and the individual adolescent met after class for a short time. The subjects were informed that the purpose of the study was to obtain a sample of relevant events in the everyday life of adolescents as adolescents themselves perceive them.

The Event Exploration Interview, Part 1: Event Sampling. The Event Exploration Interview, in which the adolescents were used as experts for generating universal events, was divided into four parts (see Table 3 in the appendix): (a) the collection of significant events occurring during the previous 2 weeks, (b) a description of coping, (c) specification of especially important events, and (d) evaluation of these events with the help of different event parameters. First, a general outline of "event" was elicited by asking the adolescents to tell about something that happened with which they were particularly occupied. After generating the events that had occurred in the previous 2 weeks and providing a description of coping, the adolescents were requested to identify a few of the most important events. These events were then rated according to eight dimensions. The interviewer presented the adolescents with the list of these event parameters and requested them to mark the appropriate rank for each event parameter. The Event Exploration Interview, Part 1 thus incorporated a combination of open and closed questions. The mean duration of this interview was 15 minutes with a range from 9 to 23 minutes.

Study 2b

Sample

Data was obtained from 110 adolescents (55 males and 55 females) from three age groups: 12-year-olds ($n = 37$), 15-year-olds ($n = 38$), and 17-year-olds ($n = 35$). These groups of adolescents paralleled those who participated in Study 2a (i.e., the adolescents in this study were also students in the same German high school). Study 2a and Study 2b represented the entire sample in the Grades 6, 9, and 11 in this school.

The Event Exploration Interview, Part 2: Universal Events. Ten universal events obtained in Study 2a were presented in a written questionnaire to the parallel groups of adolescents. This selection of events represented the standardized stimulus situation through which the process of coping was to be studied. The Event Exploration Interview, Part 2 was used as the instrument. Compared to the oral interview used in Study 2a, this exploration was based on a written questionnaire and contained standardized stimulus material. The written questions concerning appraisal and coping with events referred to 10 universal events (i.e., events that had been found in Study 2a to occur frequently in the everyday lives of adolescents). The questions cover the following categories: (a) depiction of events, (b) event frequency, (c) appraisal of event based on event parameters using the semantic differential, and (d) coping (see Table 4 in the appendix).

The adolescents were first asked to try to remember the respective universal event in such a way as if it had just happened. Then they had to indicate the event's frequency during the previous 2 weeks, ranging from 0 (*not experienced*) to 3 (*frequently experienced*). After this, they were asked to describe the event and to evaluate it according to a list of eight different event parameters (e.g., predictability, stressfulness, chronicity). Finally, the adolescents were asked how they handled the event. The sequence of the questions in the catalogue was the same for each of the universal events; however, the order in which the events were presented was systematically changed in order to avoid any artifactual effects due to sequence.

RESULTS

Study 2a

Event Sampling

The 54 adolescents named 1,099 events altogether. Females named more events ($e = 610$) than males ($e = 489$). Each subject reported approximately 23 stressful episodes, which ranged from minor concerns (e.g., "I got a bad haircut") to very stressful events such as recent parental divorce. These events were then systematically grouped together according to domains. First, individual categories were constructed that could be assigned to broader content domains. Content analysis of the reported events generated 99 age-dependent categories. Thirty categories each came from the event lists of the 12- and 15-year-olds, respectively, and 39 came from the 17-year-olds. The suitability of the category system was tested by presenting three independent raters with the 1,099 events and requesting them to reassign them to the 99 categories. Misclassifications ranged between 10% and 17%, which in sight of the large size of the category system, were considered justifiable.

Finally, the 99 event categories were assigned to eight domains, including such domains as "self," "school," "peers," and "parents." Events that were related to the adolescents' futures as well as political events were also present. Particularly stressful events were assigned to the category "critical life events." Table 4.1

TABLE 4.1
Percentages of Events Across Eight Domains[a,b]

Domains	12-Year-Old Adolescents		15-Year-Old Adolescents		17-Year-Old Adolescents	
	Male	Female	Male	Female	Male	Female
Self	16	23	25	29	24	18
Romantic relations	1	2	18	12	8	9
Peers/friends	30	24	12	17	16	20
School	21	27	25	13	28	19
Parents	16	13	12	16	9	17
Politics/future	10	8	6	10	12	11
Critical life events	2	3	2	2	1	3
Idiosyncratic events	5	2	1	1	4	5

Note. [a]Total number of events = 1,099.
[b]Columns may not add up to 100, due to rounding.

indicates the number of events named by the boys and girls in different age groups.

As can be seen in Table 4.1, most events belonged to the areas of peers, school, and self. It is surprising how frequently social, cultural, and political events were mentioned (e.g., "The Gulf War has made me think a lot" or "I heard on TV that youth unemployment is increasing"), here assigned to the domain "politics/future." Major events were reported only by about 2% of the adolescents (e.g., "My brother is moving out" or "My mother is starting to work again"). Idiosyncratic events were mentioned only by a few adolescents and were very heterogeneous and thus were not included in all further analyses.

Selection of Universal Events. The decision to rely on adolescents as experts was based on the assumption that they were best able to report about the events important for them and their methods of dealing with such events. A sample of 10 universal events was drawn according to the following criteria: (a) the named event should be an incident that involved an overt activity or manifest happening, (b) the event should occur independent of age and gender, (c) the event should be very important, and (d) the event should occur with high frequency. Thus, from our event pool we selected universal events (i.e., events that were rather frequent and perceived as salient, irrespective of age and gender). The seven domains to which the 10 universal events were assigned were as follows:

1. self: "I felt lonely," "I was humiliated," "I am dissatisfied with my appearance";
2. romantic relations: "I fell in love";
3. peers: "I had some trouble with my friends";

4. school: "I got a bad grade," "I had an argument with my teacher";

5. parents: "I had a quarrel with my parents";

6. politics/future: "A future/political event affected me very much"; and

7. critical life events: "I experienced something that was very stressful."

Dimensions of Coping

The Event Exploration Interview, Part 1: Event Sampling also inquired about coping strategies used in dealing with the events. It was surprising that on the average, the adolescents mentioned considerably fewer coping strategies (218) than events (1,099). Each participant reported approximately four coping strategies. We classified the coping responses according to three major dimensions: affects, cognitions, and actions. These categories have been used already in our first study (see chap. 3).

Study 2b

Sampling of Coping Strategies

Based on the answers of adolescents in Study 2b, each coping dimension was differentiated into additional categories so that the strategies could be assigned to 10 affect categories, 12 cognition categories, and 9 action categories. The following 10 types of coping strategies were subsumed under affects:

1. diffuse affects,

2. anger,

3. loathing/disgust,

4. dread/fear,

5. shame/guilt,

6. desperation,

7. disappointment,

8. joy,

9. affection, and

10. empathy.

Coping strategies subsumed under cognitions included 12 categories:

1. differentiation,

2. reflection,

3. anticipation,

4. brooding,

5. realistic assessment,

6. self-confidence,

7. self-criticism,

8. optimism,

9. pessimism,

10. trivialization,

11. derogation, and

12. intention to act.

Coping strategies subsumed under actions included the following 9 categories:

1. beginning of initiatives,

2. using social resources/discussing with somebody,

3. asking for help,

4. resistance,

5. finding a solution,

6. submission,

7. withdrawal,

8. uncertainty what to do, and

9. passivity/doing nothing.

Content analysis of the coping strategies in dealing with the universal events was conducted by five independent judges. A strategy was assigned to a coping dimension ranging from 1 (*not outstanding*), to 2 (*fairly outstanding*), to 3 (*very outstanding*). Kappa coefficients amounted to .67 for affects, .52 for cognitions, and .55 for actions across all 10 universal events.

Frequency of Universal Events

Figure 4.1 illustrates the frequency of 10 universal events during 2 weeks ranging from 0 (*not experienced*), 1 (*experienced once*), 2 (*experienced several times*), to 3 (*frequently experienced*). It can be seen that the majority of the adolescents experienced most of the stressful events at least once. Apparently, "quarrel with parents" was a rather frequent event, followed by "I got a poor grade" and "I fell in love." As expected, a major event (i.e., critical life event) occurred relatively seldom ($M = 0.2$).

Overall Estimation of Event Parameters

Multiple comparisons of the 10 universal events across eight event parameters revealed that very stressful events and falling in love were rated as being considerably more important than the other events. As can be seen in Table 4.2,

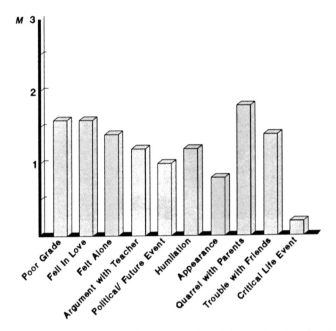

FIG. 4.1. Frequency of universal events named by adolescents in a 2-week period (n = 110).

receiving a poor grade and having trouble with parents were more predictable events than being humiliated or having trouble with friends. Events such as being in love and getting a poor grade were more likely to spur the adolescent to act, whereas events involving the self, such as being lonely, humiliated, or disappointed with one's looks had a more paralyzing effect. The feeling of being alone and the critical life event represented the events that caused the adolescents to suffer the most.

If one considers only the highest means of each of the eight event parameters measured for all the events investigated, it becomes striking that the global judgment of an event as pleasant or unpleasant represents the parameter dimension that has the highest mean. Except for Event 2, "I fell in love," all events were considered to be rather unpleasant. This again clearly shows that the adolescents mostly interpreted the events as being more aversive, stressful experiences.

Overall Estimation of Coping Strategies

How do adolescents deal with stressful, unpleasant, and paralyzing experiences? Apparently, certain events activated more emotional coping strategies, whereas others stimulated cognitive ones. Alternative actions were generally reported less often than feelings and reflections about the event. Actions were named especially for events involving social conflict, such as instances of friction

TABLE 4.2

Estimation of the 10 Universal Events According to Eight Event Parameters[a]

| The experience was for me . . . | Events | | | | | | | | | | Multiple Comparison |
	1 bad grade	2 in love	3 felt alone	4 argument w.teacher	5 fut./pol. event	6 humiliation	7 appearance	8 quarrel w. parents	9 trouble w. friends	10 critical life event	
Pleasant/unpleasant[b]	4.2	1.5	4.4	4.3	4.5	4.6	4.3	4.4	4.3	4.4	2 < 1, 3–10
Important/unimportant	2.4	1.6	1.8	2.7	1.7	2.7	2.3	2.3	2.3	1.4	2, 10 < 1, 4, 6, 7, 8, 9
Predictable/unpredictable	2.5	3.2	3.3	3.3	3.3	3.7	2.8	2.5	3.5	3.3	1, 8 < 6, 9
Motivating/paralyzing	2.5	2.1	3.4	3.0	3.5	3.5	3.0	3.0	3.2	3.7	1, 2 < 3, 5, 6, 10
Controllable/not controllable	2.7	2.3	2.9	3.1	3.2	3.1	2.6	2.6	3.0	3.2	
Minimally stressful/highly stressful	3.0	3.2	4.0	2.9	3.7	3.3	3.3	3.7	3.5	4.0	1 < 3, 0
Acute/chronic	2.1	3.4	2.6	2.8	3.3	2.0	2.7	2.3	2.3	3.4	1, 6, 8, 9 < 2, 10
Involved emotions more/ involved reasoning more	3.1	1.6	1.9	3.0	3.3	2.1	2.1	2.5	2.4	2.0	2, 3 < 1, 4

Note. [a]n = 110
[b]ranging from 1 (pleasant) to 5 (unpleasant)

TABLE 4.3
Affects, Cognitions, and Actions in Coping With 10 Universal Events
(n = 110)

	Affects		Cognitions		Actions	
Events	M	SD	M	SD	M	SD
1. "I got a poor grade."	1.41	0.51	1.62	0.35	1.40	0.26
2. "I fell in love."	1.47	0.52	1.30	0.21	1.39	0.37
3. "I felt lonely."	1.52	0.51	1.49	0.25	1.32	0.27
4. "I had an argument with a teacher."	1.37	0.46	1.54	0.42	1.02	0.24
5. "A future-political event affected me very much."	1.45	0.46	1.38	0.21	1.08	0.33
6. "I was humiliated."	1.41	0.48	1.38	0.26	1.04	0.19
7. "I am dissatisfied with my appearance."	1.36	0.38	1.43	0.21	1.10	0.29
8. "I had a quarrel with my parents."	1.40	0.43	1.46	0.26	1.38	0.26
9. "I had some trouble with my friends."	1.46	0.51	1.48	0.40	1.39	0.34
10. "I experienced something as very stressful."	1.48	0.40	1.36	0.18	1.01	0.27

between adolescents and their parents, teachers, or same-aged friends. Events that elicited a strong affective reaction in the adolescent were usually those that were very strongly related to the adolescent's self (e.g., feeling alone, being in love, being very affected by a critical life event). As a rule, such events did not result in coping efforts marked by great activity. On the other hand, we observed that for some events (e.g., having an argument with the teacher, receiving a poor grade), coping was primarily manifested in increased cognitive efforts.

Event Parameters and Coping Strategies Across Events

After having described the overall estimation of event parameters and coping dimensions, the 10 universal events are examined in more detail, as are related age and gender differences. In the following, the terms *more* and *less* are used for differences that were statistically significantly ($p < .05$).

Event 1: "I Got a Poor Grade." The event "I got a poor grade" is one of the most frequent events; it was experienced as being unpleasant yet important and transitory. Across all age groups, cognitive coping strategies were most frequently named for this event, and the adolescents also named more affects than the planning of concrete activities to tackle the problem (see Fig. 4.2).

The most frequently named affects were anger, disappointment, and shame. Anticipation, brooding, and self-criticism were the most frequently named cognitions, and beginning of initiatives and submission were the most frequently named actions. Twelve-year-olds experienced the event more seldom, yet also considered it to be very important and reported many very negative affects such as fear, feelings of guilt, and desperation. They brooded more about the event

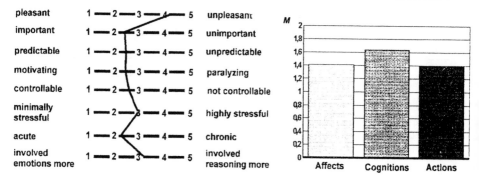

FIG. 4.2. Event parameters and coping strategies for Event 1: "I got a poor grade."

than the 17-year-olds did. It is also striking that the youngest age group took up exceptionally many initiatives in order to cope with the event that was so stressful for them.

Event 2: "I Fell in Love." Because falling in love is judged to be important and more pleasant, the majority of coping strategies related to this event were characterized more by positive affects such as joy and affection. Coping strategies that included cognitive activity and concrete actions were named with the same frequency and included high values in reflection, anticipation, optimism, intentions to act, and initiatives (see Fig. 4.3).

In the perception of the event "I fell in love," boys and girls differed only with respect to two characteristics: Girls perceived being in love as more unpleasant and paralyzing than boys. This different perception of the event (with same frequency of occurrence) was of course related to very different coping strategies. Girls expressed emotions more often, especially negative ones such as disappointment. Moreover, their preoccupation with the event was more differentiated, and they exercised more self-criticism than male adolescents. At the level of activity, they were more likely to make compromises, whereas the boys preferred to deal with the event more actively.

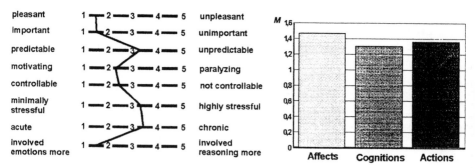

FIG. 4.3. Event parameters and coping strategies related to Event 2: "I fell in love."

Striking age differences could be observed. Compared to the older adolescents, the 12-year-olds perceived being in love as being a particularly stressful situation, which although important, could hardly be controlled. They reported very high values for one specific negative affect, namely, shame. Although they did not demonstrate much active behavior, the 15-year-olds tried to achieve a cognitive differentiation of the situation. Their final evaluations were diametrically opposed: Optimistic and pessimistic outcomes for the event were assumed in equal numbers. The 17-year-olds assessed the event most positively and showed the most initiatives in dealing with the situation.

Event 3: "I Felt Lonely." The event "I felt lonely" occurred less frequently than, for example, receiving a poor grade. However, it was experienced as being much more stressful, and the adolescents indicated that they were affected by it far more frequently. Therefore, it is not surprising that more affects were named with high values in anger and disappointment. At the same time, only few cognitive efforts were made to deal with loneliness, including self-criticism, derogation, and trivialization. Not many actions were named; high values could be observed in withdrawal and doing nothing (see Fig. 4.4).

Although male and female adolescents judged being lonely in the same manner for all eight parameters, they experienced this event with significantly different frequencies. Girls reported having felt lonely twice as often as boys. However, with respect to the coping strategies used to deal with this event, girls and boys did not differ.

A comparison of the age groups revealed no differences in the frequency with which the event was experienced by 12-, 15-, and 17-year-olds. Although the event was perceived in a similar manner by all three groups, the 15-year-olds perceived loneliness as being particularly stressful. It is interesting to note the different affective coping behaviors reported here. The 12-year-olds expressed quite diffuse affects most frequently and tended to anticipate similarly stressful occurrences. The 15-year-olds portrayed a more specific negative affect, desperation, and tended to solve the problem by trying to fit in with the group and meet their expectations. Only the 17-year-olds named positive affects such as joy and relief, and described being alone as a completely desirable situation.

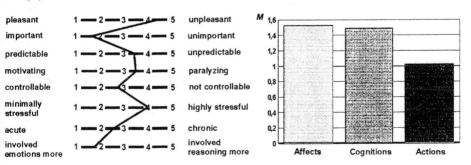

FIG. 4.4. Event parameters and coping strategies related to Event 3: "I felt lonely."

Event 4: "I Had an Argument With a Teacher."   Quarrels with a teacher occurred less often than with parents, and were also perceived to be less stressful. Most adolescents considered this event to be less predictable and saw more opportunities of being able to influence an event's outcome. It is therefore not surprising that the adolescents reacted to an argument with a teacher with fewer affects (frequent category: anger). Instead, they thought out the situation more carefully and planned more activities directed at solving the conflict than for those related to arguments with the parents. As with Event 1, "I got a poor grade," coping with this event involved more cognitive activities than other coping strategies. Frequent cognitions named were anticipation and derogation. Resistance, discussion with others, and asking for help were frequent action categories (see Fig. 4.5).

Although girls experienced arguments with teachers as being more stressful than boys, boys and girls did not differ in their choice of coping strategies for this event. Also, the age differences were not very outstanding. In this regard, the 12- and 15-year-olds named a concrete affect, the disappointment in the teacher's behavior, more often than the 17-year-olds did. The group of the oldest adolescents, however, showed an increased number of actions, in particular, resisting the teacher's behavior and settling the situation by relying on social relationships (discussions with the teacher and with other students). The individuals in this group not only undertook more action, but also devoted considerably much more time to their planning.

Event 5: "A Future/Political Event Affected Me Very Much."   The adolescents we investigated did not appear to be concerned with political events often. Nevertheless, when the adolescents were affected by a future or political event, it was considered to be very important, highly stressful, and markedly paralyzing—to the degree that was typical for events more directly related to the self, such as personal humiliation and feeling lonely. This becomes understandable as soon as one appreciates the nature of the events' contents. Events

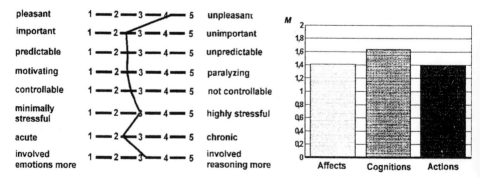

FIG. 4.5.   Event parameters and coping strategies related to Event 4: "I had an argument with a teacher."

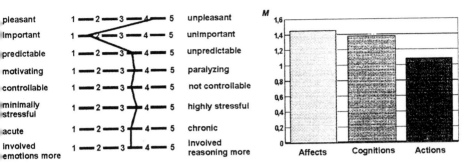

FIG. 4.6. Event parameters and coping strategies related to Event 5: "A future/political event affected me very much."

that adolescents assigned to this category involved threat, killing, and destruction of human life (e.g., visits to a concentration camp, watching a film about a massacre or bombing as well as political demonstrations) as well as events related to their personal future (e.g., TV news on youth unemployment).

It fits quite well to the characterization of these events as equally stressful and paralyzing that the adolescents reacted with strong affects (high values in fear), but carried out exceptionally few actions in connection with these events. As Table 4.3 illustrates, the reported incidence of actions is among the second lowest coping strategies of all events. This paralysis was perceived by the girls even more strongly. In addition, the oldest adolescents judged these events most pessimistically in that they ascribed a lasting quality to them (see Fig. 4.6).

Compared to boys, girls reacted to these events more with empathy; they tried to inform themselves better and exchanged their feelings with important social partners. The age differences were numerous and evident for all three dimensions of coping strategies. Younger students were generally more affected. They reported negative affects such as fear and desperation, put themselves in the roles of individuals involved in the event and brooded about the event. In addition, they tended to be passive and "keep their distance" from the event. The older adolescents appeared to be less affected by the absolute impact of such events, and although they overall also seldom named actions related to these future/political events, they did so more often than the youngest adolescents. Initiatives and talking with friends were named most frequently by these older adolescents.

Event 6: "I Was Humiliated."   The event of being personally humiliated was, in many aspects, rated similarly to feeling lonely. The frequencies with which these events were reported were similar, the adolescents gave the same weight to the event parameters for both events and they named the same coping strategies. Males believed that personal humiliation was less controllable than girls, yet girls were more troubled by it. Being humiliated caused them to feel more desperate than boys; they tried then to fit in more and stated their intentions of making changes (see Fig. 4.7).

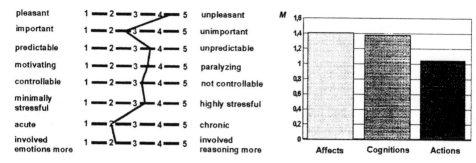

FIG. 4.7. Event parameters and coping strategies related to Event 6: "I was humiliated."

Humiliation was more disgracing for 12-year-olds and 15-year-olds than for 17-year-olds, the latter of whom showed more self-confidence and attempted to treat the event as being insignificant.

Event 7: "I Am Dissatisfied With My Appearance." This event was not reported very often yet it affected girls more often than boys. Although all adolescents considered appearance to be important, for the youngest adolescents this concern led to increased self-criticism and sulking, but also to many activities aimed at solving the unsatisfactory appearance (see Fig. 4.8).

As previously mentioned, girls were more affected by this event than boys. They were particularly desperate about having a poor outward appearance and named many more negative feelings in this connection than boys. Compared to their male peers, this assessment did not lead to an increased cognitive engagement with appearance, but results, however, in an increase in actions directed at changing appearance.

Event 8: "I Had a Quarrel With My Parents." This event was, as mentioned, the one most often mentioned by the adolescents and was rated as being very unpleasant and very stressful, similar to feeling lonely. It was, however,

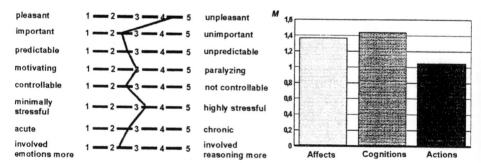

FIG. 4.8. Event parameters and coping strategies related to Event 7: "I am dissatisfied with my appearance."

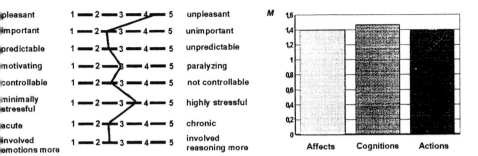

FIG. 4.9. Event parameters and coping strategies related to Event 8: "I had a quarrel with my parents."

rated as being more predictable. The contribution of cognitive, affective, and action-related strategies were relatively balanced in relation to this event. High values in positive (affection, empathy) and negative affects (anger, shame, and affection) were expressed (see Fig. 4.9).

Girls indicated that they had more quarrels with their parents and felt more emotionally affected by them. Females also developed more guilt feelings, thought a lot about the quarrel, showed more self-criticism, and expressed more intentions of solving the problem. A comparison of responses in the different age groups revealed that the 15-year-olds were especially concerned by this event, and above all stated more anger and fear. They reacted more ambivalently. On the one hand, they were more prepared to make compromises; on the other hand, they asserted themselves in the face of parental resistance. The youngest age group was most willing to give in. The 17-year-olds appeared to have the greatest distance to the event and were the most unconcerned. They had quarrels with their parents just as often as the 12-year-olds but showed considerably less emotional involvement, fear, and desperation. They attempted to bring the conflict under control through cognitive efforts (i.e., by deeming the event as more trivial, making their own position more stable, and—at the level of actions— trying to solve the problem by relying on their network of friends).

Event 9: "I Had Some Trouble With My Friends." Similar to the event "quarrel with parents," the event "I had some trouble with friends" initiated a coping process in the adolescents that involved a balanced contribution of affects, cognitions, and actions. Having trouble with friends was experienced less frequently than familial discord; however, it was described as being more important and unpleasant. According to the adolescents, problems with their friends seemed to occur more unexpectedly than family discord (see Fig. 4.10).

Girls reported having had trouble with their friends more than boys and they regarded the situation as being less alterable. The 12-year-olds felt more affected than older age groups by such an event. Corresponding differences related to age and gender were represented in the coping strategies. The group of 15-year-

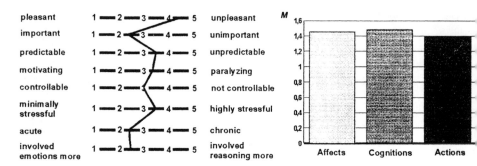

FIG. 4.10. Event parameters and coping strategies related to Event 9: "I had some trouble with my friends."

olds showed an extraordinary amount of feelings, some of which were also rather ambivalent. Their feelings ranged from fear and desperation to affection toward their friends. The 15-year-olds also indicated most clearly their intentions of doing something about the situation. It is remarkable that with increasing age, the adolescents became more willing to give in or make compromises. As has been mentioned already, girls experienced trouble with their friends more often. Their emotional disposition in relation to this event is surprisingly more diffuse than for boys. On the other hand, they mentioned feelings of affection toward their girlfriends significantly more often. In cognitions, they tended to criticize themselves more and tried to ascertain the causes for the conflict. However, in the area of actions, an avoidance of the problem seemed to dominate. In contrast, their male peers tried significantly more often to solve the conflict by taking some action.

Event 10: "I Experienced Something Very Stressful (a Critical Life Event)."

As expected, the adolescents participating in this study seldom experienced a particularly stressful event. The parameters of such critical events were comparable with those related to Event 5 (i.e., adolescents perceived the event as being very important, unpleasant, and very taxing). However, compared to political events, this event affected them more emotionally. This is understandable if one considers what kinds of events belonged to this category. Whereas most of the future/political events named by adolescents moreover were distanced from the self (war, environmental destruction, armament), the particularly stressful events named here occurred within the realms of the adolescent's immediate living environment (i.e., in the family, the neighborhood, or the residential district). Such events included serious illness; divorce and departure of family members from the home; discrimination of foreigners; witnessing or being involved in accidents; and friends or relatives being unemployed, laid off, or fired at work. The coping strategies named were similar to those indicated for Event 5. The adolescents named many affects (high values in fear, disappointment, and empathy) and reflected a great deal about the event; however,

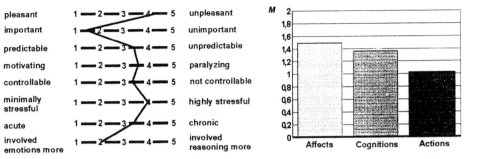

FIG. 4.11. Event parameters and coping strategies related to Event 10: "I experienced something very stressful (a critical life event)."

they felt blocked in taking any action (high values in uncertainty what to do and doing nothing). Girls indicated significantly more often that they had experienced something very stressful. They also reported their emotional involvement more than boys, in particular their concern for the individuals affected and were more intensely preoccupied with the event. Comparison of ages revealed a picture that was very difficult to interpret, due to the very wide variety of events that the adolescents assigned to this category (see Fig. 4.11).

DISCUSSION

In the second study, the focus of chapter 3 was expanded. Using two larger samples, the two major dimensions of the coping process were investigated in more detail, namely, the event side and the coping side. In a sample of 54 adolescents we attempted to collect as many everyday events that occurred relatively frequently, which were not fixed in their quality and only limited to their onset of occurrence (Study 2a). We selected those events from this set that were important for all of the adolescents, regardless of age and gender and that challenged them to cope. These universal events were then analyzed more precisely in a written interview with 110 adolescents (Study 2b). Here the efforts were directed at characterizing how the events were perceived with respect to different parameters and developing a sampling of typical coping strategies for these events.

The 1,099 events that were mentioned in Study 2a were assigned to seven different subject areas, from which we then selected 10 universal events. These events occurred relatively often independent of age and gender and were very important for the adolescents. Thus, the stressful events named covered a wide range that closely paralleled the variety of stressors identified in chapter 3. Again, most of the events entailed an interpersonal problem. Previous studies on stressful minor events have mainly focused on two different stressors: academic events and social events (see Compas, Malcarne, & Fondacaro, 1988) or family/interpersonal stressors and school/work stressors (see Stern & Zevon, 1990). These types of stressors were also highly relevant in our studies. In both the Coping Process Interview (see chap. 3) and the Event Exploration Interview detailed in this chapter, they were described as being salient and important. Most events named by adolescents in Study 2a belong to the domain "school." School-related stressors covered problems such as performance pressure, nervousness about school tests, and poor school grades. We selected two universal events from this domain, "I got a bad grade" and "I had an argument with a teacher." It was also apparent that such school-related events also involved very intense relationship stressors. Family-related stressors were ranked in fourth place for all events mentioned and covered a wide range of issues such as communication problems, limitations of individual autonomy, obligations to comply with parental demands, and so on. We assigned such events to the universal event category "quarrel with parents." A further domain of stressful events was "future/politics," which ranked fifth in our study. Compared to relationship and social stressors, only a few authors have included future-related problems (Stark et al., 1989) or future-related daily hassles (Bobo, Gilchrist, Elmer, Snow, & Schinke, 1986) as salient events that adolescents must cope with. In our study, the adolescents named anticipated personal future problems (unemployment, lack of jobs) as well as more political and social events (wars, nuclear reactor accidents, threat of nuclear energy, and environmental pollution). The universal event representing such examples was termed "A future/political event really affected me."

A very important area was "self," which encompassed such issues as difficulties in controlling emotions, depressive or aggressive moods, defiance, nervousness, as well as dissatisfaction with one's own appearance and behavior. The number of events in Study 2a assigned to this domain ranked second. Although in the literature, self-related problems generally have been considered as youth-specific stressors, specific events from this domain have been rarely investigated (see Reischl & Hirsch, 1989). Here, such events were deemed to be very stressful by our adolescents. We therefore chose three universal events from this domain: "I felt lonely," "I was humiliated," and "I am dissatisfied with my appearance." Events stemming from the domain "peers" assumed the third place in the total ranking. Above all, such events involved disagreements and communication problems with peers. We termed this universal event "I had some trouble with my friends." Concerning "romantic relationships" (ranking sixth), several events concerned jealousy and difficulties in heterosexual relations. However, more positive events were also named, for example, "I fell in love," which we chose as a universal event. The variety of minor stressors that adolescents reported having experienced (1,099 events were named, M = 23.3 per individual) was overwhelming compared to the small number of coping strategies for dealing with them (i.e., 218 coping strategies, M = 4.0 per individual). This discrepancy illustrates that in everyday life, many more stressful events are present than the ways of dealing with these events. In general, our results show that the majority of events named by adolescents in Study 2a entailed an interpersonal conflict.

Only a small percentage of the events could be assigned to the category of highly stressful events (i.e., critical life events).

The adolescents investigated in Study 2b experienced the 10 universal events quite often. They especially mentioned having had arguments with their parents, receiving poor grades in school, and falling in love. Yet at the top of the list were the reports of events that involved everyday, small spots at home. This finding corresponds to the results of Coleman et al. (1977). Based on their extensive interviews, these investigators established that most adolescents did not report a preponderance of major conflicts. Instead, it appeared that minor fights between teenagers and their parents related to issues of punctuality, neatness, clothing, noise, and so on, were most prevalent. All events, including falling in love, were described by the adolescents in Study 2b as being quite stressful. This assessment, however, is particularly evident for events involving the self such as loneliness, dissatisfaction with one's appearance, and personal humiliation. Except for falling in love, all other events showed the highest means for the parameter "pleasant/unpleasant." This again clearly shows that the adolescents interpreted all the events as being aversive and stressful experiences, including falling in love, which we thought to be positive and stimulating. This result is consistent with the results presented in chapter 3 and parallels the results of Kanner et al. (1981), who emphasized the stressful nature of everyday events.

It is striking that the 10 universal events evoked quite different coping strategies. We grouped the answers into three broad categories (affects, cognitions, and actions) which could be subdivided into 31 subcategories. Some events, such as receiving a bad grade, resulted in a more cognitive coping approach, whereas other events that involved the self mostly elicited affective reactions and hardly any concrete actions. Those events that elicited a very balanced pattern of cognitive efforts, emotional involvement, and event-related actions were those that involved conflict with significant interaction partners, such as seen in quarrels or problems with parents or friends.

It is still remarkable that cognitions and emotions reported were more differentiated than actions, irrespective of the specific topic of an event. Negative affects such as anger and fear predominated, and also negative cognitions (derogation, resignation, brooding) accounted for 25% of all cognitions reported. In addition to this major finding, it is instructive to note the quality of the reported actions. We found that 40% of the activities reported were not characterized by real actions, but instead involved submission, withdrawal, postponement of action, uncertainty about what to do, and so on.

The finding of a low incidence of actions has been reported in the literature on dealing with very stressful events (see also chap. 3). In our material, obstruction of action was also clearly seen in the case of the very stressful event, that is, the "critical life event" (Event 10). Events that were rated similarly according to the various parameters were associated with comparable coping strategies. This is especially clear when comparing the adolescents' perceptions of future/po-

litical events and the very stressful event. Both were rated as being very important, unpleasant, highly stressful, and rather immobilizing. The coping strategies
reported by the adolescents were correspondingly limited to the affective area.
They expressed many feelings and perceived many barriers to possibilities of
taking any action. However, the results also showed that when events involving
significant others such as parents, teachers, or friends were experienced in a like
manner, the coping strategies were also comparable.

The results described here are valid for the entire group of adolescents investigated in Study 2b. More differentiated analyses revealed considerable age- and
gender-related differences in the assessment of the results. For example, whereas
the event of receiving a bad grade was experienced considerably more frequently
by the older adolescents, the younger adolescents found it far more stressful and
followed up on many initiatives in order to cope with a bad grade. We may
speculate, whether this result indicates that the importance of good school performance is age-dependent or whether the decline in positive school-related
attitudes reported in the literature (cf. Schulenberg, Goldstein, & Vondracek,
1991) is also accompanied by a decrease in activity.

Feeling lonely was experienced by all the adolescents with the same frequency,
but was especially unpleasant for the 15-year-old adolescents. This event primarily evoked mechanisms of affective coping and hardly any active behaviors.
Quarrels with parents also affected adolescents in this age group the most; they
usually reacted with specific affects such as fear and anger. The actions they
undertook to cope with this event were ambivalent and entailed mechanisms
of adaptation as well as rebellion. The 17-year-olds, who reported that they had
long since distanced themselves from their parents, experienced family quarrels
with the same frequency as the adolescents in the other age groups, but they
felt clearly less affected and did little to solve the problem in question. The
12-year-olds showed a predominately submissive behavior pattern, whereas the
strategies of the 15-year-olds showed exceptionally contradictory behavior patterns. Generally speaking, also in other events a more ambivalent coping pattern
was more prevalent among the 15-year-olds. This is probably a result of many
phase-specific developmental tasks (e.g., separation from parents, development
of a new identity concept) converging together during this time. Thus, the
process where childlike behavior patterns are being replaced by more adult ones
is most intense and potentially explosive for the 15-year-old adolescent.

Concerning gender differences in dealing with events, it is surprising that the
affects shown in all groups were more specific in girls and more diffuse in boys.
Female actions were clearly limited to compromise-related, submissive, and con-
forming behaviors, whereas the male adolescents launched more independent
initiatives and were able to assert themselves in the face of resistance shown by
interaction partners. Similar gender-specific differences have been reported by
Smetana (1988) and Pearlin and Schooler (1978). According to these studies,
submission and giving in is a prevailing female mode of dealing with family

conflicts, whereas males generally experienced less conflicts with parents and showed more resistance.

In summary, the domains identified as sources of stress in our study were consistent with those reported in other studies (Daniels & Moos, 1990; Siddique & D'Arcy, 1984; Stern & Zevon, 1990). The results, however, underline the necessity of including a variety of stressors and illustrate how the selection of coping strategies is a function of stressor type. Because the majority of stressful events, even those stemming from domains such as "school" entailed relationship stressors, a precise analysis of parameters such as frequency, perceived stressfulness and predictability may further help in discriminating between these stressors and in determining subsequent coping responses.

Ways of Coping with
Everyday Problems and Minor Events

Adolescence is a developmental period in which the individual is confronted not only with a dramatic change in body contours, but at the same time, a series of complex and interrelated developmental tasks that have to be mastered, such as achieving independence from parents, establishing romantic relationships, and developing an occupational identity (Havighurst, 1953). Of special relevance is the way adolescents cope with these normative demands, which are manifested in numerous minor events. It should be acknowledged, however, that the theoretical conceptualization of stress and coping in adolescence has changed. Concerning stress, the earlier crisis model gave way to more appropriate concepts that considered the productive way of coping with stressors in various domains. Conceptualizations of adolescent coping were strongly tied to the research on adults, and the idea of adolescent-specific stressors, which were so important for the theory of stress, was not pursued. Instruments frequently were based on those developed for adults and, as a rule, they only assessed global stressors and did not consider the unique demands of this age group.

In this chapter, I present the results of the survey study (Study 3). The development of appropriate measurement techniques for assessing stress and coping in adolescent populations has high priority in this study. A major issue then is to examine different minor stressors and the ways in which adolescents cope with them. Another important question concerns individual differences among adolescents. Do youngsters in early and mid-adolescence use different strategies in coping with the same problems? And, compared to research on adults, what can be said about gender differences in coping with minor events?

STRESS IN ADOLESCENCE

In early theories of adolescent development, the transition to adulthood was considered as stressful in nature. This theory, first proposed by Hall (1904) and later elaborated upon by Blos (1964) and A. Freud (1958), claims that the biological changes occurring during the adolescent years cause severe disruption in psychological status. Empirical research, however, has not supported this view. Several studies have shown that not all adolescents pass through a tumultuous phase as has been frequently described in clinical literature. On the contrary, large-scale cross-sectional and longitudinal studies conducted during the early 1960s indicated that instead of being arrested or marked by breakdowns, development in most areas proceeds rather continuously. The degree of stress suffered by the adolescents was found to be moderate, which did not support the assumption of a generation conflict or identity crisis (Andersson, 1969; Offer & Offer, 1975). Not a major crisis, but relatively minor events, such as troubles about clothes, pocket money, or leisure time were named in the study by Douvan and Adelson (1966). Although it was acknowledged that individuals tend to become more vulnerable during periods of biological, social, and psychological transition (see Antonovsky, 1981), research has underlined for decades that adolescent development is, by and large, continuous. Furthermore, research has also emphasized the activity of the adolescent in dealing with these multiple changes (Cornell & Furman, 1984). Most studies on normative samples paint a rather rosy picture of positive development throughout adolescence, illustrating that in general, adolescents manage to tackle an impressive array of demands, conflicts, and events (see, e.g., Petersen & Ebata, 1987). Rates of prevalence for psychopathology in adolescence are not higher compared to other age groups (Earls, 1986).

Accordingly, the conceptual paradigm guiding adolescent stress research has shifted so that the adolescent is regarded as a "producer of his own development" (Lerner & Busch-Rossnagel, 1981) who masters the transition to adulthood in a productive and adaptive way. In acknowledging the major changes in all areas of functioning, Coleman's (1978) focal theory posits that adolescents successfully manage to meet the complex and interrelated demands and tasks when they have the opportunity to tackle them sequentially. In support of this view, Petersen and Crockett (1985) claimed that only early adolescence can be regarded as a period of greater stress, because so many changes have to be dealt with at the same time, such as those imposed by the transition from elementary school to middle school, junior high school to high school, or by the onset of physical maturation processes. Other research has confirmed and elaborated this perspective by showing that especially girls who mature early are at risk for developing problem behavior due to the accumulation of stressors. More specifically, adolescent girls who experienced the biological changes associated with the onset of puberty in close proximity to making the transition to junior high school were more likely to develop symptoms (Brooks-Gunn, Warren, & Rosso, 1991; Petersen, Sarigiani, & Kennedy, 1991). In summary, only the accumulation of normative events and changes resulting from accelerated maturational processes may lead to increased stress, whereas normative development leaves enough time for the individual to cope with these changes one after the other. In fact, several studies have pointed out that specific stressors can be found in each age group (i.e., each substage of adolescence has particular conflicts and inherent tasks). According to Wagner and Compas (1990), family-related stressors are reported more often by individuals in early adolescence, whereas in mid-adolescence, more network and peer stressors and in late adolescence, more achievement and school-related stressors are named. This confirms our own finding in Study 2 detailed in chapter 4 that 17-year-olds reported higher rates in getting a bad grade than younger age groups. Furthermore, the older adolescents believe that this event is more predictable and tend to play down its importance. In this Study 2, family-related stressors, such as quarrels with parents, were experienced more frequently by mid-adolescents (i.e., 15-year-olds). Furthermore, whereas relationship stressors such as quarrels with friends occurred about equally as often in both early and mid-adolescence, these stressors were perceived differently between the two age groups: 12-year-olds perceived themselves as considerably more strained by such stressors than the 15-year-olds. Also in other studies, stress originating in the domains family, school, and peer group are considered to be of particular relevance (cf. Siddique & D'Arcy, 1984). It is in these domains of life that adolescents spend most of their time and in which most of the stressful events occur (see chap. 4). In addition, our research has revealed strong gender differences in events stemming from these domains (e.g., females perceive the same events to be four times more stressful than males do; see chap. 3). Other research has also indicated that female adolescents tend to perceive greater stress in different domains. In particular, they worry more about disagreements with parents, acceptance by peers, relationships with the opposite gender, and their academic performance (Burke & Weir, 1978; Gove & Herb, 1974). There are also some studies pointing to a generally higher amount of stress in girls as compared to boys, irrespective of specific domains. For example, Petersen et al. (1991) found that adolescent girls generally experienced more challenging and stressful events than boys. Several researchers thus argue that adolescence can be considered as being more stressful for female adolescents than for males (Graham & Rutter, 1985; Siddique & D'Arcy, 1984).

One problem related to measuring adolescent stress is that the few instruments that are available are biased, because item pools were generated by sampling procedures that included not only adolescents, but also teachers, psychologists and medical doctors (see for example the SRA Youth Inventory by Remmers & Shimberg, 1954). Instruments that have generated items by asking large samples of adolescents are rare.

CONCEPTUALIZATION OF COPING

There is an increasing number of studies on coping in adolescence which, for the most part, have been based on the general paradigm used to study stress and coping processes in adults (e.g., Lazarus & Folkman, 1984). In their overview of coping approaches, Tolor and Fehon (1987) distinguished between two broad categories: problem-focused or emotion-focused coping and approach or avoidance. The classification of coping styles as approach or avoidance is found, for example, in the studies of Billings and Moos (1981), Pearlin and Schooler (1978), Kobasa (1982), and Vaillant (1977). This classification is based on the conviction that avoidance coping and poor adjustment are correlated with one another. The Lazarus group preferred to highlight the functions of coping by making the distinction between coping that is problem-focused (i.e., directed at altering the problem that causes the distress) and emotion-focused coping (i.e., directed at regulating emotional responses; Folkman & Lazarus, 1985; Lazarus & Folkman, 1991; Lazarus & Launier, 1978). Similar types of coping responses have been identified among adolescents. In their study on adolescents, Ebata and Moos (1994) have favored the approach–avoidance model (e.g., they differentiate between approach-oriented strategies including cognitive attempts to understand or change ways of thinking about the stress and behavioral attempts to deal with the stressors). Avoidance strategies include cognitive attempts to deny and minimize stress. Compas et al. (1988) favored the distinction between problem- and emotion-focused coping. Although there are some similarities between both approaches as well as an overlap in the categorization of coping strategies, they are conceptually distinct.

AGE AND GENDER DIFFERENCES IN COPING

The theoretical model of stress and coping proposed by Lazarus and Launier (1978) heavily emphasizes the role of cognitive process in determining what is experienced as stressful and how one copes (for details see chap. 3). Although developmental changes in responses to stressors might be expected, the effects of age on coping are still unclear. This situation has resulted in part from sampling procedures whereby adolescents are represented only as a subsample of larger samples with a huge age span (see, e.g., McCrae, 1982) or from the mixed samples of adolescents and students (see Folkman & Lazarus, 1985). Another reason might be that most instruments designed to assess coping deal with a nonspecific stress situation. If stress, as the literature on stress perception shows, peaks in other domains in mid-adolescence as compared to early or late adolescence, instruments that do not allow for situational variance may not be able to provide insight into developmental changes in coping behavior. All of these factors may be responsible for the divergent findings of the effect of age on coping. Several studies have shown that older youths use more emotion-focused coping or avoidance coping than younger youths (Compas et al., 1988; Hanson et al., 1989). Other studies have produced conflicting results (Blanchard-Fields & Irion, 1988; Stark et al., 1989; Stern & Zevon, 1990). In particular, no consistent age-related changes in problem-focused coping have been found to take place from childhood through adolescence. Compas, Orosan, and Grant (1993) argued that the use of problem-focused coping skills does not increase from middle childhood through adolescence because such skills have already been acquired and used at an earlier stage, whereas learning processes related to emotion-focused coping still continue through adolescence. Concerning gender differences, the overall pattern of coping seems to be similar for boys and girls. A few studies have found differences between males and females in one aspect: Girls are more likely to seek social support than boys (Patterson & McCubbin, 1987; Seiffge-Krenke, 1992; Seiffge-Krenke & Shulman, 1990; Stark et al., 1989). This is consistent with findings in adults (Billings & Moos, 1981; Stone & Neale, 1984). A trend for females to name more strategies than boys has also been reported (Compas et al., 1988). However, the question remains whether these age- and gender-specific differences apply in the same manner to all problem situations.

SITUATIONAL FACTORS IN STRESS AND COPING

Coping responses are also likely to depend on the particular situation and specific characteristics of the problem being faced. The variability observed in adolescent coping may reflect individual attempts to match coping efforts to differences in the perceived demands of stressful situations. Several studies have found that adolescents are more likely to use problem-focused efforts in order to cope with situations they deem as challenging and controllable, whereas more emotion-focused coping or avoidance responses are used in situations appraised as threatening or being uncontrollable (Compas et al., 1988; McCrae, 1984; Moos, Brennan, Fondacaro, & Moos, 1990). In the first study detailed in chapter 3 we were able to show that situations perceived as highly stressful and uncontrollable resulted in a blockade of action. It was then demonstrated in the second study detailed in chapter 4 that because adolescents must deal with stressors stemming from different fields (e.g., school, parents, or peers), coping in these same domains depend on different event parameters. Compas et al. (1988) found that both boys and girls reported that they had more control over the causes of academic events than social events. However, although Stern and Zevon (1990) were not able to relate type of situation to gender-specific coping strategies, they found that adolescent coping responses varied as a function of age and type of stressor experienced. Younger adolescents used emotion-based coping strategies (tension reduction, denial, or wishful thinking) to a greater extent than did older adolescents for stressors involving family problems. But there was no difference in using coping strategies as a function of age in response to school-related stressors.

Coping may also be influenced by the accumulative effect of stressful events. This may occur more frequently in younger adolescents and females, especially when the development is greatly accelerated. As previously mentioned, early maturing girls may simultaneously have school-related stressors and many conflictive interactions with parents and consequently develop dysfunctional coping styles that manifest themselves in problem behavior. But also for adolescents with normative development, some domains of stress may be related (e.g., achievement problems and problems with parents), which leads to higher levels of stress overall. In addition, challenges stemming from one area (e.g., search for a profession) may result in conflictive expectations and actions in light of changes occurring in other areas (e.g., developing a female sex role behavior).

Given that each substage of adolescence has particular tasks inherent to it (see Erikson, 1970) and that most adolescents manage to tackle the relevant problems sequentially, as the focal theory suggests (see Coleman, 1978), we need to know more about problem-specific coping strategies. Thus, the general approach in assessing coping style under the perspective of approach and avoidance has to be differentiated across situations, because different situations are characterized by various challenges and possibilities of reaction for adolescents of different ages and gender. Most research, with the exception of some recent studies (Ebata & Moos, 1994), has not placed much emphasis on identifying the type of situations that adolescents typically perceive as stressors. Moreover, the manner of coping with these situations warrants further investigation.

RESEARCH QUESTIONS

In the growing literature on stress and coping in adolescence, most researchers have neglected to consider the variability of situations that may cause stress and elicit coping efforts. Despite the existence of numerous complex and interrelated problems characteristic for this developmental phase, only a small number are usually selected for investigation. Moreover, the event or situation parameters of these problems have been largely overlooked.

Another related deficit in the research concerns the assessment of coping. Although in recent years there has been considerable progress in the development of tools for assessing major and minor events that are considered to be youth-specific stressors (see Compas et al., 1987; J. Johnson, 1986, for a summary), techniques appropriate for measuring coping are sorely lacking. Early research efforts were particularly marked by the method of assessing coping indirectly by inference from other variables or based on adult judgments. The deficit in the methods available for the assessment of coping is also associated with the problem outlined earlier concerning the limited variety of stressors incorporated into coping research paradigms. As demonstrated in the previous studies detailed in chapters 3 and 4, coping is dependent on the situational characteristics of the stressor, a largely neglected perspective in coping research. Indeed, most measures developed for the assessment of coping are marked by the mismatch of a huge number of coping strategies and a limited variability in situations. In the majority of studies, even in recent coping research, individuals are presented with a few unspecific or global stressful situations and then requested to describe their subsequent coping by selecting appropriate strategies provided in a comparatively extensive list (between 30 and 60), for example, as provided by the Ways of Coping Checklist from Lazarus and Folkman (1984), which has been used also on adolescent samples (see also Forsythe & Compas, 1987; Stern & Zevon, 1990), the Coping Response Inventory (Roos, 1988), or the measure developed by Glyshaw et al. (1989) and Bird and Harris (1990). This mismatch in proportions stands in contrast to the spontaneous descriptions of adolescents who report numerous stressful events yet only a restricted range of coping strategies (see chap. 4).

Given these shortcomings in research, we recognized that a necessary prerequisite for studying stress and coping in adolescents involved the development of appropriate, sensitive, and reliable tools for measuring stress and coping. This included not only defining the domains of minor stress or everyday problems typical for this age group, but also the types of coping strategies used by adolescents in dealing with these problems. An important part of this chapter thus deals with instrument development and the assessment of psychometric properties. Having developed instruments to investigate minor stress and coping, four issues warranted further investigation. First, domains of minor stress typical for this age group have to be assessed. Second, the types of coping strategies in dealing with these problems must be examined. Age and gender differences in stress perception and coping styles represent a further area to be investigated. Finally, cross-situational consistency or variability in stress and coping should be determined.

METHOD

Subjects

Participants in the survey study were 479 males and 549 females ($n = 1,028$). The sample was subdivided into 225 early adolescents (12- to 14-year-olds), 339 mid-adolescents (15- to 16-year-olds) and 464 late adolescents (17- to 19-year-olds). The sample was selected according to representative criteria for German adolescents, based on the Yearbook of Statistics (Statistisches Bundesamt, 1990). Due to changes in birth rates in Germany during the last decade, a somewhat lower percentage of early adolescents took part in the study. The selection of the sample was based on sociodemographic factors such as age, gender, family structure, number of siblings, parental education, and occupation. Eighty-nine percent of the adolescents were of German origin, 11% from mixed ethnic background (e.g., Turkish, Italian, Spanish), most of whom were raised in Germany as second-generation adolescents of foreign residents. The mean parent education level was 13.2 years for fathers and 12.8 years for mothers. The professions of the adolescents' mothers and fathers showed the following distribution: (a) 25% of the fathers were semiskilled workers, 54% technicians and clerical workers, 14% self-employed, and 7% were academics; and (b) 38% of the mothers worked full time, 62% were housewives and/or worked part time. Seventy-eight percent of the adolescents were raised in two-parent families, 22% were raised in single-parent families, with 18% stemming from divorced families. The average family size was 1.8 children. From the sample of the survey study ($n = 1,028$), on which the main body of cross-sectional analysis was conducted, two subsamples were created for (a) statistical analysis of scale properties of the instruments developed ($n = 675$) and (b) longitudinal analysis of stress and coping ($n = 94$). Individuals were selected according to the aforementioned sociodemographic factors in order to create representative subsamples with equal proportions of early, mid, and late adolescents.

Measures

Adolescent stress was measured by the Problem Questionnaire, and coping was measured by the Coping Across Situations Questionnaire (CASQ) for adolescents. The development of these research instruments is detailed here.

Procedure

Adolescents completed the Problem Questionnaire and the CASQ anonymously at school during one school lesson in small groups of 20 students each. Research assistants were present to explain questions if necessary. From this survey study involving 1,028 adolescents, 94 adolescents were selected to complete the two questionnaires again after 6 and 12 months. The questionnaires were then mailed to the adolescents, who completed them at home and returned them in a sealed envelope. Adolescents were identified in all three measurements by code numbers.

RESULTS

Overview of the Analyses

The results reported in this chapter were obtained by means of several different analyses that were conducted in three steps. First, the process of developing the appropriate scales for assessing stress and coping (the Problem Questionnaire and the CASQ) including the scale properties and statistical values for the dimensions of both instruments is outlined, followed by results of factor analysis based on these scales on a subsample of 675. Second, the results of cross-sectional data on 1,028 participants are presented. Results of MANOVAs of the Problem Questionnaire and the CASQ, including age (split into three age groups) and gender with subsequent univariate analysis of age and gender are reported. In addition, special emphasis is placed on problem-specific forms of coping. Pearson correlation coefficients were calculated between the CASQ and the Problem Questionnaire in order to assess the relationship between various domains of stress and types of coping. Finally, the results of the longitudinal study on stress and coping are presented, based on a subsample of 94, which was investigated three times in a year.

Instrument Development

The instrument and scale development of the Problem Questionnaire and the CASQ proceeded in four steps. In the first stage, relevant stressors and coping strategies for creating an item pool were identified. The majority of the items selected for the pool were selected from the list of events/problems and coping strategies named by adolescents in Study 2; these were supplemented by other items adapted from Study 1. An item pool was drafted and two preliminary instruments were developed. In the second stage, item response formats were specified and each item was examined for its appropriateness, content, and clarity. The next stage involved conducting a pilot test on 40 adolescents of various ages (12 to 17 years) to ensure the applicability of the instrument. Open-ended questions were included to check for completeness of the item set. In the third stage, minor revisions were made, resulting in the final form of the Problem Questionnaire and the CASQ as they were implemented in the survey study on 1,028 adolescents. Finally, in the fourth stage, factor analysis was conducted on a subsample of the survey study ($n = 675$), which led to the construction of seven dimensions of the Problem Questionnaire and three dimensions of the CASQ, across eight domains, with sufficient scale properties. In the following, this unified approach is specified for both questionnaires. It becomes clear how interrelated both questionnaires are and which emphasis is placed on the differentiation in various domains of stress.

Minor Stressors. The first step in the development of a measure of adolescent stress involved the identification of items. Because hardly any major events were named in our previous studies, we concentrated on minor events or everyday stressors. As detailed in chapters 3 and 4, minor stressors or everyday events frequently involved a problem. We analyzed the list of problems generated in these two studies and eliminated problems that were too specific, idiosyncratic, or redundant. The total number of problems named in both studies could be subsumed into seven problem domains: problems with school, problems with future, problems with parents, problems with leisure time, problems with peers, problems with romantic relationships and self-related problems. According to a ranking of the most frequently reported minor stressors, achievement pressure and exam-related nervousness were important items in problems with school. Fear of becoming unemployed, worries about the lack of places for vocational training, and worries about the destruction of the environment were important items assigned to problems with future. In problems with parents, difficulties in yielding to parental demands, communication problems, and a lack of understanding on the part of the parents were frequently named. Self-related problems included, for example, difficulties in affect control (being in a bad mood, anxious, nervous, or depressed), worries about one's body, and discontent with one's behavior or with specific personal traits. Problems in leisure time involved restricted leisure-time activities due to parental influence and a limited range of offers, but also dealt with passivity and a lack of interests. Problems with peers encompassed fear of peer rejection, desire for peer approval, and communication problems between friends. Finally, problems in romantic relationships covered discrepancies in emotions, jealousy, and contact problems. Of the variety of problems named in these two studies, we selected 64 items that occurred most frequently for the Problem Questionnaire with the wording based very much on the adolescents' wording. This preliminary version was complemented by formulating a structured response format (including a 5-point scale of perceived stressfulness). The pilot test on 40 adolescents thus resulted in a final instrument consisting of 64 items that had been frequently named as typical and salient problems in our previous studies. They were divided into the aforementioned seven developmentally relevant domains. The adolescents were asked to indicate the stressfulness of a specific problem, ranging from 1 (*not stressful at all*) to 5 (*highly stressful*). The final instrument can be found in Table 5 in the appendix.

Adolescent Coping. Studies 1 and 2 demonstrated the necessity of assessing coping in different developmentally relevant domains. Based on the domains of the Problem Questionnaire, we chose the following seven domains for which coping is frequently needed and highly useful for solving the underlying problems: school, parents, peers, romantic relationships, self, and future. In Study 2 it became clear that school-related events often deal with relationship stressors (e.g., problems with teachers in particular) thus, these seven domains were supplemented by a further domain, teacher. Altogether eight domains were found to represent the issues usually considered by adolescents as age-specific, salient, and conflictive. After having identified the relevant problem domains, we analyzed the coping strategies spontaneously named by adolescents in previous studies (see chaps. 3 and 4) as an item pool for constructing an instrument to assess adolescent coping. As noted already, the adolescents had spontaneously quoted much fewer coping strategies than the variety of stressors named. Also, the strategies named were highly redundant. In trying to categorize these strategies, we identified 20 coping strategies that altogether seemed to represent a comprehensive coping register. In addition, these 20 coping strategies largely corresponded to those that Westbrook (1979) also identified in a sample of adolescents as being relevant and frequently used coping strategies. They included problem-focused coping strategies (e.g., Item 3: "I try to get help from institutions [job center, youth welfare offices]"), active support-seeking (e.g., Item 19: "I try to solve the problem with the help of my friends"), emotion-focused coping (e.g., Item 12: "I let out my anger or desperation by shouting, crying, slamming doors, etc."), the reflection of possible solutions (e.g., Item 10: "I think about the problem and try to find different solutions"), as well as denial of the problem (Item 7: "I behave as if everything is alright"), active forgetting and distraction (Item 17: "I try to forget the problem with alcohol and drugs"), and withdrawal (Item 20: "I withdraw because I cannot change anything anyway"). A matrix of 160 cells was created in which the eight problem areas represented the content aspects to which the 20 coping strategies were assigned. Then, the adolescents were instructed to check, problem by problem, which of the coping strategies he or she used when, for example, problems with the school arose. The adolescents were then requested to mark which strategy they used if, for example, they experienced problems with teachers, and so on. This approach emphasizes the anticipatory character of coping. For each problem domain, the subjects could choose any number of coping strategies. In order to ensure the applicability of the CASQ, 40 adolescents completed the questionnaires as a pilot test. Open categories for other problems and coping strategies were included to ensure completeness. The pilot test revealed that the item format was clear and the contents appropriate both with respect to problem domains and coping strategies. Whereas the older adolescents had no problems in working with the matrix format, it was necessary to advise the younger participants to fill in their answers step by step (e.g., problem by problem). The necessity of providing such careful instructions, especially for the younger groups up to the age of 14, resulted in the practice of administering the CASQ in small groups (20 students maximum) with a research assistant available. The final version of the CASQ can be found in Table 6 in the appendix. By analyzing the 20 × 8 matrix, it is possible to evaluate problem-specific coping strategies as well as general coping style across situations.

Dimensions of Stress and Coping

Separate factor analyses were conducted for the Problem Questionnaire and the CASQ in order to determine dimensions of stress and coping. Both factor analyses were conducted on a subsample of 675 adolescents from the survey study ($N = 1,028$). The subsample included equal proportions of early adolescents (12 to 14 years, $n = 225$), mid-adolescents (15 to 16 years, $n = 225$), and late adolescents (17 to 19 years, $n = 225$).

Factor Structure of Minor Stress. A factor analysis of the 64 items of the Problem Questionnaire revealed that our initial grouping into seven problem domains could be maintained to a large extent. After varimax rotations, a seven-factor solution proved to be most useful and accounted for 69% of the variance. Self-related problems as well as problems with parents and problems with peers

TABLE 5.1
Results of Factor Analysis of the Problem Questionnaire (n = 675)

Scale	Number of Items	Variance Explained (%)	$r_{i(t-i)}$	Cronbach Alpha
1. Problems with school	8	11	.47	.80
2. Problems with future	8	7	.40	.75
3. Problems with parents	10	12	.52	.84
4. Problems with peers	10	12	.50	.83
5. Problems with leisure time	7	7	.29	.70
6. Problems with romantic relationships	7	7	.39	.74
7. Self-related problems	14	13	.40	.78

contributed most to the variance explained. As can be seen in Table 5.1, Cronbach alphas ranged between .70 and .84, respectively.

The item loadings for each factor can be found in Table 7 in the appendix. The intercorrelations between the seven factors revealed several significant relationships between the different domains of minor stress (see Table 5.2), for example, between problems with school and problems with future ($r = .51$), problems with parents and problems with peers ($r = .50$), and self-related problems and problems with romantic relationships ($r = .55$). This indicates that several relationship stressors are strongly associated with each other, whereas achievement stressors and future-related stressors are more closely associated.

Factor Structure of Coping. Although the Problem Questionnaire represented seven domains of stress, eight domains were included in the CASQ, dividing up teacher and school. A factor analysis of the total scores of coping across these eight domains was computed using the data of the subsample of 675. Three factors emerged which accounted for 55% of the total variance.

TABLE 5.2
Pearson Correlations Between Different Domains of Minor Stress (n = 675)

Problem Questionnaire	1 School	2 Future	3 Parents	4 Peers	5 Leisure Time	6 Romantic Relationships
1 Problems with school						
2 Problems with future	.51					
3 Problems with parents	.19	.21				
4 Problems with peers	.23	.24	.50			
5 Problems with leisure time	.24	.28	.41	.40		
6 Problems with romantic relationships	.21	.24	.30	.47	.37	
7 Self-related problems	.25	.38	.32	.46	.51	.55

Note. $r = .08$, $p < .05$. $r = .11$, $p < .01$.

TABLE 5.3
Results of the Factor Analysis of the CASQ (n = 675)

Scale	Number of Items	Variance Explained	$r_{i(t-i)}$	Cronbach Alpha
1 Active coping	7	29.9	.57	.80
2 Internal coping	7	14.3	.59	.77
3 Withdrawal	6	10.6	.53	.73

Factor 1 was termed active coping (i.e., the mobilization of social resources in order to solve the problem) and explained 30% of the variance. Factor 2, termed internal coping, signified an appraisal of the problem and the search for its solution, and explained 14% of the variance. The third factor, withdrawal, reflected a fatalistic approach to the problem and the inability to solve it and explained 11% of the variance. As can be seen in Table 5.3, the Cronbach alphas for these factors range between .73 and .80. The item loadings on each factor are represented in Table 8 in the appendix.

As can be seen in Table 5.4, active coping is not associated with withdrawal, whereas active coping and internal coping are more closely associated ($r = .38$). This points to a conceptually important distinction between functional and dysfunctional modes of coping. *Functional coping modes*, as they are encompassed in Coping Scale 1 (active coping) and Coping Scale 2 (internal coping), refer to forms of activity such as requesting information, seeking advice, or receiving support from others, or those emphasizing the adolescent's appraisal of the situation and his or her reflections about possible solutions. Both modes of coping are therefore functional because they represent an individual's active efforts directed at dealing with and solving a problem. Functional coping is thus similar to strategies used for problem solving, in that the problem is defined, alternative solutions are generated and actions performed. Depending on the saliency of interpersonal stressors in each problem area, social skills in dealing with the problem at hand may also be relevant. In contrast, *dysfunctional modes of coping*, as represented in Coping Scale 3 (withdrawal), include defenses such as denial or repression, as well as a pessimistic attitude that ultimately leads to avoidance and retreating from the problem. This does not mean that withdrawal is not a

TABLE 5.4
Pearson Correlations Between the Three Coping Styles (n = 675)

CASQ	2 Internal Coping	3 Withdrawal
1 Active coping	.38**	−.09*
2 Internal coping		.19*

Note. $r = .08$, *$p < .05$. $r = .11$, **$p < .01$.

useful reaction, but stresses that the problem is not solved at that particular moment. Because dysfunctional coping also refers to the control of feelings, it is obvious that it may serve an important function, too.

The Relationship Between Minor Stress and Coping Style

Pearson correlation coefficients were determined between the CASQ Scales (three coping styles across problem domains) and the seven scales of the Problem Questionnaire, including the total score minor stressors.

As can be seen in Table 5.5, the relationship between stress and coping is almost exclusively limited to Coping Scale 3 of the CASQ, withdrawal. Several different problem areas of minor stress were minimally or moderately associated with withdrawal; only the correlation between self-related problems and withdrawal was more substantial ($r = .47$, $p < .001$). The correlation between the total score of minor stressors and withdrawal amounted to $r = .32$, $p < .001$.

Stability of Stress and Coping Over Time

As detailed earlier, a representative subsample of 94 adolescents was drawn from the survey study and investigated three times within 1 year. The CASQ and the Problem Questionnaire were filled out every 4 months. In addition, the adolescents were asked to report any critical life events that might have occurred in the interim periods between measurements. During that year, negative life events (e.g., moving or siblings leaving home) occurred in only 4% of the longitudinal sample. The stability coefficients for the Problem Questionnaire for all three measurement points are provided in Table 5.6.

TABLE 5.5
Pearson Correlations Between Coping Style and
Several Domains of Minor Stress (n = 675)

	Problem Questionnaire							
CASQ	1	2	3	4	5	6	7	8
Active coping	.01	.06	.04	.04	.02	.03	−.06	.04
Internal coping	.05	.13**	.09*	.14**	.16**	.11*	.14**	.12**
Withdrawal	.14**	.22**	.25**	.23**	.30**	.35**	.47**	.32**

Note. 1 = Problems with school
2 = Problems with future
3 = Problems with parents
4 = Problems with peers
5 = Problems with leisure time
6 = Problems with romantic relationships
7 = Self-related problems
8 = Total minor stressors
*$p < .05$. **$p < .01$.

TABLE 5.6
Stability Coefficients in Minor Stressors (n = 94)

Scale	$r_{1/2}$	$r_{2/3}$	$r_{1/3}$
1. Problems with school	.68	.72	.60
2. Problems with future	.66	.68	.48
3. Problems with parents	.81	.86	.76
4. Problems with peers	.61	.65	.64
5. Problems with leisure time	.58	.59	.57
6. Problems with romantic relationships	.79	.71	.80
7. Self-related problems	.83	.65	.57

On the whole, stability coefficients can be considered as being sufficient. Although problems with future showed a somewhat low degree of stability ($r = .48$), most coefficients ranged between $r = .83$ and $r = .54$. Thus, minor stress across all seven areas can be described as moderate and quite stable over time. With respect to coping behavior, stability coefficients were especially high in active coping and withdrawal, but somewhat lower in internal coping, illustrating some change in this mode of coping (see Table 5.7).

It appears therefore that adolescents, taken as a group, consistently perceive the same amount of everyday stress in most domains throughout a year, and they respond to these stressors in a comparably stable way with respect to approach or avoidance, whereas more changes are found in cognitive processes leading to coping.

In the following, the findings obtained from the cross-sectional survey sample of 1,028 adolescents are reported. I first present the relevant descriptive statistics applied for the analysis of variables under scrutiny. Then, socioeconomic status (SES), age, and gender differences in stress and coping as well as situational factors influencing coping style are examined.

Descriptive Analysis

The analysis of the answers of 1,028 adolescents across all 64 items in the Problem Questionnaire shows that most items were located in the middle range of the five-step scale.

As can be seen in Table 5.8, Item 10 had the highest average score, indicating that this issue was considered to be rather stressful, followed by items that refer

TABLE 5.7
Stability Coefficients in Coping Style (n = 94)

Scale	$r_{1/2}$	$r_{2/3}$	$r_{1/3}$
1. Active coping	.88	.87	.77
2. Internal coping	.58	.66	.47
3. Withdrawal	.75	.61	.65

TABLE 5.8
Problems Perceived as Highly and Minimally Stressful (n = 1,028)

Items With High Means	M
10. The destruction of the environment is increasing	4.02
16. I might become unemployed	3.95
13. I would like very much to discover my real interests	3.81
34. Outsiders can't join existing cliques	3.56
35. My peers are often very stubborn and intolerant towards each other	3.67
41. Adolescents often have no other opportunity to spend their free time except for hanging around in the streets or in bars	3.60

Items With Low Means	M
20. My parents think I am not "all there"	1.99
23. My parents don't approve of my friends	1.83
27. I hardly have any friends	1.65
40. I feel unable to deal with my boredom in other ways than with TV, alcohol or drugs	1.47

to the personal and professional identity of the adolescents. Across all scales, the experienced distress ranged from medium to low. The order of what was perceived as most stressful was as follows: problems with future ($M = 2.89$, $SD = .89$), self-related problems ($M = 2.58$, $SD = .78$), problems with school ($M = 2.47$, $SD = .68$), problems with peers ($M = 2.39$, $SD = .86$), problems with romantic relationships ($M = 2.35$, $SD = .73$), problems with leisure time ($M = 2.27$, $SD = .73$), and problems with parents ($M = 2.10$, $SD = .75$).

The analysis of the answers of 1,028 adolescents across the coping strategy-situation matrix revealed that Coping Strategy 19 ("I try to solve the problem with the help of friends") was named most frequently for all problems, followed by discussions with parents and other adults and the thoughtful preoccupation with the problem (see Table 5.9). The strategies named least often included affective abreaction, attempts to suppress the problem as well as pessimistic retreat from the problem situation.

This already indicates that the adolescents clearly prefer active forms of coping over evasive, problem-avoiding behaviors. This becomes more obvious after totaling those coping strategies that represent a factor (i.e., coping style) across situations. According to factor analysis, we can distinguish between three coping styles. Across all eight problem situations, the adolescents used active coping most frequently ($M = 14.7$, $SD = 7.3$) as compared to internal coping ($M = 10.6$, $SD = 4.5$) and withdrawal ($M = 4.6$, $SD = 2.9$).

Demographic Influences on Stress Perception and Coping Style

As just detailed, the sample has been selected according to representative criteria as regards SES, family structure, percentage of working parents, and number of siblings. A three-way analysis of variance including profession of father (four

TABLE 5.9
Total Frequencies for Each Coping Strategy
Across Eight Problem Situations (n = 1,028)

Coping Strategy	
19. I try to solve the problem with the help of my friends	285.7
1. I discuss the problem with my parents/other adults	256.5
10. I think about the problem and try to find different solutions	249.7
6. I try to talk about the problem with the person concerned	239.4
2. I talk straight away about the problem when it appears and don't worry much	154.8
18. I try to get help and comfort from people who are in a similar situation	143.4
13. I tell myself that there will always be problems	128.1
11. I compromise	123.4
8. I try to let my aggression out (with loud music, riding my motorbike, wild dancing, sports, etc.)	101.2
15. I look for information in magazines, encyclopedias or books	90.2
5. I accept my limits	90.1
4. I expect the worst	89.7
7. I behave as if everything is alright	73.1
14. I only think about the problem when it appears	64.5
3. I try to get help from institutions (job center, youth welfare offices)	59.4
9. I do not worry because usually everything turns out alright	58.3
16. I try not to think about the problem	50.8
12. I let out my anger or desperation by shouting, crying, slamming doors, etc.	48.3
20. I withdraw because I cannot change anything anyway	48.1
17. I try to forget the problem with alcohol and drugs	13.7

levels), family structure (two-parent, single-parent, and divorced), and number of siblings (four levels) as independent variables was conducted with the seven scales of the Problem Questionnaire and three coping styles of the CASQ as dependent variables. It revealed a tendency for a main effect of SES, here operationalized as father's profession [$F(3, 1024) = 2.4, p = .06$] in active coping. Univariate analysis revealed that adolescents from academic households scored highest in active coping. In this group there was also a tendency to report fewer problems with parents [$F(3, 1024) = 2.72, p = .06$]. Because the proportion of academic households in our sample was rather low (7%), and because the findings were only marginal, SES was not considered as having an important influence on coping.

Age and Gender Differences in Minor Stress

Multivariate analysis of variance including age (three groups) and gender was conducted with age and gender as independent variables and the seven scales of the Problem Questionnaire as dependent variables. Age was divided into three groups (12–14, 15–16, and 17–19 years). MANOVAs revealed a main effect of age in problems with school [$F(2, 1025) = 3.5, p = .03$] and self-related problems [$F(2, 1025) = 2.9, p = 0.5$] with older adolescents having higher scores than younger adolescents. A main effect of gender was found for two scales, for example, in problems with future [$F(1, 1027) = 2.7, p = .08$] and in self-related problems [$F(1, 1027) = 6.4, p < .001$] with females having higher scores than males.

For most of the problem domains, male and female adolescents did not differ in their perception of stress. This homogeneity in stress perception is illustrated in Fig. 5.1. Indeed, univariate analysis showed that there were only a few differences in age, taking each gender separately. At age 12, problems with school were reported by male adolescents significantly more frequently than by female adolescents ($t = 3.0, p = .05$). At age 14, significantly more females than males reported problems with peers ($t = 3.2, p < .02$), self-related problems ($t = 3.6, p < .001$), and problems with leisure time ($t = 2.5, p = .05$). Thus, gender differences can be observed mainly in early adolescence. Indeed, early adolescence seems to be a period that is perceived as quite stressful across different domains. School-related problems, future-related problems, problems with peers, and problems with the self peaked in early adolescence (see Fig. 5.1).

Age and Gender Differences in Coping Style

Multivariate analysis of variance (MANOVAs) were conducted with age and gender as independent variables and the three coping styles as dependent variables. An overall significant difference was found for gender [$F(1, 1027) = 31.5, p < .0001$]. This difference was accounted for by active coping [$F(1, 1027) = 63.3, p < .001$] and withdrawal [$F(1, 1027) = 3.9, p = .05$]. Female adolescents scored higher on both active coping and withdrawal than males, but the difference was much more pronounced in active coping. The MANOVA revealed a significant main effect of age, too [$F(2, 1025) = 12.3, p = .001$]. This difference was accounted for two of the coping styles, active coping [$F(2, 1025) = 17.6, p < .0001$] and internal coping [$F(2, 1025) = 7.5, p < .001$]. No significant interactions between age and gender were found across the three coping styles. Thus, the use of internal forms of coping (e.g., analysis of the problem and working out possible solutions) as well as overt activity in tackling problems increases with age.

Coping Style as a Function of Problem Domain

In order to compare coping styles across problem domains, means of the CASQ scales were transformed into percentages for each of the eight problem domains separately. As is seen in Fig. 5.2, there is a higher proportion of combined functional coping strategies (including active and internal coping) than dysfunctional coping (withdrawal) across all eight problem domains. The proportion of functional to dysfunctional coping was 4:1.

The general tendency to apply dysfunctional coping across all problem domains is low (20%); but if this response tendency is considered for specific situations, some marked differences are observable. In problems related to teachers, the percentage of withdrawal is particularly low (14%), whereas in problems

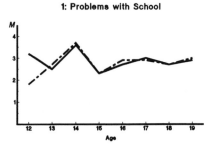

1: Problems with School

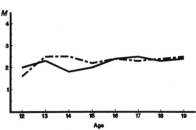

5: Problems with Leisure Time

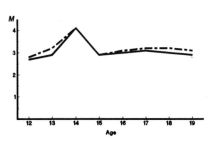

2: Problems with Future

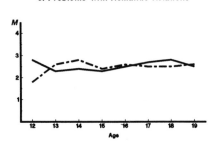

6: Problems with Romantic Relations

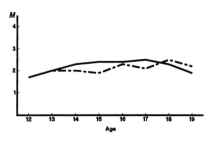

3: Problems with Parents

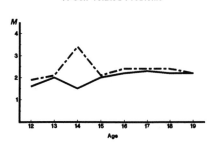

7: Self-related Problems

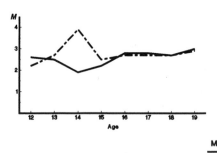

4: Problems with Peers

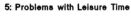

Male   Female

FIG. 5.1. Minor stressors perceived in different domains by males (*n* = 479) and females (*n* = 549).

112

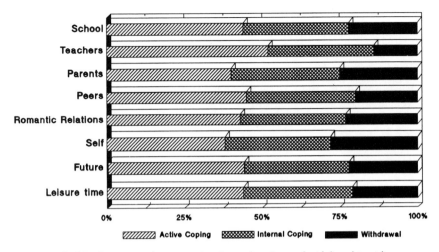

FIG. 5.2. Percentage of active coping, internal coping, and withdrawal in eight problem domains.

with parents, in future-related, and self-related problems, the use of withdrawal is comparably high (25%, 22%, and 28%, respectively). In spite of this basically functional orientation in coping, an inspection of the two functional styles of coping did reveal some differences with respect to certain problem domains. Active coping was emphasized in situations related to school and future, but played a minor role in self-related problems.

Age and Gender Differences in Coping Style by Domains

The significant gender differences that were found in active coping could be observed across situations, too. Female adolescents had significant higher scores in active coping and support-seeking for all eight situations than their male age mates: school ($t = 4.08$, $p < .001$), teachers ($t = 4.26$, $p < .001$), parents ($t = 4.34$, $p < .001$), peers ($t = 5.56$, $p < .001$), romantic relationships ($t = 5.87$, $p < .001$), self ($t = 6.71$, $p < .001$), future ($t = 4.82$, $p < .001$), and leisure time ($t = 4.73$, $p < .001$). In addition, an increase in active coping style was found in most of the eight problem domains with older age groups scoring higher than younger age groups: school [$F(2, 1025) = 2.8$, $p = .07$], future [$F(2, 1025) = 2.5$, $p = .04$], parents [$F(2, 1025) = 2.8$, $p = .06$], romantic relationships [$F(2, 1025) = 2.7$, $p = .04$], and self [$F(2, 1025) = 2.4$, $p = .05$]. Univariate analysis showed that most of these differences accounted for the youngest age group having significantly lower scores than the mid and late adolescents. With respect to internal coping total scores, no significant difference was found between genders, as detailed earlier. An inspection of internal coping across situations also revealed that boys and girls were basically similar in applying this coping style, despite a greater emphasis on reflection of females in peers [$F(1, 1027) = 2.0$, $p = .05$]. The main effect of age, found in internal coping, was accounted for in three domains, namely parents [$F(1, 1027) = 2.3, p = .05$], studies [$F(1, 1027) = 2.8, p = .05$], and self [$F(1, 1027) = 2.5, p = .03$] with mid- and late adolescents having higher score than early adolescents. With respect to withdrawal, the total scores for females was higher than for male adolescents, as has been shown. Analyzed across situations, however, significant differences in this coping style were found in only two of the eight problem domains: self ($t = 2.70, p = .01$) and parents ($t = 2.21, p = .06$).

Age and Gender Differences in Coping Strategies

By analyzing the 20 × 8 matrix, it is possible to evaluate not only the general coping styles across situations but also situation-specific coping strategies. In the following, I explore age and gender differences in specific coping strategies separately for age and gender, based on the results from a two-way MANOVA with age and gender as independent variables and the 20 coping strategies across problem domains as dependent variables. Only three coping strategies, namely, Coping Strategy 13 ("I behave as if everything was alright"), the distraction or letting out frustration through loud music, and so on (Coping Strategy 9) and avoiding thinking (Coping Strategy 14) showed neither significant age nor gender-related effects. The most significant main effects were attributed to gender and were found in 12 of the 20 coping strategies. Additional age effects appeared for 9 of the 20 coping strategies analyzed. Only in three coping strategies, namely, Coping Strategy 6 ("I try to get help and comfort from people who are in a similar situation"), Coping Strategy 11 ("I accept my limits"), and Coping Strategy 10 ("I look for information in textbooks and magazines") were significant ordinal interactions between age and gender found. This indicates that as they become older, female adolescents tend more to seek help and/or information as well as to acknowledge the scope of their abilities to change a situation. Additional aspects of this rather clear differentiation in gender- and age-related coping strategies are discussed in detail here.

Differences in Coping Strategies Between Males and Females. As detailed earlier, male and female adolescents differed with respect to their preference for two of the three coping styles, active coping and withdrawal. The more active, but at the same time, more fatalistic coping style of females as compared to males becomes even more pronounced by analyzing coping strategies across the problem areas by *t* tests. As can be seen in Table 5.10, females' scores were higher than males' in all strategies using formal and informal help, in talking about the problem with the person concerned, in the expression of emotions related to the problem and in reflecting about possible solutions. Withdrawal is also applied more frequently by females.

Males, however, scored higher than females in only two coping strategies (e.g., they worry less and try more frequently to forget the problem with alcohol

TABLE 5.10

Differences in Coping Strategies Across Domains Between Males and Females

Coping Strategy	Males (n = 479) M	Females (n = 549) M	Significance Test t
1. I discuss the problem with my parents/other adults.	3.1	4.4	6.5***
2. I talk straight away about the problem when it appears and don't worry much.	2.4	3.3	3.7**
3. I try to get help from institutions (job center, youth welfare offices).	.98	1.1	.16
4. I expect the worst.	1.5	1.7	1.4
5. I accept my limits.	1.2	1.7	.61
6. I try to talk about the problem with the person concerned.	2.0	2.9	3.7**
7. I behave as if everything is alright.	1.7	1.5	.52
8. I try to let my aggression out (with loud music, riding my motorbike, wild dancing, sports, etc.).	2.2	1.8	.13
9. I do not worry because usually everything turns out alright.	1.9	1.3	2.8**
10. I think about the problem and try to find different solutions.	3.0	3.8	4.7**
11. I compromise.	2.2	2.2	-.50
12. I let out my anger or desperation by shouting, crying, slamming doors, etc.	.95	1.9	5.7**
13. I tell myself that there will always be problems.	2.2	2.6	2.5*
14. I only think about the problem when it appears.	1.7	1.0	2.0
15. I look for information in magazines, encyclopedias or books.	1.2	1.5	2.0*
16. I try not to think about the problem.	.96	.54	1.5
17. I try to forget the problem with alcohol and drugs.	1.1	.48	3.4**
18. I try to get help and comfort from people who are in a similar situation.	1.6	2.9	8.6***
19. I try to solve the problem with the help of my friends.	2.8	4.2	9.7***
20. I withdraw because I cannot change anything anyway.	1.0	1.4	2.5*

Note. *p < .05. **p < .01. ***p < .001.

or drugs). Interestingly, in some coping strategies the discrepancies between males and females remained rather constant across age (see Strategies 12 and 20 in Fig. 5.3), whereas in others, the scores of females increased roughly in parallel with the increases seen in boys, but on a higher level (e.g., Strategies 6, 11, and 18).

Age Differences in Coping Strategies

As previously detailed, main effects of age were found in two coping styles, active coping and internal coping. Follow-up ANOVAs revealed significant age differences in 10 of the 20 coping strategies across situations, including discussion with parents, talking the problem over with the person concerned, thinking about possible solutions, making some compromise, and trying to solve problems with the help of friends or to get help and comfort from people in a similar situation (see Table 5.11). Furthermore, strategies like information seeking, seeking help in institutions, accepting one's own limits, and the anticipating negative consequences are clearly age-dependent.

It is noteworthy that certain forms of active coping are selected less often with increasing age. For one, the willingness to discuss problems with parents or other adults decreases as adolescents become older. In contrast, the increase in use of other strategies with age is striking: Older adolescents exhibit a preference for trying to solve the problem collectively with friends, seeking help from "neutral" sources such as books or making use of assistance offered by institutions. In addition to an increased tendency to think about different solutions, the willingness to make compromises and to accept the limits of one's abilities to change the situation notably increases with age. Figure 5.4 illustrates how scores in some coping strategies increased with age; especially marked changes are evident after the age of 15.

Problem-Specific Coping

Both males and females apply coping strategies differently, depending on age and problem domain. Although age and gender differences in coping style and specific coping strategies across situations have been detailed here, situation-specific effects warrant further exploration. Concerning the age differences in coping strategies described in the preceding section, it is interesting to see how the frequency of some strategies varies across domains. Some examples can be found in Fig. 5.5.

It can be clearly observed that as adolescents become older, problems in romantic relations are discussed less frequently with the parents (Strategy 1), whereas future worries remains a topic about which the adolescents are prepared to talk about with their parents or other adults. Should family-related problems exist, the willingness to discuss these directly with the parents remains substantial in all age groups. Thinking about problems and their possible solutions (Strategy

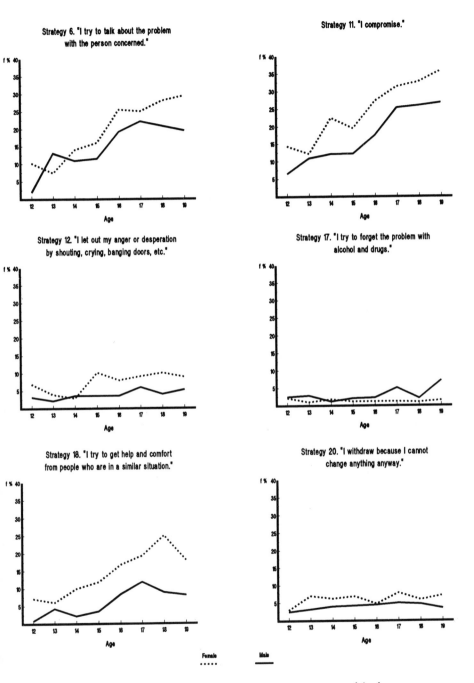

FIG. 5.3. Gender differences in 6 of the 20 coping strategies assessed (males: n = 479; females: n = 549).

TABLE 5.11

Age Differences in Coping Strategies Across Domains

Coping Strategy	12 to 14 years (n = 225) M	15 to 16 years (n = 339) M	17 to 19 years (n = 464) M	Significance Test	
				F	Duncan
1. I discuss the problem with my parents/other adults.	4.7	4.3	4.0	2.8*	1 > 2, 3
2. I talk straight away about the problem when it appears and don't worry much.	2.4	2.5	2.6		
3. I try to get help from institutions (job center, youth welfare offices).	.77	.98	.86		
4. I expect the worst.	.89	1.2	1.0	4.8**	2 > 1
5. I accept my limits.	.73	1.2	1.3	9.5**	2, 3 > 1
6. I try to talk about the problem with the person concerned.	1.4	2.0	2.6	11.6***	2, 3 > 1
7. I behave as if everything is alright.	.90	1.1	.94		
8. I try to let my aggression out (with loud music, riding my motorbike, wild dancing, sports, etc.).	1.3	1.6	1.7		
9. I do not worry because usually everything turns out alright.	.82	.84	.90		
10. I think about the problem and try to find different solutions.	2.3	3.7	4.3	12.3***	2, 3 > 1
11. I compromise.	.89	1.7	2.3	19.0***	2, 3 > 1
12. I let out my anger or desperation by shouting, crying, slamming doors, etc.	.60	.72	.76		
13. I tell myself that there will always be problems.	1.6	1.8	1.9		
14. I only think about the problem when it appears.	.97	1.0	.91		
15. I look for information in magazines, encyclopedias or books.	.75	1.4	1.6	12.4***	2, 3 > 1
16. I try not to think about the problem.	.52	.73	.64		
17. I try to forget the problem with alcohol and drugs.	.41	.49	.56		
18. I try to get help and comfort from people who are in a similar situation.	1.2	2.4	3.2	16.7***	3 > 2 > 1
19. I try to solve the problem with the help of my friends.	2.7	4.1	4.9	20.8***	3 > 2 > 1
20. I withdraw because I cannot change anything anyway.	1.0	1.2	1.1		

Note. *p < .05. **p < .01. ***p < .001.

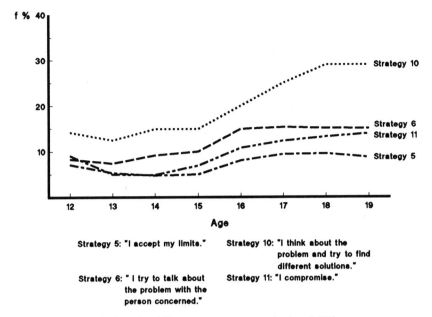

FIG. 5.4. Age differences in coping strategies (n = 1,028).

10) steadily increases with age, especially when the problems involve the self or peers. As adolescents become older, they are more prone to make compromises (Strategy 11), especially in situations involving parents and teachers. Corresponding problem-specific preferences for using a certain coping strategy are also related to gender. The following examples illustrate this point: Females tend more than males to discuss the problem directly with the involved individual, especially when the situation involves peers and romantic relationships. Females are not generally more willing to make compromises, but they are so disposed when the problems are school- or family-related. Although the means for Strategy 3 for boys and girls did not differ significantly across problems, there were some specific differences in a few areas. For example, girls sought professional help to deal with problems in the domains of self and parents more often than boys, who only resorted to this strategy in dealing with school- and future-related problems. Thus, each problem evokes a specific pattern of coping strategies, which can be differentiated according to age and gender. In the following, I summarize the results that have been presented so far, paying particular attention to the aspects of the problem situation.

School: For school-related problems, reflections about possible solutions clearly increases with age: Discussion with parents is used throughout different age groups, but seeking an emotional outlet of aggression or anger is even more common. At about the age of 16, the willingness to accept

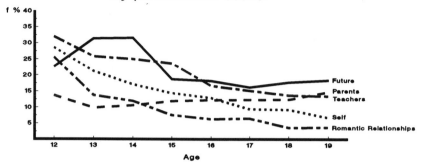

Strategy 1: "I discuss the problem with my parents/other adults."

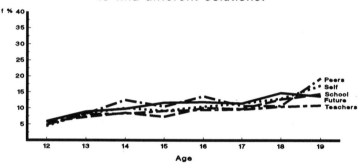

Strategy 10: "I think about the problem and try to find different solutions."

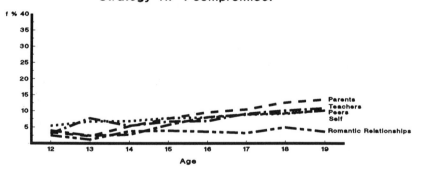

Strategy 11: "I compromise."

FIG. 5.5. Problem-specific use of coping strategies in 12- to 19-year-old adolescents (n = 1,028).

one's limits has clearly decreased, illustrating that adolescents are no longer prepared to give in with respect to problems at school (see Fig. 5.6).

Teachers: If problems with teachers arise, the adolescents talk about them with parents (decreasing with age) and peers (increasing with age). As they grow older, they more and more tend to solve these problems by direct discussion with the person concerned.

Parents: For problems with parents, the adolescents most frequently choose to address the problem directly, but attempts to cope with them by resorting to venting their emotions, seeking distractions or making some sort of compromise are also frequent. In these situations the adolescents frequently seek comfort from and discuss possible solutions with peers who have similar experiences (see Fig. 5.6).

Peers: If, on the other hand, problems with friends occur, then adolescents rarely turn to parents or other adults, but address the person concerned. Looking for consolation and understanding from other friends who are having similar difficulties is also a frequently chosen coping strategy.

Romantic Relationships: That adults are no longer trusted discussion partners is even more pronounced with respect to romantic relationships. Possible solutions are usually discussed with the partner, and the greater readiness to compromise is striking. It is also noteworthy also is that the use of alcohol and drugs as a means of forgetting problems related to heterosexual relationships increases slightly with age (see Fig. 5.6).

Self: Accepting one's own limits, finding an emotional outlet and withdrawal are comparably frequently used coping strategies in dealing with self-related problems. However, active support-seeking, which is mainly restricted to peers and close friends, and reflection about possible solutions are also exhibited, illustrating the more ambivalent coping pattern in this problem domain.

Future: Adolescents are still willing to discuss future-related problems with their parents as they get older, although to a somewhat limited extent. In contrast, the preference of adolescents to discuss such problems with their peers becomes clearly more pronounced with age. Seeking help from institutions and looking for information in literature to deal with problems in this domain are also common coping strategies.

Leisure Time: Throughout the adolescent years, problems in leisure time are hardly discussed with parents. Instead, adolescents seek support from peers, a coping strategy that increases with age. Reflections about possible solutions, but also withdrawal and behaving as if everything is alright are frequent coping strategies.

Finally, gender differences with respect to the use of social resources are especially marked in several problem areas, namely, in problems with school,

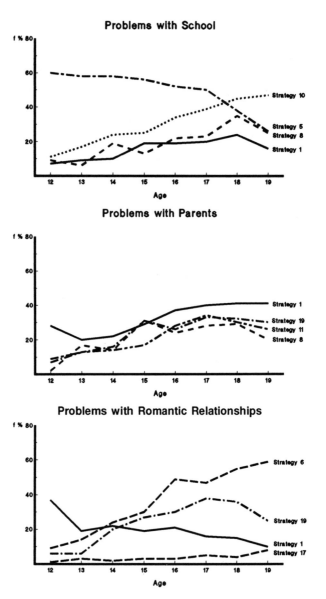

Problems with School

f % 80

Strategy 10
Strategy 5
Strategy 8
Strategy 1

Age

Problems with Parents

f % 80

Strategy 1
Strategy 19
Strategy 11
Strategy 8

Age

Problems with Romantic Relationships

f % 80

Strategy 6

Strategy 19

Strategy 1
Strategy 17

Age

Strategy 1: "I discuss the problem with my parents/other adults."

Strategy 5: "I accept my limits."

Strategy 6: "I try to talk about the problem with the person concerned."

Strategy 8: "I try to let out my aggression (with loud music, riding my motorbike, wild dancing, sports)."

Strategy 10: "I think about the problem and try to find different solutions."

Strategy 11: "I compromise."

Strategy 17: "I try to forget the problem with alcohol and drugs."

Strategy 19: "I try to solve the problem with the help of my friends."

FIG. 5.6. Problems with school, problems with parents, and problems in romantic relationships: Changes in strategy use in 12- to 19-year-old adolescents (n = 1,028).

problems with parents, and self-related problems. In these domains, girls scored much higher than boys and their scores even increase with age.

DISCUSSION

The first issue addressed in Study 3 was the identification of domains perceived as stressful by adolescents. Based on earlier studies, the Problem Questionnaire was developed. This instrument was designed to assess minor stressors in seven developmentally salient and conflictive domains revealing sufficient metric properties. Results obtained on our representative sample of 1,028 adolescents showed that the perceived stressfulness of problems and minor events in different domains was generally low to medium. The sequence of the problems cited corresponded to results found in earlier studies (e.g., McKay, 1977; Mönks, 1968; Remmers, 1962; Remmers & Shimberg, 1954; Sigal, Silver, Rakoff, & Ellin, 1973). First of all, the adolescents stated problems with future, second, self-related problems, third, achievement and school problems, and finally, difficulties in interactions with parents. The salience of these domains, especially social stressors and school-related stressors, confirmed the results of other studies (Daniels & Moos, 1990; Siddique & D'Arcy, 1984; Stern & Zevon, 1990). In our sample, problems with future were named most frequently. They consisted of items representing personal fears ("I might become unemployed") and fears regarding societal problems ("The destruction of the environment is increasing"). It is interesting to note that such a fearful future anticipation found in our sample could already be observed in other cohorts as early as 1950, although the living conditions for adolescents have obviously changed during the past 40 years. Also, in recent studies (see Klingman, Goldstein, & Lerner, 1991; Thearle & Weinreich-Haste, 1986), fears about the future were named. More specifically, nuclear threat was one of the three fears adolescents expressed most frequently in Europe and the United States. In addition, the difficulties in finding a job have been reported in several studies, especially in those countries with a high rate of youth unemployment (see Marotz-Baden & Colvin, 1989). In Germany, the youth unemployment rate at the time of the study amounted to about 20%; it is thus understandable that the adolescents in our study perceived this problem as rather stressful. Finding a job is undoubtedly related to identity. In Study 3, self-related problems (e.g., discovering what one wants, dissatisfaction with own appearance and behavior, fear of not being accepted by others) ranked second behind problems with future, thus corresponding to the relative importance that other studies have attributed to this domain (e.g., Reischl & Hirsch, 1989).

Another interesting finding was that family-related problems were only rarely reported. This applied especially to adolescents whose parents had received a higher education (7% of our sample). One may speculate whether adolescents from these families have larger living space and better financial resources. In addition, the parents in such families might also differ in their childrearing styles (e.g., they might be more tolerant), so that conflicts are minimized. Nevertheless, adolescents from other SES groups also stated only a few stressors in this domain. As adolescents grow older, females report family troubles more frequently, whereas the scores for males decrease slightly. But basically the low incidence of conflicts indicates that the orientation toward parents remains positive. This is very much in line with the research on parent–adolescent relationships showing that family relations are generally described as good and free from major conflicts (Douvan & Adelson, 1966; Hill & Holmbeck, 1986; Montemayor, 1983). Only in 10% of the sample in Fogelman's (1976) study were frequent conflicts between parents and adolescents reported. Also, in a more recent study by Richardson, Galambos, Schulenberg, and Petersen (1984), most parents and adolescents reported that they rarely argued or disagreed, generally enjoyed harmonious relations and felt close to each other.

It was somewhat surprising how uniformly problem-related strains were perceived by both genders. In contrast to the results of Petersen et al. (1991), we could not confirm that females perceive higher stress in all domains. We could only demonstrate the tendency for females of all age groups to report a higher frequency of self-related problems. This is mostly attributable to their greater concern with outer appearances and their insecurity about identity, which have also been documented in other studies (Allgood-Merten, Lewinsohn, & Hops, 1990; Gjerde & Block, 1991). Thus, we found no evidence to support the hypothesis that adolescence is generally experienced as more stressful by girls than by boys. We did find, however, some evidence that levels of stress peak in early adolescence. Younger age groups reported greater stress than older adolescents, especially in fields such as school and future, and early adolescent girls had additionally higher scores in problems with peers, leisure time, and self. This is consistent with the view that early adolescence is particularly stressful due to the transitions related to entering a new school level (Hamburg, 1974; Petersen & Spiga, 1982) and acquiring new roles. The coincidence of pubertal status, school transition, and role transition in females, due to their physical acceleration, has in several studies been held responsible for higher rates of perceived stress among females (Hamburg, 1974; Hill, 1987; Hill & Holmbeck, 1986). Thus, our data speak for higher stress only in early adolescence, with girls showing higher scores and indicating more domains causing stress than boys.

The instrument that we developed for assessing coping strategies, the CASQ, covered all relevant problem domains analyzed in the Problem Questionnaire plus an additional area, teacher. Factor analysis revealed sufficient scale properties. In analyzing coping across situations, three different coping styles were found: active coping (e.g., active problem solving and support seeking), internal coping (e.g., reflection about possible solutions), and withdrawal (including problem avoidance and emotion-focused coping strategies). Frankel (1986) reported a similar three-dimensional structure of coping after analyzing coping behavior of female adolescents. He found three factors, namely, support seeking, cognitive coping, and emotional catharsis. Moreover, the dimensions of coping identified have also been measured in other studies on adolescents employing other scales such as the A-Copes (Bird & Harris, 1990; Kurdek, 1987; Patterson & McCubbin, 1987) or The Ways of Coping Checklist (Stern & Zevon, 1990). Although most of these procedures assess the ways of coping in response to a rather unspecified stress situation while we measured coping across eight different domains, the results are quite similar. This also corresponds to the importance of these dimensions in coping research on adults (Folkman & Lazarus, 1985; Lazarus et al., 1974; Meichenbaum, 1977). Conceptually, we distinguished between functional coping modes (active coping and internal coping) and a *dysfunctional* one (withdrawal). Only the two *functional coping* styles were correlated with one another. In our approach, functional coping refers to efforts to manage a problem, either by active support-seeking, concrete actions, or reflections on possible solutions. Thus, the problem is defined, alternative solutions generated and actions performed. For internal coping, the emphasis clearly lies on using cognitive processes to modify stress and to plan activity, whereas active coping manifests itself in overt behavior such as confrontation, discussion with others, seeking social support, and so on. Dysfunctional coping in our terms includes attempts to withdraw from the stressor, the emergence of defense mechanisms to deny the existence of stressor and attempts to regulate the emotions. Basically, this type of coping results in the problem not being solved at a particular moment.

If we return to the two conceptually distinct models of coping presented at the beginning of this chapter, the approach–avoidance model and the problem versus emotion-focused model, our results speak more for the approach–avoidance model. Interestingly, some general similarities have been established in empirical findings using both models. In most studies, the adolescents choose a more active, problem-focused approach. These theoretical approaches have employed different procedures and yet have generated comparable results. Compas et al. (1988) used the Ways of Coping Checklist and Ebata and Moos (1994), the Coping Response Inventory. Whereas Ebata and Moos presented one focal stressor ("the most important problem you faced in the previous year") Compas and coworkers used a relationship stressor and an academic stressor. We could confirm the basically active and problem-focused approaches in our survey study. The young subjects presented themselves as competent copers, well able to deal with problems arising in all eight developmental areas. Functional coping modes dominated, with dysfunctional coping being employed very rarely and only for certain types of problems. This latter mode occurred particularly with self-related problems, where about 25% of responses involved withdrawal. Active coping was the dominant coping style across all eight problem areas, followed by internal coping, whereas withdrawal was applied only in about 20% of all responses.

In trying to interpret the age differences in coping style, we are confronted with poor research in this area. As several investigators have recently noted, the factor of age is critically important for understanding adolescent coping, yet has generally not been taken into consideration by the majority of researchers working in this field (J. Johnson & Bradlyn, 1988; Wagner, Compas, & Howell, 1988). Compared to the numerous studies on gender-specific differences, studies focusing on age-specific differences are rare (see McCrae, 1982, for a summary); moreover, adolescence has often not been regarded as an independent developmental phase. This is especially the case in studies in which adolescents only represent a subgroup within a population covering a broad age range, for example, 15 to 65 years (Gutman, 1970) or 18 to 64 years (Pearlin & Schooler, 1978). Accordingly, most researchers concentrate on a regression versus growth hypothesis of coping behavior (Vaillant, 1977), instead of examining differences in adolescent development. Studies using the problem-focused versus emotion-focused approach have found some evidence for developmental change of emotion-focused coping in samples of children and adolescents ranging from 5 to 17 years (Compas et al., 1988; Wertlieb, Weigel, & Feldstein, 1987), but with respect to problem-focused coping no consistent evidence of changes related to age have been found. Some authors have reported a decrease with age (e.g., Band & Weisz, 1988); others have observed a stability across age (e.g., Althuser & Ruble, 1990). These divergent findings are probably related to the fact that problem-focused coping entails strategies that cover a wide range of behaviors showing different patterns of development.

Our cross-sectional data in Study 3 do not permit any developmentally related conclusions, but some statements may be made about age-related differences. Most age-related changes occur in internal coping. As they grow older, adolescents reflect more, anticipate negative consequences and try to make compromises. These results are in agreement with research findings of increased cognitive abilities among youths related to strategy knowledge (Berg, 1989), metacognitive functions (Flavell, 1979; Miller, Kessel, & Flavell, 1970), and changes in socio-cognitive development leading to greater abilities of empathy and perspective taking (see Selman, 1980). It is also remarkable how certain forms of active coping are employed less frequently with increasing age. As adolescents grow older, discussions with parents and adults become less important except when the topics are related to areas such as school or future. At the same time, seeking social support from peers clearly increases in most domains. This result is very much in line with self-disclosure research showing that as the adolescents mature, the importance of parents as conversational partners clearly wanes, whereas at the same time, peers become more and more important (Norell, 1984). The age of 15 seems to be a turning point in that discussions with parents are drastically reduced in most domains, while at the same time, discussion with peers, reflections about problems, the tendency to compromise and to accept own limits clearly increases.

Furthermore, in our study we found striking gender differences in the use of social resources, which became even more pronounced with increasing age. As they grow older, females seek advice, help, comfort, or sympathy from others more often than boys, regardless of the nature of the problems. Girls discuss their problems with others more often and try to clarify their difficulties by talking about them openly. These trends are in line with research on adults which has indicated a general tendency among females to rely more heavily on social networks than males (Belle, 1981, 1987; Haan, 1974) or to seek help in extrafamilial settings (Ilfeld, 1980). Gender differences also emerge in dysfunctional coping. Compared to the rather uniform levels in stress perception, the gender-specific coping register is very impressive. Regardless of the type of problem, female adolescents talk about it much more frequently with parents, adults or peers than males. They address problems immediately and usually try to solve them together with the person concerned. But they also worry a lot about problems, think about possible solutions, and expect negative consequences much more frequently than boys. In addition, females show more emotional reactions like crying, slamming doors and so on, and seek more frequently consolation and empathy from friends. Accordingly, coping behavior in adolescent males show other characteristics. Male adolescents present themselves as less open and sociable, but they appraise the problem more optimistically and do not show resignation towards or withdrawal from a situation as frequently as females do. They only tackle problems when they are actually present, and do not subject themselves emotionally to so much pressure as females do. However, they also try more often to forget problems by consuming alcohol or using drugs. Taken together, boys and girls present themselves as active copers across all problem areas. Withdrawal reactions are reported significantly less frequently by both genders.

We may thus conclude that males and females do not differ much with respect to experienced stressors in different domains. The hypothesis of an accumulation of stressors in females, due to their accelerated rate of development in maturation, could only be supported in respect to early adolescence. In contrast, the differences in dealing with stressors stemming from these same domains as a function of age and gender are very pronounced. Whereas the age-related differences in coping style speak for progression in cognitive maturation and social competence, the gender differences require further explanation, especially concerning the ambivalent pattern observed in females, as marked by a more active yet more fatalistic coping style. We were able to specify that this ambivalent pattern is especially pronounced in two areas, self-related problems and problems with parents. In the latter, we also find higher scores in compromising and giving in among females. Research dealing with parent–adolescent conflict has also established that giving in is more frequent among females (see Smetana, Yau, & Hanson, 1991). In addition, research on adolescent depression has illustrated that worries about one's physical appearance, a depressive and fatalistic attitude related to the self is more frequent for young girls than for boys (Nolen-Hoeksema, 1991). The marked similarities in school- and future-related problems across gender, however, suggest these domains are basically of similar importance for both genders and elicit similar coping strategies.

Finally, I comment on problem-specific coping behavior. Due to the differentiation across eight problem areas (e.g., school, teachers, parents, peers, romantic relationships, self, future and leisure time), a problem-specific pattern of coping strategies can be identified. These results are in agreement with findings of Ebata and Moos (1994), Holahan and Moos (1987), and McCrae (1984), who have emphasized the contribution of situative variables toward explaining the differences in coping behavior. Our results elaborate this approach further in that we could demonstrate problem-specific coping behavior of males and females as well as clear age-dependent use of coping strategies in certain problem domains. Discussion with parents as a coping strategy is, for example, practiced less frequently in late adolescence, whereby the decline in females is slower than in males. Although this change was typical for relationship stressors, for school- and future-related problems, parents remain important communication partners both for males and females irrespective of age. Concerning romantic relationships, the practice of talking about the problem with the person concerned is the most important coping strategy. It occurs more frequently as adolescents grow older, yet girls have consistently higher scores than boys. After the age of 17, trying to solve the problem in romantic relationships with the help of peers no longer seems to be suitable, although again, girls generally have higher scores than boys. Interestingly, the tendency to forget this problem by consuming alcohol and using drugs was very low; but rates across adolescence increase slightly after the age of 18, and males have generally higher rates than females.

Several of our findings on adolescent coping have been reproduced in using samples from different countries. Cross-cultural studies applying the CASQ on 187 adolescents from Israel (Seiffge-Krenke & Shulman, 1990) and 537 adolescents from Finland (Seiffge-Krenke, 1992) have revealed a similar three-factorial structure. Moreover, the basically functional orientation found in the German sample has been found in these cross-cultural samples, too. The analysis of results of the CASQ in the Israeli and the Finnish samples revealed a basic similarity in the general approach marked by a focus on functional coping modes, whereas dysfunctional coping was rarely indicated. Compared with our survey study on German adolescents presented here, only some culture-specific accentuations were evident. German adolescents stress more activity and support seeking, whereas Israeli adolescents tend to show more internal reflection of problems. In the Finnish sample, active coping and internal coping are evenly balanced. Furthermore, active support seeking was found more frequently among females in all three countries. In addition, a tendency to be more reflective and active with increasing age was also found among the Finnish and German samples. Thus, the basically functional orientation as well as the age and gender differences found in our survey study largely confirmed what has been found in other samples using the same instrument. Also, in our cross-cultural studies, differences in dealing with specific problem situations were found. The most striking differences between our German sample presented here and the Finnish and the Israeli samples were found in coping with self-related problems with Germans having the highest withdrawal scores compared to Finnish and Israeli adolescents.

It is interesting to note that even when coping is assessed in response to an unspecific stressor, the results as regards the basic approach as well as age and gender differences are comparable. Herman, Stemmler, and Petersen (1992), who used a modified version of the CASQ on a sample of 603 U.S. adolescents reported only two dimensions, approach-oriented coping (e.g., active coping and internal coping) and avoidant coping (e.g., withdrawal). This reduction to two dimensions is possibly due to the fact that no specific problem domain was given in the CASQ, and the adolescents were asked to mark the usage of each coping strategy "when they have a problem." However, the basically active approach of the adolescents investigated as well as increasing scores in approach-oriented coping with age and higher scores in this coping style among females as compared to males closely parallels our findings. We lack, however, information about problem-specific coping styles, which may vary in the U.S. sample as compared to our other cross-cultural samples.

In summary, the studies have indicated that adolescents basically show a high competence in coping with minor stressors. Age and gender differences in coping strategies are striking, especially concerning certain domains. Our survey study has concentrated on elucidating those factors that influence stress and coping. Based on these results of Study 3, we may now begin to identify those adolescents who are at greater risk for dysfunctional coping as well as those salient domains which predominantly lead to withdrawal behavior in all adolescents.

Internal Resources and Their Effect on Coping Behavior

Defining parameters that constitute a more or less stressful situation is certainly important in stress and coping paradigms; but still more relevant, especially on a practical level, is often the question of how effectively an adolescent deals with a problem or stressor. The stressful encounter alone does not in itself explain why an individual responds in an adaptive or nonadaptive way. Even the threatening nature of the most severe crisis can be differently appraised because of the peculiarities of personal resources. Consequently, the manner of dealing with or the mastering of a stressful encounter will differ (Coelho, Hamburg, & Adams, 1974; Meichenbaum, 1977; Murphy & Moriarty, 1976). In coping theories (see Roskies & Lazarus, 1980), such internal resources may include interpersonal skills, personality, and self-concept variables.

Although I have reported on the relationship between self-concept and coping behavior in adolescence elsewhere (see Seiffge-Krenke, 1990a), the focus of this chapter lies on internal resources related to personality variables that may shape coping behavior. More specifically, personality variables may (a) influence the appraisal of an event by determining what is salient for an individual, (b) shape the coping response, and (c) provide the basis for evaluating possible outcomes (Lazarus & Folkman, 1991). In the study detailed here, I therefore aimed at determining the influence of personality variables on coping behavior, including their influence on stress perception. A brief outline of the research findings on the relationship between personality variables is presented first, followed by a more detailed discussion of the main research question in this chapter.

PERSONALITY VARIABLES AS COPING
DISPOSITION, INTERNAL COPING RESOURCES,
AND PROTECTIVE FACTORS

The relationship between personality variables, stress appraisal, and coping is complex. On the one hand, knowledge of personal characteristics enables a better prediction of how an encounter will be perceived and evaluated by an individual. On the other hand, personality factors may allow a more reliable prediction of whether, and with what probability, a person will be confronted with events of a certain nature. Finally, personal characteristics point toward those internal resources of an individual that may be significant for an efficient mastery of the various demands that he or she may be called to meet. People who judge themselves as inefficient in coping with stressors dwell on their personal deficiencies and imagine potential difficulties to be more formidable than they really are (Bandura, 1986; Lazarus & Launier, 1978).

The great conceptional significance of personality variables is outstanding in definitions, operalizations, and models of coping. In the process model developed by Lazarus et al. (1974), variables of the person and his or her environment are brought together. Lazarus referred to this configuration as a *unit*. He questioned, however, whether personality traits are directly associated with coping behavior (Folkman & Lazarus, 1980). Instead, the transaction between person and situation is accorded the major role in his model, whereas personality variables are regarded as influential at best. In contrast, according to the trait-oriented conceptualization of Haan (1974), certain personality traits such as productivity, fluency, introspectiveness, and high intellectual capacity covary with effective coping, defined here as reality-oriented, flexible, and emotionally appropriate responses to problems. These approaches reflect two alternative models in the role of personality variables in coping. Personality may be considered in the classical sense as traits and dispositions, or as internal resources. In a third approach, emphasis is placed on the protective factors of personality variables. In the studies of Kobasa, Maddi, and Kahn (1982) and Richman and Flaherty (1985), personality variables were most influential in the coping process, buffering the effects of stress, and played an even stronger role in warding off depressive symptomatology than social support variables. In the course of the discussion about the factors that keep individuals healthy even in the face of great stress (cf. the concepts of hardiness, Kobasa et al., 1982; and of resiliency, Rutter, 1985b) personality factors have received renewed attention. They were, for example, relevant predictors in the Cambridge Study on Delinquent Development (Farrington, 1989) and served as protective factors in the development of children belonging to high-risk groups in the longitudinal study by Werner and Smith (1982).

Historically, the issue of the influence of personality variables on coping is one of the oldest in coping research (cf. Lazarus, 1966). Despite critical discussions of the trait-oriented approaches and the shift of focus to interactionist and transactional perspectives, the issue has continued to attract the interest of researchers (cf. Panzarine, 1985), even though some basic theoretical and methodological problems are still unsolved. These include the difference in importance attributed to personality variables in models of the coping process previously indicated. Methodological difficulties in investigating the relationship between coping and personality characteristics arise from the temporal relation between the two. Personality factors may be regarded not only as antecedent or concurrent conditions affecting the coping process but can also be shown to undergo changes themselves as a result of feedback processes occurring during coping. In the field of personal control this was demonstrated impressively by Folkman (1984). Further methodological problems arise from the difficulty of determining the effects of situational and personal components (Averill, 1973).

PERSONALITY VARIABLES AND COPING STYLE

Questions concerning the relation between personality structure and coping have, however, remained marginal in research with adolescents. Research has focused almost exclusively on the analysis of how young people cope with very stressful, critical, or even traumatic events (cf. chap. 1). In these studies, personality traits have been, at best or if at all, included as side issues. In the following review it is demonstrated that this also applies to more recent research in which mastery of normative events has been increasingly emphasized.

Compared with studies on adults, studies on how adolescents come to terms with serious physical illness rarely involve close analyses of the influence of personality variables on coping. The few existing studies deal primarily with locus of control and extraversion/introversion. The most frequently investigated samples are young diabetics (e.g., Follansbee, 1984; Lipets, 1984; Meier, 1984). Although other investigators have analyzed personality variables in cancer patients (Blotcky, Raczynski, Gurwitch, & Smith, 1985; Guillory, 1983) or patients having other severe chronic illnesses with high mortality rates (e.g., Berman, 1983; Drotar et al., 1980; Dunn Geier, 1986), the samples used are very small, especially because some of the diseases studied are quite rare. Appraisal of personal control is also a frequently studied variable in analyses of how adolescents cope with critical life events such as parental divorce (Armistead et al., 1990; Farber, Felner, & Primavera, 1985), unplanned pregnancy (Coletta et al., 1981; Hussain, 1976; Panzarine, 1986), accidents (Stuart & Brown, 1981), and unemployment (Mehler, 1986), as well as traumatic events such as physical abuse (Hjorth & Ostrov, 1982), rape (McCombie, 1976), death, suicide or murder (Morawetz, 1982; Petti & Wells, 1980; Weight, 1979).

The majority of studies on coping with minor stressors are concerned with problems at school and focus on anxiety in learning situations (Gertner, 1982; Magnusson & Olah, 1983; Olah, Törestad, & Magnusson, 1984) or on achievement stressors (Hart, 1991; Schinke et al., 1987). In the studies conducted by

Richman and Flaherty (1985) and O'Hare and Tamburri (1986), the transition from leaving school to pursuing an occupation or going to university were studied with respect to personality.

The investigation of control beliefs, anxiety, extraversion/introversion, or repression/sensitization found in adolescent research corresponds to the aspects most frequently emphasized in research on adult coping (Rim, 1986; Spielberger, 1972); on the whole, very similar results have been found. Adolescents with internal control beliefs were, as a rule, better at appraising the situation and were more active in solving problems (Gatz et al., 1978; Parkes, 1984; Siddique & D'Arcy, 1984; Tyler, 1978). Studies on beliefs about one's personal efficacy revealed similar results (see, e.g., Walker & Greene, 1987).

In contrast to the very uniform results on locus of control and personal efficacy, studies of the effects of fear and anxiety on adolescent coping are very hard to compare because these constructs are associated with many different experiences and comprise a variety of behavioral components. Studies of trait anxiety and state anxiety as modifying and predictive factors in the coping process of adolescents have produced controversial results (e.g., Dowd, Claiborn, & Milne, 1985; Hart, 1991; Magnusson & Olah, 1983; Olah et al., 1984). As regards a further personality variable, repression/sensitization, controversial results were reported. Finally, it must be emphasized that the construct of extraversion/introversion has been studied almost exclusively in coping research with clinical groups, with the exception of the study by Malaviya (1977). Over the years, personality variables have remained of interest in adolescent coping research, but the importance of understanding more about the personal correlates of coping is not fully recognized in research focusing too much on selective samples and extremely stressful events. Moreover, in most studies, event appraisal has not been followed up systematically.

RESEARCH QUESTIONS

The studies described here have in common that they examine the relations between personality variables and coping within a relatively narrow field. Most deal with clinical or normal samples of adolescents who have been forced to encounter a highly damaging, non-normative experience with limited personal resources. This perspective reduces the situational variability to a minimum and stands in direct opposition to the large number of complexly interwoven problems confronting all young people in the transition to adulthood; moreover, by concentrating on extreme degrees of stress, little or no personality-specific variance is allowed for. Research questions such as whether the mobilization of certain coping strategies is more likely to be due to situational or personal factors or whether a systematic interaction of both influences may be assumed (cf. Magnusson, 1980) are not even raised in this approach. The consideration of situational characteristics in investigating the influence of personality variables on adolescent coping is rare. The work of Magnusson and Olah with their Swedish research team (e.g., Magnusson, 1980; Magnusson & Olah, 1983; Olah et al., 1984) is an example of this perspective.

In the previous chapters I analyzed coping as a dynamic process and elucidated the multidimensional nature of coping. I was able to show how appraisal processes are influenced by event parameters or situational characteristics and, furthermore, how age and gender influence stress appraisal and coping. All of these studies were based on normative samples and included a broad range of minor events that were highly salient for the majority of adolescents investigated. In this framework, I analyze personal resources for coping, because individual differences in these variables may help to explain why an event may be appraised as threatening by one person or as neutral or challenging by others.

According to the model described in chapter 2, coping is influenced by antecedent personality and stressor characteristics and may lead to adaptive and nonadaptive outcomes. In Study 3, detailed in chapter 5, I distinguished between two different modes of coping, namely, a functional one (including active coping and internal coping) and a dysfunctional one (entailing withdrawal as a main coping mode). In the following study (Study 4) I aimed at investigating the influence of personality variables on coping behavior. More specifically, I first wanted to know whether personality variables determine the manner of stress appraisal, and second, whether functional coping as compared to dysfunctional coping is related to a certain personality type and, finally, what influence situational factors have (i.e., whether personality-specific ways of coping possibly occur in a generalized manner across different problem areas).

METHOD

Subjects

Participants included 353 adolescents (153 males and 200 females), ages 15 to 19. The participants were randomly selected from the larger sample of participants in the survey study (n = 1,028), which was detailed in chapter 5. As was characteristic for the survey sample, slightly more females than males were investigated. Grade level was as follows: 117 adolescents (male: n = 50, female: n = 67) were attending the 10th grade, 115 adolescents (male: n = 54, female: n = 61) were in the 11th grade, and 121 adolescents (male: n = 49, female: n = 72) in the 12th grade.

Procedure

Adolescents completed the various questionnaires at school in small groups of approximately 15 students each, with a research assistant available to explain questions if necessary. The questionnaires were completed during two school lessons with a break of 15 minutes in between.

Measures

Adolescent Stress

Adolescent stress was measured by the Problem Questionnaire (see for details chap. 5) assessing minor stressors. The adolescents had to indicate the stressfulness of 64 items that covered frequently named and salient everyday problems ranging from 1 (*not stressful at all*) to 5 (*highly stressful*). Factor analysis revealed seven domains including problems with school, problems with future, problems with parents, problems with peers, problems with romantic relationships, problems with leisure time, and self-related problems. Cronbach alphas ranged between $r = .70$ and $r = .84$.

Adolescent Coping

Coping was measured by the CASQ (see for details chap. 5). Twenty coping strategies across eight different problem domains such as studies, teachers, parents, peers, romantic relations, self, leisure time, and future were assessed. The adolescents were free to mark several coping strategies for each area. Three factors emerged representing the following coping styles: active coping by means of social resources, internal coping, and withdrawal. The Cronbach alphas for these dimensions were $r = .80$, .77, and .73, respectively.

Personality Structure

Personality structure was assessed by the Freiburg Personality Inventory (FPI-K; Fahrenberg & Selg, 1970). It consisted of 12 subscales including nervousness, aggression, depressivity, irritability, sociability, composure, dominance, inhibition, openness, extraversion, emotional instability, and masculinity. Altogether, 76 items had to be answered with ratings ranging from 1 (*not true*), 2 (*somewhat true*), 3 (*medium*), 4 (*very true*), to 5 (*often true*). The FPI-K is a standardized short version for assessing personality variables on adolescent samples and has been frequently used in Germany. Norms for different age groups can be found in Fahrenberg and Selg (1970). The Cronbach alphas for these scales ranged between $r = .75$ and $r = .89$.

Self-Concept

The German version of the Offer Self Image Questionnaire (OSIQ) was used (Seiffge-Krenke, 1989). The adolescents had to agree to 73 items concerning different domains of self-concept ranging from 1 (*not true at all*) to 5 (*fully agree*). Factor analysis revealed five dimensions: general satisfaction with oneself and the world, good relations with parents, confidence in one's own abilities, social relationships with peers, and depressed self-concept. The Cronbach alphas for these scales were $r = .81, .75, .68, .67,$ and $.80$, respectively.

Clinical Service Use

As a general criterion for adaptation or dysfunction, the adolescents were asked if they had ever sought out or made use of counseling services.

RESULTS

Overview of Analysis

The question of whether our subsample of 353 adolescents showed a stress and coping pattern similar to that found in the survey sample was examined by applying descriptive statistics and MANOVAs to the results of the Problem Questionnaire and the CASQ's including age (split up in three age groups) and gender. Descriptive statistics and MANOVAs were also calculated for the FPI-K and OSIQ. The question of whether certain personality variables are related to stress perception and coping behavior was evaluated by correlation analysis.

The main question addressed in Study 4 concerned the relation between personality type and coping behavior. First, the FPI-K scale values were calculated for the adolescents being studied. To determine personality type from the FPI-K scale values, cluster analysis methods were employed. We selected the partitioning procedure according to the K-means method of MacQueen (1967); this procedure divides the samples to be analyzed by maximizing the Euclidean distance of cluster centers. We chose a three-cluster solution that divided the sample into comparably sized, homogenous subgroups. Finally, MANOVAs were calculated in order to analyze the degree of stress and the coping behavior of the adolescent depending on personality type. In order to achieve a problem-specific differentiation in coping behavior, MANOVAs for the three coping scales, separated according to the eight different problem areas were calculated as well. Multiple comparison of means according to the Scheffé test was implemented. Additional characterization of the three personality types was achieved by evaluating self-concept through ANOVAs and multiple comparison of means according to Scheffé. In order to avoid random effects, the significance level for each test was adjusted according to the procedure suggested by Dunn (1961) to $.05/45 = 0.0011$. The significance of variations in the frequency between the three personality types found in association with the additional, dichotomously coded question (clinical service use) was established by means of a chi square test.

Preliminary Analysis

Means and standard deviations for the Problem Questionnaire and the CASQ, broken down by age and gender, confirmed the adolescent stress and coping pattern found in the survey study limited to the age groups 15 to 19 years. Again,

MANOVAs revealed a significant effect of age in active coping [$F(2, 350) =$ 10.3, $p < .001$] and internal coping [$F(2, 350) = 7.8$, $p < .001$] with older age groups having higher scores in both active coping [$M_{10th\ grade} = 15.0$; $M_{11th\ grade} =$ 19.6; $M_{12th\ grade} = 20.3$] and internal coping [$M_{10th\ grade} = 6.0$; $M_{11th\ grade} = 7.8$; $M_{12th\ grade} = 8.9$]. In addition, girls scored higher in active coping [$F(1, 351) =$ 7.6, $p < .001$; $M_{male} = 10.5$, $M_{female} = 19.5$] and withdrawal [$F(1, 351) = 1.5$, $p =$ .05; $M_{male} = 4.1$, $M_{female} = 4.8$].

The personality structures of the adolescents were quite unexceptional in all seven dimensions measured. Comparing them with the standard scores based on German samples (see Fahrenberg & Selg, 1970), the raw scores of our subjects were all located in the second quartile, which can be taken as an indication of the high degree of normality of our sample. The slightly raised scores in the scale Openness illustrate that our sample was relatively self-critical and tended not to provide warped information. Means and standard deviations of the FPI-K, broken down by gender, can be found in Table 6.1.

Male and female adolescents differed in 8 of the 12 personality dimensions. Females described themselves as more nervous, irritable, depressed, and emotionally unstable, but also as more sociable than their male counterparts. Male adolescents, on the other hand, had significantly higher scores in aggression, dominance, composure, and masculinity.

In 9 of the 12 dimensions of the FPI-K of female adolescents no differences were found between the three age groups. Changes were only evident in depressivity and nervousness (increase with age) and in composure (decrease with age). In contrast, among the males a considerable degree of variability was observable over all age groups. A comparison of the scores of the 15- to 19-year-old males

TABLE 6.1
Differences in Personality Structure Between Males and Females

FPI-K Dimensions	Male (n = 153)		Female (n = 200)		Significance Test F(1,351)
	M	SD	M	SD	
1 Nervousness	2.3	1.5	2.9	1.6	2.7**
2 Aggression	2.8	1.6	2.2	1.5	3.6***
3 Depressivity	3.5	2.0	4.2	1.8	3.1***
4 Irritability	3.0	2.1	3.9	2.1	4.2***
5 Sociability	3.6	1.9	4.2	2.0	2.8**
6 Composure	3.9	1.8	2.9	1.9	4.7***
7 Dominance	2.2	1.8	1.9	1.5	1.7*
8 Inhibition	3.3	1.9	3.8	1.9	
9 Openness	4.4	1.5	4.2	1.6	
10 Extraversion	3.3	2.0	3.3	2.1	
11 Emotional instability	3.5	2.0	4.3	1.9	3.6***
12 Masculinity	3.5	1.6	2.6	1.7	3.8***

Note. *$p < .05$. **$p < .01$. ***$p < .001$.

revealed that only four dimensions (i.e., masculinity, emotional instability, extraversion, and sociability) remain unchanged. Here too, as with the females, most changes could be observed in early to mid-adolescence.

Pearson correlations were determined between the CASQ and FPI-K dimensions and the sum score of the Problem Questionnaire (total minor stressors) and FPI-K dimensions. Only three of the personality dimensions (i.e., nervousness, depressivity, and emotional instability) showed low but significant correlates with the sum score of total minor stressors, whereby depressivity showed more substantial relationships ($r = .41$).

As can be seen in Table 6.2, the relation found between coping and personality structure was almost exclusively limited to Scale 3 of the CASQ, withdrawal. Thus, the personality dimensions depressivity and inhibition correlated positively ($r = .38$ and $r = .32$, respectively) with the CASQ scale withdrawal, whereas negative correlations were found between withdrawal and sociability, composure and extraversion ($r = -.39$, $-.34$, and $-.32$, respectively).

Description of Personality Types

Through a cluster analysis using the K-means method according to MacQueen (1967), a three-cluster solution was established that divided the sample into homogeneous, comparably sized subgroups characterized by different personality structures. The clusters were controlled for age, gender, and socioeconomic background. As indicated in Table 6.3, the distribution according to age and gender in the cluster groups is more or less balanced (chi square n.s.).

In the following, the characteristics of these clusters are outlined, whereby the terms *high* and *low* are used to characterize the relative size of scale values of the cluster in question as compared to the other clusters.

Cluster 1: Sociable, extraverted adolescents ($n = 115$). The adolescents in this cluster were, compared with those in the other clusters, relatively composed, extraverted, and sociable. As shown in Fig. 6.1 their excitability took a midway position between the other two clusters. The adolescents in this cluster hardly mentioned psychosomatic complaints, they were content, and their mood was balanced.

Cluster 2: Emotionally unstable, depressed adolescents ($n = 127$). Adolescents in this cluster described themselves as rather unstable, moody, and insecure. They saw themselves as rather introverted, withdrawn, and lacking in enterprise. They felt depressed and named more physical complaints than those in the other clusters.

Cluster 3: Normal, controlled adolescents ($n = 111$). Adolescents belonging to this cluster on the whole had very average, balanced FPI profiles. They present themselves as calm, self-controlled, and not dominant at all. It has

TABLE 6.2

Pearson Correlations of Personality Dimensions, Stress Perception, and Coping Style (n = 353)

	FPI-K											
	1	2	3	4	5	6	7	8	9	10	11	12[a]
CASQ												
Active coping	-.03	.07	-.10	.03	.15*	.03	-.07	-.05	.06	.08	.09	.10
Internal coping	.06	.01	.01	.03	.05	.03	.02	.09	.06	.05	.02	.04
Withdrawal	.26**	.06	.38**	.18	-.39**	-.34**	-.03	.32**	.15*	-.32**	.29**	-.33**
Problem Questionnaire												
Minor stressors	.29**	.15*	.41**	.16*	.03	.07	.01	.11	.08	.19**	.23**	.07

Note. [a]1. Nervousness
2. Aggression
3. Depressivity
4. Irritability
5. Sociability
6. Composure
7. Dominance
8. Inhibition
9. Openness
10. Extraversion
11. Emotional instability
12. Masculinity
*p < .05. **p < .01.

139

TABLE 6.3
Age and Gender Distribution in the Three Personality Clusters

Age	Cluster 1 (n = 115)		Cluster 2 (n = 127)		Cluster 3 (n = 111)	
	Males	Females	Males	Females	Males	Females
15–16	15	18	20	30	17	17
17	15	21	16	19	26	18
18–19	20	26	18	24	16	17
Total	50	65	54	73	59	52

to be stressed, however, that lower scores on the Openness scale indicated a less open self-presentation.

Personality Type and Stress Perception

An analysis of how adolescents in the sample perceived stress revealed significant differences in all seven Problem Questionnaire scales. As can be seen in Table 6.4, emotionally unstable, depressed adolescents stood out in perceiving minor stressors in all domains analyzed as significantly more stressful. Particularly great are the discrepancies between the personality types in self-related problems.

Personality Type and Coping Style

A MANOVA revealed that adolescents belonging to the three clusters with different personality types differed only slightly from one another with respect to active coping using social resources [active coping: $F(2, 350) = 2.63$, $p = .07$]. With re-

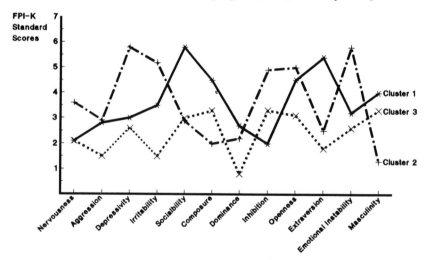

FIG. 6.1. Mean scores of three personality types across different personality scales.

TABLE 6.4
Stress Perception of Adolescents With Different Personality Types

| | Personality Type | | | | |
| Minor Stressors Across Different Domains | Cluster 1 Sociable/ Extraverted (n = 115) M | Cluster 2 Emotionally Labile/Depressed (n = 127) M | Cluster 3 Unexceptional/ Controlled (n = 111) M | Significance Test | |
				MANOVA F(2, 350)	Scheffé
Scale 1: problems with school	2.75	3.21	2.85	10.46***	2 > 1, 3
Scale 2: problems with future	2.98	3.43	3.01	10.84***	2 > 1, 3
Scale 3: problems with parents	2.29	2.73	2.12	14.40***	2 > 1, 3
Scale 4: problems with peers	2.45	3.18	2.71	22.34***	2 > 1, 3
Scale 5: problems with leisure time	2.23	2.69	2.29	22.39***	2 > 1, 3
Scale 6: problems with romantic relations	2.36	2.94	2.63	20.04***	2 > 3 > 1
Scale 7: self-related problems	2.87	3.94	3.01	84.17***	2 > 1, 3

Note. *p < .05. **p < .01. ***p < .001.

spect to certain problem domains, the active coping style of adolescents from Cluster 1 differed significantly in two problem areas from that exhibited by adolescents in other clusters. In problems with teachers [F(2, 350) = 2.23, p = .04] the adolescents belonging to Cluster 1 were significantly more active than the subjects in Cluster 2; in self-related problems they tended to be more active than those in Clusters 2 and 3 [F(2, 350) = 2.85, p = .05]. With respect to internal coping, adolescents with different personality types did not differ at all. The MANOVA revealed, however, significant differences between the three groups in Scale 3 of the CASQ that assesses withdrawal [F(2, 350) = 21.13, p < .0001]. The emotionally unstable, depressed adolescents from Cluster 2 had significantly higher scores here than those in the other two clusters. As can be seen in Table 6.5, these striking differences found in dysfunctional coping traverse all problem domains investigated.

In all analyzed problem domains the emotionally unstable, depressed adolescents showed two to three times higher scores in withdrawal than the sociable, extraverted and the unexceptional, self-controlled adolescents. Particularly strik-

TABLE 6.5
Significant Differences in Means in CASQ Scale 3, Withdrawal, of Adolescents
With Different Personality Types, Broken Down for Eight Problem Areas

| | Personality Type | | | | |
| | Cluster 1 Sociable/ Extraverted (n = 115) | Cluster 2 Emotionally Labile/Depressed (n = 127) | Cluster 3 Unexceptional/ Controlled (n = 111) | Significance Test | |
Problem Domains	M	M	M	MANOVA $F(2, 350)$	Scheffé
School	5.4	10.2	4.2	8.72***	2 > 1, 3
Teachers	1.8	7.2	4.2	8.55***	2 > 1
Parents	3.0	6.8	2.4	5.29***	2 > 3
Peers	3.6	8.4	3.6	7.82***	2 > 1, 3
Romantic relations	4.2	10.8	6.0	10.74***	2 > 1, 3
Self	4.9	11.4	3.6	19.94***	2 > 1, 3
Leisure time	3.0	6.6	2.4	5.90***	1 > 1, 3
Future	3.0	9.0	4.2	4.62**	2/1, 3

Note. $*p < .05.$ $**p < .01.$ $***p < .001.$

ing are the discrepancies in self-related problems, romantic relations, and school. Thus, adolescents with different personality structures neither differ very much with respect to their active coping and support seeking, nor in their internal reflection of possible solutions; however, they do differ in respect to the degree of withdrawal. Adolescents from Cluster 2 had the highest scores in dysfunctional coping which proved to be a generalized response across all problem domains.

Characterization of Personality Types Based on Additional Variables

The findings from the OSIQ presented in Table 6.6 show that the self-concept of the emotionally labile, depressed adolescent is significantly different in practically all the self-concept-relevant dimensions. These adolescents perceive themselves as very depressed and less satisfied with themselves and the world, as less efficient in their achievements and more strained in their relationships with parents and peers.

With respect to actual contact with counseling services or psychotherapists, no significant differences between adolescents with different personality types were revealed: Eight percent of the social and extraverted, 12% of the emotionally labile, and 12% of the unexceptional, controlled adolescents had already made contact with health professionals and had received counseling or completed therapy.

DISCUSSION

The personality structure of the adolescents we studied is unexceptional; its characteristics parallel the age and gender differences reported in the findings of other German studies (cf. Merz, 1982). Such findings have included more

TABLE 6.6
Significant Differences in OSIQ Scales of Adolescents
With Different Personality Type

	Personality Type			Significance Test	
	Cluster 1	Cluster 2	Cluster 3		
	(n = 115)	(n = 127)	(ns = 111)	MANOVA	
OSIQ Scale	M	M	M	F(2, 350)	Scheffé
1. General satisfaction with oneself and the world	36.1	28.9	33.6	62.20***	2 < 3 < 1
2. Good relations with parents	39.7	36.9	42.3	18.65**	3 < 1 < 2
3. Confidence in one's own abilities	33.0	29.9	32.3	13.98**	2 < 1, 3
4. Social relationships with peers	26.9	28.2	27.5	3.98*	2 > 1
5. Depressed self-concept	37.3	48.1	38.3	72.07***	2 > 1, 3

Note. *p < .05. **p < .01. ***p < .001.

differences related to gender than to age and earlier stabilization of personality structure in the females than the males, and frequently have been interpreted in terms of maturation processes. An analysis of stress perception and coping behavior parallels the results of Study 3 reported in chapter 5.

Cluster analysis revealed three different personality types that varied according to stress, coping behavior, and other variables. One group of adolescents was particularly energetic, sociable, and gregarious; another group described their moods as rather gloomy, they were less able to deal with strain and were socially withdrawn; the third group was characterized by an unexceptional personality structure. It must be mentioned, however, that this group was less eager to disclose information and revealed an increased number of problems in a few problem areas (e.g., in romantic relationships), which indicates that not all aspects of their lives functioned smoothly. Self-concepts and the degree of perceived burden of problems varied correspondingly with the different personality types. Consequently, differences in coping style could be found between the different personality types. In general, the preferred forms of coping in all of the adolescents included use of social resources, discussion with concerned others, the seeking of advice and help, regardless of the type of problem the individual was confronted with. Adolescents with socially oriented, extraverted personality structures, however, only showed a tendency to prefer this coping style in a few problem areas and thus did not differ from their same-aged peers having other personality types. Absolutely no differences between adolescents with different personality types were observed in relation to another coping style, namely, internal coping. According to our findings, a noteworthy influence of the personality structure of the adolescents studied on either general functional coping or problem-specific differentiation of the functional coping could not be established. However, the personality differences were striking concerning aspects of defense as found in the dimension of withdrawal (i.e., in dysfunctional coping according to our conceptualization). We were able to establish that significant differences between the three groups not only existed at the level of all problem domains but also covaried with differences in perceived stressors and self-concept.

Outstanding in this respect were the adolescents in Cluster 2, who were characterized as depressed and emotionally unstable. In particular, the rather negative self-image that these adolescents portrayed of themselves was striking. They also reported significantly higher rates of minor stressors across all seven domains assessed as compared to adolescents with other personality types. Thus, our results clearly show that depressed and unstable adolescents perceive the same problems as considerably more stressful. In line with this altered appraisal, we registered a higher frequency of dysfunctional coping (i.e., withdrawal), which was evident across all eight problem domains investigated. The withdrawal rates found in emotionally unstable and depressed adolescents were twice as high as those of sociable and extraverted adolescents and three times higher than those found in normal, controlled adolescents. Our measure of assessing minor stressors has been carefully developed and includes stressors with comparable parameters for the vast majority of adolescents investigated (see chap. 5), thus this result deserves attention. Folkman (1984) claimed that differences in personality variables are helpful in explaining why stressors are perceived as different. We have substantial evidence that personality type not only influences stress perception but also subsequent coping.

On the other hand, situational influences were apparent, too. This specific relationship becomes particularly clear with respect to stressors related to the self. Adolescents from Cluster 2 have the highest scores in perceived stressfulness in all scales of the Problem Questionnaire, particularly striking are the high scores in self-related problems. Moreover, an inspection of their coping behavior revealed that withdrawal rates were highest for self-related problems. This points to a special vulnerability and coping deficit, which is also supported by the finding of a negative self-concept in this group. Due to their depressive self-concept and their depressed and unstable personality structure, these adolescents lack internal resources needed to adequately deal with stressors. Their appraisal is quite impaired and withdrawal may result. This combined deficit is most clearly seen in coping with self-related problems. Rather unexpected, however, was the finding that there were no differences in the preference for active coping and internal coping between the three groups differing in personality type. Taking into consideration the results of depression research (e.g., Nolen-Hoeksema, 1991), we would expect that emotionally unstable, depressed adolescents resort more frequently to internal reflections of possible solutions. It should not be forgotten, however, that even the personality scores of the adolescents in Cluster 2 were by and large in the normal range, which may explain the unexpected result concerning internal coping.

The relationship between perceived stress and dysfunctional coping found in our study parallels the finding of a strong relationship between the increase of stress and a corresponding increase in defense reported by Folkman (1984) and Rim (1985) on adult samples. These same relationships were found to exist in adolescent samples studied in Sweden by Olah et al. (1984). These authors reported an association between high stress and high defense, and a corresponding association between low stress and predominantly constructive coping. A similar but less pronounced effect can be observed in our data concerning Cluster 1. Adolescents characterized as sociable and extraverted reported fewer minor stressors and also showed more active coping in some domains. Olah et al. (1984) interpreted this finding in two ways: Either it could be that those who think they know how to handle stressful situations may not see them as potentially harmful and thus not label them as "stressors" or there could also be an ability in functional copers to foresee and fend off impending threats. Our cross-sectional design does not permit us to address the question of causal relationships. However, we may be in a position to have a closer look at the relationships between functional or dysfunctional coping, personality variables and subsequent adaptation.

In chapter 1, I introduced a controversial issue in coping research, the conceptual distinction between coping, defined as successful mastery, and defending, which is regarded as dysfunctional. Nearly all authors differentiate between these two concepts, although they only rarely give precise criteria for their definition. Haan (1977) posited 10 underlying ego functions, the definition of which depend on the degree to which a person is able to perceive the situational demands in a realistic manner and to coordinate an adequate response. Besides distinguishing between coping (reality-oriented, adaptive functioning) and defense (denial of reality), which can be quantitatively defined according to the criteria emotional expression, reality orientation, and purposefulness, Haan added the mechanism of fragmentation (failure of ego-functions) as a qualitatively distinct expression of pathological behavior. She took the viewpoint that coping, defending, and fragmentation are to be regarded as permanent features of an individual's disposition. In contrast, Lazarus' transactional approach emphasizes the situational determinants of coping, and proceeds without an explicit differentiation between these two forms. It is an important feature of his definition (see Lazarus & Launier, 1978) that coping is defined independently of its outcome (i.e., coping refers to the efforts made to manage demands, regardless of the success of these efforts). Defense processes are subsumed under intrapsychic coping patterns that, along with information seeking, direct action, and inhibited action, are conceived as an independent coping modality. Defensive reappraisal is seen as a further coping form. Apart from their different emphasis on transaction between person and situation and their differing evaluation of coping styles, the differences between the approaches of Haan and Lazarus can also be demonstrated through their criteria of coping. Although for Haan, defense is a nonadaptive misinter-pretation of reality and leads to an unsuccessful outcome, Lazarus' conception concedes that an event may well be "distortedly" perceived but still contribute to successful coping from the point of view of functionality and efficacy. In this case, the criterion of optimal outcome begins on the level of action and is judged according to functionality or dysfunctionality. Apart from the criteria for differ-entiating between defending and coping, a series of attempts have been made to separate the two concepts by focusing on appraisal aspects. Folkman (1984) found that individuals showed more problem-focused coping in situations ap-praised as changeable, and more emotion-focused coping in situations appraised as unchangeable realities that have to be accepted. In addition, right from the beginning, personal characteristics have been regarded as relevant, leading to a search for those personality factors that constitute a "good coper" (Haan, 1974, 1977). In Haan's trait-oriented approaches, effectivity criteria played a major role and were expressed in the differentiation between coping and defense, be-tween productive adaptation and defense processes.

Our findings would appear at first to favor the concept of Haan, because the defensive behavior of the depressed and emotionally unstable adolescents is generally increased for all problems. The similarly high scores in functional coping nevertheless show that this group cannot simply be classified as "defend-ers." The simultaneous occurrence of both functional and dysfunctional forms of coping in this group could possibly be an important protection against physical or psychological symptoms. This is an important aspect, because due to its higher perceived stress level in all problem domains investigated, this group may be regarded as being at risk. The items subsumed under withdrawal include such aspects as active forgetting, emotional outlet, and avoiding, described by Folkman and Lazarus (1980) as emotion-focused coping. Especially in situations of high stress they represent a reasonable means of controlling the subject's emotional state and protecting him or her against further overtaxation. Here, withdrawal can be a very adaptive coping response as Ebata and Moos (1994) showed.

The analysis of clinical service use revealed no difference between the three groups of adolescents with different personality types. This means that despite greater burdens of stress, the adolescents in Cluster 2 were not prepared to accept professional help right away. Their mixture of withdrawal as a preventive initiative against future stress and the more offensive forms of tackling the problems is possibly very efficient. On the other hand, our findings on the adolescents showing an especially normal personality structure suggest a certain denial in stress perception. Our results of both adolescents with normal personality structure and those describing themselves as depressed and emotionally unstable converge and necessitate a revision of the classical division drawn by Haan. In summary, findings on Study 4 show that active approaches also exist among defenders and thus, caution is warranted in stereotyping somebody as "coper." We have to concede that defensive approaches may be successful at least in the short run.

Changes in Stress Perception and Coping Style as a Function of Perceived Family Climate

Social support provided to individuals by their close relationships serves as a buffer against the negative effects of stress (Caplan, 1974). Research has shown that parent–adolescent relationships contribute to an individual's ability to cope with various sources of stress such as stressful life events (Dean & Lin, 1977) and life transitions (Cauce, Felner, & Primavera, 1982). Adolescents' interpersonal resources, combined with intrapersonal factors such as age, gender, intelligence, and temperament, are perceived as crucial predictors of coping and adaptation (Rutter, 1985a; Werner & Smith, 1982). The interpersonal resources emphasized in adolescence are close relationships including the nuclear and extended family, peers, teachers, social groups, and the social context. According to Skinner and Wellborn (1993), in relationships where adolescents sense that support is available and their psychological needs are being met, they cope with stress in more active, flexible, and positive ways. In contrast, when relationships are coercive and adolescents' needs are ignored, adolescents react to challenges in passive and rigid ways. Certainly, the level of perceived stress is also linked to parent–adolescent relationships. In the past, adolescent development was viewed in terms of transformations in the reciprocal nature of parent–child relationships. Even more important with respect to coping was the evidence found in several studies showing that the quality of family relations was linked to the degree of adolescent competence in problem solving.

In this study (Study 5), I address the interface between adolescent coping and perception of family processes. More specifically, I relate the adolescent perception of family climate to his or her appraisal of stress and coping style. There is a growing consensus that the family environment has a significant influence on coping behavior. However, not only do families affect adolescents' coping behavior, but aspects of adolescent development (e.g., dysfunctional coping) may affect the life of the family. This is apparent if the adolescent and his or her family has to cope with major events such as chronic illness or parental divorce. But even for minor events, the contribution of families to adolescent adaptation and the impact of adolescent development on families may be quite marked.

FAMILY RELATIONS AS A SOURCE
OF SUPPORT AND STRESS

In evaluating 60 years of research, Montemayor (1983) reported that empirical studies have been unable to document the existence of universal distress among nonclinical families with adolescents. On the contrary, most studies have indicated that the degree of interpersonal discord between parents and adolescents varies considerably. Although in most families, interpersonal relations are usually harmonious, in a smaller number of families, disagreements and misunderstandings between parents and adolescents are frequent (Montemayor, 1983; Richardson et al., 1984). Communication problems, emotional withdrawal, and conflicts are particularly typical in disordered adolescents and their families. Rutter, Graham, et al. (1976) reported that such families are three times more likely to experience alienated relationships than normal families. According to their findings, confrontations between parents and adolescents occurred once a month for 11% of the boys and 7% of the girls. Nearly 25% of the boys' parents and 9% of the girls' parents reported some emotional withdrawal or communication difficulty. In previous studies, serious disagreements with parents were found to be a relatively common event, which, however, were perceived as moderately stressful by most adolescents. The issues viewed by adolescents as leading to conflict with parents were not very serious and corresponded to the examples provided by Csikszentmihalyi and Larson (1984). Other studies have also shown that when conflicts do occur between adolescents and parents that their causes are predominantly related to mundane issues. Family chores, curfews, dating, school grades, personal appearance, and eating habits were the matters of concern, or as Hill and Holmbeck (1986) stated ironically, instead of being about basic values, conflicts were related to "hair, garbage, dishes and galoshes" (p. 158). In addition, it appears that the causes for parent–adolescent conflicts do not change much over time. A replication of the Middletown study by Lynd and Lynd (1929) and later by Caplow, Bahr, Chadwick, Hill, and Williams (1982) showed that the points of contention have not changed much for 60 years. If we regard the parent–child relationship as an enduring bond that continues throughout life span (D. Moore, 1987; Youniss & Smollar, 1985), but undergoes significant transformations in early childhood and adolescence (see Collins, 1990, for a review), frequency of parent–adolescent problems and modes of coping with these problems may be of relevance. However, typical modes of resolution of family conflict do not represent optimal models of coping. Montemayor and Hanson (1985) have shown that 47% of adolescent conflicts with parents are solved by walking away and only 15% are marked by negotiation. In analyzing conflict resolution strategies, Smetana (1988) found two types of unilateral solutions (a parent or child either actively concedes or does so passively by walking away) and two types of bilateral solutions (compromise or no solution, as demonstrated either by actively agreeing or passively by walking away). Parents and children did not differ significantly in their reports that adolescents conceded to parental demands in 56% of all conflicts, whereas parents acceded to child demands in only 18% of conflicts. Similar to Montemayor and Hanson (1985), joint discussion accounted for only 13% of all conflict resolutions. Similar trends were found in a study by Vuchinich (1987), who analyzed conflicts occurring at the dinner table in families with adolescents. The study revealed that in only 14% of the cases did parents and adolescents reach a compromise. In other cases, partners either resisted, withdrew, or submitted. These "solutions" undoubtedly are not indicative of an active mode of coping.

Several authors (e.g., Blos, 1967; Collins, 1990; L. Steinberg, 1981) suggested that these apparent perturbations in relationships may serve the positive function of facilitating adolescents' independence and diminishing dependence on parents. In open conflicts, family members allow themselves to express their distinctive and separate views. In addition, family conflicts are only one facet of parent–adolescent relationships. In adolescence, parents are also expected to be aware of and support the adolescent's process of individuation yet maintain the adolescent's confidence that he or she can turn to them in time of need (Grotevant & Cooper, 1986). Empirical studies on a sample of maladjusted adolescents have indicated that parents that lacked closeness or support for adolescents' striving toward independence were common (Shulman & Klein, 1982). Such families employ counterseparation attitudes either by portraying the external world as hostile and uncontrollable or by undermining the adolescent's own initiatives when interacting with extrafamilial agencies or exerting independence. Families of normal adolescents reveal interaction patterns that foster both individuation and connectedness in relationships. These qualities of family relationships have been found to be associated with adolescents' status in identity exploration, role-taking skills, and ego-development (e.g., Grotevant & Cooper, 1985, 1986; Hauser et al., 1984). When separation is allowed, adolescent expressions of individuality and self-assertion are possible. Combined with a context of connectedness, these independent tendencies are acknowledged and supported by other family members.

THE INFLUENCE OF FAMILY CLIMATE
ON COPING BEHAVIOR

Coping reflects a condition where an individual effectively regulates his or her own behavior, emotions, and motivational orientation during periods of stress. However, the mechanisms by which a family enhances or undermines coping are still not clearly defined. According to Reiss (1981), each family establishes a "family paradigm," namely, a structure of its intrafamilial interaction, as well as a perception of and a set of assumptions about the external world. Following the work of Lazarus (1976), Reiss and Oliveri (1980) proposed a model for linking the family paradigm to the ways in which the family responds to stress (i.e., how it copes). A family that possesses appropriate problem-solving skills is able to reappraise an external threat, thus supporting the search for a favorable solution. The functional coping process is marked by a family's belief in its ability to deal with the world, along with an integration of responses from all family members. On the other hand, a hostile attitude toward the world and an emphasis on family unity against external threats may impede coping strategies; the family may be left with only its former mode of responding that may not be suitable for a present set of circumstances. This type of family obviously does not offer a model for functional coping. In addition, perception of the external world as dangerous and hostile may lead parents to prevent their youngsters from dealing autonomously with other persons or external entities, such as peers or school.

Thus, the family may serve as a guide or model for adolescent functioning. Various studies have emphasized the roles that family interaction or family type play in adolescent development and adaptation (Hauser et al., 1984; Russel, Olson, & Sprenkle, 1979; Shulman & Klein, 1982). Due to the distancing process, the adolescent may develop his or her own model of the family, which may not exactly reflect parental perceptions. Barnes and Olson (1985) found that adolescents perceive their family differently than their parents. Thus, despite the family's role as a guide or model, the adolescent's own perception of the family may also be related to his or her level of functioning.

Moos (1974) introduced the concept of family climate in which each individual's perceptions of the family milieu are assessed. Several studies in the past have analyzed the influence of family climate on coping behavior. Shulman, Seiffge-Krenke, and Samet (1987) compared adolescent coping styles across different perceived family climates. Family climate was measured by the FES (Moos, 1976) and coping by the CASQ (see chap. 5). Participants included 187 Israeli adolescents aged 15 to 17. Four distinctive types of family climates were found that were related to the preferred coping styles of the adolescents. Two types of family climates enhance coping, whereas two other types of family climates had negative effects on coping. The analysis indicated that the perception of family cohesion and organization, combined with respect for individual development, was related to a higher level of functional coping in the adolescent. A lack of family support as well as a lack in structure and organization, however, was related to a higher level of dysfunctional coping. A replication of this study on a strictly parallel sample of 521 Scandinavian adolescents revealed similar results, especially with respect to perceived family climate and dysfunctional coping (Seiffge-Krenke, 1990b). The cross-cultural comparison of adolescents from Tel Aviv and Helsinki shows that families whose offspring have the highest withdrawal rates are uniformly characterized by poor cohesion, minimal expression of feelings, highly conflictual interactions, and (especially in the Finnish sample) a high control over their adolescent members, accompanied by neglecting the individuality of their offspring.

In a recent study by Stern and Zevon (1990), this research was extended by assessing the specific coping responses of adolescents as a function of age, type of stressor, and quality of family environment. Seventy-three adolescents aged 15 to 18 completed the revised Ways of Coping Scale (WCS; Folkman & Lazarus, 1985) and the FES (Moos, 1976). The adolescents named recent encounters they experienced as being stressful and were asked to consider these stressors in answering the WCS. Problem-focused coping and seeking social support were the coping responses most frequently reported. Younger adolescents used emotion-based coping strategies to a greater extent than older adolescents. The relationship between adolescent coping and perceived family climate showed similar results to the aforementioned study by Shulman et al. (1987) and my recent cross-cultural replication in Finland (Seiffge-Krenke, 1990b). Negative perception of the family environment was associated with the use of more emotion-based coping strategies such as withdrawal, denial, and tension reduction.

RESEARCH QUESTIONS

As illustrated, parent–adolescent relationships may serve as a source of stress or as a source of support. Our previous studies have shown that parent–adolescent problems, although not perceived as very stressful, represented a considerable amount of the minor events adolescents have to cope with. As mentioned already, Montemayor (1986) reported that 15% to 25% of parents complained about conflicts with their adolescents. Estimates about the frequency of arguments between parents and adolescents amounted to about two arguments per week with the parents, usually the mother, and about three arguments with siblings. In Laursen's (1993) study, the adolescents reported an average of seven disagreements a day, the majority involving family members. In our Coping Process Study, the adolescents came about once a week to report about quarrels with parents (see chap. 3). In the Event Exploration Study, problems with parents constituted between 9% and 17% of the minor events named (see chap. 4). It is therefore apparent that although conflict exists even in the most positive, close relationships, extremely high levels of problems are not characteristic of "normal" families. We may find, however, more conflicts and manifestations of parent–adolescent stress in families with a certain type of family climate. Although in Study 3 (see chap. 5) we have been unable to demonstrate the existence of universal distress, the age- and gender-related differences in parent–adolescent conflicts and problems point to differences in stress perception. Moreover, we would expect that frequency and intensity of problems differ, depending on family climate.

In dealing with coping more specifically, it is unclear which modes of adolescent coping are related to family relationships. Undoubtedly, nonsupportive relationships are probably related to passive and inefficient encounters with the environment. It would be reasonable to assume that supportive relationships may enable active information seeking and provide a source of advice and assistance. Yet the question remains whether supportive family relationships are also related to better appraisal and analysis of events. In the studies reported here we were able to show that the relationship between family climate and coping is much more distinct for dysfunctional coping styles than for active coping and support seeking. Internal coping, however, was not related to types of family climate. This may suggest that family climate influences coping styles differently. In pursuing this line of thought, we may ask how consistent this relationship across various problem domains is. Is the perceived family climate related to the adolescent coping across domains or is it associated with adolescent coping only in certain family-related areas? It is possible that coping with issues related to the individuation process that are mostly controlled by the adolescent, such as relationships with peers and the opposite gender, are not greatly affected by the nature of the family climate.

A further important issue to consider are changes in stress perception and coping style over time. Our previous studies have demonstrated that family relations are rather harmonious overall, and that over time, parent–adolescent problems increase only slightly. Our studies also show that although discussion with parents is one of the most important coping strategies for adolescents, its use declines over the adolescent years, and in late adolescence, is restricted to certain domains (see chap. 5). Thus, changes in coping style or specific coping strategies over time may also vary according to the type of families the adolescents belong to.

The aims of the Study 5 presented here were threefold. The first aim was to investigate differences in stress perception between adolescents stemming from different family types. The second aim was to analyze the relationship between the family climate perceived by the adolescent and his or her functional or dysfunctional style of coping. This included the analysis of the association between styles of coping and family climate across the various problem domains the adolescent would be expected to be confronted with. Finally, we intended to follow-up adolescents assigned to groups with a specific family climate longitudinally and compare their stress perception and coping style over years.

METHOD

Subjects

Participants were 215 adolescents aged 12 to 16. They constituted the healthy control group of a 4-year longitudinal study on chronic illness and coping, which included healthy and diabetic adolescents and their parents. The sample consisted of 109 males and 106 females, attending Grades 6 to 10 in a German high school. Seventy-three percent of the adolescents were raised in two-parent families, 27% were raised in single-parent or divorced families. The average family size was 1.7 children. Mean parent education level was 12.8 years for fathers and 12.4 years for mothers. The families came from a broad socioeconomic strata.

Measures

Adolescent Stress

Adolescent stress was measured by the Problem Questionnaire (for details see chap. 5) assessing minor stressors. The adolescents had to indicate the stressfulness ranging from 1 (*not stressful at all*) to 5 (*highly stressful*) of 64 items that covered frequently named and salient everyday problems.

Adolescent Coping

Coping was measured by the CASQ for adolescents (for details see chap. 5). Twenty coping strategies across eight different problem domains such as school, teachers, parents, peers, opposite gender, self, leisure time, and future were assessed. The adolescents were free to select several coping strategies for each area.

Family Climate

The FES (see Moos & Moos, 1981) was administered to assess the adolescents' perceptions of their families. Ten subscales were included: cohesion, expression, conflict, independence, achievement orientation, intellectuality, recreation, moral, organization, and control. Each of the 91 items were rated according to a 5-point scale: 1 (*very false*), 2 (*somewhat false*), 3 (*partly true*), 4 (*mainly true*), and 5 (*very true*). Cronbach alphas for the German version of the FES yielded the following coefficients (see Schneewind, 1987): cohesion, .81; expression, .76; conflict, .62; independence, .68; achievement orientation, .78; intellectuality, .80; recreation, .76; moral, .77; organization, .80; and control, .71.

Procedure

The adolescents completed the various questionnaires after personal contact with the researchers at school during one school lesson. A research assistant was available to explain the details of our longitudinal approach, to answer questions if necessary, and to supervise the adolescents in small groups of approximately 15 students each. Additional assessments following the same procedure and on the same sample took place during 2 consecutive years with 12 months time in between. Thus, the first phase of the study in summer 1991 was followed by two further waves in summer 1992 and summer 1993. Adolescents were identified at all three measurement points by code numbers. The drop-out rate was 3% (i.e., from the 215 adolescents, 207 could be identified in all three waves). Results were based on the values of 207 adolescents with complete data sets.

RESULTS

Overview of the Analysis

The question of whether our longitudinal sample showed stress and coping patterns similar to those found in the survey sample (see chap. 5) was examined at Time 1 by applying descriptive statistics and MANOVAs to the Problem Questionnaire and the CASQ, including age (split up into three age groups) and gender. Descriptive statistics and MANOVAs were also calculated for the FES. The question of whether family climate dimensions were related to stress perception and coping behavior was evaluated by correlation analysis.

The main question addressed in this study concerned the relationship between family type and coping behavior. The building of groups was achieved by employing cluster analysis methods to the FES scores of Time 1. We selected the partitioning procedure according to the K-means method of MacQueen (1967) that divides the sample to be analyzed by maximizing the Euclidean distance of cluster centers. A four-cluster solution was chosen that divided the sample into comparably sized, homogenous subgroups. Then, MANOVAs were calculated in order to analyze minor stressors and coping behavior of the adolescents stemming from different family types for Time 1. In order to evaluate problem-specific differentiation in coping behavior due to family type, MANOVAs for the three coping scales, separated according to the eight different problem areas, were calculated as well. Multiple comparison of means according to the Scheffé Test was also implemented.

Then, means and standard deviations of the variables measured at each time of measurement were determined. Changes over time for the whole sample were analyzed by autocorrelations. These correlations suggested a moderate to high degree of stability in perceived family climate, minor stressors, and coping style. Finally, a series of analyses examined the changes in stress perception and coping style for adolescents stemming from different family clusters. Based on the cluster analysis of FES scores of Time 1, the adolescents were assigned to four groups of different family types and their mean level changes in the Problem Questionnaire and the CASQ were analyzed longitudinally. MANOVAs repeated measurements and follow-up ANOVAs were computed with time as a within-subject factor and family type as a between-subject factor, including the data set of all three waves of the Problem Questionnaire and the CASQ. Repeated measurement MANOVAs included a Greenhouse–Geisser correction for variance heterogenity.

Preliminary Analysis

Means and standard deviations for the Problem Questionnaire and the CASQ (see Table 7.5) generally confirmed the adolescent stress and coping pattern found in the survey study (see chap. 5). Multivariate analysis of variance with respect to age (three groups) and gender was conducted with age and gender as independent variables and the seven scales of the Problem Questionnaire as dependent variables. MANOVAs revealed a tendency for a main effect of age only in school-related problems [$F(2, 204) = 2.8$, $p = .08$] with younger adolescents perceiving these problems as being more stressful than older adolescents. Significant main effects of gender, however, were found in four of the seven scales of the Problem Questionnaire. Females scored higher in future-related problems [$F(1, 205) = 6.1$, $p = .01$], self-related problems [$F(1, 205) = 14.8$, $p < .001$], problems with romantic relationships [$F(1, 205) = 3.9$, $p = .04$] and problems with peers [$F(1, 205) = 16.8$, $p < .001$]. Concerning the CASQ, MANOVAs revealed a significant effect on age only in internal coping [$F(2, 204) = 3.5$, $p = .05$] with older age groups having higher scores in internal coping ($M_{youngest} = 6.9$; $M_{middle} = 7.3$; $M_{oldest} = 7.9$). In addition, girls scored higher in active coping [$F(1, 205) = 5.48$, $p = .02$; $M_{male} = 13.1$, $M_{female} = 17.6$] and tendentially in withdrawal [$F(1, 205) = 3.1$, $p = .08$; $M_{male} = 4.8$, $M_{female} = 5.8$].

For family climate, MANOVAs revealed significant main effects of age only in 2 of the 10 FES dimensions, achievement [$F(2, 204) = 3.4$, $p = .05$] and independence [$F(2, 204) = 5.4$, $p = .02$]. Besides a tendency among females to perceive less achievement orientation in the family than males [$F(1, 205) = 3.0$, $p = .08$], no significant effects of gender could be observed.

Correlational Analysis

Correlation coefficients between dimensions of family climate and stress and coping were calculated. Pearson correlation coefficients of the total score of minor stressors, the seven domains of the Problem Questionnaire, the 3 dimensions of the CASQ and the 10 FES dimensions can be found in Table 7.1.

The analysis revealed that several of the subscales of the Problem Questionnaire were substantially related to dimensions of the FES. For example, problems with parents was negatively associated with perceived independence in the family ($r = -.51$) and positively with conflicts in the family ($r = .39$). In addition, cohesion and expression both showed negative associations with total scores of minor stressors, and control was positively related to the total score of minor stressors, illustrating the saliency of these family climate variables for stress levels. As illustrated, from the dimensions of the CASQ, active coping was moderately related to some family dimensions signifying personal growth (e.g., independence, achievement orientation, and intellectuality). It is also apparent from Table 7.1 that withdrawal was rather positively associated with conflict and control and negatively with cohesion. Internal coping style was not related to any of the FES dimensions.

Description of Family Types

In order to determine family climate as perceived by the adolescents, a K-means clustering procedure was applied on the 10 Moos scales. Cluster analysis revealed four distinctive types of perceived family climates. As indicated in Table 7.2, the distribution according to age and gender in the cluster groups is more or less balanced.

TABLE 7.1
Pearson Correlations Between Stress, Coping, and Perceived Family Climate (n = 207)

	Perceived Family Climate									
	Coh	Expr	Confl	Indep	Achie	Intel	Recre	Moral	Organ	Contr
Problem Questionnaire										
Total minor stressors	-.49**	-.55**	.27**	-.34**	.14*	-.19**	-.31**	.13*	.01	.41**
Problems with school	-.16*	-.25**	.10	-.15*	.01	-.05	-.26**	.11	.08	.17*
Problems with future	-.22**	-.33**	.06	-.19**	.16*	-.03	-.17*	.12	.10	.27**
Problems with parents	-.64**	-.69**	.39**	-.51**	.19**	-.27**	-.31**	.08	.01	.64**
Problems with peers	-.30**	-.35**	.20*	-.22*	.06	-.19*	-.25**	.13*	-.02	.16**
Problems with leisure time	-.45**	-.46**	.31**	-.24**	.08	-.08	-.29**	.15*	-.09	.38**
Problems with romantic relationships	-.21**	-.22**	.02	-.09	.09	-.15*	.19**	-.11	-.01	.04
Self-related problems	-.45**	-.45**	.26**	-.28**	.11	-.16*	-.15*	.17*	-.09	.36**
CASQ										
Active coping	.06	.03	.04	.20**	.19**	.36**	.09	.02	.24**	.12
Internal coping	.14*	.12	.10	.08	.03	.20**	.05	.09	.02	.16*
Withdrawal	-.37**	-.29**	.44**	-.18**	.04	.09	.03	.08	.05	.37**

Note. *p < .05. **p < .01.

TABLE 7.2
Age and Gender Distribution in the Four Family Clusters

Age	Cluster 1 (n = 53)		Cluster 2 (n = 32)		Cluster 3 (n = 65)		Cluster 4 (n = 57)	
	Males	Females	Males	Females	Males	Females	Males	Females
12–13	14	14	5	6	17	10	9	10
14–15	9	9	7	10	18	12	13	13
16–17	3	4	2	2	4	4	6	6
Total	26	27	14	18	39	26	28	29

Mean standard score profiles are graphed in Fig. 7.1. In the following description of clusters, the term *high* or *low* refer to the relative status of the mean standard score of the cluster among the four clusters. The characteristics of the four clusters are described here:

Cluster 1: Achievement- and control-oriented families (53 adolescents). In this cluster, adolescents perceived their families as achievement-oriented and emphasizing control. Intellectual and recreational activities were many, reflecting the pressure for a structuring of family activities and explicitness of family rules. This structuring, however, existed in an atmosphere marked by friction, and family members were not perceived as close and expressing feelings. As well, there was not much leeway provided for the adolescent to express his or her individuality.

Cluster 2: Disengaged and conflict-oriented families (32 adolescents). In this cluster, adolescents perceived a high degree of conflictive interaction and lack of support within the family context. Adolescents described their families as having a comparably low intellectual and achievement orientation, and not providing much room for individual development. The degree of emotional bonding perceived was the lowest in this cluster compared to all other clusters. The families were depicted as being aggressive and showing extreme control.

Cluster 3: Structured, cohesive, and moral-oriented families (65 adolescents). Adolescents in this cluster described their families as being cohesive and having little conflict. In addition, family members were described as supporting each other while refraining from expression of emotions. This is probably related to the low degree of conflict in such a family. In addition, the family was described as highly organized with pressure for achievement. Clear rules and guidance were accompanied by strong emphasis on family morals that might be part of the family's organization. Individuality, however, was not encouraged in these families.

Cluster 4: Cohesive, expressive, and individuated families (57 adolescents). Adolescents in this cluster, as in Cluster 3, described an emphasis on

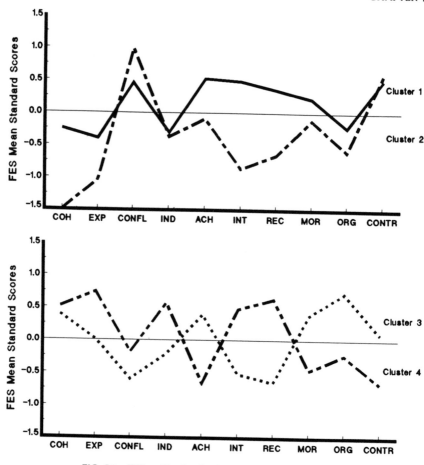

FIG. 7.1. FES profiles for the four perceived family clusters.

intrafamilial relationships. Compared to adolescents from other clusters, they perceived the family cohesion and unity to be the highest. An open expression of feelings was encouraged. Also, individuality was highly encouraged in an intellectually oriented atmosphere, which might reflect a tendency towards openness to the external world. Achievement orientation as well as organization and control were lowest compared to the other clusters, which might be indicative of a laissez-faire atmosphere or a great trust in the structuring abilities of its members.

Family Type and Stress Perception

A MANOVA was performed on the seven scales of the Problem Questionnaire across the four perceived family clusters. It revealed significant differences in six of the seven problem domains.

As can be seen in Table 7.3, adolescents from the four family climate clusters uniformly reported low numbers of school-related problems. Adolescents from disengaged and conflict-oriented families reported higher stress than adolescents from the other family types in all problem domains except school. The discrepancies in stress perception were particularly high in adolescents from Cluster 2 who showed the highest stress levels with respect to problems with parents. However, adolescents from Cluster 1, who had also described their families as being achievement- and control-oriented, reported more minor stressors than adolescents from Clusters 3 and 4 in problems with future, problems with parents, and problems with leisure time.

Family Type and Coping Style

A MANOVA was performed on the three coping styles across the four family clusters. It revealed that adolescents belonging to different family types differed significantly from one another with respect to active coping and withdrawal. As can be seen in Table 7.4, adolescents from Cluster 4, who had described their families as being cohesive, expressive, and allowing individuality, exhibited the highest level of active coping and the lowest level of withdrawal. In contrast, dysfunctional coping style was the highest and active support seeking the lowest among adolescents stemming from disengaged and conflict-oriented families. No difference emerged with respect to internal reflection of possible solutions.

Another MANOVA was performed on the coping styles of adolescents from the various family climates across the eight domains of the CASQ. With respect to these problem domains, the more active coping styles of adolescents from Cluster 1 and 4 differed significantly from those exhibited by adolescents in Clusters 2 and 3 in four problem areas. They were significantly more active in the domains parents [$F(3, 203) = 3.49$, $p = .01$], peers [$F(3, 203) = 5.54$, $p = .001$], leisure time [$F(3, 203) = 3.66$, $p = .01$], teachers [$F(3, 203) = 2.71$, $p = .04$], and future [$F(3, 203) = 3.75$, $p = .01$]. With respect to internal coping, adolescents stemming from families with different family climates did not differ at all. However, significant differences in withdrawal among the four groups were found for the problem domains school [$F(3, 203) = 5.68$, $p < .001$], parents [$F(3, 203) = 5.16$, $p < .001$], and peers [$F(3, 203) = 2.91$, $p = .06$]. Adolescents from disengaged and conflict-oriented families had significantly higher withdrawal scores in these domains compared to the other three cluster groups. Adolescents from cohesive, expressive and individuated families reported the lowest withdrawal rates in these domains, even lower than adolescents from Clusters 1 and 3.

Changes in Stress Perception and Coping Style Over Time

Table 7.5 displays the means and standard deviations of the measures of family climate, adolescent stress, and coping across the three measurement points.

TABLE 7.3
Stress Perception of Adolescents Stemming From Different Family Types

Minor Stressors Across Different Domains	Family Type				Significance Test	
	Cluster 1 Achievement/ Control-Oriented (n = 53) M	Cluster 2 Disengaged/ Conflict-Oriented (n = 32) M	Cluster 3 Structured/Cohesive Moral-Oriented (n = 65) M	Cluster 4 Cohesive/Expressive Individuated (n = 57) M	MANOVA $F(3, 203)$	Scheffé
Scale 1: Problems with school	1.61	1.43	1.62	1.54	$F = .59$	
Scale 2: Problems with future	2.94	2.98	2.54	2.72	$F = 3.84^*$	1, 2 > 3, 4
Scale 3: Problems with parents	2.23	2.62	1.85	1.61	$F = 24.4^{***}$	1 < 3, 4 2 < 1, 3, 4
Scale 4: Problems with peers	2.48	2.66	2.12	2.20	$F = 5.29^{**}$	2 > 3, 4
Scale 5: Problems with leisure time	2.42	2.70	1.99	1.94	$F = 17.30^{***}$	1, 2 > 3, 4
Scale 6: Problems with romantic relationships	2.31	2.70	2.11	2.13	$F = 4.61^*$	2 > 3, 4
Scale 7: Self-related problems	2.16	2.46	1.90	1.80	$F = 8.51^{**}$	2 > 3, 4

Note. $^*p < .05$. $^{**}p < .01$. $^{***}p < .001$.

TABLE 7.4
Coping Style of Adolescents Stemming From Different Family Types

	Family Type				Significance Test	
	Cluster 1 Achievement/ Control-Oriented (n = 53) M	Cluster 2 Disengaged/ Conflict-Oriented (n = 32) M	Cluster 3 Structured/Cohesive Moral-Oriented (n = 65) M	Cluster 4 Cohesive/Expressive Individuated (n = 57) M	MANOVA F(3, 203)	Scheffé
CASQ						
Active coping	16.47	12.81	12.92	17.24	F = 3.65*	1, 4 > 2, 3
Internal coping	8.41	7.96	8.01	8.56	F = −.30	
Withdrawal	4.24	7.18	4.37	3.12	F = 3.57*	2 > 1, 3, 4 1, 3 > 4

Note. *p < .05.

161

TABLE 7.5

Means and Standard Deviations of Family Climate, Stress Perception,
and Coping Style at Each Time of Measurement (n = 207)

	Time 1 M (SD)	Time 2 M (SD)	Time 3 M (SD)
FES			
Cohesion	3.41 (.49)	3.47 (.57)	2.87 (.51)
Expression	3.14 (.51)	3.05 (.47)	2.95 (.53)
Conflict	2.45 (.49)	2.50 (.54)	2.47 (.55)
Independence	3.17 (.61)	3.24 (.67)	3.43 (.48)
Achievement orientation	2.68 (.44)	2.90 (.48)	2.63 (.68)
Intellectuality	3.02 (.71)	3.06 (.70)	3.09 (.74)
Recreation	3.29 (.51)	3.34 (.59)	3.39 (.56)
Moral	2.18 (.58)	2.09 (.54)	2.03 (.56)
Organization	2.94 (.50)	2.94 (.48)	2.93 (.47)
Control	2.19 (.55)	2.22 (.54)	2.21 (.51)
Minor Stressors			
Problems with school	1.63 (.33)	2.29 (.66)	2.31 (.68)
Problems with future	2.81 (.77)	2.78 (.64)	2.89 (.71)
Problems with parents	1.99 (.65)	2.02 (.66)	1.98 (.64)
Problems with peers	2.40 (.77)	2.23 (.61)	2.20 (.62)
Problems with leisure time	2.21 (.65)	2.10 (.54)	2.08 (.64)
Problems with romantic relationships	2.30 (.82)	2.21 (.68)	2.29 (.79)
Self-related problems	2.16 (.68)	2.12 (.59)	2.14 (.54)
CASQ			
Active coping	15.2 (6.0)	16.1 (8.1)	16.2 (7.9)
Internal coping	7.3 (3.2)	9.8 (4.1)	10.2 (5.8)
Withdrawal	5.2 (2.1)	6.0 (2.3)	6.2 (3.1)

It is interesting to note that, overall, the variables measured did now show much variability across time. School-related problems seemed to increase, as well as functional coping styles (e.g., active coping and internal coping). Regarding family climates, most of the FES dimensions, besides cohesion, independence, and achievement orientation, remained stable over the 2 years. This impression was validated by calculating autocorrelations of the three measurements including Time 1 to Time 3. These correlations suggest a moderate to high stability of the family climate scales (r range from .59 to .83, all $p < .01$), of the perceived stress (r range from .46 to .81, all $p < .01$) and of coping style (r range from .43 to .77, all $p < .01$).

Changes in Stress Perception Depending on Family Type

As was found in Time 1, the pattern of family types was replicated at Time 2 and Time 3. Then, a series of analyses examined the pattern of mean changes in stress perception and coping style among adolescents stemming from different family types. The adolescents were assigned to four groups with different family types on the basis of their scores obtained in the cluster analysis of the FES in Time 1. Repeated measurement MANOVAs and follow-up ANOVAs were computed with time as one factor (three levels) and family type (four levels) as the other. These analyses were run separately for the scores of the CASQ and Problem Questionnaire. Repeated measurement MANOVAs revealed significant main effects of family type across all seven domains of minor stressors. In four of the seven scales interactions between family type and time could be observed; Greenhouse-Geisser values indicate the significance of these interactions after correcting for variance heterogeneity: problems with school [$F(3, 203) = 11.7$, $p < .02$, interaction family type × time $F(6, 406) = 4.1$, $p = .01$, Greenhouse-Geisser $= .02$]; problems with future [$F(3, 203) = 39.4$, $p < .001$, interaction family type × time $F(6, 406) = 3.5$, $p = .04$, Greenhouse-Geisser $= .04$]; problems with parents [$F(3, 203) = 44.4$, $p < .001$, interaction family type × time $F(6, 406) = 4.9$, $p < .001$, Greenhouse-Geisser $= .02$]; problems with peers [$F(3, 203) = 87.1$, $p < .001$]; problems with leisure time [$F(3, 203) = 48.8$, $p < .001$, interaction family type × time $F(6, 406) = 4.0$, $p = .01$, Greenhouse-Geisser $= .05$]; problems with romantic relationships [$F(3, 203) = 65.0$, $p < .001$]; and self-related problems [$F(3, 203) = 98.9$, $p < .001$].

Follow-up ANOVAs indicated that the discrepancies in stress perception between adolescents stemming from different family types remained constant in some problem domains and increased in others over time. The high stress levels of adolescents from Cluster 2 reported in problems with peers, problems with leisure time, problems with romantic relationships, and self-related problems as compared to the stress levels reported by adolescents from Clusters 3 and 4 were found for all three times of measurement, illustrating a highly stable discrepancy in stress perception.

In problems with school, which in general were rarely indicated by our sample, no differences between adolescents stemming from different clusters emerged at Time 1. At Time 2, however, increases in school-related problems in Cluster 1 and Cluster 3 could be observed, which remained stable for Time 3 only for Cluster 1 ($t_{1/3} = 2.3$, $p = .01$; $t_{1/2} = 1.8$, $p = .07$; $t_{2/3} = 1.2$, $p = .20$). Concerning problems with future, the scores of adolescents stemming from Clusters 1 and 2 increased over time. At Time 1, problems with parents were strongly indicated in Cluster 1 and Cluster 2. In contrast, in Clusters 3 and 4 very low means indicated a low level of problems with parents. The discrepancies between Cluster 2 (having the highest mean) and Cluster 4 (having the lowest mean) became even more obvious over time. Although the means of adolescents in Cluster 2 increased over time ($t_{1/3} = 2.2$, $p = .04$; $t_{1/2} = 2.0$, $p = .04$; $t_{2/3} = 2.0$, $p = .04$), the means of adolescents of Cluster 4 decreased or remained stable ($t_{1/3} = 2.1$, $p = .05$; $t_{1/2} = 2.0$, $p = .06$; $t_{2/3} = 1.6$, $p = .08$). Figure 7.2 illustrates the changes over time in the four cluster groups in the domains problems with school, problems with future, and problems with parents.

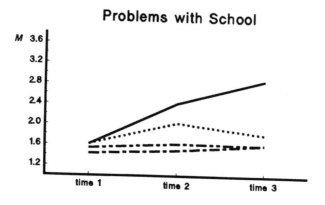

Problems with School

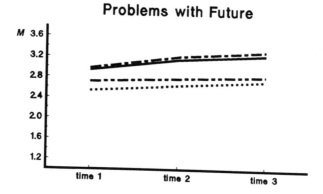

Problems with Future

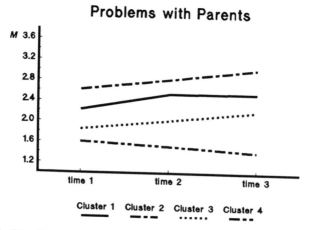

Problems with Parents

Cluster 1   Cluster 2   Cluster 3   Cluster 4

FIG. 7.2. Changes in stress perception over time: Discrepancies between adolescents stemming from different family clusters.

TABLE 7.6
Means of Coping Style Depending on Family Type
at Each Time of Measurement

	Active Coping M	Internal Coping M	Withdrawal M
Cluster 1 (n = 53)			
Time 1	16.47	8.41	4.24
2	17.10	9.01	4.27
3	17.90	9.24	4.32
Cluster 2 (n = 32)			
Time 1	12.81	7.96	7.18
2	12.41	8.26	7.27
3	12.19	8.57	7.36
Cluster 3 (n = 65)			
Time 1	12.92	8.01	4.37
2	12.85	8.80	4.18
3	13.01	9.14	4.31
Cluster 4 (n = 57)			
Time 1	17.24	8.56	3.12
2	18.04	9.08	3.24
3	18.70	9.36	3.18

Changes in Coping Style Depending on Family Type

Table 7.6 shows the means in the three coping styles, broken down by adolescents stemming from different family clusters across time.

Repeated measurement MANOVAs revealed a significant main effect of family type and a significant interaction of family type and time in active coping $[F(3, 203) = 20.1, p < .001$, interaction family type × time $F(6, 406) = 7.1, p < .001$, Greenhouse-Geisser $p < .001]$. Follow-up ANOVAs indicated that active coping increased over time in Cluster 1 ($t_{1/3} = 1.9, p = .06; t_{1/2} = 2.3, p = .04; t_{2/3} = 2.9, p = .01$) and Cluster 4 ($t_{1/3} = 2.1, p = .05; t_{1/2} = 3.0, p = .01; t_{2/3} = 3.3, p = .01$), and, tendentially, decreased in Cluster 2 ($t_{1/3} = 1.9, p = .06$). As regards internal coping, a main effect of time was found $[F(2, 204) = 2.8, p = .05]$. This significant main effect of time indicated an increase in internal coping over all three measurement points irrespective of the group the adolescents were assigned to. In withdrawal, a significant main effect of family type $[F(3, 203) = 9.3, p < .001]$ was found. Separate follow-up ANOVAs revealed that for the most part, the discrepancies measured at Time 1 remained constant. The means of adolescents in Clusters 1 and 3 did not change over time, and the strong discrepancies between adolescents from Cluster 2 (having the highest means in withdrawal) and adolescents from Cluster 4 (having the lowest means in withdrawal) could be traced from Time 1 ($t = 11.1, p < .001$) to Time 2 ($t = 12.0, p < .001$), and Time 3 ($t = 12.7, p < .001$). Thus, the initial discrepancies in coping style between adolescents stemming from families with different perceived family climate became even stronger over time.

DISCUSSION

The main issue of Study 5 was to analyze the influence of family climate on stress perception and coping behavior. The four distinctive types of family climates perceived by the adolescents which emerged in the cluster analysis reflected different levels of family functioning. The four clusters resembled family climate clusters reported in other studies (Billings & Moos, 1982; Mink, Nihira, & Meyers, 1983; Moos & Moos, 1976). Our results show that an adolescent's appraisal of stress and style of coping is related to the type of his or her perceived family climate. Adolescents stemming from disengaged and conflict-oriented families (Cluster 2), a climate that Billings and Moos (1982) considered least optimal, reported a high level of stressors. Especially high were the scores in problems with parents, but many problems with peers and in romantic relationships are also named. Thus, many more relationship stressors were reported in this group. Concerning coping style, adolescents from disengaged and conflict-oriented families exhibited a low level of active coping and a high level of withdrawal. It has been well documented that this family climate neither serves as a model for functional coping nor supports or even may interfere with the adolescent's ability to deal with the external world and developmental demands. These families did not provide an environment suitable for the stimulating development of individual autonomy or for the promotion of adolescent development in general. Rather, the family climate was marked by aggressive intrafamiliar conflicts. We identified another family type that contributed to a particularly high level of stress in the adolescents, although it certainly did not have such negative consequences for the style of coping. Adolescents from achievement- and control-oriented families (Cluster 1) also reported a very high level of minor stressors, especially in the domains parents, future, and leisure time. The intense achievement pressure in these families and the rigid organization apparently is related to the many problems with parents concerning issues of autonomy and individuation. Adolescents from these families have the fewest possibilities to develop autonomy, yet the stress level in leisure time and the amount of apprehensions about the future (likelihood of unemployment, difficulty in finding a job) emphasize that these families burden adolescents with high expectations and exert a great influence on their future performance. We may expect that a family that is perceived as being less supportive and that exerts pressure on the adolescent to achieve represents a source of higher stress and thus impedes the development of functional coping. However, although an increased stress level was found in adolescents stemming from achievement- and control-oriented families, their coping style was not so dysfunctional. These adolescents did not show especially high values in withdrawal rates, and more importantly, they exhibited a high level of active coping. We may speculate that even in nonsupportive family environments, a high level of structure (e.g., clear rules and fixed expectations) may contribute to adolescent adaptation. In such families, young people are probably induced to rely on family decisions, and the way the adolescents cope may reflect a high level of dependency on the family (Deci & Ryan, 1985). Similar results have been reported by Guay and Dusek (1992), who demonstrated a relation between authoritative parenting and efficacious coping strategies.

This hypothesis is further supported by the results in the group of adolescents who described their families as being cohesive, structured, and moral-oriented (Cluster 3). Achievement orientation and control was also high in these families, albeit lower than in families stemming from Cluster 2. In these families, a sense of family support and organization contributed to low stress and low levels of withdrawal. However, active support seeking was comparably low and matched levels seen in disengaged and conflict-oriented families. Adolescents from Cluster 3 did not exhibit particular noteworthy levels of stress, and they also were not as withdrawn as the adolescents in Cluster 2. Given the marked avoidance of intrafamiliar conflicts and the strong emphasis on ethical standards seen in these families the question may be ventured whether these families provide adequate models of autonomous development and functional coping. A family lacking the ability to tolerate confrontation and in which conflictual issues are suppressed may prevent adolescents from actively dealing with conflict and taking positions in response to dissonance and opposition. Pursuing this line of thought, I suggest that a supportive family atmosphere is not sufficient in itself for an adolescent's functional coping, but that there also must be an opportunity for the adolescent to exercise this form of coping and to benefit from the adaptive functions of parent–adolescent conflicts or problems in general.

An inspection of stress perception and coping style of adolescents stemming from Cluster 4 further elucidates our perspective. These adolescents, stemming from cohesive, expressive and individuated families, not only showed a comparably low level of stress (aside from a realistic anticipation of future-related problems), they also exhibited the highest level of active coping and the lowest level of withdrawal. These findings highlight the positive contributions that support in the family, an enriching family environment and the advancement of autonomy make toward adolescent adaptation. In our study, such families exhibited a comparably low level of organizational structure. On the other hand, the adolescent's independent mode of dealing with the world was respected. The ability to act individually might increase the sense of mastery. In such a family, members might serve as models for functional coping. By advocating the importance of maintaining positive intrafamilial relationships without prohibiting conflict in a "facilitating environment" (Shulman & Klein, 1982), the development of competent methods for coping with stressful situations may be fostered (see also Wrubel, Brenner, & Lazarus, 1981).

Thus, results in Study 5 specify and elaborate earlier findings on family climate and coping behavior (see Seiffge-Krenke, 1990b; Shulman et al., 1987). In this study, four family types were also found, but the differential contributions of cohesion and expression (the relationship dimensions) and control, organization, and achievement orientation (as system maintenance) became much more obvious. Family support and commitment as such are important because they contribute to a lower level of stress overall, especially concerning that caused by relationship stressors and in so far are definite stress buffers. However, to develop functional coping styles characterized by an active approach, two additional requirements must be met: Family life must be clearly organized and structured, providing rules and procedures that may also guide adolescent coping behavior, or a family climate must encourage the adolescent's autonomous behavior and responsibility. This latter aspect is very much in line with the work of Grotevant and Cooper (1985), which shows that separateness combined with closeness and support facilitates the adolescent's exploration of the world. It can be seen that the sense of family cohesion and support in asserting individuality are the precursors of adolescent adaptive coping. It has been stated that well-functioning families allow both separateness and attachment (Lewis, 1986). The encouragement of separateness becomes the analogue of individuality and autonomy. The parents in such families are models for adequate coping in their day-to-day interaction. A family climate in which cohesion and individuality are emphasized may serve as a model of a support system for functional coping when the adolescent is faced with external demands. In a way, the clear organization, control, and achievement orientation we found in some families might also serve as guidelines for dealing with stress—while at the same time remaining a continuous source of stress. We emphasize, however, that adolescents across the four family types did not differ in a further dimension of functional coping, internal coping. This cognitive-centered coping style represents the initial stage of appraisal in the process of coping as outlined by Lazarus and Launier (1978). Considering the fact that this study was conducted on a nonclinical sample of adolescents, it can be suggested that adolescents, irrespective of family climate, are able to appraise a stressful situation in a similar mode and reflect on possible solutions. It is in the latter stages of the coping process, namely active support-seeking and withdrawal, where the distinction between family climates will emerge. This is supported by the findings of our longitudinal study. Whereas the basic differences in stress perception and coping style among adolescents stemming from the different family types remained constant over time, cognitive development was expressed in the changes in internal coping styles. With increasing age the adolescents became more flexible and reflected upon their perspective of the problem. However, active coping and withdrawal may be influenced by the perceived family climate. Adolescents from families that demonstrate either an actively structuring approach or which promote adolescent autonomy and responsibilities showed further gains in active coping over time. Adolescents who have either low or high scores in withdrawal retain this pattern over time. Thus, the adolescents from Cluster 2 who showed low activity and high withdrawal scores at Time 1 developed poorly over time, in that the already low scores in active coping showed further decreases and the tendency to withdraw remained stable, thus narrowing their coping register. This group, burdened by a considerably high level of stressors at the beginning, showed a parallel increase in stress levels over time. This demonstrates quite impressively how increase in stress is accompanied by increased withdrawal and inactivity. The overall picture of the results concerning changes in stress perception and coping style points to both continuity (in terms of stability of the variables assessed over time) and change (in terms of mean changes in groups stemming from different family types). Study 5 has contributed to our understanding of the relationship between family variables and functional and dysfunctional coping. Our understanding would be further advanced through research that incorporates the perception of family climate by fathers and mothers into the longitudinal approach and limits the age range of the adolescents investigated to one age in order to better control for age-dependent changes in family climate over time.

The Unique Contribution
of Close Friends
to Coping Behavior

As shown in the preceding chapter, the parent–adolescent relationship may serve as a source of stress or a source of support and encouragement for coping behavior. However, the increasing saliency of peer relationships during adolescence cannot be ignored (Sullivan, 1953; Youniss, 1980). For many adolescents, relationships with friends are critical interpersonal bridges that move them toward psychological growth and social maturity (Savin-Williams & Berndt, 1990). Having friends is an indication of healthiness, and parents are often worried if their children do not have close friends (Achenbach & Edelbrock, 1981). Several authors emphasized the positive effects of peers and close friends for adolescents. The peer group is seen as important in the transition to a new identity and close friends help each other to validate their views. Peers, and more specifically close friends, are not only willing to help each other, but invest their personal time and resources (Bigelow, 1977; Wright, 1984). Friends support perceptions of oneself as competent and enhance one's self-esteem. The exchange of ideas within a secure and accepting relationship is thus an additional provision and the hallmark of close relations between friends.

In this chapter, I present and discuss the findings from Study 6, which illustrate some of the unique contributions of friendship relationships for coping. In the past, help-seeking behavior, discussion with friends and peers was mainly analyzed via survey methods, questionnaires, and interviews. In Study 6, we were interested in studying coping by investigating selected attributes of adolescent diarists and their nonwriting peers and, furthermore, by analyzing the contents of adolescents' diaries in the search for problems and events dealt with in the diaries and how diarists tackle them. In addition, the contribution of close friends providing support and coping assistance was analyzed.

CLOSE FRIENDS AS SOURCES OF SUPPORT
AND COPING MODELS

Family relations are altered in the course of adolescence, and the role of friendships as a source of activities, influence, and support increases rather dramatically. According to Sullivan (1953), friends serve several related functions. They offer consensual validation of interests, hopes, and fears, bolster feelings of self-worth and provide affection and opportunities for intimate disclosure. Similarly, Hartup (1992) listed three friendship functions: providing emotional security and support, serving as a context for growth in social competence, and acting as prototypes for later relationships.

Research on parent–adolescent relationships and adolescent relationships with friends has demonstrated important links between these two socialization contexts. Given the multiple functions of friendship, however, it should be stressed that friendships differ from other attachments in being less exclusive and marked by a more equal power balance (Hartup, 1983).

Several authors stress the adolescent's perception of friendship as a supportive relationship (Berndt & Perry, 1986) and underline that the friendship relationship provides a totally new perspective by which the adolescent may discover his or her own power to co-construct ideas and receive validation through the exchange between his or her peers (Youniss & Smollar, 1985). This implies that adolescents can learn about aspects of themselves from friendship, aspects that are barred from the parental relationship by the fear of judgment and need for approval. Research on aspects of privacy and self-disclosure confirms this view (Broughton, 1981; Laufer & Wolfe, 1974). In fact, studies using interviews, questionnaires, and observational data have rather consistently indicated that adolescents emphasize reciprocal disclosure, intimate sharing, and social support as salient criteria of close friendship (Berndt, 1981; Parker & Gottman, 1989; Selman, 1980). Among all changes, the increased intimacy of adolescent friendship gains most attention (Buhrmester, 1990; Buhrmester & Furman, 1987; Craig-Bray & Adams, 1986) and is often treated as the prototypical feature of adolescent friendship, especially among girls. As Furman and Robins (1985) pointed out, these relationships involve engagement in mutual activities, self-disclosure, and reciprocal feelings of satisfaction with the relationship. The benefits of close friendship may also depend further on similarity among friends (Savin-Williams & Berndt, 1990). Several empirical findings support this view. From mid-adolescence onward, parents are replaced by coevals as trustworthy partners for sharing personally relevant experiences and events (Andersen & Ross, 1984; Rivenbark, 1971). With parents, adolescents are likely to talk about school and career goals; with friends they talk about problems with dating or sexuality and about personal experiences, interests, and aims (see chap. 5). In addition, the increased importance of friendship is reflected generally in an increased amount of time spent with friends and, more specifically, in time spent talking with friends. Meetings with friends take up a substantial proportion of adolescents' daily free time (Crokett, Losoff, & Petersen, 1984), covering companionship in a wide range of activities (Buhrmester & Furman, 1987). "Just talking" (Raffaelli & Duckett, 1989, p. 567), that is, extensive conversation, also increases dramatically. Moreover, increased social support seeking and social comparison processes with friends may point to the growing function of friends as coping models (Seiffge-Krenke, 1993b).

THE FUNCTION OF DIARY WRITING

Adolescent diaries are highly relevant in this respect, because they may provide us with insight not only into the problems and events adolescents are concerned with but also the function of close friends in tackling these problems. Again, secrecy and confidential self-disclosure are important prerequisites of these private documents.

Diary writing (i.e., the regular writing down of personal experiences, thoughts, and feelings and the collecting of these secret, dated notes) is regarded as a typical activity among adolescents. Studies from Europe, the United States, and Russia have all found that diary writing is mostly limited to early and mid-adolescence (Allport, 1942; Küppers, 1964; Roscoe, Krug, & Schmidt, 1985; Seiffge-Krenke, 1985; Thompson, 1982). A recent German study, for example, illustrated that diary writing typically begins in early adolescence, increases toward mid-adolescence, when about 45% of the sample was keeping diaries, and diminishes again as the transition to adulthood draws to a close (Seiffge-Krenke, 1985). The practice of keeping a diary in adults is practically negligible (5% of the sample). Pronounced gender differences were also observed: Girls practiced this form of self-reflective activity much more often than boys. Since the early research of the Vienna School (see Bühler, 1925), not only frequency of diary writing but also motives for writing in adolescence and characteristics of adolescent diarists have been investigated. According to Bühler (1934) and Küppers (1964), a diary fulfills at least three different functions: as a memory aid, an emotional outlet, and a friend substitute. Other investigations have identified the additional motives such as following a current fad or working out critical life events. Several authors have concerned themselves with the questions of special giftedness and creativity of adolescent diarists (Myers, 1976, 1979; Piers, Daniels, & Quakenbush, 1960).

One may ask what contribution, if any, writing makes to successful coping and adaptation in adolescence. Apparently, due to sociocognitive development (Piaget, 1951, 1972), the adolescent is able to deal with situations as they are as well as how they could be, and has a greater ability to reflect and contemplate upon his or her life and activities. Compared to children, he or she develops a subjective sense of continuity and change of the self (Handel, 1987), both in the retrospective and prospective dimension (Handel, 1980) and is able to monitor, through self-observation and self-control, expressive behavior and self-presentation (Snyder, 1987). Because of their more complex level of thinking, adolescents can conceptualize the thoughts of others and anticipate how others will act and react.

Thus, adolescent diaries are highly relevant from a developmental point of view. Considered across the life span, adolescence is a period marked by prolific writing activity. Compared to younger age groups, adolescents have excellent prerequisites for expressing themselves in a private document; they show a greater ability to reflect upon life, to conceptualize their own thoughts and those of others, and to anticipate how others will act. Furthermore, they seem to have a particular interest in documenting events and experiences.

STUDY 6A

Research Questions

Study 6a focused on examining what kinds of coping functions diary writing might have. The frequency, motives, and functions of diary writing as well as the characteristics of diary writers were investigated. Aside from numerous studies conducted at the beginning of this century—most of which were carried out by investigators belonging to the Vienna School—there are only a few recent studies on diary writing. These mostly concentrate on frequency distributions with respect to incidence, gender patterns, and motives of writing. Systematic comparisons have been lacking, as well as data supporting the hypothesis that adolescents who keep diaries have special characteristics compared to their nonwriting agemates. Most authors have concentrated on the diary itself as the sole source of information and stressed the considerable methodological problems regarding authenticity, selection, and transformation of memories (Neisser, 1976) or representativeness (Bernfeld, 1927). Yet, the developmental function of diary writing itself needs further clarification. As I tried to illustrate earlier, due to numerous developmental changes adolescents possess the ability, need, and desire for private, personal self-expression. Thus, the general topic of Study 6a is the contribution of diary writing to coping in adolescence.

Two converging lines of thought are given special attention—the deficit hypothesis and the coping hypothesis. According to the deficit hypothesis, the diary is a substitute for trustworthy partners in the family or among friends (e.g., adolescents with a deficit in intimacy and companionship are especially prone to use a diary). The coping hypothesis proposes that the diary itself helps in dealing with everyday conflicts, in that events are described, possible solutions are reflected on and reactions of others anticipated.

METHOD

Subjects

The study included 241 adolescents aged between 12 and 17. They attended Grades 6–11 in a German high school and represented the entire sample of these grades in this school. About 40 adolescents per age group were investigated, half male, half female (male: $n = 112$, female: $n = 129$). Eighty-two percent of the adolescents came from intact families; 18% were from divorced families or lived in a single-parent household. The mean number of siblings reported was 1.8; the mean number of friends reported ranged between two and five. The adolescents predominantly belonged to lower and upper middle-class families.

Instruments

A semi-structured questionnaire was used to inquire about several general aspects related to keeping a diary. The absolute frequency of diary keeping, the motives for beginning a diary as well as the regularity of the entries were registered.

Several additional questionnaires were also employed:

1. Minor Stressors: Adolescent stress was measured by the Problem Questionnaire (for details, see chap. 5) that assesses minor stressors. The adolescents had to indicate the stressfulness of 64 items ranging from 1 (*not stressful at all*) to 5 (*highly stressful*), which covered frequently named, salient everyday problems.

2. CASQ: Coping was measured by the CASQ for adolescents (for details, see chap. 5). Twenty coping strategies across eight different problem areas such as school, teachers, parents, peers, opposite gender, self, leisure time, and future were assessed.

3. A German version of the OSIQ was also used (Seiffge-Krenke, 1987, 1990a). Factor analysis revealed five dimensions: general satisfaction with oneself and the world, good relations with parents, confidence in one's own abilities, social relations with peers, and depressed self-concept. The Cronbach alphas for these scales ranged between $r = .68$ and $r = .86$.

4. Role-Taking: As a measure of the social abilities of the adolescents, the Role-Taking Test by Feffer (1970) was administered. This instrument determines the ability to decenter. The extent to which the informant is able to coordinate the different perspectives of persons acting in a school situation is regarded as an index of role-taking ability. Two dimensions were included: simple role-taking (self-entry) and perspective coordination (self-elaboration according to Feffer, 1970).

5. Self-Disclosure: Because diary writing is likely to be kept secret, the Letter Test (Koch, 1977) was administered to measure readiness for self-disclosure. The adolescents were asked to imagine disclosing seven specific topics to a given

group of nine persons. The adolescents were requested to select which of the letters (each containing information about themselves) they would send to a person they felt close to.

6. Creativity: A further test aimed at finding out whether adolescents are particularly creative. Both a verbal and a figural subtest of the Torrance Test of Creative Thinking were administered (Torrance, 1966; see German version by Seiffge-Krenke, 1974): The adolescents were asked to imagine the possible consequences of an unusual situation ("Just Suppose . . .") and to transform drawn circles into as unusual a picture as possible ("Circles"). Three scores were obtained assessing fluency, flexibility, and originality.

Procedure

The adolescents filled in the semi-structured questionnaire inquiring about diary keeping as well as the other questionnaires during two school lessons. A research assistant was available to answer questions if necessary and to supervise the adolescents in small groups of approximately 15 students each.

RESULTS

Preliminary Analysis

The content analysis of the open-ended answers concerning diary keeping was carried out by two independent judges. Concerning the motives of adolescents for diary writing, four different categories were found: (a) current trend/chance, (b) memory aid, (c) lack of a confidant/confidante, and (d) working out critical life events. Concerning the regularity of the entries, three categories emerged: regularly (i.e., at least once a week), irregularly (i.e., when there is some spare time), and only in case of pressing problems. The style of writing was found to be characterized either by an unnamed, impersonal format or by a letter format, whereby the diary was personally addressed by name. The concordance coefficient for the nine categories of diary writing according to Kappa (cf. Fleiss, 1971), amounted to $k = .71$, $p < .001$.

With the help of the Letter Test (Koch, 1977), the topics of self-disclosure, the disclosure partners, and the relation between these two were assessed. The productions in the creativity test were scored according to the criteria developed by Torrance (1966) for the three creativity dimensions. For the evaluation of role-taking, the answers were calculated according to Feffer (1970) for simple role-taking and perspective coordination.

Due to imbalances of individuals per cell, differences between writers ($n = 94$) and nonwriters ($n = 147$) as well as male ($n = 13$) and female diarists ($n = 81$) were tested separately. For the interval-scaled data, the t test for independent samples was used. For the significance test of the ordinally scaled parameters, the chi-square test and Fisher's Exact-Test were used.

Characteristics of Adolescents Who Keep a Diary

Of the adolescents investigated, 40% kept a diary. In analyzing the social network including size of family, number of female and male friends in general, and number of close friends in particular, no differences between adolescent diarists and their nonwriting agemates were found. The number of close friends was lower in girls than boys (mean number of 1.2 and 2.3, respectively). The subgroup of diary-keeping adolescents ($n = 94$) did not show any distinctive characteristics with respect to age, social class, family structure, number and closeness of friends in comparison to the total group of adolescents, except that the female diarists outnumbered the male diarists by far.

Concerning the self-concept, two significant differences emerged between diarists and nondiarists across the five self-concept dimensions. Diarists scored higher on general satisfaction with oneself and the world ($t = 2.0$, $p = .01$) and social relations with peers ($t = 2.8$, $p < .001$), indicating generally a more positive self-esteem among diarists and a higher relevance of personal topics concerning friendships for diarists than for nonwriting peers. Moreover, as Table 8.1 shows, the diarists scored significantly higher on all three creativity dimensions. Especially pronounced was the difference in originality, which measured statistically rare ideas.

With respect to self-disclosure, diarists have higher scores in total self-disclosure than their nonwriting agemates ($t = 5.2$, $p < .001$). A close look at target persons and topics of self-disclosure revealed that the preferred target persons were comparable for diarists and nondiarists. Regarding topics, diarists showed a noticeable readiness to disclose especially intimate, private issues irrespective of the addressee, i.e., they had higher disclosure rates than nondiarists in Personal Thoughts and Feelings ($t = 3.4$, $p < .001$), and disclosed more frequently Past Personal Experiences ($t = 2.7$, $p = .001$) and Topical Personal Experiences ($t = 3.1$, $p < .001$), as well.

TABLE 8.1
Significant Differences Between Diarists and Nonwriting
Agemates in Three Creativity Dimensions

	Diarists (n = 94)		Others (n = 147)		Significance Test
	M	s	M	s	t
Fluency	12.6	4.0	11.1	3.0	2.3*
Flexibility	8.9	3.0	7.5	2.6	2.1*
Originality	7.9	4.0	3.8	2.4	2.6**

Note. *$p < .05$. **$p < .01$.

TABLE 8.2
Significant Differences Between Diarists and
Nonwriting Agemates in Coping Style

	Diarists (n = 94)		Others (n = 147)		Significance Test
	M	s	M	s	t
Active coping	18.2	8.1	13.8	7.5	2.54**
Internal coping	7.5	3.9	7.2	3.4	.59
Withdrawal	4.9	2.8	5.2	1.7	1.0

Note. *p < .05. **p < .01.

As can be seen in Table 8.2, the coping style of the diarists was significantly more active, relative to nondiarists. With respect to all eight problem areas under consideration (i.e., studies: $t = 2.6$, $p < .001$; teachers: $t = 2.2$, $p < .01$; parents: $t = 2.3$, $p < .01$; peers: $t = 2.8$, $p = .001$; opposite sex: $t = 2.4$, $p = .01$; self: $t = 2.3$, $p < .01$; leisure time: $t = 2.0$, $p = .04$; and future: $t = 2.5$, $p < .01$) diarists chose active coping strategies (e.g., asking others for help or advice, discussion or attempting to "talk it all over" with the person concerned) more frequently than nondiarists. In two further coping dimensions, internal coping and withdrawal, no significant differences between diarists and nondiarists were found.

An analysis of the results of the Role-Taking Test by Feffer indicated a positive predisposition of diarists on both the analyzed dimensions. In simple role-taking $[\chi^2(n = 241) = 7.6$, $p = .02]$ and perspective coordination $[\chi^2(n = 241) = 4.9$, $p = .05]$ diarists surpassed their nondiarist peers.

Differences Between Male and Female Diarists

One of the striking findings is the rather similar personality structure of male and female diarists concerning the majority of parameters under scrutiny. No differences between male and female diarists were found with respect to coping behavior, role-taking, creativity, and self-concept, except for a marginally higher score of male diarists in Originality ($t = 1.9$, $p = .06$) and in the OSIQ-Scale 3: confidence in one's own abilities ($t = 2.1$, $p = .04$).

Diary Writing: Gender Differences in Frequency, Motives, and Style of Writing

In our sample, diary keeping started in early adolescence, reached its peak in mid-adolescence, and lost its appeal thereafter. Among the 12-year-olds, 32% kept a diary; among the 13-year-olds, 42%; and among the 14-year-olds, 47%. For the 15-, 16-, and 17-year-olds, the percentages were 46%, 36%, and 32%, respectively. However, the percentage of female diarists was much greater than the percentage of male diarists [63% vs. 12%, $\chi^2(n = 94) = 59.9$, $p < .001$]. In mid-adolescence, diary keeping reached levels of 70% to 80% among the 14- and 15-year-old girls, but only 25% to 30% among the 14- and 15-year-old boys. These remarkable gender differences are probably related to the function the diary fulfills in the lives of the adolescents.

This function, as illustrated by Fig. 8.1, was judged differently by boys and girls [$\chi^2(n = 94) = 9.8$, $p = .02$]. Male adolescents emphasized external causes like boredom, current trend ("I want to have a diary like my friends"), or mere chance ("I was given a diary") and also the function of a possible memory aid. It was quite remarkable that as many as 37% of the adolescents—boys more than girls—found it important to document events, especially to have a souvenir. The lack of a trustworthy communication partner, on the other hand, was mentioned only by female diarists. For 26% of the female diarists, this was the reason for starting a diary. For 13% of the total group of diarists, critical life events (e.g., "I fell in love," "My family had moved and consequently, I felt lonely") were reasons to start keeping a diary. With respect to critical life events, no gender differences could be observed.

One third of the diarists wrote on a regular basis (i.e., every day or at least once a week), another third irregularly (i.e., when they happened to have some spare time), and another third only in case of pressing problems. Most of the female diarists belonged to the latter category, whereas male diarists tended to make entries regularly. More female than male writers addressed their diary

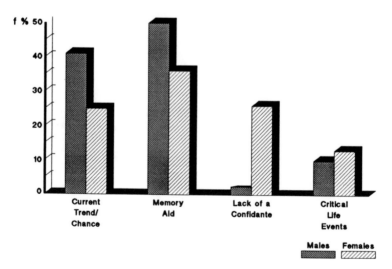

FIG. 8.1. Motives for starting a diary described by male ($n = 13$) and female ($n = 81$) diarists.

TABLE 8.3
Multiple Regression Analysis to Predict Diary Writing (n = 241)

Variables	F-Value	Beta-Coefficient	Multiple r	r p/c
Role-taking	8.8***	−.64	.36	.34
Self-disclosure	5.6***	−.58	.46	.33
Creativity Scale 2: Flexibility	3.9**	−.54	.50	.23
OSIQ-Scale 3: Confidence in one's own abilities	2.9**	−.46	.61	.17
CASQ-Scale 1: Active coping	2.5*	−.42	.65	.16

Note. *$p < .10$. **$p < .05$. ***$p < .01$.

personally by naming it and used a letter format as if they were writing to an imaginary companion [56% and 17%, χ^2 ($n = 94$) = 39.1, $p < .001$].

Prediction of Diary Writing

In order to establish which of the considered variables was most likely to predict the readiness to write a diary, a stepwise multiple regression analysis was carried out on the data of all subjects. A total of 14 variables were entered as predictors, including 5 self-concept scales, 3 coping scales, 3 creativity scales, the sum scores for minor stressors, self-disclosure, and role-taking ability. Diary writing was used as a dependent variable.

Table 8.3 shows that role-taking ability represented the most efficient predictor, followed by self-disclosure and creativity (flexibility of ideas). Positive self-esteem concerning one's own abilities, measured with Scale 3 of the OSIQ, as well as active coping made additional contributions. Apparently, adolescents who kept a diary were competent, open-minded, and more willing to tackle problems together with interaction partners. Two aspects of the exchange were evident, namely empathy with the partner and openness.

STUDY 6B

Research Questions

In a consecutive study, the contents of adolescent diaries were analyzed. The first question addressed concerned identifying what kinds of problems and events adolescents are concerned about in their diaries and how they are tackled. Second, we were interested in discovering how relationships with close friends are described in the diary, especially with respect to aspects of emotional support and coping assistance. Adolescent diaries are private documents and normally not made available for others to read. The few adolescent diaries that have been published (see for a summary Seiffge-Krenke, 1989) were done so exclusively after the author's death and have often been considerably edited or condensed by relatives, editors, and other adults. Already in the beginning phase of diary research, methodological problems involved in using such documents were discussed (see Allport, 1942). Accordingly, the individuals who do make such a secret document available to others must be investigated with respect to various relevant variables. The questionnaires and variables, which have been used in Study 6a, to distinguish diarists and nondiarists were used to select the diarists taking part in Study 6b. Thus, participants in Study 6b were carefully selected from a larger sample of diarists and screened with regard to these variables. Then, the contents of their private documents were analyzed with respect to stress, coping and relationships with a special emphasis on close friendship relations.

METHOD

Obtaining Diarists

The basic material for Study 6b consisted of 87 diaries written by 20 subjects during their adolescence, from which a sample of entries was drawn for closer examination by content analysis. The diaries were offered on a voluntary basis following personal contact with the writers. Every writer taking part in Study 6b answered an extensive battery of questionnaires covering such subjects as role-taking, self-concept, self-disclosure, minor stressors, coping strategies, and creativity. In Study 6a, these psychological variables had been shown to be relevant for characterizing adolescent diarists as compared with their contemporaries who do not keep a diary. For Study 6b only those 20 diarists from a larger sample were selected who were comparable with the diarists in Study 6a with respect to the aforementioned variables.

The subjects who allowed us to use their diaries for this study were older than those in Study 6a. This time the age range of the participants extended from 17 to 28 years, the majority being between 21 and 26 years (i.e., in the transition period between adolescence and adulthood). A common reason for allowing us to see the diaries was the writer's feeling that they represented something "historical," a document of their youth that occurred months, sometimes years, or in the case of the young adults, even a decade ago. No participant was prepared to submit a current diary. A pronounced difference was found between the genders with regard to their readiness to share their diaries with us: 17 women but only 3 men complied to participate in the study. The women came from a broad occupational spectrum (nurse, nursery school teacher, secretary, lawyer's clerk, student, housewife, etc.), whereas the men all came from scientific and artistic spheres (chemical scientist, actor, student). With regard to the stability of their family backgrounds and number of siblings, the sample did not deviate from the expected norm. At the time of the study, 11 participants had a stable relationship with a partner. Two thirds no longer kept a diary; these were mainly young adults who had kept a diary as a specifically adolescent activity and then given it up. A subgroup of adolescents, aged between 17 and 20 years, was still keeping a diary. For the main body of young adults who offered their old diaries (having given up writing in the meantime) the average duration for keeping a diary—beginning between the ages of 11 and 13—was 5 years.

Analysis of Entries

From the mass of material thus made available we selected two diary years per writer beginning at the age of 13. The database therefore included 40 diaries, 20 per diary year. A diary year was not identical with a calendar year, because as a rule, the diaries commenced at some date in the middle of the year. A diary year was therefore defined as starting on the date of the first entry and ending exactly 12 months later, which amounted to a standardization of the texts over time. The number of entries was limited to 40 per diary year, as most writers kept within this frequency range. Thus 80 entries of 2 consecutive years were analyzed for each writer. This procedure was chosen in order to be able to include developmental changes occurring over a considerable period of time.

The content analysis of the 80 entries per writer was carried out using categories based on units of meaning that could well include several sentences. A system consisting of 60 subcategories was developed that allowed for an adequate content analysis of the entries. In this chapter, I deal only with 15 main categories and, more specifically, with the subcategories of everyday events, critical life events, self, and close friendship. Two independent judges categorized the material. Their average rate of agreement over 15 categories and all subjects was k = .69, which can be considered as satisfactory. In the following, we refer mainly to the diaries of females. In the first diary year, mean age of writers was 13.6 years; in the second diary year, the mean age was 14.6.

RESULTS

Categories in Adolescent Diaries: An Overview

With respect to the content, the diaries covered a broad range of 15 main categories. These are illustrated in Fig. 8.2.

We found that self and others, that is the diarist and his or her social relationships, were the main topics in 85% of all entries. Close friendship, social comparison, empathetic reflections about significant others, and heterosexual relationships were additional important categories, contrasting with descriptions and evaluations of the self and the body of the writer. School and work were of minor significance. Diaries of male writers contained the same categories, but

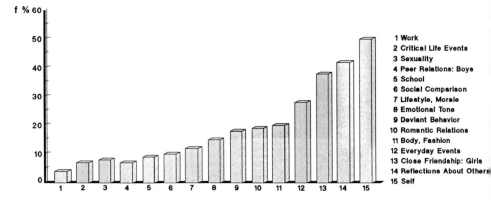

FIG. 8.2. Frequency of categories named in the diaries (sum score across 80 entries in 2 diary years).

slightly different frequencies. For example, body and close friendship relationships were mentioned less frequently, whereas work, school, and lifestyle were mentioned more frequently. Thus, the diarist and his or her social relations were the main theme in most entries, increasing from 71% in the first diary year (self: 38%, others: 33%) to 89% (self: 45%, others: 44%) in the second diary year [$\chi^2(n = 20) = 5.9, p < .001$]. Social comparison processes represented another important category, increasing from 7% in the first diary year to 18% in the second diary year. Two thirds of these social comparison processes included references to peers, one third to adults.

Events and Coping

The diaries mostly focused on everyday events and activities (28%). Special social events like birthday parties (13%) or critical life events (4%) were rarely mentioned. Critical life events included, for example, loss of friends and relatives, accidents, getting pregnant, divorce or remarriage of parents. In both diary years, special social events and critical life events were reported with the same frequency. In contrast, descriptions of everyday activities and events significantly decreased from the first diary year (46%) to the second diary year (18%) [$\chi^2(n = 20) = 45.5, p < .001$]. The following example illustrates an account of everyday activities and events.

Anne, 13.4 years:
My parents left to go hiking this morning at 6 a.m. I had breakfast with the Hermanns. I didn't go swimming because I have a cold. In the evening we played in the garden and then watched TV. It was a nice day. Bye! Love, Anne.

Thus, the entries in the diaries primarily dealt with descriptions of the events and activities making up the day which were not directly related to conflict.

Conflicts and disagreements with others were mainly represented as a subcategory of the main category empathetic reflections about others; they accounted for 10% of the entries in this main category. As a rule, direct reference to coping strategies in dealing with these everyday events were missing. However, references to coping strategies could be found in the main category self, which encompassed the following subcategories: self-doubt, self-confidence, self-criticism, and self-educating appeals. Among the coping perspectives, the subcategories self-criticism (the author criticizes his or her own behavior and attitudes) and self-educating appeals (the writer expresses his or her desire for change, encourages oneself to act, or directs disciplinary remarks at oneself) were particularly relevant. The following are examples of entries containing self-criticism and self-educating appeals:

> Self-Criticism: Anita, 13.9 years:
> I was really angry at Karla yesterday. I let too much steam off.

> Self-Educating Appeal: Conny, 14.4 years:
> All in all, I am not concentrated enough in my piano playing; this has to change. From now on I'm going to practice 10 minutes longer every day. Also, I've got to stop all my blabbering. I will try as best I can to watch my words, suppress my spontaneity and work on developing my ideal.

As can be seen in Fig. 8.3, self-educating appeals increase in the second year of writing [$\chi^2(n = 77) = 1.9$, $p = .05$].

Dimensions of Close Friendship

The functions of close friends as providers of support and assistance, however, is dealt with more directly in the diary under the main category close friendship. As noted already, close friendship between girls was mentioned in 38% of all entries, whereas peer relations with boys were dealt with only in 7% of all entries.

How are relationships to close friends described in female diaries? We found that dyadic relationships were the preferred form of close friendship between girls, whereas triads were mentioned far less often. According to the content analysis of the diarists' descriptions of how and where they spend their leisure time with friends, it was apparent that females spent much more time together with other girls ($M = 46$ activities) than with males ($M = 17$ activities). The activities shared by girls (e.g., the main category: close friendship: girls) could be assigned to the following six categories: (a) doing things together, for example, keeping each other company in doing chores, homework, or going shopping together (mentioned in 19% of the entries); (b) intimate, symbiotic, or homoerotic activities, for example, changing clothes together, staying in the bathroom together, making each other up, holding hands (mentioned in 45%); (c) symbolic approach to the opposite gender, for example, fantasizing together about boys or making plans how to meet them (22%); (d) real approach to the opposite gender, for example, making real

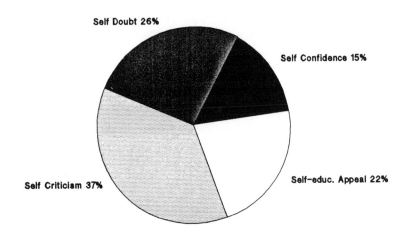

First Year

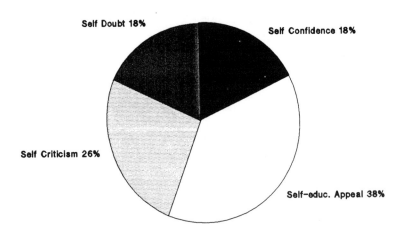

Second Year

FIG. 8.3. Self-evaluations and self-educating remarks in the first and second years of diary keeping.

contact with boys by writing love letters together, double-dating, and so on (10%); and (e) shared norm-breaking, for example, taking drugs or stealing together (seldom mentioned). Talking together as an exclusive activity was coded separately as (f) just talking and amounted to 5% of all the entries. Selected examples of each type of entry are provided in the following:

1. Examples of doing things together/companionship:
   Elisabeth, 14.6 years: In the afternoon I went to see Jutta. We did German together. That was fun.
   Judith, 15.2 years: During the break I went to make a phone call together with Nicole.

2. Examples of intimate, symbiotic, or homoerotic activities:
   Isabel, 14.3 years: Last night I stayed overnight at Nanni's place. We just hung around and giggled and so on. At midnight we decided to eat a bar of chocolate in bed and of course got crap all over the bed. Nanny just phoned to remind me not to forget the grey trousers tomorrow. I'm going to lend them to her and she's giving me her beige trousers in return.
   Caroline, 14.2 years: It was really no fun watching the film without Christine. So empty. I usually lay my hand on her knee when it becomes scary and exciting. The first time she looked at me with surprise, but then she understood. When I feel her close by, I calm down.

3. Examples for symbolic approach to the opposite gender:
   Friederike, 13.9 years: Anja and I wanted to try it first with her older brother because he is really gorgeous. We have already devised a strategy.
   Elisabeth, 14.2 years: Jutta and I looked at photos of Bernd and we talked for a long time. Topics: Frogs and princes in fairy tales.

4. Examples for real approach to the opposite gender:
   Sabine, 14.1 years: Went to Ute's in the afternoon. She'd written a letter to Rolf. Not bad, but between us we made it even better. She really should be more straightforward. When I told her this she got angry.
   Anja, 14.8 years: On the way home we went past U's. She desperately wanted to show me his house, but she got in a real state, worrying that he'd come out and see us. We got off the bus and waited for him around the next corner, but nothing happened, so we went on after half an hour.

5. Examples for shared norm-breaking:
   Isabel, 14.3 years: And then we did another round of trips.
   Ingrid, 14.6 years: Today we really let rip and nicked quite a few things.

6. Examples for just talking:
   Friederike, 13.9 years: We spent the whole day talking about God and the world.

As can be seen in Fig. 8.4, intimate symbiotic or homoerotic activities [$\chi^2(n = 7) = 2.4$, $p < .05$] and just talking [$\chi^2(n = 7) = 1.9$, $p = .05$] increased from

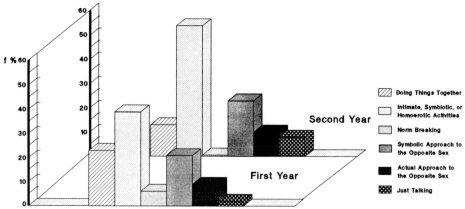

FIG. 8.4. Changes in close friendship activities shared by female diarists in their first and second diary years.

the first to the second diary year, whereas doing things together decreased [χ^2(n = 7) = 4.1, p < .01].

We found that intimate activities between close friends were very much related to the body, the external appearance and the female role; high proximity and close body contact was frequent. The symbolic approach to males centered very much around fantasies, wishful thinking, and potential encounters, whereas examples of real approach showed concrete initiations of contact mainly under the protection of the same gender friend, where sometimes feelings of rivalry could be observed. The first contacts to romantic partners are generally characterized by a relatively large physical distance, whereby the friend functioned as a third object obviously exerts a fear-reducing and protective function.

DISCUSSION

Our study confirms that diary keeping is a phenomenon typical of this age group that has hardly changed over the years. The findings of Bühler (1925, 1927, 1932, 1934), Abegg (1954), Küppers (1964), and Thompson (1982) are all comparable in this respect. The finding that diary keeping is far more frequent among adolescent girls than boys is also in accordance with other studies. The percentage of female diarists (63%) in our study was four times higher than that of male diarists (12%), thus similar to earlier research findings (see Allport, 1942; Bühler, 1925; Küppers, 1964; Roscoe et al., 1985; Seiffge-Krenke, 1985; Thompson, 1982). Most authors placed the proportion of diarists among females between 40% and 60%, and the proportion among males between 20% and 30%. This striking difference, which has been consistently found since the beginning of the century, has led to the hypothesis that diary writing is a gender-specific behavior (see Thompson, 1982). Given the gender differences in self-disclosure (Chelune, Sultan, & Williams, 1980), the perception of self (Tobin-Richards, Boxer, & Petersen,

1983), and friendships (Berndt & Hoyle, 1985; Buhrmester, 1990; Buhrmester & Furman, 1987), we may speculate whether keeping a secret document such as a diary, which allows for intimate sharing, is more important for female adolescents. At this point, further research is required to clarify whether diary writing is a very common transient activity of female adolescents (cf. Thompson, 1982), and if it is chosen by male adolescents only under exceptional conditions (e.g., high originality), as was the case for the male diarists in our sample.

Our results do not support a deficit hypothesis (i.e., that adolescents with a deficit in social interaction are especially prone to diary writing). On the contrary, diarists did not differ from nondiarists with respect to family structure (intactness, number of siblings) or the number and closeness of friends. According to our results, the diary is but one among many interlocution partners and is addressed in combination with other trustworthy partners in the family and among friends, but is by no means a substitute for them. Furthermore, we may underline the positive self-esteem and the good coping abilities of the diarists as compared to their nonwriting agemates. Various authors investigated the correlation between personal traits, especially creativity, and diary writing (Myers, 1976, 1979; Piers et al., 1960; Schaefer, 1969). Our results confirm that creativity, especially flexibility in thought, contributes to diary writing. In addition, perspective-taking and perspective coordination, which was especially high among diarists, are reflective of an individual's tendency to entertain the psychological point of view of another person, frequently in coordination with one's own perspective. Someone who is willing and able to see things from another person's point of view should be better able to anticipate feelings, needs, and behavior of others and thus optimize interpersonal relationships. Thus, we may, in accordance with Partington and Grant (1984), regard diary writing as a sign of positive growth and efficient coping. Rather unexpectedly, however, was the fact that internal coping did not contribute to diary writing (e.g., the internal reflection about possible solutions was not related to diary writing). Moreover, minor stressors (i.e., the total scores of everyday stressors in different fields such as school, parents, friends, etc.) did not contribute to promoting diary writing. However, as the analysis of motives for starting a diary shows, even major stressors such as critical life events are not an important motive for beginning a diary. It was striking how uniform the subgroup of diarists was. We did not find gender differences for almost all investigated variables, except for male writers being even more creative and writing more regularly than females. However, we did find significant differences in the motives behind and functions of the diary. The diary as a replacement for a confidante was only mentioned by female diarists. They wrote less regularly, in most cases when they had a pressing problem or something special happened. Male diarists wrote very regularly and gave a continuous report of their days. Thus, diarists represent a relatively homogeneous, developmentally advanced group but use the diary as a tool quite differently.

We may summarize from our results obtained in Study 6a so far that diary writers possess more advanced social skills and are more flexible in thinking. Regarding the possible coping function of adolescent diarists, it is unclear why active coping (e.g., the solving of the problem by using social resources) contributes to diary writing and internal coping (e.g., the reflection about possible solutions) does not. Research on written self-expression has been remarkably slow in examining the ways in which writing about a topic may be related to thinking (see, e.g., Applebee, 1984). In an earlier study analyzing the diary-writing process (Seiffge-Krenke, 1989), we found that epistemic forms of writing (e.g., the cognitive restructuring and reframing of experiences) was developed by diarists mainly in late adolescence, whereas communicative forms of writing dominated during mid-adolescence when writing activity was highest. This result emphasizes that cognitive restructuring contributes to writing, but communicative exchange and narrative forms of expression are much more important, especially at certain ages. In Study 6a, the individuals in the group of diarists were distinguished by their increased flexibility, including their ability to consider various possible solutions or perspectives simultaneously, albeit more under the aspect of creativity than coping. With respect to coping, only those dimensions of coping were relevant that stressed problem solving with the help of others. The great significance of empathy and perspective coordination was also apparent in Study 6a. The way in which flexibility of thought fulfills the function of integrating present experiences and anticipating future situations, thus helping the diarist to cope with everyday problems, remains an issue warranting further research. Study 6b only addresses this topic in part, apparently because a diary is not primarily kept in order to cope with minor or major stressors. Although a diary contains stressful events—much more minor events than critical life events—it is more a form to reflect on the self and social relationships.

I outlined at the beginning the protective function of close friendship relationships in adolescence. Two major benefits were emphasized: the fulfillment of emotional needs for closeness and intimacy, and the functions of social support and coping assistance. In general, the results here demonstrated the benefits of close relationships. Close friends provide consensual validation, social support, and coping assistance, particularly against potential stressors (like body changes, sexuality, dating), many of which cannot be comfortably discussed with parents (see also Buhrmester & Furman, 1987). The most efficient predictors for writing a diary (i.e., role-taking ability and flexibility in thought) provide substantial support for positive growth and coping functions. In addition, the results of Study 6a can be seen as a validation of the results of the diary research in Study 6b, which do not support the hypothesis that adolescents with a deficit in social interaction are especially likely to keep a diary. On the contrary, diarists and nondiarists do not differ with respect to family structure and the number and closeness of friends in both studies. An analysis of diary entries concerning close friendship behavior vividly illustrates the significance of intimacy, shared activity and mutual disclosure between close friends of the same gender.

As the results illustrate, close friends uniquely contribute to the development of social competence and help to prepare adolescents for romantic love. Close friends assist each other in understanding their sexual and personal identities by mirroring and shaping their behavior on a very concrete level, for example, with respect to clothing, hairstyle, interests, leisure activities, and dating. If we relate this, first, to the fact that close friends in diaries are mentioned in every third entry and, second, to the broad variety of activities in same gender dyads, we may well conclude that the diarists are very much concerned about and active with their best friends. The quality of close friendship behavior between females as described in the diary supports findings of Buhrmester and Furman (1987) and Sharabany, Gershoni, and Hofman (1981) who have demonstrated the special significance of intimacy in girls' close friendship. Our results further confirm other findings pointing to the exclusiveness of female friendships (Berndt & Hoyle, 1985). Buhrmester and Furman suggested, however, that the gender difference may be more one of style than of substance, in that boys achieve a sense of worth through actions rather than through reciprocal disclosure. Because in our studies girls outnumbered boys by far, we have to postpone confirming this suggestion following future research including equal numbers of both genders.

Much of the behavior, activities, and reflections reported in the entries seemed to give a permanent answer to the question "Who am I?" (Gottman & Parker, 1986). The diary material makes it clear that this process of defining who one is and will be is also the central theme in close friendships. We may add at this point that social comparison processes, discussing similarities and differences, were rather frequent in the diaries. We know from social comparison theory (Hormuth & Archer, 1986) that comparisons in vaguely defined situations are necessary and particularly helpful with similar others. Furthermore, perceived similarity and shared activity as well as modeling female gender role behavior are basic elements in close friendship between girls as described in the entries.

Apparently, diaries are private and intimate documents that adolescents address frequently and very personally. However, diary writing is not predominantly started when friends are gone. A diary may not supply very much coping assistance compared to real close friends. What are therefore the developmental benefits of keeping a diary? Our findings, especially from Study 6b, speak for an active restructuring of self while keeping the relationship with friends very close. Conceptually, we may suspect that both diary writing and close friendship behavior may help in coping with demands during the transition to adulthood, providing some support, clarification, and coping assistance on direct and indirect levels. Consequently, both lose their significance when the restructuring of identity has taken place. Age-dependent changes in diary writing and close friendship behavior were very obvious in both studies. An additional analysis of diary entries in the third diary year (Seiffge-Krenke, 1994) revealed that intimate homoerotic activities as mentioned in the entries decreased and real contacts with the other gender increased. Furthermore, Studies 6a and 6b confirmed our own results in chapter 5 that showed that mid-adolescence can be regarded as a turning point in development, where progress in cognitive and social development becomes especially apparent, which for certain subgroups, is even more pronounced.

Stress, Coping, and Relationships as Risk and Protective Factors in Explaining Adolescent Depression

The skills and resources that adolescents bring to bear on trying to cope with the stressors they face are important determinants of the course of their psychological adjustment during adolescence and adulthood. Efforts to alter stressful conditions, strategies for managing negative emotions experienced under stress, and support received from family and friends will further contribute to successful resolution of stress. The studies presented so far provided some guidelines for understanding adaptive coping with stress during adolescence. Adaptive coping or *functional coping*, as it is termed here, appears to involve matching one's appraisal of stress with the use of active support-seeking and internal reflection of possible solutions. Maladaptive or *dysfunctional coping* may be characterized at least in part by the use of withdrawal and problem avoidance and a focus on reducing negative affects. In addition, the appraisal of stress is distorted. Study 5 (see chap. 7) shows that certain aspects of perceived family climate covary with a more dysfunctional, less adaptive coping style among adolescents. Concerning internal resources, Study 4 (chap. 6) provided substantial evidence that adolescents with depressive personality structure are more prone to dysfunctional coping styles.

In the last study to be presented here (Study 7), stress, coping, and relationships are analyzed with a major focus on adaptation. I focus on adolescent depression as a frequently occurring outcome. It is my aim to understand factors that contribute to adolescent depression as well as protective factors that may buffer the effects of stress. An integrated view of stressors and protective factors may be crucial for prevention and treatment of other health problems, too, because a striking feature of depressive phenomena in adolescence is the degree to which they are associated with other maladaptive behaviors.

DEPRESSION AS A PROTOTYPE
OF ADOLESCENT MALADAPTATION

Depressive phenomena increase sharply in adolescence and show a marked gender pattern. In contrast to the relatively low rates of clinical depression in children, rates of depression are high and approximate the adult rates (Kovacs, 1989). Several studies indicate about a fourfold increase in the incidence of adolescent depression compared to childhood depression (Rutter, 1985b) with an exceptionally sharp increase for girls emerging by mid-adolescence (Kandel & Davies, 1982; Merikangas & Angst, 1992). Diagnostic problems in assessing adolescent depression have been reported frequently (see, e.g., Achenbach, McConaughty, & Howell, 1987) and lead to a differentiation between several types with varying severity. Empirical studies have established that depressive mood, depressive syndromes, and depressive disorders are related but distinct manifestations of depression (Compas, Ey, & Grant, 1993; Kovacs, 1989; Petersen et al., 1991). These three constructs are unique representatives of depressive phenomena in adolescence and show different rates of prevalence.

Depressive mood refers to the presence of sadness, unhappiness, or blue feelings for an unspecific period of time. As Offer and Offer (1975) showed, depressive mood is reported by 30% to 70% of nonclinical subjects during some time in adolescence. *Depressive syndrome*, however, refers to a set of emotions and behavior that statistically have been found to occur together in an identifiable pattern. They are identified empirically through reports of adolescents and for example their parents or teachers (Achenbach, 1985, 1991). The characterization of *depressive disorder* is based on a disorder model of psychopathology and currently reflected in the diagnostic system of *DSM-III-R* or *ICD 10*. According to Merikangas and Angst (1992), the prevalence rates of depressive disorders are rather low, about 3%, whereas depressive syndromes are diagnosed more frequently (10%). Compas and Hammen (1993) demonstrated a high degree of comorbidity of depressive phenomena with other symptoms and disorders. For example, the overlap with anxiety disorders was highest (30%–70%), but the overlap with conduct disorders and eating disorders was also substantial (10%–21%). It is thus safe to say that with regard to all three manifestations of depressive phenomena, comorbidity is the rule rather than the exception during adolescence. Due to these characteristics, the analysis of factors that contribute to depression as well as the analysis of protective factors may be highly relevant because they may reflect a more general association between stress, coping, relationships, and psychopathology.

DEPRESSION AND STRESSFUL EVENTS

Psychosocial stress plays a prominent role in most models of depression throughout the life span. As a rule, the interaction of psychosocial stress with individual vulnerability or predisposition has been considered, for example, with the diathesis–stress model of depressive disorders (Monroe & Simons, 1991). In examining research on stress and depression it is important to address the question of specifity in the stress–depression relation (i.e., to analyze whether and to what degree stress is associated with depressive phenomena). A related question is concerned with the specific contribution of different types of stressors.

Concerning the general issue of whether stressful events are related to depression, more than 40 recent studies have established that there is a cross-sectional association between stressors and depressed mood, depressive syndromes and depressive disorders (see for a summary Compas, Orosan, & Grant, 1993). Compared to other forms of psychopathology, however, this association is not unique to depression. Compas, Howell, Phares, Williams, and Giunta (1989) found that the association was higher for internalizing problems (variance explained 11%) than with externalizing problems (5%). This may suggest that stressful events are more strongly related to depression than to other disorders, but the difference in variance explained is not that high and speaks more for a general association between stress and symptomatology. Studies trying to determine whether certain types of stress are related to depression have revealed quite uniform results with correlations for major events being typically lower than those for minor events or hassles. Several studies found modest to moderate correlations between negative life events and depression (see, e.g., Barrera, 1981; Compas & Phares, 1986; Friedrich, Reams, & Jacobs, 1982; Grennberger, Steinberg, & Vaux, 1982; Siddique & D'Arcy, 1984; Swearingen & Cohen, 1985; Thomson & Vaux, 1986). More specifically, an investigation by Newcomb, Huba, and Bentler (1981) analyzed the occurrence of 39 major events during the past few years of life of 1,000 adolescents. A general correlation of $r = .20$ between negative events and depression was found; events from the parent/family cluster were most closely associated with distress and depression ($r = .30$). Research on adults has already shown that daily hassles and minor events play a critical role in understanding stress and symptoms within individuals. That daily stress and everyday problems may play an equally important role in adolescents' symptomatology has been also established (Baer et al., 1987; Compas et al., 1987). Compas and colleagues favored an integrative model of stress that includes major and minor events. As in other studies, correlations have been found between major negative events (ranging between $r = .23$ and $.32$), but the correlation between daily stressors and symptomatology is even more substantial (ranging between $r = .54$ and $.68$; see Wagner et al., 1988). Both types of stressors were analyzed according to their associations with depression. Additional studies by Compas et al. (1989) and Rowlinson and Felner (1988) have confirmed the differential contribution of minor and major events to adolescent depression.

These results are rather unexpected, because for a long time, a special type of major event involving loss had been regarded as highly significant in explaining depression. Since the early theories of S. Freud (1917) and Abraham (1911/ 1927), loss of a loved one was considered to be a major etiological factor. Although there is evidence of a link between events involving loss and depressive reactions (Malmquist, 1986; Payton & Krocker-Tuskan, 1988), it is important to recognize that individuals exposed to such events are also likely to exhibit other forms of psychopathology. Moreover, other types of stress, including minor events and everyday problems and hassles seemed to contribute strongly to depressive feelings. In those studies in which major and minor stressors have been compared, minor stressors have been found to be more strongly related to depressive phenomena than major events. Further correlations between both types of stressors have been found illustrating that major events may lead to an increase in daily or minor stressors that in turn leads to depressive outcomes. This points to a reciprocal influence between stress and depression. It has also raised the question of confusing stress and depression with similar items appearing on measures of both constructs (Dohrenwend & Shrout, 1985). Yet, longitudinal studies have indicated that the association between stress and depression is not simply an artefact of self-report of these two variables (Compas et al., 1989; Walker & Greene, 1987). The relations are weaker than in cross-sectional studies, which suggests an influence of other factors. Even prospective longitudinal studies do, however, not provide definite proof of the causal relationships between the two variables. While the aforementioned studies have found that initial stress predicts subsequent depression, other studies have reported that initial levels of depressive mood and syndromes are predictive of increased stress at a later point of time (L. Cohen, Burt, & Bjorck, 1987; Roosa, Beals, Sandler, & Pellow, 1990).

COPING STYLE AND COPING RESOURCES

Several current models of depression suggest that depressed individuals differ in their coping responses to stressful events (Billings & Moos, 1984). Studies of community groups indicate that people with little depressive symptomatology are more likely to use problem-focused coping, whereas reliance on avoidance and emotion-focused coping characterize those with a high symptom level (Folkman & Lazarus, 1980; Lazarus & Folkman, 1984; Pearlin & Schooler, 1978).

There are also some studies that support a link between childhood depression and problem-solving deficits (see, e.g., Mullins, Siegel, & Hodges, 1985). Consistent with the coping skills deficit model, Asarnow, Carlson, and Guthrie (1987) found that depressive children generated significantly fewer cognitive mediational strategies for coping with stressful events than nondepressed children. In addition, a reduction in general activity in depressed adults has been well documented (see, e.g., Lewinsohn & Talkington, 1979). Also, an association between activity and childhood depression has been found; depressed children are less active and more withdrawn (Peterson, Mullins, & Ridley-Johnson, 1985).

Although coping style has been thus linked to the emergence or amelioration of depression in adults and children, there has been little work suggesting that coping style plays a role in depression of adolescents. Only few researchers have directed attention toward evaluating the role of activity in the development or maintenance of depression in adolescence. In one of the rare studies conducted, Carey, Kelly, Buss, and Scott (1986) found in a nonclinical sample of adolescents that those individuals who reported being engaged in more unpleasant activities rated themselves as being more depressed. Other studies, most of them involving nonclinical samples, have demonstrated a gender difference in stress appraisal that may lead to differences in coping style. Adolescent girls have been found to rate negative life events as more stressful than boys (e.g., Newcomb, Huba, & Bentler, 1986; Siddique & D'Arcy, 1984). My own research (see chaps. 3 and 4) has demonstrated that these gender differences could be also found in the appraisal of minor stressors with girls perceiving the same minor stressors as four times more threatening. In a clinical sample, Cramer (1979) found that adolescent girls reported using internalizing defense mechanisms (e.g., turning against the self, intellectualization, and rationalization) more often than boys did. In contrast, boys reported using externalizing mechanisms like projection or turning against others more than girls did. These findings are consistent with Nolen-Hoeksema's (1987) hypothesis that men and women are socialized into different coping styles according to the gender role stereotype. In reviewing the relevant literature on gender differences in unipolar depression, she concluded that "men are more likely to engage in distracting behaviors that dampen their mood when depressed, but women are more likely to amplify their mood by ruminating about their depressed states and the possible causes of these states" (p. 259).

Despite the important conceptual role of coping in models of depression and the saliency of minor stressors found in empirical studies, little research has considered how depressed adolescents cope with minor stressors. Our research on nonclinical subjects has revealed gender differences in coping with minor events, which probably can be regarded as a predecessor of a more clinical coping pattern (see Seiffge-Krenke, 1993a). The results from the survey study reported in chapter 5 show a strong need among females to solve problems by discussing them with parents and peers or, more generally, by seeking their support. This trend increases with age and is in line with research on adults, indicating a higher tendency among females than males to rely heavily on social networks or seek help in extrafamiliar settings (Belle, 1987). In addition, females worry a lot about a problem and expect negative consequences more frequently than males (see chap. 3). Males, on the other hand, present themselves as more carefree. If, however, a serious problem occurs, they try more often to forget about it by using alcohol and drugs (see chap. 5). Similar gender differences in coping style have been reported by Larsson, Melin, Breitholtz, and Andersson (1991).

Whether these gender differences in stress perception and coping style explain the differential emergence of depressed affect in adolescence requires further investigation. There is also a notable change in girls' self-concept and body image; they are more dissatisfied with their physical appearance and have more negative self-esteem than boys (Allgood-Merton et al., 1990; Seiffge-Krenke, 1990a).

PARENT AND PEER RELATIONSHIPS AND SUPPORT

Among the factors that moderate the relationship between stressors and dysfunction, the availability of social resources such as family support has received the most attention (Patterson & McCubbin, 1987). The role of family variables as protective factors that moderate a youngster's response to stress has been emphasized in the invulnerability research (Garmezy, 1983; Garmezy & Rutter, 1983). Several variables in the life situation of depressed adolescents, including family structure (intact vs. nonintact), parental health (nonclinical vs. disturbed), and dimensions of parent–adolescent relationships such as attachment, perceived family climate, and parent–adolescent conflict have been addressed.

Generally, only weak relationships between variables of family structure (e.g., single parenting or divorce) and adolescents' depressive symptoms have been found (Baron & Perron, 1986; Gibbs, 1985; Wolchik, Braver, & Sandler, 1985). However, the perceived quality of parent–adolescent relations contributes significantly to depressive symptoms in adolescents, whether they are from divorced or intact families. Farber et al. (1985) found that adolescents who reported experiencing a greater degree of family conflict due to divorce-related reorganization were more anxious, depressed, and hostile. Baron and MacGillivray (1989) analyzed depressive symptoms in nonclinical adolescents as a function of perceived parental behavior. For both male and female adolescents, a higher level of depressive symptoms was associated with father's rejection and mother's control, the former accounting for about 26% of the variance in the BDI scores. Perceived parental rejection and family conflict as factors contributing to depression were also analyzed in the study by Robertson and Simons (1989), who compared participants in a substance abuse program and nonclinical agemates. Perceived parental rejection showed both a direct and an indirect effect on depression, whereas family conflict failed to reach significance. The latter variable was related to depression only insofar as it was associated with parents who failed to provide love, understanding, and support. Positive qualities of parent–adolescent relationships such as attachment to parents, support, and family cohesion, were investigated by Greenberg, Siegel, and Leitch (1983); Barrera (1981); Burke and Weir (1978); and Kaplan, Robbins, and Martin (1983). The overwhelming majority of these studies showed a beneficial effect of positive parent–adolescent relationships.

Until recently, the stress-moderating effects of peer relationships and friendships in adolescent psychopathology have been sadly neglected. With respect to adolescent depression, only some studies deal with perceived support from friends and peer relationships (e.g., Asarnow, 1988; Camarena, Sarigiani, & Petersen,

1990; Vernberg, 1990). Poor peer relationships have been viewed alternatively as incidental manifestations of some underlying disturbance, as playing a causal role in the emergence of dysfunction, and as part of a reciprocal process in which symptomatology both leads to and flows from poor experiences with peers (Parker & Asher, 1987). According to a study by Achenbach and Edelbrock (1981), in which children and adolescents referred to child guidance clinics were compared with a matched nonreferred sample, no other cluster of symptoms differentiated the groups more clearly than disturbances in peer relations. Moreover, poor peer relations in childhood are among the best predictors of adult disorders (Sroufe & Rutter, 1984). Thus, Parker and Asher (1987) claimed in a study of peer relationships that children who are less accepted are at risk of becoming depressive later on. Regrettably, comparatively few investigators have studied adolescent friendship and peer relationships with respect to psychopathology so far.

As I demonstrated in chapter 8, peers and friends serve important functions during adolescence in that, for example, they are good models for coping and provide help and assistance. Moreover, friends provide a rich and possibly unique source of information about the self during a period of heightened concern about the judgments of others. Peer relations influence various elements of self-perception (Furman & Robins, 1985; Harter, 1983), and thus active rejection by peers may be related to feelings of distress. There is some evidence beginning to emerge that points to the relationship between depression and difficulties in peer relationships. The study by Feldman, Rubenstein, and Rubin (1988) demonstrated an association between poor peer relations and depressive symptoms. In the study by Faust, Baum, and Forehand (1985) social rejection and isolation were characteristic features in the self-perception of depressed adolescents. Social stress in friendship relationships accounted for a significant amount of the variance in depression scores for adolescents aged 14 and younger, but not for the older group (15 to 18 years) in the study by Moran and Eckenrode (1991). Female adolescents were significantly more affected by stress in friendship relationships than males.

The study by Camarena et al. (1990) on a nonclinical sample illustrated as well, that low social support from friends was associated with depressive mood for girls but not for boys. All studies show impressively how much adolescents are oriented toward friends and rely on them both for their self-worth and coping behavior. Yet, the stress-moderating function of friends or peers with respect to depression warrants further investigation.

RESEARCH QUESTIONS

In this study, stress perception, coping processes, and social resources are analyzed with respect to symptomatology. I attempted to investigate the potential moderating functions of parent and peer relationships in depressive symptomatology in adolescents. Because depressive manifestations are widespread in this age group and show a high comorbidity with other disorders, we hoped to gain insight into the general interrelationships of risk and protective factors in adolescent psychopathology. Among the different depressive manifestations detailed earlier, I focus on depressive syndromes. As argued at the outset, different appraisals of the same stressful situation may contribute to depressive feelings and consequently lead to differences in the practice of seeking support and advice as a coping strategy. In addition, interpersonal relationships may possibly buffer the effects of stress. Although the central role of the family in adolescence has been well documented and parents continue to be important providers for social support (see chap. 7), emotional support and coping assistance from friends and peers becomes increasingly important (see chap. 8). A central issue of this study thus deals with the relative contribution of parents and peers in protecting the adolescent against potential pathogenetic influences of stressful events. To address this question, we have to face two controversial hypotheses about the interrelationships between stress, relationships, and adaptive outcome.

As viewed by Cohen and Wills (1985), social support functions are incorporated in two theoretical models. The main effect model posits that social support has a beneficial effect irrespective of whether individuals are under stress. The buffering or interaction effect model proposes that social support buffers or protects individuals from the potentially pathogenetic influence of stress. Some measures of adolescents' social support have marginally included family relations, but according to Moos and Moos (1981), family climate encompasses a wider range of processes, including relationships, personal growth, and system maintenance dimensions that all seemed to be important for adolescent well-being. Several studies on adolescence have used the FES and documented direct effects, that is, the benefits of a positive family environment, for example in nonclinical samples of adolescents (e.g., Billings & Moos, 1983; Farber et al., 1985; Friedrich et al., 1982), in adolescent psychiatric samples (e.g., Asarnow et al., 1987), and in adolescents whose parents have been identified to be at risk for psychiatric illness (e.g., Hirsch, Moos, & Reischl, 1985). Concerning social support by peers or friends, a lack of instruments is apparent, whereas the benefits of positive peer and friendship relationships have been well documented and the criteria for assessing positive adolescent friendships are universal (Berndt & Hoyle, 1985; Selman, 1980). Our study on adolescent friendship and its contribution to coping (see chap. 8) vividly illustrates that closeness, frequency of contact, talking together, and shared activity are all important indicators of friendship relationships.

In Study 7, a wide range of family and peer relationships were included. Besides family climate, including social support, attachment to parents and frequency of interaction with both parents were assessed. Both qualitative and quantitative components of peer relationships were assessed by sociometric ranking, evaluations of the degree of attachment to peers as well as the extent and quality of peer contact; however, it is not certain which of these indices is more salient for the inquiry at hand.

In order to adequately address the question of stress-buffering, different types of stressors such as minor and major stressors should be included. Coping processes that may also moderate the relationship between stressors and outcome have to be analyzed in order to test the deficit hypothesis (e.g., the contribution of dysfunctional coping style for depression). In summary, stress, coping, and relationships as protective and risk factors associated with adolescent depression are investigated. Again, a nonclinical sample was chosen, although the same processes are analyzed in clinical samples elsewhere (Seiffge-Krenke, 1990b, 1995).

METHOD

Subjects

The participants included 136 adolescents ($n = 79$ females, $n = 57$ males) and their parents ($n = 136$ mothers, $n = 121$ fathers). The adolescents ranged in age from 13 to 17 years and attended high school Grades 7 to 11. Criteria for participation were that the parents and adolescents agreed to take part in the study. Seventy-six percent of the entire sample of these grades in school participated. The mean age of the fathers was 41 years ($SD = 2.0$); the mean age of the mothers was 39 years ($SD = 3.5$). Although all fathers worked full time, 54% of the mothers in the sample were not working. Family SES was based on education and occupation. Fathers possessed an average of 12.1 years of education ($SD = 3.1$), and mothers a mean of 11.8 years of education ($SD = 2.4$). Forty-two percent of fathers had received a graduate degree, 21% of them were semiskilled workers, 28% were technicians and clerical workers, and 11% were self-employed. Ninety percent of the adolescents had intact families, 10% came from divorced or single-parent families. Thirteen percent of the adolescents were single children, 55% had one sibling, 32% had two or more siblings.

Measures

Adolescent Symptomatology

Both parents were asked to fill in the Child Behavior Checklist (CBCL; Achenbach & Edelbrock, 1987), which consists of 118 problem behavior items and 20 competence items. The scored behavior describes the child within the past 6 months. We used the German version of the CBCL by Lösel, Bliesener, and Köferl (1991), who reported high internal consistency (mean $r_{tt} = .80$) and test–retest reliability over 1 week (mean $r_{tt} = .71$) on a sample of 870 adolescents aged 11 to 17.

The adolescents reported on 12 measures, including two different indices of stress, three measures of relationships with parents, and three measures of relationships with peers. Additionally, self-concept, coping, and clinical service use were measured as indices of psychological adaptation.

Adolescent Stress

Two different measures were used to analyze perceived stress. They were as follows:

1. Major stressors: As a measure of major stressors, the Life Events Checklist (LEC; Johnson & McCutcheon, 1980), which consists of 46 events, was used. For this task, the adolescents have to mark which of the events they have experienced during the past year and indicate whether they would rate the event as "good" or "bad." Finally, they have to indicate how much they feel the event has had an impact or effect on their life. The measure taps a range of events likely to be experienced by young people and yields two scores: a positive life change score and a negative life change score. The LEC has been used frequently in research with adolescents. Johnson (1986) reported mean test–retest correlations for positive and negative life change scores of .69 ($p < .001$) and .72 ($p < .001$).

2. Minor stressors: The Problem Questionnaire including 64 daily stressors from different developmental fields such as school, future, parents, peers, leisure time, romantic relationships, and self-related problems was applied. Psychometric properties have been reported in chapter 5.

Parent–Adolescent Relationships

Three different measures were used to analyze the parent–adolescent relationship. The measures are as follows:

1. FES (Moos & Moos, 1981): This scale was administered to assess the adolescents' perception of their families. Ten subscales were included (cohesion, expression, conflict, independence, achievement orientation, intellectuality, recreation, moral, organization, and control). Each of the 91 items was rated on a 5-point scale, ranging from 1 (*very false*), 2 (*somewhat false*), 3 (*partly true*), 4 (*mainly true*), and 5 (*very true*).

2. The Inventory of Adolescent Attachment (IAA; Armsden & Greenberg, 1987): The IAA assesses the quality of affect toward parents and peers. Attachment toward mother and toward father was investigated separately, including 28 items each. Both were summed up to a total score.

3. Interaction density: Frequency of interaction with father or mother including frequency with which the respondents turned to their mother or father to discuss problems was assessed.

Peer Relationships

To gain a more complete view of the adolescents' peer relationships, several aspects of experiences with peers were assessed.

1. Sociometric procedure: The adolescents were asked (a) to rate each pupil in the classroom for overall likeability on a 5-point scale, (b) list the three pupils whom he or she liked most, and (c) list the three pupils whom he or she liked least. The number of nominations for the most liked and least liked pupil were totaled for each adolescent.

2. Amount of peer contact: Following the form used by Berndt and Hawkins (1984), the adolescents were asked to state (a) the number of and closeness to best friends, (b) how frequently they talk with their friends on the telephone, (c) how often they share activities, (d) how often they visit each other's home, and (e) whether they attend a youth club. Frequency of responses were coded on a 4-point scale, ranging from 1 (*less than once a week*), 2 (*about once a week*), 3 (*a few times a week*), and 4 (*every day*). Attendance in a youth club or organization was coded by 1 (*no attendance*), 2 (*in one organization*), 3 (*in two or three organizations*), and 4 (*in more than four organizations*). A total score of amount of peer contact was computed by summing up the frequency of contact scores across the different areas.

3. Peer attachment: From the IAA, the Peer Attachment scale was used, including 25 items.

For validation purposes and as indicators for general adaptation of the adolescent, several variables were assessed, including self-concept, coping style, and clinical service use.

1. OSIQ: A German version of the OSIQ was used (Seiffge-Krenke, 1987). Factor analysis revealed five dimensions: (a) general satisfaction with oneself and the world, (b) good relations with parents, (c) confidence in one's own abilities, (d) social relationships with peers, and (e) depressed self-concept. The Cronbach alphas for these scales ranged between $r = .68$ and $r = .86$.

2. CASQ: Coping was measured by the CASQ for adolescents (see for details chap. 5).

3. Clinical service use: The adolescents were asked if they had ever made use of or received counseling services.

Procedure

The adolescents completed the various questionnaires after personal contact with the researchers at school during two school lessons. A research assistant was available to explain questions if necessary and to supervise the adolescents in small groups of approximately 15 students each. The adolescents were given an envelope containing the CBCL for their parents and were instructed to take these materials home and return the completed parent forms in a sealed envelope the following week.

RESULTS

Overview of Analyses

The question whether both critical life events and minor stressors are related to depressive symptomatology in adolescents was evaluated by correlation analysis. From the two measures of stress used, it revealed that the relationship between critical life events and depression was low. All further analyses conducted also included the total score of the problem questionnaire as a measure of minor stress, because it showed substantial correlation with depression.

The second question addressed in this study concerned the relative contribution of family versus peer relationships as a buffer in minimizing stress. Out of the six different measures of family and peer relationships, only one dimension of the perceived family climate (FES cohesion), the total score of amount of peer contact, entered the multiple regression analysis to predict depression. Two different models for analyzing buffer effects were used: the main effect model and the interaction model. Separate regression analyses tested the main and interactive effects of stress.

To describe the sample with respect to all variables used, means and standard deviations were calculated in a preliminary analysis, and a two-way MANOVA was conducted, analyzing the effect of age and gender. The total sample was divided into three age groups, up to 14 years of age, 15 to 16, and 17 to 18 years of age.

Preliminary Analysis

As a dependent measure, we obtained the CBCL scores of both parents. Scores of the CBCL completed by mothers were compared with those completed by fathers. Mothers' ratings revealed a higher score in adolescent symptomatology, but the difference was not statistically significant. We thus combined fathers' and mothers' ratings into a parents' CBCL score for further analysis.

The CBCL total score was 46.79 for female and 41.83 for male adolescents, indicating that this sample was relatively symptomless. The scores are comparable to total scores gained in other studies on non-clinical populations in the United States and Germany (Lösel et al., 1991). With respect to depressive symptomatology, standardized means for female and male adolescents were calculated, taking into account different numbers of items per gender. Again, the scores gained were comparable to those reported in other German samples (see Lösel et al., 1991). With respect to depressive symptomatology, our sample can thus be considered as comparable to other nonclinical samples. Means and standard deviations of depressive syndromes as well as stress, parent and peer relationships can be found in Table 9.1.

Two-way MANOVAs including age (split up into three age groups) and gender revealed several differences between males and females. A main effect of gender was found in the depression score [$F(1, 134) = 3.58$, $p < .06$], with girls

TABLE 9.1
Means and Standard Deviations of Stress, Parent
and Peer Relationships, and Depression

	Total Sample (n = 136)		Female (n = 79)		Male (n = 57)	
	M	SD	M	SD	M	SD
Major Stressors						
Positive change	6.28	3.24	6.39	3.71	6.18	3.50
Negative change	5.12	3.19	5.38	2.78	5.01	3.12
Minor Stressors						
Problems with school	2.63	.78	2.63	.86	2.62	.66
Problems with future	2.86	.77	2.87	.82	2.85	.70
Problems with parents	2.15	.73	2.15	.75	2.14	.62
Problems with peers	2.46	.75	2.55	.87	2.33	.68
Problems with leisure time	2.23	.69	2.26	.78	2.18	.60
Problems with romantic relations	2.39	.86	2.36	.88	2.43	.83
Self-related problems	2.72	.68	2.81	.72	2.67	.58
Perceived Family Climate						
Cohesion	3.61	.72	3.60	.81	3.61	.59
Expression	3.32	.64	3.36	.68	3.21	.55
Conflict	2.68	.43	2.74	.47	2.60	.33
Independence	3.54	.50	3.54	.56	3.54	.40
Achievement	3.05	.55	2.97	.54	3.16	.53
Intellectuality	2.91	.83	2.83	.83	3.02	.77
Recreation	3.54	.58	3.51	.61	3.51	.56
Moral	2.40	.73	2.39	.72	2.41	.75
Organization	3.23	.58	3.27	.62	3.18	.53
Control	2.56	.76	3.52	.86	2.61	.62
Amount of Peer Contact						
Number of friends	1.98	.55	2.02	.52	1.90	.59
Frequency of telephone calls	2.16	.73	2.24	.68	2.03	.77
Frequency of shared activities	2.41	.67	2.37	.65	2.46	.69
Number of visits at home	2.23	.56	2.17	.62	2.31	.77
Attendance in a club	1.42	.83	1.33	.83	1.53	.84
Depressive Syndrome[a]	15.9	6.9	16.8	7.3	13.3	5.7

[a]Combined parents' rating.

having slightly higher scores than boys; age and age × gender interaction was nonsignificant. No age and gender differences appeared with respect to major stressors. Furthermore, only some gender differences with respect to perceived minor stressors across different areas were found. A main effect of gender in self-related problems [$F(1, 134) = 5.6$, $p = .02$] and a main effect of age in problems with school [$F(2, 133) = 3.5$, $p = .03$] were found. This shows that minor stressors in different areas are perceived comparably similarly across age and gender. In order to test age and gender differences with respect to perceived family climate, the 10 subscales of the FES were assigned to three general dimensions: relationships (cohesion, expressiveness, conflict); personal growth (independence, achievement orientation, intellectual–cultural orientation, active–recreational orientation, moral–religious emphasis); and system maintenance (organization and control) according to Moos and Moos (1976). No age and gender differences appeared with respect to relationship and personal growth. With respect to system maintenance, a MANOVA revealed only a trend indicating an interaction between age and gender [$F(6, 130) = 2.58$, $p = .08$].

Amount of contact with peers did not differ significantly between age and gender; attendance in a youth organization revealed a main effect of age [$F(2, 133) = 4.2$, $p = .02$] illustrating decreasing activity of the older adolescents in formally organized peer organizations.

Correlational Analysis

Scatter plots were generated relating the depression score to all variables measured in the sample. Pearson correlation coefficients were calculated including the total score of major stressors, minor stressors, amount of contact with peers, attachment with parents and peers, sociometric ranking, and density of interaction with both parents. Three general dimensions of the FES were included, as well as three dimensions of coping and five dimensions of self-concept. The relationship between clinical service use and depression was calculated using tetrachoric correlation coefficients.

Table 9.2 shows that the association between depression and major stressors such as positive or negative life changes was significant but not substantial. In contrast, daily stress in different developmental fields (i.e., the total score of minor stressors) was substantially related to depression ($r = .61$). Among the subscales of the Problem Questionnaire, self-related problems ($r = .60$), problems with parents ($r = .52$), problems with peers ($r = .46$), and problems with school ($r = .42$) contributed most to depression, whereas the association between problems with future ($r = .29$), problems with romantic relations ($r = .35$), and problems with leisure time ($r = .38$) and depression was somewhat lower. A closer inspection of the instruments intended to measure relationships with parents showed that mere frequency of interaction was not related to depression, whereas attachment to both parents correlated negatively with depression ($r = -.41$). Of the FES general dimensions, relationship was negatively related to depression ($r = -.37$), too, showing an overlap in concepts.

Two of the three measures employed to analyze peer relationships showed only low correlations with depression; again, frequency of interaction was not related to depression, whereas positive quality of relationship was negatively related to depression ($r = -.35$). Thus, a comparable pattern could be established in the domains of parent and peer relationships and activity.

Finally, Table 9.2 shows that withdrawal as a coping style was significantly associated with depression ($r = .31$). Clinical service use (e.g., having undergone counseling/treatment) showed a low but significant correlation with depression

TABLE 9.2
Intercorrelation Between Measures of Stress, Parent and Peer
Relationships and Activities, and Depression (n = 134)

	Depression
Stress	
Total major stressors	.18*
Total minor stressors	.61**
Total developmental pressure	.10
Parent relationship and activity	
FES relationship	−.37**
personal growth	−.16
system maintenance	.06
Total parent attachment	−.45**
Total density of interaction	−.06
Peer relationship and activity	
Sociometric ranking	−.11
Amount of contact with peers	−.18*
Total peer attachment	−.35**
Coping	
CASQ active coping	.02
internal coping	.04
withdrawal	.31**
Self-concept	
OSIQ general positive self-esteem	−.51**
good relations with parents	−.49**
confidence in own abilities	−.25**
social relations with peers	.12
depressed self-concept	.61**
Clinical service use	.23**

Note. *$p < .05$. **$p < .01$.

($r = .23$), too. The substantial correlations between positive self-esteem ($r = -.51$) or a depressed self-concept ($r = .61$) as well as the considerable correlation between good relations with parents and depression ($r = -.49$) provided some information for validation purposes.

In the next step, we selected variables that were highly correlated with depression for the subsequent analyses. As can be seen in Table 9.2, minor stressors were more strongly related to depressive symptomatology than critical life events. The subscale intercorrelations between parent and peer attachment were substantial ($r = .61$) so that we could not expect them to contribute independently to the measure of outcome. In our subsequent analysis, we used amount of peer contact as a predictive variable because conceptually it represents the most accurate measure of an adolescent's perception of social support and positive peer relationships. As expected, several of the FES dimensions assigned to FES relationships showed considerable negative correlations with depression. We chose cohesion, not only because of its greater correlations with depressive symptomatology ($r = -.42$; see Table 9.3), but also according to the theoretical grounds detailed earlier, illustrating that cohesion is a central variable in describing perceived family climate.

Thus, given the interrelations and partial redundancy among the variables included in Table 9.2, minor stressors, amount of contact with peers, and FES cohesion were selected for the subsequent analyses.

Regression Analyses

As the first step for regression analysis, the intercorrelations between the measures of parent and peer relationships and depression were determined as well as the interaction term. The analysis revealed that positive family dimensions such as cohesion and expression were negatively related to depression, and negative family dimensions such as conflict and control were positively related to depression. Interaction between minor stressors and conflict or control revealed an increase in correlation with depression, pointing to a stress-inducing effect. A stress-moderating effect was apparent in some of the positive family dimensions, too, and was especially pronounced in cohesion and expression (see Table 9.3). The high correlation between depression and minor stressors ($r = .61$; see Table 9.2) was lowered by including the interaction term cohesion × minor stressors,

TABLE 9.3
Correlation Between Depression and FES Scales and
Minor Stressors × FES and Depression ($n = 134$)

	Depression
Cohesion	−.42**
Cohesion × minor stressors	.22*
Expression	−.39**
Expression × minor stressors	.27**
Conflict	.30**
Conflict × minor stressors	.60**
Independence	−.17
Independence × minor stressors	.47**
Achievement	.02
Achievement × minor stressors	.45**
Intellectuality	−.12
Intellectuality × minor stressors	.29**
Recreation	−.22*
Recreation × minor stressors	.42**
Moral	−.01
Moral × minor stressors	.34**
Organization	−.16
Organization × minor stressors	.37**
Control	.23**
Control × minor stressors	.44**

Note. *$p < .05$. **$p < .01$.

or expression × minor stressors. As described earlier, I selected FES cohesion for all further analyses. Mean correlations between depression and amount of peer contact amounted to $r = -.18$. As well, the interaction term minor stressors × amount of peer contact accounted for a significant lowering of the effects of stress ($r = .44$).

Then, multiple regression analyses were conducted with depression as the criterion, analyzing the main and the stress-moderating effects of parent and peer relationships. Minor stressors, the FES dimension cohesion, and amount of contact with peers were used as predictors. Furthermore the interaction terms between the measure of stress and relationships were included.

In order to determine the relative contributions of parent and peer relationships, two hierarchical multiple regression analyses were conducted with the FES dimension cohesion and the amount of peer contact as predictors and depression as dependent variable. In both analyses, the adolescent's age, gender, and total minor stressors were entered first, followed by the FES cohesion and then the interaction terms minor stressors × FES cohesion and minor stressors × amount of peer contact. The results are presented in Table 9.4.

Age and gender were initially entered as demographic control variables. Age did not significantly predict depression. The significant R of gender accounted only for 3% of the variance. Stress, measured by minor stressor total score, predicted 36% of the variance in depressive symptomatology. The two separate models were next entered testing the FES predictor cohesion or amount of peer contact predictor variable and their interaction terms. Of the two models, amount of peer contact was not significant, and cohesion was marginally significant. In addition, the stress × relationship interaction term was significant for minor stressors × cohesion, but only marginally for minor stressors and amount of peer contact.

Thus, cohesion was found to have statistically significant main effects on depressive symptomatology with buffering interaction effects of cohesion and minor stressors. The significant interaction effect was graphed in accordance with Cohen and Cohen (1975). As can be seen in Fig. 9.1, the positive rela-

TABLE 9.4
Two Separate Multiple Regression Analyses for
the Prediction of Depressive Symptomatology

Predictor Variable and Step	Multiple R	Cumulative R^2	R^2 Change	Significance Level
1) Age	.11	.01	.01	.19
2) Gender	.21	.04	.03	.05
3) Minor stressors	.64	.40	.36	.00
4) Cohesion	.65	.42	.02	.06
5) Cohesion × Minor Stressors	.67	.45	.03	.02
4) Amount of Contact with Peers	.64	.41	.01	.25
5) Peer Contact × Minor Stressors	.65	.42	.02	.08

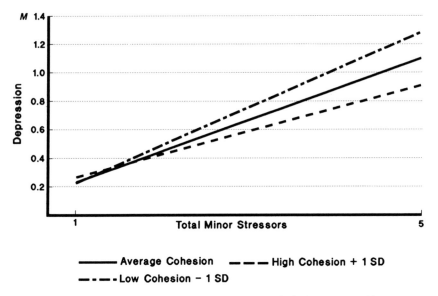

FIG. 9.1. Regression of depression on minor stressors for high, average, and low cohesion values.

tionship between minor stressors and depression becomes lower at higher levels of cohesion.

DISCUSSION

The relation between both major and minor stressors and depression was the first question addressed in this study. Several studies in the past have underlined the saliency of everyday hassles and minor stressors for predicting symptoms, showing that minor stressors play a similar important role in adolescents (Compas, Davis, Forsythe, & Wagner, 1987) and adults (Kanner, Coyne, Schaefer, & Lazarus, 1981). Using his life events scale, Newcomb et al. (1981) found that negative life events account for only 6% of the variance in adolescent symptomatology. In the studies summarized by Compas et al. (1993), the variance explained by minor events is three times higher than that by major events. That minor stressors were more closely related with adolescent depression than major life events, was a further important finding in the studies conducted by Cohen et al. (1987) and Glyshaw et al. (1988) and Compas et al. (1993).

Consistent with research on adults and adolescents, the results in Study 7 confirm the important relation between minor stressors and psychological symptoms. In our study, a significant positive correlation between major events and depressive symptomatology was found ($r = .18$), accounting for 9% of the variance in depression. Minor stressors such as bad grades, quarrels with parents, arguments with close friends, feelings of loneliness, and worries about one's own future, which were summed up to a total minor stress score, accounted for four times as much variance in depression ($r = .61$, $r^2 = .36$) than did life events. In general, the present findings indicate that self-reported stressful events were a significant risk factor and thus speak for an integrative model of stress, as has been developed by Wagner et al. (1988). Although major events are related to depression, the considerably stronger relation between minor stressors and depression is striking. From a cognitive appraisal perspective, Lazarus, DeLongis, Folkman, and Gruen (1985) also argued that daily hassles may predict depressive symptomatology more accurately than major life events.

Not all of the minor stressors we measured are related to depressive symptomatology in the same way. With respect to the sequence of minor stressors perceived as stressing, future-related problems ranked first in the present sample, followed by self-related problems and school-related problems. Problems with peers and romantic relationships were more important than problems with parents. The special significance of future-related problems has been demonstrated already in chapter 5. However, it should be noted that self-related problems ($r = .60$) and problems with parents ($r = .52$) and peers ($r = .46$) are more closely associated with depressive symptomatology than future-related problems ($r = .29$). This parallels findings of Siddique and D'Arcy (1984), who reported that for middle and late adolescence, perceived family and peer stress was the most significant predictor of psychological adjustment. Our results thus speak for differential effects of various sources of stress with minor stressors exceeding the influence of major stressors, and, among the minor stressors, with identity stressors and relationship stressors contributing most toward explaining depression.

Another purpose of this study was to investigate the potential main and interaction effects of various domains of parent and peer relationships that moderate the effects of minor stressors. With respect to stressful events and parent–adolescent relationships, it was hypothesized that the adolescents' perception of family climate as being cohesive, open and allowing for independence would be related to positive outcome (i.e., low depression), whereas their perception of familial rejection, conflict, and control would be related to negative psychological functioning (i.e., high depression). Furthermore, significant interactions between stressors and family environment were expected in that adolescents under stress should be protected when the family is cohesive and expressive and exhibits low conflict and low control.

In general, a negative relationship between positive family dimensions and depression could be established in our study. Family dimensions referring to the quality of emotional bonding such as family cohesion and expression of emotions correlated moderate negatively with depression in the total sample ($r = -.42$ and $r = -.39$, respectively). Furthermore, negative aspects of the family climate such as control (e.g., the extent to which set rules and procedures are used to run family life) and conflict (e.g., the amount of openly expressed anger, aggression, and conflict among family members) showed moderately positive associations with adolescent depression, amounting to $r = .23$ and $r = .30$. The saliency of these family dimensions corresponds with retrospective accounts of family relations provided by individuals who were already depressed. Compared to nondepressed individuals, depressed individuals remembered their parents as hostile and authoritarian (Raskin, Boothe, Reatig, Schulterbrandt, & Odel, 1971), rejecting (Lamont & Gottlieb, 1976), affectionless (G. Parker, 1979), and using negative control techniques (Lewinsohn & Rosenbaum, 1987). Furthermore, parents do not provide emotional support (Jackobson, Fasman, & DiMarcio, 1975) and lack abilities to nurture or show affection (Blatt, Wein, Chevron, & Quinlan, 1979). We have, however, to acknowledge that depressive persons may construe past experience congruent with present mood, as Beck (1967) found. Interestingly, Gjerde and Block (1991) were able in a longitudinal study to relate depressive symptoms at age 18 to parental interactive behavior, which was assessed when the children were 5 years old, thus confirming the strong association between positive family dimensions as protective factors. Although in our study several positive family dimensions, including cohesion, expression, and independence, were negatively related to depression, cohesion (e.g., the degree of commitment, help, and support family members provide for each other) showed a considerably stronger association with depressive symptomatology. We found a significant main effect of cohesion, which is consistent with previous research (Burt, Cohen, & Bjorck, 1988; Felner, Aber, Primavera, & Cance, 1985), pointing to the centrality of this relationship dimension. Thus, the perceived degree of commitment, help and support from the family is related to low levels of depressive symptomatology. It is important to recognize that these associations were found without controlling for adolescents' minor stressors. Entered as a predictor after minor stressors, the additional variance explained by FES cohesion was generally low, accounting only for 2% (R^2 change). Controlled for age, gender, and minor stressors, the R amounted to .42 ($R = 21\%$). The significant main effect of FES cohesion found in our study was qualified by a significant interaction with minor stressors ($p = .02$), supporting the hypothesized stress-buffering role of positive family climate. A few other published studies to date have tested the stress moderating effects of adolescents' perceived family environment, mostly on samples with chronically ill adolescents.

Burt et al. (1988) tested the main effect model and the buffer model in a cross-sectional and longitudinal study with a nonclinical adolescent sample. Significant main effects for positive family climate, measured by the FES, were found, a positive family climate score, e.g., high cohesion was negatively related to depression. Whereas none of their statistically significant interactions between negative life events and perceived family environment supported the stress-buffering role of positive family climate on depression, in analyzing psychological distress in adolescents with spina bifida Murch and Cohen (1989) found main effects of perceived family climate, comparable to those mentioned by Burt et al. (1988). Murch and Cohen also reported a stress-buffering effect of the interaction term of cohesion with life events. In both these studies negative family climate was positively related to distress, and conflict was positively related to depression, as was found in our study, too. The study of Varni, Rubenfeld, Talbot, and Setoguchi (1989) analyzed stress, social support, and depressive symptomatology on a sample with congenital and acquired limb deficiencies. They found that minor stressors and parental support were all significant predictors of depressive symptomatology, but limb loss was not a significant predictor. The authors found evidence for the main or direct effect model. However, the stress–parent support interaction was not significant.

Another question in our study concerned the relative contribution of parent and peer relationships in stress-buffering. Regarding peer relationships, it was hypothesized that positive friendship relationships, characterized by a high frequency of contact and high attachment would have a beneficial effect and serve as a stress-buffer, whereas low attachment and low frequency of contact was expected to correlate highly with dysfunction. Because peer attachment was highly correlated with attachment to parents, we concentrated on amount of peer contact as a valid indicator of peer relationships. We did not find a main effect of peer support, but we could demonstrate that the interaction between peer contact and minor stressors contributes toward predicting depression. Thus, the amount of peer contact tended to exert a minor stressor buffering effect. Taken together, both parent and peer relationships showed a buffer effect, but the effect was much more pronounced as regards perceived family cohesion. Because cohesion also was effective as a predictor of symptomatology in testing the main effect model, it may be perceived as a strong protective factor. Thus, a high level of family cohesion, in general and under the conditions imposed by daily stressors, was associated with lower levels of depressive symptomatology. Alternatively, low levels of family cohesion may be viewed as a risk factor. The relationship with peers, however, does not have beneficial effects irrespective of whether the adolescents are under stress, and, moreover, the buffer effect is somewhat lower than the buffer effect of perceived family cohesion. This result is consistent with several studies that show that although the transition from childhood to adolescence is mainly characterized by the increasing importance of peer relations, the family continues to play a central role in the life of adolescents and to remain important providers of social support (Greenberg et al., 1983; Hunter & Youniss, 1982).

With respect to the differential effect of various sources of social support, the study of Varni et al. (1989) mentioned earlier analyzed several sources of social support, including classmates, friends, parents, and teacher support. The three sources of support, including classmate, parent, and teacher support, were significant predictors of depressive symptomatology; support from friends was not. The main effect model could thus be tested on three of the four sources of social support investigated, however, none of the stress × social support interactions were significant.

Although the results of Varni et al. (1989) support the main model for both parental and peer support, Vernberg (1990) upheld the interaction model, although only for peer support. He analyzed the relationship with parents and peers over time including three types of experiences with peers (i.e., amount of contact with friends, intimacy with best friend, and rejection by peers). Data were collected twice on a sample of 73 seventh and eighth graders with a 6-month interval between measurements. The causal analysis involving depressive affect and peer experiences shows consistently that less contact with friends, less closeness with best friend, and greater rejection contributed over time to increases in depressive affect. In summary, the controversial findings reported here suggest the need to measure various sources of support for their potential differential influence on psychological adjustment. Although the effect of peer contact in our study was not that substantial compared to family cohesion, the need to explore the various contributions of different relationships is obvious.

The results of the present study indicate that demographic variables such as age and gender are not significant predictors of depressive symptomatology. Besides, in Study 7 not many age and gender differences were found with respect to the variables examined. Those differences found paralleled earlier findings, for example, regarding higher rates of depression in females. The adolescent scores in stress and coping were similar to those obtained in previous studies on normal samples (see chaps. 5, 6, and 7). Additionally, the FES values for normal samples are similar to those reported elsewhere (see chap. 8 and Burt, Cohen, & Bjorck, 1988). There are some other findings that add to our picture obtained with previous samples. It should be noted that the CASQ-Scale 3, withdrawal, was positively correlated with depression ($r = .31$). This shows that the coping strategies such as emotional withdrawal and problem avoidance, which may be regarded as dysfunctional in the sense that no immediate solution is reached, were related to depression. Higher withdrawal rates have been found in many clinical samples of adolescents, too (see Seiffge-Krenke, 1995). This may support the coping deficit hypothesis previously mentioned. Furthermore, a small but significant correlation between depression and clinical service use was found ($r = .23$), illustrating a certain disposition to accept therapeutic advice with respect to depressive symptomatology. Because the tendency to accept or reject psychotherapy and counseling is not simply a function of problem pressure, especially not for adolescents who were stereotyped as "unmotivated patients" (Rogers, 1970), this result deserves attention. Although our findings are cross-sectional, they nonetheless are consistent with other cross-sectional and longitudinal studies in child, adolescent, and adult stress research that have rather consistently found that minor stressors and social resources are significant predictive variables of depressive symptomatology. However, longitudinal studies are needed to adequately explain the causal process of the stress–relationship–depression association. They may also enlighten the possible changing role of peer support. In our study, the parents' support (e.g., cohesive family relationships), contribute sub-

stantially more, both directly and through interaction to depressive symptomatology. With increasing age, the possible buffering effect of peer relationships
may increase, too, and exceed that of family cohesion in the long run. Our
analysis of the significance of friendships for females outlined in chapter 8 also
suggests that with increasing age, friendship support possibly becomes more important for girls as compared to boys so that in the future we should explore
different models of depression for males and females. Finally, whether our findings
based on a nonclinical sample can be also generalized for more severely depressed
groups, requires additional study. A second volume has been reserved to examine
this question (see Seiffge-Krenke, 1995).

Conclusions

This chapter fulfills three purposes: (a) it provides a summary of the key findings obtained in the seven studies detailed in this book, and (b) in relation to these findings, it proposes a number of emerging theoretical interpretations and future research issues. Finally, some concluding thoughts about interventions are provided.

This contribution started with a review of research on adolescent coping. Then, a model that brought together the constructs of stress, coping, and relationships was described. Using coping as the key construct in this model, I integrated a broad range of variables that one would expect on theoretical and empirical grounds to be associated with coping and to contribute to adolescent adaptation. The empirical studies designed to test this model thus included major conceptual issues related to stress (type of stressor, event appraisal, event parameters), coping (coping process, coping dimensions, functional and dysfunctional coping), internal resources (self-concept and personality variables), and relationships (emotional support, coping assistance, and coping models provided by parents and peers). All of these factors may influence the outcome (depression).

REVIEWING THE FINDINGS

This volume has been based on an approach that attempts to allow adolescents to express their perceptions of and reactions to the world around them as they progress through adolescence. Several interrelated questions have been under scrutiny: What type of stressors are salient for the vast majority of adolescents? How do adolescents cope with the special and complex demands that arise during this phase of development? How do age and gender differences shape coping behavior? How does the family influence and respond to the adolescent's attempts at coping? What do we know about the role of close friendship in adolescence and its contribution to individual coping? How can we understand adolescents who are unable to overcome the challenges during these years as well as those who are highly effective in dealing with the transitions?

The seven studies designed to answer these research questions were planned after a careful analysis of research activities in adolescent coping and included a variety of methods and designs.

Research Trends in Adolescent Coping: A Review

Our analysis of research activities in adolescent coping since 1967 indicated the existence of two different phases in coping research. Until quite recently, research activity was very modest and limited to certain issues. During the first phase of research in adolescent coping, which lasted until the middle of the 1980s, two thirds of the studies were concerned with investigating responses to traumatic events and critical life events. When compared with studies carried out on adults during the same period, studies on adolescent coping in this phase shared the following peculiar characteristics: (a) The prototypical approach was clinical. In general, small, homogeneous groups of adolescents were studied after they had experienced a very stressful, critical, or even traumatic event. (b) Compared to studies on coping with critical life events in adulthood, the events studied in adolescents were clearly damaging and possessed an inevitable finality yet had a low incidence and a particularly low level of controllability. Little thought was given to how the occurrence of these extremely stressful events might hinder, delay, or make it impossible to cope with age-typical developmental tasks. (c) Most studies assessed defense rather than coping aspects. (d) Given the strong clinical orientation, important developmental questions, for example, those related to aspects of age-related changes, played a negligible role.

At around 1985, a second phase of coping research began to emerge that was clearly developmentally oriented. It provided the starting point for a broader definition of events, for the development of more refined research methods, and for the analysis of factors that modify the impact of stressors. By going beyond individual coping patterns and investigating how families as a unit deal with stress, additional light has been thrown on developmental interrelationships. Studies belonging to this second phase of coping research on adolescents were conducted on large and representatives samples of a broad range, including adolescents at risk. Not only did research efforts in this phase incorporate a more refined and systematic assessment of stressors and coping processes but major and minor events were simultaneously assessed as well, taking into consideration their interdependency. Thus, a unification of developmental and clinical research questions was apparent in nearly all studies. A consideration of the role of social support in coping and an integration of individual and family coping approaches further characterized this second phase of coping research. Thus, on the whole, the major limitations of the early phase of coping research were largely overcome.

Our Own Approach

Based on this literature review and the major limitations of early coping research, we developed a theoretical model to guide our own research efforts that brought together the constructs stress, coping, internal resources, and relationships and related them to adaptation. As described in chapter 2, this model was placed in a developmental context. Accordingly, the samples investigated were normal ones in a comparable developmental context. The adolescents we investigated were aged between 12 to 19 years and came from a broad socioeconomic strata. All adolescents participating in our studies were still in school and had not yet started upon a transition to employment. They were sampled for the seven studies at different times since the mid-1980s.

In order to enhance the developmental perspective in our studies on stress, coping, and relationships new assessment procedures and research methods had to be created. Seven studies were designed to establish a cumulative knowledge base that would systematically enlarge our understanding of the underlying processes and mechanisms involved in adolescent coping. In our research we tried to integrate different types of stressors and corresponding coping responses. Although we examined coping with both major and minor stressors, this book has predominantly dealt with findings related to coping with minor stressors (i.e., daily hassles and everyday problems) because these turned out to be the normative type of developmental stress for most of our adolescents investigated. This normative stress was measured by the Problem Questionnaire, which covers 64 minor stressors in eight different developmental fields such as school, parents, peers, romantic relationships, and future. In addition, we analyzed the actual occurrence of such everyday problems by interviewing the adolescents immediately after the event had taken place. Correspondingly, we chose two different methods in analyzing coping behavior. Coping after confrontation with problems was investigated by several process-oriented interviews immediately after the stressor had occurred. Anticipatory coping was assessed by the CASQ, a two-dimensional matrix including 20 coping strategies across eight age-specific problem areas, such as school, teachers, parents, peers, romantic relationships, self, future, and leisure time. In assessing relationships, we attempted to incorporate many new approaches. For instance, we combined the application of more standardized procedures (such as instruments assessing perceived family climate) with the content analysis of diary entries, focusing on relationships. And because there are many reasons to believe that stress, coping and relationships may not be stable throughout adolescent years, longitudinal designs were added to the cross-sectional designs (e.g., developmental and differential perspectives were integrated into a coherent whole). The replication of the same measurement procedures in several studies over the years, the assessment of the same variables using different methods and the variety of different methods used (interviews, questionnaires, surveys, and content analysis) are thus main characteristics of our approach.

Altogether, 2,176 German adolescents and more than 1,000 adolescents from Israel, Finland, and the United States participated in our studies. In reviewing the main findings of the seven studies, I bring together here results obtained in different samples and with different methods in order to validate our multivariate–multimethod approach.

What Are the Stressors That Required Adolescents' Coping Responses?

Initially we left the question open of how events and stressors were defined. From the results generated by the adolescents in free answers in various studies we found that events and stressors shared the following traits: (a) events that demanded coping were comparatively common and occurred at least once a week, (b) they were predominantly threatening yet only one third of them were experienced as challenging. This applied also to events that, at first thought, would be regarded as positive (e.g., "being in love"), (c) two thirds of the events involved social conflicts that had to be resolved by the adolescent, and (d) minor events named by males belonged to domains such as leisure time and school, whereas females named more often problems with their own self, their parents, or their friends. These gender-specific encounters covaried with number and kind of involved persons. Generally, males indicated a larger number of involved individuals who were qualitatively different from those named by girls. Females named twice as many friends and peers involved than males, whereas male adolescents indicated a higher number of involved adults such as trainers, teachers, and group leaders. The most frequently experienced stressors for both genders belonged to the category "quarrel with parents," followed by "I got a poor grade."

As mentioned already, in attempting to determine which dimensions make events stressful we discovered that most events were perceived as threatening and rather unpleasant, but also very important. From the mass of events named by the adolescents we selected 10 "universal events" (i.e., events that had been named by most adolescents, irrespective of age and gender). Again, most of universal events involved relationship stressors (arguments with teachers, quarrel with parents, trouble with friends, humiliation, being in love). Interestingly, events related to the self (being lonely, being dissatisfied with own appearance and behavior) were reported as occurring rather frequently and being distressing. In addition, political and social events that might affect the adolescent's future were named. Although the saliency of school-related stressors and family stressors has also been documented in other studies (see, e.g., Stern & Zevon, 1990), little attention has been devoted to the variety of relationship stressors we found. Conflicts with close friends, disagreement and communication problems with peers as well as feeling left out and ignored by peers were important events named by our adolescents. Rather unexpectedly, romantic relations also entailed considerable stress. Concern about the future or political events was quite marked, a result that validates the findings obtained with the Problem Questionnaire.

In summary, the adolescents named a variety of stressors they had to deal with in their everyday lives and reported considerable strain caused by these minor events. Although our results are thus in line with the findings of Compas (1987a) and Compas and Phares (1986) concerning the perceived stressfulness of minor events, they represent a considerably wider range of possible stressors. Given that most of the stressors reported occurred rather frequently, and that we analyzed only the most salient among the numerous events reported, we may assume that there is a continuous flow of stressful events that have to be tackled and mastered.

What conclusions may be drawn from such findings? We should be very wary about societal and common-sense tendencies to downplay the distress stemming from minor events. Implicit in such a trivialization of distress is that the latter is treated as unworthy or even pathological (see Lazarus, 1985). Although we have not yet discussed coping with these events, we must acknowledge here that the sheer number of events experienced and, especially, their synchronicity (i.e., their simultaneous appearance) may well have an impact on adolescents' well-being. Furthermore, stressors related to friendship and romantic love as well as identity-related stressors have been neglected so far.

Indication of a Universality in Stress Perception

No study has attempted to compare how stress is perceived today with that of, say, 20 to 50 years ago. High youth unemployment, high divorce rates, and a continual migration from Eastern to Western countries may suggest that living conditions have changed considerably. At present we have no data comparing the perceived stressfulness inherent in major events (such as unemployment, divorce, or immigration) in different cohorts. But we are quite well informed about how everyday problems and minor stressors have been perceived in different cohorts since 1950.

Based on our interviews with adolescents about distressing events, we developed the Problem Questionnaire, which assesses minor stressors in different areas such as problems with school, within the family, with friends, with romantic relationships, and also future-related problems. This instrument was then applied in five of our studies including altogether 1,992 adolescents aged 12 to 19 years. From these studies it was observed that future-related problems ranked highest, followed by self-related problems and problems associated with the family and friends. The ranking of problems basically paralleled the ranking of salient and distressing events spontaneously quoted by adolescents in the interviews (e.g., relationship stressors and identity stressors were very important). The high ranking of future-related problems, however, needs further clarification. These future-related problems included personal fears (e.g., about unemployment), insecurity about choosing a suitable occupation as well as more general worries (e.g., about environmental pollution). It is striking that these fearful anticipations about the future were already documented in earlier investigations (see, e.g., McKay, 1977; Mönks, 1968; Remmers, 1962; Remmers & Shimberg, 1954; Seiffge-Krenke, 1990b). It is thus interesting to note that these fears about the future seemed to be present in totally different cohorts, although the living conditions for adolescents have apparently changed over the past 30 to 40 years. As far as we can tell within the limitations of our research methodology, young people are very much concerned about their own future and the general development of society. Political and future events were, by the way, also quoted spontaneously in our interviews. As expected, we found age and gender differences in stress perception, which is discussed later.

In dealing with change and continuity, we have to consider that the more things change, the more they stay the same. Although adolescents show differences in what they perceive as stressful, the marked continuity in basic rankings of stressors is remarkable and suggests a universality of stress perception over time. Irrespective of concrete living conditions, the sequence of what is experienced as most stressful has remained constant over decades. This is a remarkable finding that has been identified in other domains, too, for example, in sexual attitudes (see, e.g., S. Moore & Rosenthal, 1993) and in types of conflict between parents and adolescents (see Montemayor, 1986). Since the early Middletown Study in 1929, such conflicts have been strikingly similar (see Hill & Holmbeck, 1986; Lynd & Lynd, 1929).

Coping Styles and Coping Strategies

Our research explored the role of daily stressors in the lives of adolescents from two different approaches: (a) anticipatory coping, which was assessed in large, representative samples; and (b) coping after an event has happened, which was investigated by process-oriented interviews conducted in small groups. Major events were included according to their real occurrence in the lives of adolescents. Heretofore the importance of examining coping in the context of naturally occurring stressors had been underestimated and thus the interviews with adolescents immediately after a stressor had happened provided rich data. Most of these results are discussed in the following section on "The Coping Process." Here I only highlight the differences in coping when using a different approach. We found that action blockade or passivity was much more prominent in coping after an event has taken place than in anticipatory coping. This suggests, that adolescents in real transactions may be influenced by social norms. Nevertheless the adolescents were dealing with the emotions aroused by the problem, which was an effective coping mode. In other studies, cognitive and behavioral efforts to alter the source of stress, as well as attempts to regulate the negative emotions associated with stressful circumstances, were found to be important in reducing the negative effects of a range of stressful events (see Compas, 1987b). In anticipatory coping, the adolescents present themselves as competent copers, well able to deal with problems from different domains. It is important to note that the results on anticipatory coping were obtained on large samples and also included cross-cultural comparisons. Factor analysis of the CASQ in different cross-cultural samples yielded similar structures. In most cross-cultural samples, two *functional* coping styles (active coping and internal coping) and one dysfunctional coping style (withdrawal) were found. As argued here, the classification of a coping style as *dysfunctional* refers to the characteristic that the problem at hand is not solved immediately.

Despite differences found in the closeness of the relationship between functional and dysfunctional coping styles, we have to consider that in all cross-cultural samples, the two functional modes of coping (i.e., active support-seeking and internal reflection of possible solutions) were principally employed, whereas defenses such as denial or withdrawal were applied to a lesser extent. More precisely, the proportion of functional to dysfunctional coping modes was approximately 4:1 and cross-culturally comparable. Thus, the normative demands typical of this age group are approached in an adaptive way. Our subjects presented themselves as competent copers, well able to deal with problems arising in different fields such as school, parents, peers, and romantic relations. This generally positive and adaptive way of dealing with minor stressors could be confirmed with different methods. Apart from a greater emphasis on active support-seeking in anticipatory coping and a less active, more internal approach in coping immediately after the stressor occurred, the similarities in coping styles measured via these two methods were impressive. In using different methods, however, we uniformly found that a differentiation in coping must be made according to age and gender. Furthermore, each problem evoked a specific pattern of coping strategies. Thus, context effects or situational dependencies were clearly evident.

The Coping Process

Among the most interesting results are those that allow us to test assumptions based on Lazarus' coping model. They also bring together the three constructs we investigated, stress, coping, and relationships, in a unique and rich way. The analysis of the different phases in the coping process, in particular, the differentiation between aspects of coping and appraisal, revealed the following findings: The first global appraisal of events (primary appraisal) was generally followed by initial reactions that included confusion, preliminary cognitive coping efforts, and first action impulses (e.g., leaving the area). In the secondary appraisal of the situation, which accompanied the coping process, very precise analysis of the adolescent's own coping resources, scope of action, and expectations of success could be observed. As well, intentions were contemplated and obstacles analyzed. Causal attribution was focused on the situation. Also in the tertiary appraisal process after coping, situational changes were named. These results are in accordance with social psychology research. In the perception of social situations, individuals view their own behavior as being dependent on the situation, whereas the behavior of others is attributed to their personality (Nisbett et al., 1973). Argyle et al. (1981) interpreted this observation in terms of the different foci of agents and observers: Agents do not observe their own behavior, but focus on situational stimuli that are important for planning of action. In accordance with the findings of Sanchez-Craig (1976), in our own studies we also observed a decrease in negative emotions after coping (e.g., during reappraisal).

Although each adolescent was characterized by a flexible pattern that was applied for a specific event, situational consistency among those adolescents who had experienced a similar event could be demonstrated. High concordances in the affects and cognitions of adolescents' coping with structurally similar events were found. Only actions displayed greater variability. This finding can be attributed to the different barriers in the scope of action of various adolescents (cf. Lewin, 1968). Mechanic (1962) and Kossakowski (1974) already directed attention to the fact that social norms (i.e., specific behaviors prescribed by a culture for responding to specific events) may also come into effect.

Apart from this considerable homogenization of coping responses to thematically similar events, we were impressed by the limited extent to which actions were applied to deal with everyday events. Without question, coping with very stressful events may frequently result in defense and passivity. However, in mildly stressful events of everyday life such passivity requires explanation. It can be found in the analysis of primary and secondary appraisal, where two thirds of the adolescents regarded these events as threatening and their possibility of control as limited.

The Age of 15: A Turning Point in the Use of Coping Strategies and Social Resources

In our research, we considered the age differences in the definition of stressful events and in those parameters that allow an event to be perceived as stressful. Then we examined the extent to which coping differences are a function of changes in context or situation, or are clearly age-dependent. As previously outlined, stress appraisal differs not so much as a function of age, but as a function of relevant event parameters. General stress in different domains was observed to be rather homogeneous across adolescent years, apart from a peak in early adolescence. By limiting our studies to the age span of 12 to 19 years in all samples, and, furthermore, by only including adolescents from a comparable context (e.g., all attending high school), our results permit us to differentiate between early, middle, and late adolescence. Among all these adolescents, who lived under comparable conditions, only the group of early adolescents perceived greater stress. This is in line with the research of Hamburg (1974), who pointed to early adolescence as a specifically stressful stage in the life cycle. As regards coping behavior, our results verify the presence of changes in cognitive functions across the adolescent years, both with respect to the analysis of the components of situations (i.e., the thinking in terms of possibilities and probabilities; Piaget, 1972) and in a relational perspective (Miller et al., 1970; Selman, 1980). As adolescents become older, the perspectives of the interaction partners can be better understood empathetically, leading to more discussion and compromising. Generally speaking, our results suggest that age differences in coping are both developmentally and contextually determined.

In addition, in all our studies we found that mid-adolescence is rather outstanding in that the age of 15 seemed to represent a turning point in the use of certain coping strategies and in the way relationships are perceived and dealt with. It is well known that compared to children, adolescents are more involved and intimate with peers and friends, turning to them for support formerly provided by the family. In our studies we observed that after the age of 15, adolescents not only addressed the person concerned in order to solve a problem more frequently, they discussed the problem with people who were in a similar situation increasingly and more frequently tried to obtain help from their peers and friends. These developmental changes in the use of social support are intertwined with changes in social and cognitive development that lead to increased cognitive complexity and social maturity. We observed that after the age of 15, the perspective of significant others was increasingly adopted, which led to increases in compromising and giving in. Also, a higher frequency in reflecting about possible solutions led to a richer inner picture of coping options, although not necessarily to more actions. Knowledge about social conventions and higher impulse control are partly responsible for constraint on acting. Moreover, increased acceptance of own limits enhance the stronger reality orientation.

Central to our hypothesized link between level of social cognitive maturity and functional coping style is the recognition that cognitive structures serve as information-processing filters through which adolescents organize and respond to their world. By integrating these various perspectives we may describe adolescence as being marked by the development of cognitive processes from simple, concrete, and more self-centered thinking to complex, abstract, and relational thinking. Early adolescents who operate at an earlier level of social cognitive maturity are, for example, unlikely to differentiate between sources of support. They are less able to recognize links between current behavior and long-range outcomes and they are possibly more motivated by self-centered needs. In contrast, late adolescents, having already reached a more mature social cognitive level, select social support strictly in accordance to the problem at hand, consider current options more often, think about the future consequences of their actions, and reflect about their position with respect to the perspectives of others. Among other things, these qualities lead to their being more likely to regulate compromising and resistance very specifically according to person and problem. Furthermore, they show increased respect for a person's autonomy together with an interest in genuine mutuality. That the age of 15 is a turning point between the early and the later, more mature social cognitive levels, becomes especially evident in the heterogenous and partly very contradictory coping strategies that adolescents employ. Resistance and giving in may be demonstrated in rapid alternation, as was impressively illustrated in respect to problems with parents. The transition to a more advanced level is accordingly marked by instable and contradictory coping behavior.

Gender Differences in Stress and Coping: Are Females More at Risk?

We found that female adolescents reported more relationship stressors and felt four times more threatened by these same stressors than males. In addition, they were more fatalistic in their approach to solving underlying problems. What is more, females reported a higher percentage of ongoing stress even after the coping process drew to a close. Especially early adolescent females reported many stressors in quite different domains such as school, future, self, and relationships.

There are a number of research findings that could be interpreted as supporting the notion of a greater vulnerability of females to social stress. For example, research by Gilligan (1982) indicated that female adolescents tend more than male adolescents to depend on others in assessing their abilities. Hunter and Youniss (1982) observed that females were affected more negatively by the stressors that occurred within their social worlds. Other authors have found that females experience changes in their environment and in themselves as being very stressful and threatening (Allgood-Merton et al., 1990; Gjerde & Block, 1991). This is in line with our results showing that females perceived the same everyday events as being more stressful and more permanent than males did. Several researchers have observed that an accumulation of stressors is more pronounced among early adolescent girls than boys (see Hamburg, 1974; Rice, Herman, & Petersen, 1993). In their coping strategies, female adolescents relied more heavily on social networks (e.g., they discussed problems more freely with the person concerned, talked them over with others, and asked for help and assistance). In all our studies, the preference for talking and conversation as a means of using social resources was remarkably high among females. These trends are in line with research findings on adults, indicating a general tendency among females to rely more heavily on social networks than males (Belle, 1981; Haan,

1974) or to seek help in extrafamilial settings (Belle, 1987). What was striking, however, were gender differences both in active coping and in withdrawal: Females had higher scores in both coping styles. The more active, but at the same time also more fatalistic coping style of females became even more pronounced when analyzing coping strategies across problem areas. We found gender differences in 14 of the 20 strategies investigated. Regardless of the type of problem, female adolescents addressed problems immediately, talked about them much more frequently with significant others than males, and usually try to solve the problem with the person concerned. In addition, they worried a lot about the problem, thought about possible solutions, and expected negative consequences much more frequently than boys. Due to these fearful anticipations, they seem to be additionally stressed. This often resulted in higher rates of emotional reactions like crying, slamming doors, and so forth, or in turning to friends for consolation and sympathy.

Male adolescents, on the other hand, presented themselves as less open and sociable, but evaluated the problem situation more optimistically and did not withdraw resignedly from a situation as frequently as females did. They only tackled problems when imminently present, and did not subject themselves emotionally to as much pressure as females did. However, if a serious problem occurred that could not be solved easily, they tried more often to forget it with alcohol or drugs.

Thus, the appraisal of minor stressors as well as coping with these stressors revealed strong gender differences. Moreover, females seemed to be caught up in a special dilemma. On the one hand, it appeared that females felt more stressed than boys by the same event—entailing interpersonal conflicts with significant others. On the other hand, they more often applied coping strategies that required using these same social relations. We would suggest that this social and psychological dependency of females causes an irresolvable dilemma for them. Possibly, the greater social and psychological dependency in female adolescents is one factor which may account for the nature of their stress perception and its relationship to symptomatology. Several authors have found substantial gender differences in both the perception of family and peer-related stressors as well as in the level of psychological distress (Compas et al., 1993; Moran & Eckenrode, 1991; Siddique & D'Arcy, 1984). This may indicate that differences in the impact of stress from interpersonal relations may also be relevant to understanding gender differences in emotional well-being.

The Changing Influence of Parents and Peers

Several developmental changes serve to alter the way in which adolescents interact with their main partners, parents and friends, including changes in cognitive, verbal, and social reasoning abilities. In addition, many developmental tasks encountered in adolescence involve relationships and require new and more complex interpersonal skills (Hartup, 1989). Early theories discussing the relative and shifting influence of parents and peers have been related to socio-logical research (Coleman, 1961), whereas more recent theories stress the con-tinuity perspective (Grotevant & Cooper, 1986). The early findings underlined the shift in orientation of the adolescent towards his or her peers, as parents are abandoned as trustworthy communication partners. Subsequent research has con-siderably revised this view, showing that parent and peer influences are not necessarily counteractive, but may work synergistically with, and potentiate, peer influence (Kandel, 1986). Furthermore, parents' counsel is often preferred in situations involving future decision making. Burke and Weir (1978) examined adolescents' psychological health and its relationship to satisfaction with help from parents and peers. Although adolescents were more likely to turn to peers for help, satisfaction with parental assistance was more strongly related to their psychological health and well-being than was satisfaction with help from peers.

Our own research has shown that parents are highly valued for their remarks and counsel on school and future-related problems, and they continued to remain important discussion partners for their children throughout adolescence. On the other hand, with peers, very personal problems (such as dating and romantic relationships) are discussed, many of which cannot comfortably be discussed with parents. Thus, during the transition period, marked changes become obvious in the choice of discussion partners as well as a careful selection of what topic is to be discussed with or disclosed to whom. Closely intertwined with the question of the changing influence of parents and peers across the adolescent years and their differential influence as communication partners is the issue of continuity or discontinuity in the quality of relationships with parents and peers. According to the literature, two opposing pathways may be suggested. The continuity model stresses the transfer of skills and emotional bondings within the family into new relationships with friends (Cooper, Carlson, Keller, Koch, & Spradling, 1991), whereas the compensatory model suggests that adolescents with negative expe-riences in their families may use friends to compensate this deficit (Jacovetta, 1975). It would be interesting to analyze in future if adolescents coming from families with dysfunctional coping models will necessarily exhibit this same coping style or try to compensate by modeling their coping behavior according to a good peer model.

Benefits and Costs of Close Relationships

In many studies, both on adult and adolescent samples, a major assumption has been that having a good relationship with someone is equivalent to getting support from them. Implicitly, larger networks are assumed to be better than smaller ones. These assumptions are particularly problematic when dealing with adolescents, and they are made without any differentiation according to age and gender. Despite the evidence that social relationships can be both supportive and yet represent a source of stress, most research has focused only on the positive aspects. In this volume, we tried to overcome this unilateral perspective by demonstrating not only the benefits, but also the costs of close relationships in coping with stress.

Across all seven studies, there is ample evidence for this double function. First, more than 74% of all spontaneously reported events adolescents had to cope with involved an interpersonal conflict with significant others, most frequently with parents and peers. This event was described as rather common, aversive, and distressing. Even if the affects named were not that strong as for major events, these permanent arguments bother the adolescents at least once a week. Rather unexpectedly, even events involving romantic relations, which at first sight might be imagined as being positive and challenging, turned out to be perceived as stressing by the adolescents. Second, adolescents were very much engaged in their close relationships. They spent a considerable amount of time with their friends and reflected a great deal about their partners. More than 40% of the entries in adolescent diaries could be described as empathic reflection about others, another 38% deal with friendship relationships and activities. Third, among all coping dimensions, active coping (e.g., discussion of the problem with the person concerned or other individuals, the seeking of social support, help, and assistance as well as the talking about stressful experiences with others) was the strongest coping factor and explained most of the variance in coping in all of our studies. Relationship stressors made up a substantial proportion in minor stressors, and seeking support and help from others was the most common way of dealing with these stressors. Thus, perceiving friends solely as "good medicine" (Lazarus, 1985, p. 38) would tell us only half of the story. Without question, the vital role friendship plays in the life of adolescents was clearly evident. Furthermore, we were able to demonstrate that family dimensions enhance functional coping style. Nevertheless, the negative and distressing character of these relationships was also very clear.

The Relationship With Parents

I have tried to demonstrate that the shift from childhood to adolescence is marked by changes in many aspects of social relationships. In addition to maintaining the continuity in affection and warmth, parent–adolescent relationships begin, over time, to involve more mutuality, less intimacy, and greater equality in the balance of power. The frequent arguments with their parents that the adolescents reported in the interviews are an indication of this change in the direction of increased reciprocity and balance of power. Many of these arguments were centered around the central theme "autonomy" (i.e., the adolescents struggled with their parents about curfews, traveling alone, staying overnight at a friend's house, or visiting somebody abroad). More females than males reported that they had quarrels with their parents or felt more emotionally affected by them. A higher level of family conflict among females as compared to males has been documented elsewhere as well (Smetana et al., 1991). This might be interpreted as an indication that parents impose stricter rules for their daughters and that the latter have to fight harder to achieve independence. Among all age groups investigated, the 15-year-olds had the highest rates of parent–adolescent conflicts and showed the most ambivalent reactions. On the one hand, they were more prepared to make compromises than younger adolescents; on the other hand, they showed more resistance and aggression toward their parents than older age groups. Interestingly, across the adolescent years the emotional involvement in parent–adolescent quarrels decreases, which can be seen as an indication of continual separation.

In our studies, we also found evidence for the significant influence of the family environment on stress perception and coping style. Four distinct types of family clusters were identified. Adolescents coming from disengaged and conflict-oriented families reported the highest stress levels, were very withdrawn, and did not show many active efforts to solve a problem. In this group, the avoidance approach basically increased over time, as well as the level of perceived stress. In another family type, the achievement and control-oriented families, adolescents reported high stress levels, too, but their coping styles were not that dysfunctional. Adolescents belonging to such families exhibited quite a high level of active coping, which can be taken as proof that a high level of structure and clear rules in the family may at least enhance some functional coping behavior. Two other family types were identified in which high levels of family cohesion and support contributed to low stress and low levels of withdrawal. Among these two types, a family cluster was outstanding insofar as adolescents belonging to these families exhibited the highest level of active coping and the lowest level of withdrawal compared to all other cluster groups. We found that the combination of family cohesion and support with an emphasis on individuation for the adolescents contributed to these results. Furthermore, adolescents belonging to these cohesive, expressive, and individuated families developed their functional coping modes further over the 3 years of this longitudinal study. Structuring and clear rules as well as the encouragement of the adolescent's autonomous development contribute most to a functional and active coping style. In contrast, stress perception was more influenced by other variables such as a lack of closeness and support and a high level of conflict in the family. The great importance of the family in coping with stress was also made clear in our study on the buffering effects of social support.

The Relationship With Peers and Close Friends

In our studies, the rapid shift in the functions and needs that adolescents' relationships with agemates fulfill was reflected in the changes in the pattern of activities and interaction partners, as well as in the distribution of these needs across different persons or groups at the same time. Moreover, the quality of friendships seemed to differ across gender in that females preferred more close, intimate relationships and limited the number of friends to one or two. Males enjoyed having more friends and being active in several different leisure contexts. Other research has also found that girls' friendships are focused on meeting the emotional needs of the females and that intimacy is more important (Burhmester & Furman, 1987). In contrast, boys' friendships are based more on shared activities (Steinberg, 1989).

In this book, I illustrated that adolescents behave in quite different ways in their friendships than in their relationships with parents, and that they gain a lot, although not necessarily consciously, from being with peers and friends. The important role of close friends in guiding and shaping coping behavior was especially apparent in friendships between female peers. Developmental tasks such as establishing a female role or engaging in romantic relationships were tackled and solved in close contact with the female friend. Close friends helped each other in making the transition to a new identity by validating each other's views. Modeling of a female identity and coping assistance in everyday activities and problems were closely related to the body, the appearance, and concrete behavior. As we have seen in our studies, talking together was a frequent activity between friends that increased throughout adolescent years. Other authors also reported that daily meetings with friends account for a substantial portion of how adolescents spend their free time (Crockett et al., 1984; Montemayor, 1982). Indeed, adolescents spend more time talking to peers than for any other activity and are most happy when doing so (Csikszentmihalyi, Larson, & Prescott, 1977). The finding that adolescents themselves tend to play down this activity ("We are just talking," Raffaelli & Duckett, 1989, p. 567) should not hide the fact that this represents a new facet of their social world and is especially important with respect to coping. The analysis of a problem situation, the sharing of possible ideas about how to solve a conflict as well as empathetically discussing the perspective of persons involved are all important precursors of functional coping.

In this context, we have to stress that research on the function of peers for coping has often emphasized the negative influence of friends and peers in developing problem behavior such as drug and alcohol abuse, dangerous driving, or premature sexual activity. However, such problem behavior tapers off as adolescence comes to a close (Kandel, 1986). The great susceptibility to peer pressure decreases throughout these years, making room for other, more mature criteria of friendship such as reciprocity, mutuality, and intimacy. In our research, we did not find much evidence for a "contagious model" or a "bad boys model," as we may ironically term the idea of a negative influence of peers on coping. On the contrary, the positive, stimulating, and supporting functions of close friends and peers became obvious, both on a concrete behavioral level (via imitations and concrete actions) as well as on a more disguised and indirect level (via identification processes). This does not necessarily imply low stress in friendships. Having trouble with friends was experienced less frequently than, for example, quarrels with parents. However, it was described in comparison to family discord as being more important and unpleasant and rather unexpected. This underscores again the increasing importance friendships have for adolescent coping while still representing a source of strain should conflict arise in these relationships.

Successful Coping: A New Look at an Old Paradigm

A further problem to be aware of, especially with respect to coping and development, is the problem of confounding coping with outcome (Lazarus & Folkman, 1991). In this context, we may raise the question of which coping strategies are effective or ineffective. In answering this question, we have to take a new look at an old paradigm based on the concepts of coping and defense.

In this book I outlined that the coping skills of young people in dealing with age-specific problems have been considerably underestimated. This was at least partly due to the clinical orientation that dominated early research on adolescent coping. After 1985, research efforts began to study more representative samples and normative events. The focus of interest shifted from examining only highly stressful and unusual events to include the whole range of demands and problems encountered in adolescence. Measurement procedures differentiated between various forms of coping. In this regard, defense no longer played a dominating role, but was one aspect among many.

As noted earlier in this volume, Haan (1977) considered coping to be more adaptive than defense, because it allows choice and is reality-oriented, whereas defenses are rigid, compelling, and misdirect an individual's experience. However, based on our results on normal samples, we were not able to make such a clear distinction. In the first place, females showed higher withdrawal rates but at the same time were "good copers" in that they applied functional and efficacious strategies in order to solve a problem. Second, some domains gave rise to more "defensive" coping reactions. Self-related problems, for example, elicited quite a high rate of dysfunctional coping in all our studies. Third, the choice of a coping style was not only dependent on situational factors, but on temporal factors as well. More precisely, an event that an individual is immediately confronted by aroused more "defensiveness" than an anticipated event, because he or she must first cope with negative emotions. According to our results, it became apparent that this behavior supported relaxation and was thus functional. In Lazarus' terms, this behavior positively altered the "mismatch" between the individual and his or her environment. Fourth, in all our studies on normal samples in different cultures, functional coping modes (e.g., active support-seeking and internal reflection of possible solutions) were primarily applied, whereas dysfunctional coping modes (withdrawal and other defenses) were applied less frequently. Only about 16% to 20% of all coping responses found in our different samples and across several problem domains were characterized by such defense processes.

As pointed out by Roth and Cohen (1986), in evaluating the effectiveness of coping process one must consider the point in time at which effectiveness is evaluated, whether the stressful situation can in fact be controlled, and the degree of correspondence between the coping style and the demands of the stressful situation. Even though some researchers (e.g., Kobasa, 1982; Vaillant, 1977) insist that avoidance coping and poor adjustment are related, such a relationship may be weakened when factors such as the specific moment of evaluating effectiveness, the individual's degree of control over the event, and the demand characteristics of the event are considered. Clearly, strategies such as denial and distraction are sometimes seen as less effective forms of coping, because they treat the symptoms rather than the cause of the problem. Yet, as Hauser and Bowlds (1990) showed, in certain circumstances, they may lead to a positive outcome contributing to an emotional equilibrium. How does one determine which of the ways a teenager copes are adaptive? Coping processes cannot simply be labeled as inherently good or bad; rather, the specific context has to be considered. A strategy that is effective for one problem or person may not work at all for another. The effectiveness of a given response may also vary over time. A coping strategy that is at first beneficial may become maladaptive if used continuously. In general, our results point to remarkable competencies in dealing with stressors. They illustrated the abilities of adolescents to appropriately apply their coping reactions according to the situation, and to make an age- and gender-specific selection from the coping register. Thus, situational and contextual variables as well as social norms and conventions were much more influential than a "coping trait." The flexible shift in coping according to these various demands is thus a prerequisite of successful coping.

Stress, Coping, and Symptomatology

The relation between stress management and adaptation was a further research issue in our studies. What precisely is the relation between stressors and psychological dysfunction? The outcomes following the impact of stressors appear to be a function of several interacting factors such as timing and synchronicity of stressors as well as the availability of options and social networks that may help in buffering the effects of stress (Kessler, Price, & Wortman, 1985). In light of this complexity, stressors do not necessarily lead to problematic outcomes. Neither may it be concluded that troubled adolescents automatically experience greater stress or simply lack abilities to cope with stressful situations or events. Because coping is regarded as an attempt to alter demands (see Kessler et al., 1985), it can be seen as a key to understanding stress reactions and the relation between stress and symptomatology.

In one of our studies, we analyzed the stress-buffering effects of close relationships. More specifically, we asked if parents or peers are more efficient in buffering stress. According to S. Cohen and Wills (1985), two models may be distinguished, the main effect model and the buffer model. The concept of the buffer model focuses on the perceived availability of social resources. According to this model, social support may intervene between the stressful event and stress reaction by reducing or preventing a stress appraisal. That is, the perception that others can and will provide necessary resources may redefine the potential for harm posed by a situation. In contrast, the main effect model expects a positive outcome of close relationships irrespective of the stress at hand.

Our results very clearly demonstrated a stress-buffering effect of parent and peer relationships. The effect was, however, stronger for parent support. Furthermore, our data impressively showed the strongly stressful nature of minor events. Minor events were more strongly related to dysfunction $(r = .61)$ than major events $(r = .19)$. This again emphasizes the importance of these recurring, everyday, distressing events for adolescent dysfunction. Although we tested this association primarily in respect to depressive symptomatology, due to high comorbidity among most disturbances in adolescence, this result deserves a general attention.

SOME CONSIDERATIONS AND ISSUES FOR FURTHER RESEARCH

Our theoretical model was not able to take into account in a detailed way all important influential factors on adolescents that come from within the individual and from the variations of context that young people find themselves in. Individual characteristics of an adolescent such as perceptions of self or saliencies of a stressor may interact with social influences such as living conditions, parenting styles, school, peer group, leisure context, and the wider cultural background. The processes by which functional and dysfunctional coping strategies are acquired in these different contexts are not fully clear. We encountered less intentional processes, which seemed to be significant components in some domains, especially in friendship relations. Furthermore, our original model and empirical approach did not allow us to examine important aspects of adolescence that impinge on aspects of stress, coping, and relationships such as being depressed, being unemployed, coming from broken homes, or being involved in problem behavior.

Acknowledging Different Cultural Contexts

Depicting stress management as a dynamic process where relationships between the adolescent and his or her environment constantly change meant that contextual factors assumed an important role in our approach. This was already clear in the research issues and studies that concentrated on the situational determinants of coping. Cross-cultural comparison, however, offers a broader framework for the general understanding of stress, coping, and relationships in adolescence. For one, cultural norms, rules, and attitudes regulate perception and interpretation of events (Magnusson, 1982). I would, therefore, suggest that the degree of stress inherent in a situation will be perceived differently by different ethnic and social groups. Also, different cultural standards may exist between cultures that prescribe the "adequate" way of dealing with stressors. Furthermore, individual variations in coping may reflect the traditional styles of childrearing and the unique experiences encountered in the context of a particular culture. Relationships with parents and friends may be perceived differently in different cultures, and the norms for using social support may vary.

So far, only a few cross-cultural studies have been concerned directly with adolescent coping. Diaz-Guerrero's (1973) studies tried to identify "active" and "passive" cultures, based on a comparison of eight countries in 1960. The results showed that active modes of coping were more widespread among adolescents in highly industrialized nations like the United States, Great Britain, or Italy, and that passive modes of coping were typical of agricultural societies such as Mexico. A replication of this study on adolescents in the United States and Mexico by the same investigator in the 1980s (Emmite & Diaz-Guerrero, 1983), however, failed to confirm the original results. Cohort differences must be considered here.

Apparently, cross-cultural comparison is only useful if it includes countries having reached comparable levels of modernization and educational opportunities; otherwise interpretation of the results may be blemished by problems of validity. In addition, cross-cultural comparison necessitates the application of standardized assessment procedures to enhance our knowledge about coping in different cultures. Although the seven studies presented in this book were carried out in Germany, the results may be applicable to a more general context. From the beginning, the issue of the generalizability of my results was very important, and so I initiated my first studies in 1986 in Israel (Seiffge-Krenke & Shulman, 1990). Later studies were conducted in Finland (Seiffge-Krenke, 1992) and in the United States (Herman et al., 1992). Currently, research with the Problem Questionnaire and the CASQ is underway in France, Holland, Canada, Japan, Poland, and India.

The studies that we have published so far have indicated a certain universality in stress perception and coping style across cultures. Besides a basically functional coping approach in the cross-cultural samples investigated so far, differences in dealing with specific problem domains in the Finnish, Israeli, and German samples have been found that were related to the unique experiences encountered within the context of these particular cultures. As we were able to show, the family plays a significant role in shaping the adolescent's repertoire of coping, for it can serve as a model and can have the effect of inhibiting coping resources. Nevertheless, family coping behavior cannot be seen apart from a broader cultural context (see Bronfenbrenner, 1986; Shulman et al., 1987). More research is needed to explain why adolescents may respond—or are encouraged to respond—to the same stressor with different modes of coping. We are now able to use our present findings to move to a deeper level of understanding of the variations in the adolescent experience with different stressors within different social and cultural contexts.

The Need for Clinical Samples

At this point I find it important to emphasize that in future research, all of the main research questions dealt with in this book should be addressed by comparing normal and clinical samples. Why, one may ask, would clinical samples be of any interest for the study of stress, coping, and relationships? To begin with, the extent is limited to which we can generalize from studies of normative development and parents and peer contexts to clinical populations, which may differ in all these aspects. Second, in adolescence, normal and pathological development occasionally merge. Results on clinical populations may thus contribute to our knowledge of both and help to discriminate between them. Finally, there are good, clinically important reasons to pursue questions regarding coping with everyday stressors. Virtually most of the published literature on clinical samples have narrowed their perspective by emphasizing critical life events and major stressor as grounds for referral. Too many studies have focused on the inability to solve a problem as the cause behind seeking professional help while ignoring other types of stressors. Case studies often tend to be idiosyncratic and lack insight into the more general social and cognitive development of the adolescent patient, his or her coping options, and available social support systems. Studies on the therapeutic efficacy, on the other hand, focus too intensely on the cooperation involved in treatment, which is an overly restricted aspect of coping (Tramontana, 1980). Among clinically referred adolescents, disturbed relationships with parents and peers are frequent (Achenbach & Edelbrock, 1987). Social resources that may buffer the effect of stress are limited and may add to deficiencies in internal resources such as inefficacious coping strategies or low self-esteem. According to the model of Lazarus and Launier (1978) and as we have observed ourselves, the perception of possible resources (secondary appraisal) can dramatically alter the perceived degree of stress. It is likely that a multiple deficit in internal and social resources in dealing with stressors may be accompanied by a relatively high level of stress. Perhaps there are other areas as well in which even clinically referred adolescents are quite competent. A lack of information about frequency and quality of minor and major events, however, as well as ignoring coping resources and potentialities in other, nonclinical areas, is a poor starting point for intervention.

In my ongoing research, I was therefore interested in knowing more about those different stressors that clinically referred adolescents are faced with and their ways of dealing with these demands. Is there empirical evidence for a clustering of stressful events, and if so, is this clustering related to symptomatology? Adolescent patients facing numerous stressful events may elicit different coping strategies than those who live under more stable and less stressful living conditions. If stressors are too numerous, require too much change, or offer too little time to develop coping strategies, they may produce negative outcomes. In accordance with one prominent approach, the focal theory (see Coleman, 1978), we need to prove if those individuals who have more than one issue to cope with at one time are most likely to have problems in adjustment. Moreover, there is evidence of diversity in coping style depending on type of patient and we should therefore clarify this point. In a second volume (see Seiffge-Krenke, 1995), I have tried to answer these questions. A further question that should be addressed in future work is the possible coping function of problem behavior. Since the early work of Kandel (1986) and Labouvie (1986), little attention has been devoted to addressing this question in research. Yet, such knowledge might represent an important contribution to understanding the relationships between stressors and symptomatology. It is well known that problem behavior such as dangerous driving, alcohol and drug abuse as well as delinquency, which is widespread during a certain period in adolescence, especially among males, fades out as adolescence comes to a close. Motive analysis of adolescent drug users has shown that drug abuse serves as a coping strategy only for a small proportion of young people (Jessor & Jessor, 1977). The same holds true for alcohol abuse. Peer pressure and attempts to reach an adult status are frequent motives for starting to drink (Hawkins, 1982). This possibly may place adolescents, especially males, at risk, but additional factors certainly play a role in transforming an occasional drinker or nonproblem drinker into a problem drinker. The slightly elevated scores in the coping strategy "I try to forget the problem with the help of alcohol or drugs" we found among males over the adolescent years does not offer a clear answer to this question. A more thorough analysis in the future should clarify whether such increased scores are reflective of social conventions (drinking, especially for males, becomes more and more socially accepted), or whether this expresses the increased tendency of males to use alcohol and drugs as a coping strategy.

PROBLEMS AND LIMITATIONS IN STUDYING STRESS, COPING, AND RELATIONSHIPS: DO WE NEED A BETTER METHODOLOGY?

Conducting research about stress, coping, and relationships is fraught with difficulties. How can we tell what adolescents are thinking? Do they know the motives and reasons why they use a certain coping strategy? Are they prepared to share with researchers the details of their private lives? Nisbett and Wilson (1977) wrote insightfully about problems that arise when using verbal reports on mental processes. We tried to solve some of these problems by using various methods to approach the adolescents' everyday lives as closely as possible, as for example, by studying their private written documents about these experiences. In the following section of this chapter, I review the methods and research designs we used in our studies, and discuss their strengths and limitations.

In several of our studies we used self-report measures such as questionnaires and interviews. In order to clarify certain aspects of coping, such as the stress appraisal and the coping process, these were, by definition, the only measures we could use. For aspects such as event appraisal, affects, or cognitions in dealing with the stressor there were no clear objective checks on validity. In principle, only the actions named as coping strategies can be verified through appropriate observations. Obtaining direct observations of adolescents' coping behavior in natural settings seemed to us an important new approach to apply in further research. In this book, we chose to validate the interview data by comparing it with data obtained on different samples, using more circumscribed and standardized instruments such as questionnaires and surveys. Applying the same instrument to larger and new samples helped to overcome the difficulties of relying on a "shotgun approach."

The extent to which questionnaires can provide valid information about processes and mechanisms underlying behavior depends on the skill of selecting items that adequately sample the universe of content that make up these behaviors or constructs. In item sampling, we used the adolescents' reports from earlier studies as a starting database. Because problems in the wording of questions and items might contribute to poor reliability and validity, we attempted to retain the original wording as recorded in our interview studies as much as possible. Without question, conscious and unconscious distortion of responses are possible. We tried to reduce such distortions by posing questions that offered a great deal of freedom for definition and description to the adolescents themselves. For example, we asked them to define constructs or we used open-ended questions. Also, we were careful to formulate our items so that value judgments were not implied. In addition, in our survey study, a scale to measure socially desirable responses was included. Furthermore, although some techniques for acquiring information relied on producing spontaneously elicited verbal material, we also used material originally not intended to be read or analyzed by others. The fresh reports about stressors that had just happened as well as the analysis of diary entries are examples of these techniques. The face-to-face interviews we conducted allowed us to explain problematical questions and request clarification of unclear responses. The comfortable conversational setting between interviewer and adolescent increases the potential for a more reliable access to information in general and, especially in the open-ended questions, of obtaining a greater amount of detail. After the initial, personal contact between interviewer and adolescents had been established, the telephone interviews used in follow-up stages provided more information. Even in our survey study on a large sample and in the other studies using questionnaires, it was important to maintain close contact between research assistants and adolescents, who were supervised in small groups. Longitudinal studies, which trace the same adolescents over a period of time, overcame some of the problems inherent in cross-cultural data and allowed us to assess the same individual several times, thus obtaining a deeper insight into individual development. In summary, because we wished to explore stress, coping, and relationships from as many perspectives as possible, it was important for us to employ a wide variety of data collection techniques. Accordingly, we are now beginning to understand what influences coping across a variety of stressful situations.

Because so many stressors are related to interpersonal relationships and so many coping strategies involve relationships, we intend to pursue our "natural setting approach" (as exemplified by our content analysis of adolescent diaries) in order to understand these interrelationships more clearly. Thus, we would like to broaden our future research endeavors by also including direct observations of adolescents in natural settings. This approach requires that we are able to make systematic observations of individuals and of interactions between them, such as those that take place in leisure context. Indeed, some of these may be of a quite private nature and thus extremely difficult to obtain access to. Conceptually we assume that social relationships and modeling processes in the friendship context are particularly well suited for observation studies. This elaboration upon our previous multi-method approach is also necessary to be able to make exact statements about stress, coping and relationships in male adolescents. In contrast to females, male friendship is considerably more characterized by instrumental behavior. Thus, we hope that especially observational studies will provide us with more insight on this group.

PRACTICAL APPLICATIONS

In our literature review on training programs for the development of coping abilities, we criticized the heterogenity of the different approaches as well as the fact that the majority of such programs were based on inadequate and global definitions of coping that could not be distinguished from general adaptation. After clarifying constructs and developing instruments that allow the assessment of stress and coping as multidimensional constructs, we are now in a better position to start thinking about the practical applications of our research.

As I tried to demonstrate in this book, outcomes following the impact of stressors are a function of multiple interaction factors such as type of stressor, coping abilities, developmental stages, and internal and social resources. The findings of our survey study demonstrated that adolescents employ a range of coping strategies in response to naturally occurring stressors. Furthermore, these coping strategies are orderable and vary as a function of type of stressors, event parameters of these stressors as well as age and gender of the adolescents. Internal resources such as self-concept, personality variables, and perception of the family environment play an important role in coping behavior, leading either to more functional or more dysfunctional coping. In particular, close friends become increasingly more important as coping models in a variety of tasks that cannot be comfortably solved with the help of adults.

The present results have numerous clinical applications for programs that are intended to improve the abilities of adolescents in managing stress and using social resources. It has become clear that coping is best evaluated in the context of a particular stressor. Intervention programs that focus on the development of global coping behavior intended to be applied according to a variety of stressor types and may be less effective than programs that are specific to a particular stressor. From a developmental perspective, the selection of which coping strategies are most suitable for dealing with a specific stressor is a sign of positive growth. Program planners would be well advised to be aware of the underlying developmental processes and to provide the opportunity to learn and practice a diversity of coping strategies suitable for different problems. Taking into account that internal reflections on possible solutions are further important hallmarks of developmental progression, anticipatory coping and training in hypothetical situations might be advisable. Creativity research has provided numerous inspirations on how to analyze a problem, developing alternative solutions, hypothetically test them, and communicate about them (see Seiffge-Krenke, 1974; Torrance, 1962, 1975). Training in flexibility of thought and action might be helpful if the coping register is too narrow or too much biased by, for example, gender-specific behavior. It is plausible to expect that males and females may be socialized to use different strategies for managing their emotions under stress. Also, their active approach in dealing with a stressor may vary. We should be aware of the distinctive way male and female adolescents deal with stressors; however, it should be ascertained whether or not these gender-specific ways of coping become too rigid or lead to negative outcome.

If differences in stress perception and coping processes do play a critical role in gender differences in depression or externalizing syndromes, intervention programs should devote attention to the early origins of these differences. The focus on negative emotional status, the stronger dependency on relationships as well as more negative self-evaluations among females increase the chances of developing depressive mood. Males, on the other hand, may be more protected from depression by their prototypical response of emotional distraction or by purposely turning their attention away to more pleasant and neutral activities. Males are, however, more prone to becoming involved in instrumental behavior so that the chances may increase that they lose sensitivity to problems and the persons involved in these problems and develop externalizing symptoms. Making adolescents more sensitive to the various facets of a problem, encouraging various ideas and thoughts, offering the opportunity to try out new coping strategies are goals that serve both male and female adolescents when facing stress.

Last, but not least, tolerance for individual limitations and an empathy for shortcomings originating from a certain coping or relationship history should be demonstrated. Adolescents belonging to ethnic or racial minority groups as well as adolescents coming from troubled milieus may lack a rich repertoire of coping and stress management skills or may, due to different values and family backgrounds, prefer certain coping strategies. Also, their way of using social resources may differ. A deep understanding for these adolescents at risk should be developed as well as respect for their ability to face a comparably higher number of stressors. Possibly, a general intervention program for all adolescents followed by more specific intervention courses for risk groups, as Compas et al. (1993) suggested, is a helpful tool.

Adolescent peer and friendship relationships were found to contribute uniquely to stress management and coping behavior. Intervention programs should therefore strengthen rather than weaken adolescents' peer support network. It is time to change from the "contamination model" or "bad boys model" of peer support, which was a major conceptualization in research on problem behavior to friends as a positive model of social support and coping assistance. It is important to see that this is the major function that close friends and peers have for the majority of adolescents in the transition to adulthood. Our findings also highlight the importance of examining how perceptions of the family serve as a moderator of coping strategy. It would seem, therefore, that the family context of the adolescent must be included when trying to change the way adolescents cope with stress and use social resources. Working with troubled adolescents is a growing, changing and demanding field (see Coleman, 1987). Yet, practitioners need to know as much as possible about normal development in adolescence. Thus, it has been one intention of this book to assist them by providing them with solid and extended results in this field.

Appendix

TABLE 1
Interview Guide for Coping Process Study

Deep Structure	Surface Structure	
Intention	Explanation	Sample Questions
Definition of situation	The cognitive representation of the situation is to be described	Please tell me again about what happened.
Situative and social context	Situative and social framework in which event occurred to be recorded, whether for example in the family, in school, with boy/girlfriend and which persons were involved	Can you describe the event in detail? Where did it happen? Who was also present/involved?
Causality	Whereas in the previous point the framework in which the event occurred is to be recorded, here the course of events leading to the final one in question is to be recorded. Closely related here is the subjective interpretation of the causes	What led to this situation/event? What happened before? How do you account for this event?
Appraisal	From this point on the subjective appraisal of the event should be recorded. Of importance here are the evaluation of the event and the evaluation of the own inductive competence to cope	I wonder what the event meant to you. As this event was taking place, what were you thinking? What did you think of first? Did you feel you are able to cope with the situation? (nondirective statements also possible: And then?)

(Continued)

TABLE 1
(Continued)

Deep Structure	Surface Structure	
Intention	Explanation	Sample Questions
Coping	Recording of efforts to cope with the event following appraisal. Separation of appraisal and coping may be difficult for some adolescents. It is also possible that the perception is not very differentiated or that the coping reactions have been so automatic or impulsive that a distinction between both aspects may be difficult to make. Therefore, in this phase of the interview the interviewer should encourage the adolescents to continue further self-exploration by providing a few nondirective statements and should maintain a rather "wait-and-see" attitude.	What did you do then? How did you solve the problem/conflict/matter? How did you deal with this (feelings, thoughts)? (nondirective statements also possible: And then? I see!)
Effect	Here one is dealing with the *intended* and the *achieved* effect of the coping reaction.	What did you expect to achieve by this? How did your actions change the situation? Did you intend to do something else? In retrospect, would you have rather done something else? If so, what? Do you think this event will have any influence on future events? Do you expect this?
Reappraisal	Whereas in the previous step the description of the effect was dealt with, here the aspects of reappraisal are of interest: Did he or she view the situation differently now, did his or her feelings change after coping? Was the event over for him or her or were the coping efforts ongoing?	Could you see the event differently afterward? Is the event now over for you? Would you react the same way if such an event happened again?

TABLE 2
Example of a Coping Process Interview (Summary)

Meike, female, 12 years old
Interviewer: Claudia, female, 27 years old

Topic: Fear of being excluded by girlfriend and then being alone

Time 1: Interview duration = 15 minutes

During the break the other girls took her girlfriend to the side and whispered something to her. She wondered what the hush-hush was all about. If she approached them, they would send her away. The main thing was that she was afraid of losing her friend and then being all alone. She recalled a similar situation during a school sports class. The other girls, who were all a year older than she, also whispered about something and made her think that she was too young to understand. One really couldn't do much, so she just didn't say anything and went away. If she got angry, the others might completely reject her.

Time 2: Telephone interview, 2 days later, duration = 6 minutes

Meike is still very upset. She didn't have enough nerve to speak with her friend openly about the situation. The event doesn't bother her as much as it did 2 days ago. Nevertheless, Meike thinks something like this could happen again at any time. She is unsure how she will be able to deal with it.

TABLE 3
Event Exploration Interview, Part 1: Event Sampling

Questions in the Exploration of Adolescent Experts

1. Can you tell me if something important has happened to you recently, let's say, in the last 2 weeks?
2. How did you deal with this?
3. Which of the named events were particularly important? Let's look first at event X more carefully.
   (Presentation of five-level importance scale.)
4. Now try to rate the event.
   (Presentation of the list with event parameters.)

I thought the event . . .

was pleasant	1	2	3	4	5	was unpleasant
was important	1	2	3	4	5	was not important
was predictable	1	2	3	4	5	was unpredictable
was motivating	1	2	3	4	5	was paralyzing
was controllable	1	2	3	4	5	wasn't controllable
was minimally stressful	1	2	3	4	5	was highly stressful
was acute	1	2	3	4	5	was chronic
involved my emotions more	1	2	3	4	5	involved my reasoning more

240

TABLE 4
Event Exploration Interview, Part 2: Universal Events

Questions Used for Generating Event Parameters and Coping Strategies
(Written Interview)

1. Event: "I got a bad grade."

(a) First of all we would like to know if such an event has recently taken place, that is, in the last couple of weeks. Please mark the answer that applies with a large X.

During the last 2 weeks, I have experienced this event

(0) *not at all*, (1) *once*, (2) *several times*, (3) *quite often*

(b) Now please describe exactly what happened.

(c) I thought the event

was pleasant	1	2	3	4	5	was unpleasant
was important	1	2	3	4	5	was not important
was predictable	1	2	3	4	5	was unpredictable
was motivating	1	2	3	4	5	was paralyzing
was controllable	1	2	3	4	5	wasn't controllable
was minimally stressful	1	2	3	4	5	was highly stressful
was acute	1	2	3	4	5	was chronic
involved my emotions more	1	2	3	4	5	involved my reasoning more

(d) Now we would like to know what you did when the event took place. What did you think about? How did you feel? What did you do?

TABLE 5
Problem Questionnaire[a]

On the following pages you will find a list of worries and difficulties that adolescents of your age have identified as their problems.
Among these there will be certainly some that apply to you personally and some that hardly apply or not at all. Please indicate honestly and spontaneously how stressful the problems are for you.

I found this problem to be . . .	*highly stressful*				*not stressful at all*
Problems related to *school*					
1. There is great pressure to get the best marks in school.	5	4	3	2	1
2. There is no comradeship in my classes, only competition.	5	4	3	2	1
3. The interaction with other students and the teacher is impersonal.	5	4	3	2	1
4. The school's prescribed learning material is difficult.	5	4	3	2	1
5. The teachers aren't interested in my problems.	5	4	3	2	1
6. Graduation seems so far away.	5	4	3	2	1
					(Continued)

[a]Copyright 1995 by Inge Seiffge-Krenke.

TABLE 5
(Continued)

	I found this problem to be . . .	highly stressful				not stressful at all
7.	Differences in opinions with my teacher could result in bad marks.	5	4	3	2	1
8.	I don't have anything to say in the classroom.	5	4	3	2	1
Problems related to the *future*						
9.	I might not get into the training program or college/university of my choice.	5	4	3	2	1
10.	The destruction of the environment is increasing.	5	4	3	2	1
11.	It may be difficult to combine my studies and job with marriage and family.	5	4	3	2	1
12.	I might lose myself in the daily humdrum of life, in social norms and pressures.	5	4	3	2	1
13.	I would like very much to discover my real interests.	5	4	3	2	1
14.	I don't know what I am going to do after I finish school.	5	4	3	2	1
15.	I am unsure which profession I am best suited for.	5	4	3	2	1
16.	I might become unemployed.	5	4	3	2	1
Problems related to *life with parents at home*						
17.	My parents show little understanding for my problems in school.	5	4	3	2	1
18.	My parents are only interested in my getting good marks in school.	5	4	3	2	1
19.	I fight with my parents because my opinions about many things differ from theirs.	5	4	3	2	1
20.	My parents think I'm "not all there."	5	4	3	2	1
21.	My parents don't let me make my own decisions.	5	4	3	2	1
22.	I can't talk with my parents.	5	4	3	2	1
23.	My parents don't approve of my friends.	5	4	3	2	1
24.	My parents don't have very much time for me.	5	4	3	2	1
25.	It's difficult for me to pursue my own interests because I don't want to disappoint my parents.	5	4	3	2	1
26.	I wish I wasn't so dependent on home (on my parents).	5	4	3	2	1
Problems related to *relationships with peers*						
27.	I hardly have any friends.	5	4	3	2	1
28.	It's difficult for me to approach others.	5	4	3	2	1
29.	I'm having difficulties combining my interests with those of my friends.	5	4	3	2	1
30.	I don't have a real friend with whom I can also talk about personal worries and problems.	5	4	3	2	1

(Continued)

242

TABLE 5
(Continued)

	I found this problem to be . . .	highly stressful				not stressful at all
31.	Some of my acquaintances are dishonest and underhanded.	5	4	3	2	1
32.	Many of my acquaintances are only willing to have superficial contact with me.	5	4	3	2	1
33.	I am unsure if the others will accept me.	5	4	3	2	1
34.	I don't like the fact that outsiders can't join existing cliques.	5	4	3	2	1
35.	My peers are often very stubborn and intolerant toward each other.	5	4	3	2	1
36.	I have too little time for my friends.	5	4	3	2	1
	Problems related to *leisure* time					
37.	I don't get enough pocket money.	5	4	3	2	1
38.	School and home obligations don't leave me enough free time.	5	4	3	2	1
39.	I am often unable to get started on something.	5	4	3	2	1
40.	I feel unable to deal with my boredom in other ways than with television, alcohol, and drugs (smoking marijuana).	5	4	3	2	1
41.	Adolescents often have no other opportunities to spend their free time except for hanging around in the streets or in bars.	5	4	3	2	1
42.	My parents try to influence how I spend my leisure time.	5	4	3	2	1
43.	I don't have anyone with whom I can spend my free time.	5	4	3	2	1
	Problems that are related to *romantic relations*					
44.	I don't have a boyfriend/girlfriend.	5	4	3	2	1
45.	I feel insecure in dealing with the opposite sex.	5	4	3	2	1
46.	I am afraid of losing contact with my other friends if I pair up with a boyfriend/girlfriend.	5	4	3	2	1
47.	I sometimes have to make pretenses just to please others.	5	4	3	2	1
48.	I am afraid of hurting others because I am unsure of their feelings.	5	4	3	2	1
49.	It's difficult for me to develop a truly equal and balanced relationship.	5	4	3	2	1
50.	I am afraid that my jealousy could ruin my friendships.	5	4	3	2	1
	Problems related to my *own self*					
51.	I feel lonely.	5	4	3	2	1
52.	Even little things enrage me.	5	4	3	2	1
53.	I am dissatisfied with my appearance.	5	4	3	2	1
54.	I am not very politically involved.	5	4	3	2	1
55.	I am often sad and dejected.	5	4	3	2	1

(Continued)

TABLE 5
(Continued)

	I found this problem to be . . .	highly stressful — not stressful at all
56.	I find it difficult to talk about my feelings with others.	5 4 3 2 1
57.	I am different than my friends and acquaintances.	5 4 3 2 1
58.	I am dissatisfied with my behavior, my own traits and abilities.	5 4 3 2 1
59.	I don't trust myself to say anything in the presence of others.	5 4 3 2 1
60.	I have guilty feelings about a few things I have done.	5 4 3 2 1
61.	I would like to discover what I really want.	5 4 3 2 1
62.	I sometimes behave contrary to my opinions and beliefs just to bother others.	5 4 3 2 1
63.	I find it difficult to live up to my own decisions.	5 4 3 2 1
64.	All new things make me afraid.	5 4 3 2 1

TABLE 6
CASQ[a]

	When this problem comes about . . .	School	Teachers	Parents	Peers	Romantic Relations	Self	Future	Leisure Time
1	I discuss the problem with my parents/other adults.								
2	I talk straight away about the problem when it appears and don't worry much.								
3	I try to get help from institutions (job center, youth welfare offices).								
4	I expect the worst.								
5	I accept my limits.								
6	I try to talk about the problem with the person concerned.								
7	I behave as if everything is alright.								
8	I try to let my aggression out (with loud music, riding my motorbike, wild dancing, sport, etc.).								
9	I do not worry because usually everything turns out all right.								

(Continued)

[a]Copyright 1995 by Inge Seiffge-Krenke.

TABLE 6
(Continued)

When this problem comes about . . .	School	Teachers	Parents	Peers	Romantic Relations	Self	Future	Leisure Time
10	I think about the problem and try to find different solutions.								
11	I compromise.								
12	I let out my anger or desperation by shouting, crying, slamming doors, etc.								
13	I tell myself that there always will be problems.								
14	I only think about the problem when it appears.								
15	I look for information in magazines, encyclopedias, or books.								
16	I try not to think about the problem.								
17	I try to forget the problem with alcohol and drugs.								
18	I try to get help and comfort from people who are in a similar situation.								
19	I try to solve the problem with the help of my friends.								
20	I withdraw because I cannot change anything anyway.								

TABLE 7
Item Loadings of the Problem Questionnaire

Item No.	Item	Loading	Communality
Factor 1: Problems related to *school*			
1	There is a great pressure to get the best marks in school.	.65	.40
2	There is no comradeship in my classes, only competition.	.63	.41
3	The interaction with other students and the teachers is impersonal.	.62	.41
4	The school's prescribed learning material is difficult.	.49	.35
5	The teachers aren't interested in my problems.	.52	.28
6	Graduation seems so far away.	.45	.21
7	Differences in opinions with my teacher could result in bad marks.	.59	.39
8	I don't have anything to say in the classroom.	.43	.20

(Continued)

TABLE 7

(*Continued*)

Item No.	Item	Loading	Communality
Factor 2: Problems related to the *future*			
9	I might not get into the training program or college/university of my choice.	.60	.44
10	The destruction of the environment is increasing.	.81	.48
11	It may be difficult to combine my studies and job with marriage and family.	.50	.41
12	I might lose myself in the daily humdrum of life, in social norms and pressures.	.49	.29
13	I would like very much to discover my real interests.	.62	.38
14	I don't know what I am going to do after I finish school.	.69	.40
15	I am unsure which profession I am best suited for.	.65	.41
16	I might become unemployed.	.43	.23
Factor 3: Problems related to *life with parents at home*			
17	My parents show little understanding for my problems in school.	.79	.40
18	My parents are only interested in my getting good marks in school.	.75	.39
19	I fight with my parents because my opinions about many things differ from theirs.	.65	.34
20	My parents think I'm "not all there."	.51	.27
21	My parents don't let me make my own decisions.	.52	.30
22	I can't talk with my parents.	.60	.33
23	My parents don't approve of my friends.	.60	.30
24	My parents don't have very much time for me.	.48	.20
25	It's difficult for me to pursue my own interests because I don't want to disappoint my parents.	.43	.27
26	I wish I wasn't so dependent on home (on my parents).	.49	.29
Factor 4: Problems related to *relationships with peers*			
27	I hardly have any friends.	.59	.30
28	It's difficult for me to approach others.	.48	.27
29	I'm having difficulties combining my interests with those of my friends.	.41	.20
30	I don't have a real friend with whom I can also talk about personal worries and problems.	.60	.31
31	Some of my acquaintances are dishonest and underhanded.	.51	.29
32	Many of my acquaintances are only willing to have superficial contact with me.	.61	.33
33	I am unsure if the others will accept me.	.60	.32
			(*Continued*)

TABLE 7
(Continued)

Item No.	Item	Loading	Communality
34	I don't like the fact that outsiders can't join existing cliques.	.50	.29
35	My peers are often very stubborn and intolerant toward each other.	.49	.20
36	I have too little time for my friends.	.39	.17
Factor 5: Problems related to *leisure* time			
37	I don't get enough pocket money.	.39	.20
38	School and home obligations don't leave me enough free time.	.40	.21
39	I am often unable to get started on something.	.52	.30
40	I feel unable to deal with my boredom in other ways than with television, alcohol, and drugs (smoking marijuana).	.41	.20
41	Adolescents often have no other opportunities to spend their free time except for hanging around in the streets or in bars.	.44	.23
42	My parents try to influence how I spend my leisure time.	.49	.25
43	I don't have anyone with whom I can spend my free time.	.50	.29
Factor 6: Problems that are related to *romantic relations*			
44	I don't have a boyfriend/girlfriend.	.60	.32
45	I feel insecure in dealing with the opposite sex.	.70	.48
46	I am afraid of losing contact with my other friends if I pair up with a boyfriend/girlfriend.	.41	.22
47	I sometimes have to make pretenses just to please others.	.50	.30
48	I am afraid of hurting others because I am unsure of their feelings.	.48	.29
49	It's difficult for me to develop a truly equal and balanced relationship.	.51	.31
50	I am afraid that my jealousy could ruin my friendships.	.59	.35
Factor 7: Problems related to my *own self*			
51	I feel lonely.	.79	.48
52	Even little things enrage me.	.80	.50
53	I am dissatisfied with my appearance.	.53	.35
54	I am not very politically involved.	.41	.29
55	I am often sad and dejected.	.81	.49
56	I find it difficult to talk about my feelings with others.	.72	.37
57	I am different than my friends and acquaintances.	.61	.35
58	I am dissatisfied with my behavior, my own traits and abilities.	.65	.39
59	I don't trust myself to say anything in the presence of others.	.60	.31
60	I have guilty feelings about a few things I have done.	.48	.30
			(Continued)

TABLE 7
(Continued)

Item No.	Item	Loading	Communality
61	I would like to discover what I really want.	.49	.22
62	I sometimes behave contrary to my opinions and beliefs just to bother others.	.30	.15
63	I find it difficult to live up to my own decisions.	.40	.20
64	All new things make me afraid.	.30	.16

TABLE 8
Item Loadings of the CASQ

Item No.	Item	Loading	Communality
Factor 1: Active coping (29.9%/57%)			
15	I look for information in magazines, encyclopedias, or books.	.69	.39
3	I try to get help from institutions (job center, youth welfare offices).	.62	.39
2	I talk straight away about the problem when it appears and don't worry much.	.61	.55
6	I try to talk about the problem with the person concerned.	.58	.62
19	I try to solve the problem with the help of my friends.	.55	.62
1	I discuss the problem with my parents/other adults.	.51	.42
18	I try to get help and comfort from people who are in a similar situation.	.49	.40
Factor 2: Internal coping (14.3%/27.3%)			
5	I accept my limits.	.70	.64
11	I compromise.	.70	.68
10	I think about the problem and try to find different solutions.	.61	.40
13	I tell myself that there always will be problems.	.56	.56
14	I only think about the problem when it appears.	.40	.43
4	I expect the worst.	.50	.49
Factor 3: Withdrawal (10.6%/10.7%)			
7	I behave as if everything is alright.	.64	.50
16	I try not to think about the problem.	.64	.32
20	I withdraw because I cannot change anything anyway.	.66	.39
17	I try to forget the problem with alcohol and drugs.	.48	.41
12	I let out my anger or desperation by shouting, crying, slamming doors, etc.	.43	.39
8	I try to let my aggression out (with loud music, riding my motorbike, wild dancing, sport, etc.)	.40	.35

References

Abegg, W. (1954). *Aus Tagebüchern und Briefen junger Menschen* [From diaries and letters of young people]. München: Reinhardt.

Abraham, K. (1927). Notes on the psychoanalytical investigation and treatment of manic-depressive insanity and allied conditions. In K. Abraham (Ed.), *Selected papers on psychoanalysis* (pp. 137–156). London: The Hogarth Press. (Original work published 1911)

Abrams, D. M. (1977). Conflict resolution in children's storytelling: An application of Erikson's theory and the conflict-enculturation model. *Dissertation Abstracts International, 38,* 2335.

Achenbach, T. M. (1985). *Assessment and taxonomy of child and adolescent psychology.* Beverly Hills, CA: Sage.

Achenbach, T. M. (1991). The derivation of taxonomic constructs: A necessary stage in the development of developmental psychopathology. In D. Chicchetti (Ed.). *Rochester Symposium on Developmental Psychopathology, Vol. 3.* Hillsdale, NJ: Lawrence Erlbaum Associates.

Achenbach, T. M., & Edelbrock, C. S. (1981). Behavioral problems and competencies reported by parents and normal and disturbed children aged four through sixteen. *Monographs of the Society for Research in Child Development, 46,* No. 1.

Achenbach, T. M., & Edelbrock, C. S. (1987). *Manual for the Youth Self-Report and Profile.* Burlington: University of Vermont, Department of Psychiatry.

Achenbach, T. M., McConaughty, S. H., & Howell, C. T. (1987). Child/adolescent behavioral and emotional problems: Implications of cross-informant correlations for situational specificity. *Psychological Bulletin, 101,* 213–232.

Allgood-Merton, B., Lewinsohn, P. M., & Hops, H. (1990). Sex differences and adolescent depression. *Journal of Abnormal Psychology, 99,* 55–63.

Allport, G. W. (1942). The use of personal documents in psychological science. *Social Science Research Council Bulletin, 49.*

Althuser, J. L., & Ruble, D. N. (1990). Developmental changes in children's awareness of strategies for coping with uncontrollable stress. *Child Development, 60,* 1337–1349.

Anastasi, A. (1975). Commentary on the precocity project. *Journal of Special Education, 9*(1), 93–103.

Andersen, S. M., & Ross, I. (1984). Self-knowledge and social inference: The diagnosticity of cognitive, affective, and behavioral data. *Journal of Personality and Social Psychology, 46,* 280–293.

Anderson, J. F. (1979). Adjustment of adolescents to chronic disability. *Rehabilitation Psychology*, 46, 177–185.

Andersson, B. E. (1969). *Studies in adolescent behavior*. Stockholm: Almquist & Wiksell.

Andrews, G. (1981). A prospective study of life events and psychological symptoms. *Psychological Medicine*, 11, 759–801.

Antonovsky, A. (1981). *Health, stress, and coping*. San Francisco: Jossey-Bass.

Applebee, A. N. (1984). Writing and reasoning. *Review of Educational Research*, 54, 577–596.

Argyle, M., Furnham, A., & Graham, J. A. (1981). *Social situations*. Cambridge: Cambridge University Press.

Armistead, L., McCombie, A., Forehand, R., Wierson, M., Long, N., & Tauber, R. (1990). Coping with divorce: A study of young adolescents. *Journal of Clinical Child Psychology*, 19, 79–84.

Armsden, G. C., & Greenberg, M. T. (1987). The inventory of parent and peer attachment: Individual differences and their relationship to psychological well-being in adolescence. *Journal of Youth and Adolescence*, 16, 427–454.

Asarnow, J. R. (1988). Peer status and social competence in child psychiatric inpatients. A comparison of children with depressive, externalizing, and concurrent depressive and externalizing disorders. *Journal of Abnormal Child Psychology*, 16, 151–162.

Asarnow, J. R., Carlson, G. A., & Guthrie, D. (1987). Coping strategies, self-perceptions, hopelessness, and perceived family environments in depressed and suicidal children. *Journal of Consulting and Clinical Psychology*, 55, 361–366.

Averill, J. R. (1973). Personal control over aversive stimuli and its relationship to stress. *Psychological Bulletin*, 80, 286–303.

Bachman, J. G., O'Malley, P. M., & Johnston, J. (1978). *Youth in transition. Vol. VI: Adolescence to adulthood*. Ann Arbor: University of Michigan Social Research.

Baer, P. E., Garmezy, L. B., McLaughlin, R. J., Pokorny, A. D., & Wernick, M. J. (1987). Stress, coping, family conflict and adolescent alcohol use. *Journal of Behavioral Medicine*, 10, 449–466.

Band, E. B., & Weisz, J. R. (1988). How to feel better when it feels bad. Children's perspectives on coping with everyday stress. *Developmental Psychology*, 24, 247–253.

Bandura, A. (1986). *Social foundations of thought and action*. Englewood Cliffs, NJ: Prentice-Hall.

Barnes, H. L., & Olson, P. H. (1985). Parent-adolescent communication and the circumplex model. *Child Development*, 56, 428–432.

Baron, P., & Labrecque, C. (1988). Conceptions and coping strategies related to depression in adolescents in a clinical setting. *Enfance*, 41, 449–466.

Baron, P., & MacGillivray, R. G. (1989). Depressive symptoms in adolescents as a function of perceived parental behavior. *Journal of Adolescent Research*, 4, 50–62.

Baron, P., & Perron, L. M. (1986). Sex differences in the Beck depression inventory scores of adolescents. *Journal of Youth and Adolescence*, 15, 165–171.

Barrera, M. (1981). Social support in the adjustment of pregnant adolescents: Assessment issues. In B. H. Gottlieb (Ed.), *Social networks and social support* (pp. 69–96). Beverly Hills, CA: Sage.

Beardslee, W. R., Jacobson, A. M., Hauser, S. T., Noam, G. V., Powers, S. J., Houlihan, J., & Rider, E. (1986). An approach to evaluating adolescents' adaptive processes: Validity of an interview-based measure. *Journal of Youth and Adolescence*, 15, 355–375.

Beck, A. T. (1967). *Depression: Clinical, experimental, and theoretical aspects*. New York: Hoeber.

Belle, D. E. (1981). *The social network as a source of both stress and support to low-income mothers*. Paper presented at the biennial meeting of the Society for Research in Child Development, Boston, MA.

Belle, D. E. (1987). Gender differences in moderators of stress. In R. D. Barnett, L. Biener, & G. K. Baruch (Eds.), *Gender and stress*. New York: The Free Press.

Bem, D. J., & Allen, A. (1974). On predicting some of the people some of the time: The search for cross-situational consistency in behavior. *Psychological Review*, 81, 506–520.

Berg, C. (1989). Knowledge of strategies for dealing with everyday problems from childhood through adolescence. *Developmental Psychology*, 25, 607–618.

Berman, S. J. (1983). The effects of perceived control on adolescent coping with hospitalization and major illness. *Dissertation Abstracts International, 44*, 297.

Berndt, T. J. (1981). Relations between social cognition, nonsocial cognition, and social behavior: The case of friendship. In J. H. Flavell & L. Ross (Eds.), *Social cognitive development: Frontiers and possible futures* (pp. 128–143). Cambridge: Cambridge University Press.

Berndt, T. J., & Hawkins, J. (1984). *Friendship interview.* Unpublished manuscript, Purdue University at West Lafayette, IN.

Berndt, T. J., & Hoyle, S. G. (1985). Stability and change in childhood and adolescence friendships. *Developmental Psychology, 21*, 1007–1015.

Berndt, T. J., & Perry, T. B. (1986). Children's perceptions of friendships as supportive relationships. *Developmental Psychology, 22*, 640–648.

Bernfeld, S. (1927). Die heutige Psychologie der Pubertät. Zur Kritik ihrer Wissenschaftlichkeit [Contemporary adolescent psychology. A criticism on its scientific approach]. *Imago, 13*, 1–56.

Bigelow, B. J. (1977). Children friendship expectations: A cognitive development study. *Child Development, 48*, 246–253.

Billings, A. G., & Moos, R. H. (1981). The role of coping responses and social resources in attenuating the stress of life events. *Journal of Behavioral Medicine, 4*, 157–189.

Billings, A. G., & Moos, R. H. (1982). Psychosocial theory and research on depression: An integrated framework and review. *Clinical Psychological Review, 2*, 213–237.

Billings, A. G., & Moos, R. H. (1983). Comparisons of children of depressed and nondepressed parents: A social-environmental perspective. *Journal of Abnormal Child Psychology, 11*, 463–486.

Billings, A. G., & Moos, R. H. (1984). Coping, stress and social resources among adults with unipolar depression. *Journal of Personality and Social Psychology, 46*, 877–891.

Bird, G. W., & Harris, R. L. (1990). A comparison of role strain and coping strategies by gender and family structure among early adolescents. *Journal of Early Adolescence, 10*, 141–158.

Blanchard-Fields, F., & Irion, J. (1988). Coping strategies from the perspective in two developmental markers: Age and social reasoning. *Journal of Genetic Psychology, 149*, 141–151.

Blatt, S. J., Wein, S. J., Chevron, E., & Quinlan, D. M. (1979). Parental representation and depression in normal young adults. *Journal of Abnormal Psychology, 88*, 388–397.

Blos, P. (1964). Die Funktion des Agierens im Adoleszenzprozeß [The function of acting out during adolescence]. *Psyche, 18*, 120–138.

Blos, P. (1967). The second individuation process of adolescence. *Psychoanalytic Study of the Child, 22*, 162–186.

Blotcky, A. D., Raczynski, J. M., Gurwitch, R., & Smith, K. (1985). Family influence on hopelessness among children early in the cancer experience. *Journal of Pediatric Psychology, 10*(4), 479–493.

Bobo, J. K., Gilchrist, D., Elmer, J. F., Snow, W. H., & Schinke, S. P. (1986). Hassles, role strain, and peer relations in young adolescents. *Journal of Early Adolescence, 6*, 339–352.

Bosma, H. A., & Jackson, A. E. S. (Eds.). (1990). *Coping and self-concept in adolescence.* Berlin: Springer.

Briedis, I. (1978). The facilitation of social competence through the implementation of an interpersonal coping skills program. *Dissertation Abstracts International, 39*, 1430.

Brim, O. G. J., & Ryff, C. D. (1980). On the properties of life events. In P. B. Baltes & O. G. J. Brim (Eds.), *Life-span development and behavior* (pp. 368–389). New York: Academic Press.

Bronfenbrenner, U. (1986). Ecology of the family as a context for human development: Research perspectives. *Developmental Psychology, 22*, 723–742.

Brooks-Gunn, J., Warren, M. P., & Rosso, J. T. (1991). *The impact of pubertal and social events upon girls' problem behavior.* Unpublished manuscript.

Broughton, J. M. (1981). The divided self in adolescence. *Human Development, 24*, 13–32.

Brown, S. A., Stetson, B. A., & Beatty, P. A. (1989). Cognitive and behavioral features of adolescent coping in high-risk drinking situations. *Addictive Behaviors, 14*, 43–52.

Bühler, Ch. (1925). Zwei Knabentagebücher, mit einer Einleitung über die Bedeutung des Tagebuchs in der Jugendpsychologie [Two boys' diaries, with an introduction on the significance of diaries in youth psychology]. *Quellen und Studien zur Jugendkunde, No. 3,* Jena: Fischer.

Bühler, Ch. (1927). Zwei Mädchentagebücher [Two girls' diaries]. *Quellen und Studien zur Jugendkunde, No. 1,* Jena: Fischer.

Bühler, Ch. (1932). Jugendtagebuch und Lebenslauf. Zwei Mädchentagebücher mit einer Einleitung [Adolescent diary and life-span development. Two girls' diaries, with an introduction]. *Quellen und Studien zur Jugendkunde, No. 9,* Jena: Fischer.

Bühler, Ch. (1934). Generationen im Jugendtagebuch [Generations in adolescent diary]. *Quellen und Studien zur Jugendkunde, No. 11,* Jena: Fischer.

Buhrmester, D. (1990). Intimacy of friendship, interpersonal competence and adjustment during preadolescence and adolescence. *Child Development, 61,* 1101–1111.

Buhrmester, D., & Furman, W. (1987). The development of companionship and intimacy. *Child Development, 58,* 1101–1113.

Bulman, R. J., & Wortman, C. B. (1977). Attributions of blame and coping in the "real world": Severe accident victims react to their lot. *Journal of Personality and Social Psychology, 35,* 351–363.

Burke, R., & Weir, T. (1978). Benefits to adolescents of informal helping relationships with their parents and peers. *Psychological Reports, 42,* 1175–1184.

Burt, C., Cohen, L. H., & Bjorck, J. (1988). Perceived family environment as a moderator of young adolescents' life stress adjustment. *American Journal of Community Psychology, 16,* 101–122.

Camarena, P. M., Sarigiani, P. A., & Petersen, A. C. (1990). Gender-specific pathways to intimacy in early adolescence. *Journal of Youth and Adolescence, 19*(1), 19–32.

Caplan, G. (1974). *Support systems and community mental health.* New York: Behavioral Publications.

Caplow, F., Bahr, H. M., Chadwick, B. A., Hill, R., & Williams, M. H. (1982). *Middletown families.* Minneapolis: University of Minnesota Press.

Carducci, D. J. (1980). Positive peer culture and assertiveness training: Complementary modalities for dealing with disturbed and disturbing adolescents in the classroom. *Behavioral Disorders, 5,* 156–162.

Carey, M. P., Kelley, M. L., Buss, R. R., & Scott, W. O. (1986). Relationship of activity to depression in adolescents: Development of the adolescent activities checklist. *Journal of Consulting and Clinical Psychology, 54*(3), 320–322.

Carlsmith, J. M., Ellsworth, P. C., & Aronson, E. (1976). *Methods of research in social psychology.* Reading, MA: Addison-Wesley.

Cauce, A. M., Felner, R. D., & Primavera, J. (1982). Social support in high-risk adolescents: Structural components and adaptive impact. *American Journal of Community Psychology, 10,* 417–428.

Chatterjee, R. N., Mukherjee, S. P., & Nandi, D. N. (1981). Life events and depression. *Indian Journal of Psychiatry, 23,* 333–337.

Chelune, G. J., Sultan, F. G., & Williams, C. L. (1980). Loneliness, self-disclosure, and interpersonal effectiveness. *Journal of Counseling Psychology, 27,* 462–468.

Coddington, R. D. (1972). The significance of life events as etiological factors in the diseases of children: A study of a normal population. *Journal of Psychosomatic Research, 16,* 205–213.

Codega, S. A., Pasley, B. K., & Kreutzer, J. (1990). Coping behaviors of adolescent mothers: An exploratory study and comparison of Mexican-Americans and Anglos. *Journal of Adolescent Research, 5,* 34–53.

Coelho, G. V., Hamburg, D. A., & Adams, J. E. (Eds.). (1974). *Coping and adaptation.* New York: Basic Books.

Cohen, J., & Cohen, P. (1975). *Applied multiple regression/correlation analysis for the behavioral sciences.* Hillsdale, NJ: Lawrence Erlbaum Associates.

Cohen, L. H., Burt, C. E., & Bjorck, J. P. (1987). Life stress and adjustment: Effects of life events experienced by young adolescents and their parents. *Developmental Psychology, 23,* 583–592.

Cohen, S., & Wills, T. A. (1985). Stress, social support and the buffering hypothesis. *Psychological Bulletin, 98*, 310–357.

Cole, D. A. (1989). Psychopathology of adolescent suicide: Hopelessness, coping beliefs, and depression. *Journal of Abnormal Psychology, 98*, 248–255.

Coleman, J. S. (1961). *The adolescent society*. New York: The Free Press of Glencoe.

Coleman, J. S. (1978). Current contradictions in adolescent theory. *Journal of Youth and Adolescence, 7*, 11–34.

Coleman, J. S. (Ed.). (1987). *Working with troubled adolescents*. London: Academic Press.

Coleman, J. S., George, R., & Holt, G. (1977). Adolescents and their parents: A study of attitudes. *Journal of Genetic Psychology, 130*, 239–245.

Coletta, N. D., Hadler, S., & Gregg, C. H. (1981). How adolescents cope with the problems of early motherhood. *Adolescence, 16*, 499–512.

Collins, W. A. (1990). Parent child relationships in the transition to adolescence: Continuity and change in interaction, affect, and cognition. In R. Montemayor, G. Adams, & J. Gullotta (Eds.), *The transition from childhood to adolescence*. Beverly Hills, CA: Sage.

Compas, B. E. (1987a). Stress and life events during childhood and adolescence. *Clinical Psychological Review, 7*, 275–302.

Compas, B. E. (1987b). Coping with stress during childhood and adolescence. *Psychological Bulletin, 101*, 393–403.

Compas, B. E., Davis, G. E., Forsythe, C. J., & Wagner, B. M. (1987). Assessment of major and daily stressful events during adolescence: The adolescent perceived events scale. *Journal of Consulting and Clinical Psychology, 55*, 534–541.

Compas, B. E., Ey, S., & Grant, K. E. (1993). Adolescent depression: Issues of assessment, taxonomy, and diagnosis. *Psychological Bulletin, 4*, 323–344.

Compas, B. E., Forsythe, C. J., & Wagner, B. M. (1988). Consistency and variability in causal attributions and coping with stress. *Cognitive Therapy and Research, 12*, 305–320.

Compas, B. E., & Hammen, C. L. (1993). Depression in childhood and adolescence: Covariation and comorbidity in development. In R. J. Haggerty, N. Garmezy, M. Rutter, & L. Sherrod (Eds.), *Risk and resilience in children: Developmental approaches*. New York: Cambridge University Press.

Compas, B. E., Howell, D. C., Phares, V., Williams, R. A., & Giunta, C. T. (1989). Risk factors for emotional/behavioral problems in young adolescents: A prospective analysis of adolescent and parental stress and symptoms. *Journal of Consulting and Clinical Psychology, 57*, 732–740.

Compas, B. E., Malcarne, V. L., & Fondacaro, K. M. (1988). Coping with stressful events in older children and young adolescents. *Journal of Consulting and Clinical Psychology, 56*, 405–411.

Compas, B. E., Orosan, P. G., & Grant, K. E. (1993). Adolescent stress and coping: Implications for psychopathology during adolescence. *Journal of Adolescence, 16*, 331–349.

Compas, B. E., & Phares, V. (1986). Stress during childhood and adolescence: Source of risk and vulnerability. In A. L. Greene, E. M. Cummings, & K. H. Karraker (Eds.), *Life-span developmental psychology: Perspectives on stress and coping* (pp. 111–129). Hillsdale, NJ: Lawrence Erlbaum Associates.

Cooper, C., Carlson, C., Keller, J., Koch, P., & Spradling, V. (1991). *Conflict negotiation in early adolescence. Links between family and peer relational patterns.* Paper presented at the annual meeting of the Society for Research in Child Development, Chicago.

Cornell, J. P., & Furman, W. (1984). The study of transitions. In R. Emde & R. Harman (Eds.), *Continuity and discontinuity in development* (pp. 418–433). New York: Plenum Press.

Craig-Bray, L., & Adams, G. R. (1986). Measuring social intimacy in same-sex and opposite-sex contexts. *Journal of Adolescent Research, 1*, 95–101.

Cramer, P. (1979). Defense mechanisms in adolescence. *Developmental Psychology, 15*, 476–477.

Crockett, L., Losoff, M., & Petersen, A. C. (1984). Perception of the peer group and friendship in early adolescence. *Journal of Early Adolescence, 4*, 155–181.

Csikszentmihalyi, M., & Larson, L. (1984). *Being adolescent: Conflict and growth in the teenage years*. New York: Basic Books.

Csikszentmihalyi, M., Larson, L., & Prescott, S. (1977). The ecology of adolescent activity and experience. *Journal of Youth and Adolescence, 6,* 281–294.

Daniels, D., & Moos, R. H. (1990). Assessing life stressors and social resources among adolescents: Applications to depressed youth. *Journal of Adolescent Research, 5,* 268–289.

Dean, A., & Lin, N. (1977). The stress buffering role of social support: Problems and prospects for systematic investigation. *Journal of Nervous and Mental Disease, 165,* 403–417.

Deci, E. L., & Ryan, R. M. (1985). *Intrinsic motivation and self-determination in human behavior.* New York: Plenum Press.

Delamater, A. M., Kurtz, S. M., Bubb, J., & White, N. H. (1987). Stress and coping in relation to metabolic control of adolescents with type 1 diabetes. *Journal of Developmental and Behavioral Pediatrics, 8,* 136–140.

Diaz-Guerrero, R. (1973). Interpreting coping styles across nations from sex and social class differences. *International Journal of Psychology, 8,* 193–203.

Dohrenwend, B. P., & Shrout, P. E. (1985). "Hassles" in the conceptualization of and measurement of life stress variables. *American Psychologist, 40,* 780–785.

Dohrenwend, B. S., & Dohrenwend, B. P. (1974). *Stressful life-events: Their nature and effects.* New York: Wiley.

Dohrenwend, B. S., & Dohrenwend, B. P. (Eds.). (1981). *Stressful life events and their contexts.* New York: Prodist.

Donovan, A. M. (1988). Family stress and ways of coping with adolescents who have handicaps: Maternal perceptions. *American Journal on Mental Retardation, 92,* 502–509.

Douvan, E., & Adelson, J. (1966). *The adolescent experience.* New York: Wiley.

Dowd, E. T., Claiborn, C. D., & Milne, C. R. (1985). Anxiety, attributional style and perceived coping ability. *Cognitive Therapy and Research, 9,* 575–582.

Drotar, D., Owens, R., & Gotthold, J. (1980). Personality adjustment of children and adolescents with hypopituitarism. *Child Psychiatry and Human Development, 11,* 59–66.

Dunn, O. J. (1961). Multiple comparisons among means. *Journal of the American Statistical Association, 56,* 52–64.

Dunn Geier, J. (1986). Childhood chronic pain. The ability to cope. *Dissertation Abstracts International, 46* (8-B), 2802.

Dweck, C. S., & Wortman, C. B. (1982). Learned helplessness, anxiety, and achievement motivation: Neglected parallels in cognitive, affective, and coping responses. In H. W. Krohne & L. Laux (Eds.), *Achievement, stress, and anxiety* (pp. 93–125). Washington, DC: Hemisphere.

Dzegede, S. A., Pike, S. W., & Hackworth, J. R. (1981). The relationship between health-related stressful life events and anxiety. An analysis of a Florida metropolitan community. *Community Mental Health Journal, 17,* 294–305.

Earle, E. M. (1979). The psychological effects of mutilating surgery in children and adolescents. *Psychoanalytic Study of the Child, 34,* 527–546.

Earls, F. (1986). Epidemiology of psychiatric disorders in children and adolescents. In G. L. Klerman, M. M. Weissman, P. S. Applebaum, & L. H. Roth (Eds.), *Psychiatry: Social epidemiological and legal psychiatry* (pp. 125–152). New York: Basic Books.

Easson, W. A. (1970). *The dying child.* Springfield, IL: Charles C. Thomas.

Ebata, A. T., & Moos, R. H. (1994). Personal, situational and contextual correlates of coping in adolescence. *Journal of Research in Adolescence, 4,* 99–125.

Eisen, P. (1986). Adolescence: Coping strategies and vulnerabilities. Seminar on psychiatric vulnerability in adolescence. *International Journal of Adolescent Medicine and Health, 2,* 107–117.

Eiser, C. (1989). Coping with chronic childhood disease: Implications for counselling children and adolescents. Special Issue: Health Psychology: Perspectives on Theory, Research and Practice. *Counselling Psychology Quarterly, 2,* 323–336.

Elash, D. D. (1977). At risk for Huntington's disease. *Psychiatric Annals, 7,* 410–418.

Elias, M. J. (1983). Improving coping skills of emotionally disturbed boys through television-based social problem solving. *American Journal of Orthopsychiatry, 53,* 61–72.

Elliott, G. R., & Eisdorfer, C. (Eds.). (1982). *Stress and human health: Analysis and implications for research*. New York: Springer.

Emmite, P. L., & Diaz-Guerrero, R. (1983). Cross-cultural differences and similarities in coping style, anxiety and success-failure on examinations. *Series in Clinical & Community Psychology, 2*, 191–206.

Erikson, E. H. (1970). *Jugend und Krise: Die Psychodynamik im sozialen Wandel* [Adolescence and crisis: The psychodynamics of social change]. Stuttgart: Klett.

Everhart, R. B. (1982). The nature of "goofing off" among junior high school adolescents. *Adolescence, 17*, 177–188.

Fahrenberg, H., & Selg, H. (1970). *Das Freiburger Persönlichkeitsinventar FPI* [The Freiburger Personality Inventory FPI]. Göttingen: Hogrefe.

Farber, S. S., Felner, R. D., & Primavera, J. (1985). Parental separation/divorce and adolescents: An examination of factors mediating adaptation. *American Journal of Community Psychology, 13*(2), 171–185.

Farrington, D. P. (1989). Long-term prediction of offending and other life outcomes. In H. Wegener, F. Lösel, & J. Haisch (Eds.), *Criminal behavior and the justice system* (pp. 26–39). New York: Springer.

Faust, J., Baum, C. G., & Forehand, R. (1985). An examination of the association between social relationships and depression in early adolescence. *Journal of Applied Developmental Psychology, 6*, 291–297.

Feffer, M. (1970). A developmental analysis of interpersonal behavior. *Psychological Review, 77*, 197–214.

Feldman, S. S., Rubenstein, J. L., & Rubin, C. (1988). Depressive affect and restraint in early adolescents: Relationships with family structure, family process and friendship support. *Journal of Early Adolescence, 8*, 279–296.

Felner, R. D., Aber, M. S., Primavera, J., & Cauce, A. M. (1985). Adaptation and vulnerability in high-risk adolescents: An examination of environmental mediators. *American Journal of Community Psychology, 13*(4), 365–379.

Fend, H., & Helmke, A. (1981). Die Konstanzer Untersuchungen über Verbreitung und Bedingungen psychischer Risikofaktoren [The Konstanz research on prevalence and conditions of psychological risk factors]. In G. Zimmer (Ed.), *Persönlichkeitsentwicklung und Gesundheit im Schulalter. Gefährdungen und Prävention* (pp. 87–112). Frankfurt: Campus.

Fend, H., & Schroer, S. (1989). Depressive Verstimmungen im Jugendalter [Depressive moods during adolescence]. *Zeitschrift für Sozialisationsforschung und Erziehungssoziologie, 4*, 264–284.

Finlay-Jones, R., & Brown, G. W. (1981). Types of stressful life event and the onset of anxiety and depressive disorders. *Psychological Medicine, 11*, 803–815.

Flavell, J. H. (1979). *Kognitive Entwicklung* [Cognitive development]. Stuttgart: Klett-Cotta.

Fleiss, J. L. (1971). Measuring nominal scale agreement among many raters. *Psychological Bulletin, 76*, 378–382.

Fleming, D., & Lavercombe, S. (1982). Talking about unemployment with school-leavers. *British Journal of Guidance and Counseling, 10*, 22–33.

Fogelman, K. (1976). Bored eleven-year-olds. *British Journal of Social Work, 6*(2), 201–211.

Folkman, S. (1984). Personal control and stress and coping processes: A theoretical analysis. *Journal of Personality and Social Psychology, 46*(4), 839–852.

Folkman, S., & Lazarus, R. S. (1980). An analysis of coping in a middle-aged community sample. *Journal of Health and Social Behaviour, 21*, 219–239.

Folkman, S., & Lazarus, R. S. (1985). If it changes it must be a process: Study of emotion and coping during three stages of a college examination. *Journal of Personality and Social Psychology, 48*, 150–170.

Folkman, S., Lazarus, R. S., Gruen, R., & DeLongis, A. (1986). Appraisal, coping, health status and psychological symptoms. *Journal of Personality and Social Psychology, 50*, 571–579.

Follansbee, D. J. (1984). Coping skills training for adolescents with insulin dependent diabetes mellitus. *Dissertation Abstracts International, 44,* 2554–2555.

Forsythe, C. J., & Compas, B. E. (1987). Interaction of cognitive appraisals of stressful events and coping: Testing the goodness of fit hypothesis. *Cognitive Therapy and Research, 11,* 473–483.

Frankel, K. (1986). *The relationship of coping and social milieu perception to self-reported depression in middle school girls.* Paper presented at the first biennial meeting of the Society for Research in Adolescence, Madison, WI.

Freud, A. (1958). Adolescence. *Psychoanalytic Study of the Child, 13,* 255–278.

Freud, S. (1917). *Trauer und Melancholie* [Grief and melancholia]. In Gesammelte Werke, Band X.

Friedrich, W., Reams, R., & Jacobs, J. (1982). Depression and suicidal ideation in early adolescents. *Journal of Youth and Adolescence, 11,* 403–407.

Furman, W., & Robins, P. (1985). What's the point: Selection of treatment objectives. In B. Schneider, K. H. Rubin, & J. E. Ledigham (Eds.), *Children's peer relations: Issues in assessment and intervention* (pp. 41–54). New York: Springer.

Garcia, D. M. (1987). *The transactional model of stress and coping: Its application to young adolescents.* Unpublished doctoral dissertation, Denver University at Denver, CO.

Garmezy, N. (1983). Stressors of childhood. In N. Garmezy & M. Rutter (Eds.), *Stress, coping and development in children* (pp. 43–84). New York: McGraw-Hill.

Garmezy, N., & Rutter, M. (Eds.). (1983). *Stress, coping and development in children.* New York: McGraw-Hill.

Garrison, W. T., & McQuiston, S. (1989). Chronic illness during childhood and adolescence. *Developmental Clinical Psychology and Psychiatry, 19.*

Gatz, M., Tyler, F. B., & Pargament, K. I. (1978). Goal attainment, locus of control, and coping style in adolescent group counseling. *Journal of Counseling Psychology, 25,* 310–319.

Geist, R. A. (1979). Onset of chronic illness in children and adolescents: Psychotherapeutic and consultative intervention. *American Journal of Orthopsychiatry, 49,* 4–23.

Gertner, C. R. (1982). Personality variables associated with response in dissonant situations. *Dissertation Abstracts International, 42,* 4558–4559.

Gibbs, J. T. (1985). Psychosocial factors associated with depression in urban adolescent females: Implications for assessment. *Journal of Youth and Adolescence, 14,* 47–60.

Giddan, N. S., & Whitner, P. A. (1989). Implications of cognitive psychology for the coping behavior of youth. *Journal of Human Behavior and Learning, 6,* 36–45.

Gilligan, C. (1982). *In a different voice: Psychological theory and women's development.* Cambridge, MA: Harvard University Press.

Gjerde, P. F., & Block, J. (1991). Preadolescent antecedents of depressive symptomatology at age 18: A prospective study. *Journal of Youth and Adolescence, 20,* 217–232.

Glyshaw, K., Cohen, L. H., & Towbes, L. C. (1989). Coping strategies and psychological distress: Prospective analyses of early and middle adolescents. *American Journal of Community Psychology, 17,* 607–623.

Goetz, A. A., & McTyre, R. B. (1981). Health risk appraisal. *Nursing Research, 30,* 307–313.

Goode, W. J., & Hatt, P. K. (1966). Beispiel für den Aufbau eines Fragebogens [Examples of the organization of a questionnaire]. In R. König (Ed.), *Das Interview* (pp. 115–124). Köln: Kiepenheuer & Witsch.

Gottlieb, B. H. (1975). The contribution of natural support systems to primary prevention among four social subgroups of adolescent males. *Adolescence, 10*(38), 207–220.

Gottman, J. M., & Parker, J. G. (Eds.). (1986). *Conversations of friends: Speculations on affective development.* Cambridge, England: Cambridge University Press.

Gove, R. R., & Herb, I. R. (1974). Stress and mental illness among the young: A comparison of sexes. *Social Forces, 53,* 256–265.

Graham, P., & Rutter, M. (1985). Adolescent disorders. In M. Rutter & L. Hersov (Eds.), *Child and adolescent psychiatry: Modern approaches* (pp. 351–367). Oxford: Blackwell Scientific.

Greenberg, M. T., Siegel, J. M., & Leitch, C. J. (1983). The nature and importance of attachment relationships to parents and peers during adolescence. *Journal of Youth and Adolescence, 12,* 373–386.

Gregory, E. H., & Stevens-Long, J. (1986). Coping skills among highly gifted adolescents. *Journal for the Education of the Gifted, 9,* 147–155.

Grennberger, E., Steinberg, L. D., & Vaux, A. (1982). Person-environment congruence as a predictor of adolescent health and behavioral problems. *American Journal of Community Psychology, 10,* 511–526.

Grinder, R. E. (1982). Isolationism in adolescent research. *Human Development, 25,* 223–232.

Grotevant, H. D., & Cooper, C. R. (1985). Patterns of interaction in family relationships and the development of identity exploration in adolescence. *Child Development, 56,* 415–428.

Grotevant, H. D., & Cooper, C. R. (1986). Individuation in family relationships. A perspective on individual differences in the development of identity and role-taking skill in adolescence. *Human Development, 29,* 82–100.

Guay, J. A., & Dusek, J. B. (1992, March). *Perceived childrearing practices and styles of coping.* Paper presented at the fourth biennial meeting of the Society for Research on Adolescence, Washington, DC.

Guillory, P. (1983). Impact of cancer on adolescents and their families. An exploration of coping responses. *Dissertation Abstracts International, 43,* 3114.

Gutman, D. L. (1970). Female ego styles and generation conflict. In J. M. Bardwich (Ed.), *Female personality and conflict* (pp. 187–196). Belmont: Brooks-Cole.

Haan, N. (1974). The adolescents' ego model of coping and defense and comparisons with Q-sorted ideal personalities. *Genetic Psychology Monographs, 89,* 273–306.

Haan, N. (1977). Coping and defending. *Processes of self-environment organization.* New York: Academic Press.

Hall, G. S. (1904). *Adolescence.* New York: Appleton.

Hamburg, B. A. (1974). Early adolescence: A specific and stressful stage of the life cycle. In G. V. Coelho, D. A. Hamburg, & J. E. Adams (Eds.), *Coping and adaptation* (pp. 101–124). New York: Basic Books.

Handel, A. (1980). Perceived change of self among adolescents. *Journal of Youth and Adolescence, 9,* 507–519.

Handel, A. (1987). Personal theories about the life-span-development of one's self in auto-biographical reconstruction of his past self. *Human Development, 33,* 289–303.

Hanson, C. L., Cigrang, J. A., Harris, M. A., & Carle, D. L. (1989). Coping styles in youths with insulin-dependent diabetes mellitus. *Journal of Consulting & Clinical Psychology, 57,* 644–651.

Hart, K. E. (1991). Coping with anger-provoking situations. *Journal of Adolescent Research, 3,* 357–370.

Harter, S. (1983). Developmental perspectives on the self-system. In P. H. Mussen & E. M. Hetherington (Eds.), *Handbook of child psychology: Socialization, personality, and social development* (Vol. 4, pp. 275–386). New York: Wiley.

Hartup, W. W. (1983). The peer system. In P. H. Mussen (Series Ed.) & E. M. Hetherington (Vol. Ed.), *Handbook of child psychology: Vol. 4. Socialization, personality and social development* (pp. 103–106). New York: Wiley.

Hartup, W. W. (1989). Social relationships and their developmental significance. *American Psychologist, 2,* 120–126.

Hartup, W. W. (1992). Conflict and friendship relations. In C. U. Shantz & W. W. Hartup (Eds.), *Conflict in child and adolescent development* (pp. 186–215). Cambridge: Cambridge University Press.

Hauser, S. T. (1991). *Adolescents and their families. Paths of ego development.* New York: The Free Press.

Hauser, S. T., Borman, E. H., Jacobson, A. M., Powers, S., & Noam, G. (1991). Understanding family contexts of adolescent coping: A study of parental ego development and adolescent coping strategies. *Journal of Early Adolescence, 11,* 96–124.

Hauser, S. T., & Bowlds, M. K. (1990). Stress, coping and adaptation. In S. S. Feldman & G. R. Elliot (Eds.), *At the threshold. The developing adolescent* (pp. 388–413). Cambridge, MA: Harvard University Press.

Hauser, S. T., DiPlacido, J., Jacobson, A. M., Willett, J., & Cole, C. (1993). Family coping with an adolescent's chronic illness: An approach and three studies. *Journal of Adolescence, 16*, 305–329.

Hauser, S. T., Jacobson, A. M., Noam, G., & Powers, S. (1983). Ego-development and self-image complexity in early adolescence. Personality studies of psychiatric and diabetic patients. *Archives of General Psychiatry, 40*, 325–332.

Hauser, S. T., Powers, S., Noam, G., Jacobson, A. M., Weiss, B., & Follansbee, D. (1984). Family contexts of adolescent ego development. *Child Development, 55*, 195–213.

Hauser, S. T., & Shapiro, R. L. (1976). An approach to the analysis of faculty-student interactions in small groups. *Human Relations, 29*, 819–832.

Havighurst, R. J. (1953). *Human development and education.* New York: Longmans, Green.

Hawkins, R. O. (1982). Adolescent alcohol abuse: A review. *Journal of Developmental and Behavioral Pediatrics, 3*(2), 83–87.

Hendricks, L. E. (1980). Unwed adolescent fathers: Problems they face and their sources of social support. *Adolescence, 15*, 861–869.

Herman, M. A., Stemmler, M., & Petersen, A. C. (1992). *Approach versus avoidant coping: Implications for adolescent development.* Unpublished manuscript, Pennsylvania State University at University Park.

Herzog, W. (1987). Problemschilderung und Problembewältigung bei Jugendlichen mit erhöhter Problembelastung [Problem description and coping with adolescents with increased stress]. *Zeitschrift für Entwicklungspsychologie und Pädagogische Psychologie, 19*, 143–157.

Hetzer, H. (1982). Kinder- und jugendpsychologische Forschung am Wiener Psychologischen Institut von 1922 bis 1938 [Research on child and adolescent psychology at the Psychological Institute of Vienna from 1922 to 1938]. *Zeitschrift für Entwicklungspsychologie und Pädagogische Psychologie, 14*, 175–224.

Hill, J. P. (1987). Research on adolescents and their families: Past and prospect. In C. E. Irwin (Ed.), *Adolescent social behavior and health* (pp. 13–31). San Francisco: Jossey-Bass.

Hill, J. P., & Holmbeck, G. N. (1986). Attachment and autonomy. *Annals of Child Development, 3*, 145–189.

Hirsch, B., Moos, R. H., & Reischl, T. (1985). Psychosocial adjustment of adolescent children of a depressed, arthritic, or normal parent. *Journal of Abnormal Psychology, 94*, 154–164.

Hjorth, C. W., & Ostrov, E. (1982). The self-image of physically abused adolescents. *Journal of Youth and Adolescence, 11*, 71–76.

Hofmann, A. D., & Becker, R. D. (1979). Psychotherapeutic approaches to the physically ill adolescent. *International Journal of Child Psychotherapy, 2*, 492–511.

Holahan, C. J., & Moos, R. H. (1987). The personal and contextual determinants of coping strategies. *Journal of Personality and Social Psychology, 52*, 946–955.

Holbrook, S. M. (1978). Coping in adolescence: Some differences between males and females. *Issues in Ego-Psychology, 1*(1), 9–10.

Holmes, T. H., & Rahe, R. H. (1967). The Social Readjustment Rating Scale. *Journal of Psychosomatic Research, 11*, 213–218.

Holsti, O. R. (1969). *Content analysis for the social sciences and humanities.* Reading, MA: Addison-Wesley.

Honess, T., & Edwards, A. (1990). Selves in relation: School-leavers' accommodation to different interpersonal and situational demands. In H. Bosma & A. E. Jackson (Eds.), *Coping and self-concept in adolescence* (pp. 69–86). Heidelberg: Springer.

Hormuth, S. E., & Archer, R. I. (1986). Selbstenthüllung im Lichte der sozialpsychologischen Selbstkonzeptforschung [Self disclosure in the light of social-psychological research on self concept]. In A. Spitznagel & I. Schmidt-Atzert (Eds.), *Sprechen und Schweigen. Zur Psychologie der Selbstenthüllung* (pp. 123–142). Bern: Huber.

Houston, J. P. (1977). Cheating behavior, anticipated success-failure, confidence, and test importance. *Journal of Educational Psychology*, 69(1), 55–60.

Hultsch, D. F., & Cornelius, S. W. (1981). Kritische Lebensereignisse und lebenslange Entwicklung: Methodologische Aspekte [Critical life events and life-span development: Methodological aspects]. In S. H. Filipp (Ed.), *Kritische Lebensereignisse* (pp. 72–91). München: Urban & Schwarzenberg.

Hunter, F. T., & Youniss, J. (1982). Changes in functions of three relations during adolescence. *Developmental Psychology*, 18, 806–811.

Hurrelmann, K. (1990). Health promotion for adolescents: Preventive and corrective strategies against problem behavior. *Journal of Adolescence*, 13, 231–250.

Hurrelmann, K., & Engel, U. (1989). *The social world of adolescents. International perspectives*. Berlin: De Gruyter.

Hussain, S. E., Gulati, P. V., Singh, K. P., & Moni, G. S. (1976). Psychological background of unwed motherhood. *Indian Journal of Clinical Psychology*, 3, 183–187.

Ilfeld, F. W. (1980). Coping styles of Chicago adults: Description. *Journal of Human Stress*, 6, 2–10.

Isherwood, J., Adam, K. S., & Hornblow, A. R. (1982). Life event stress, psychosocial factors, suicide attempt and auto-accident proclivity. *Journal of Psychosomatic Research*, 26, 371–383.

Jacks, K. B., & Keller, M. E. (1978). A humanistic approach to the adolescent with learning disabilities: An educational, psychological and vocational model. *Adolescence*, 13, 59–68.

Jackson, S., & Rodriguez-Tomé, H. (1993). Adolescence: Expanding a social world. In S. Jackson & H. Rodriguez-Tomé (Eds.), *The social worlds of adolescence* (pp. 47–66). Hillsdale, NJ: Lawrence Erlbaum Associates.

Jacobson, S., Fasman, J., & DiMarcio, A. (1975). Deprivation in the childhood of depressed women. *Journal of Nervous and Mental Disease*, 160, 5–14.

Jacovetta, R. G. (1975). Adolescent–adult interaction and peer group involvement. *Adolescence*, 10, 327–336.

Jerusalem, M. (1992). Akkulturationsstreß und psychosoziale Befindlichkeit jugendlicher Ausländer [Stress of acculturation and psychosocial well-being of adolescent foreigners]. *Report Psychologie*, 2, 16–23.

Jessor, S. J., & Jessor, R. (1977). *Problem behavior and psychosocial development: A longitudinal study of youth*. New York: Academic Press.

Johnson, J. H. (1986). *Life events as stressors in childhood and adolescence*. Beverly Hills, CA: Sage.

Johnson, J. H., & Bradlyn, A. S. (1988). Assessing stressful life events in childhood and adolescence. In P. Karoly (Ed.), *Handbook of child health assessment: Biopsychosocial perspectives* (pp. 303–331). New York: Wiley.

Johnson, J. H., & McCutcheon, S. M. (1980). Assessing life stress in older children and adolescents. Preliminary findings with the Life Events Checklist. In O. Sarason & C. D. Spielberger (Eds.), *Stress and anxiety* (pp. 230–241). Washington, DC: Hemisphere.

Johnson, R. (1978). Youth in crisis: Dimensions of self-destructive conduct among adolescent prisoners. *Adolescence*, 13, 461–482.

Kahn, R. L., & Antonucci, I. C. (1980). Convoys over life course: Attachment, roles, and social support. In R. V. Baltes & O. G. J. Brim (Eds.), *Life-span development and behavior* (Vol. 3, pp. 254–287). New York: Academic Press.

Kandel, D. B. (1986). Processes of peer influences in adolescence. In R. K. Silbereisen, K. Eyferth, & G. Rudinger (Eds.), *Development as action in context* (pp. 203–228). Berlin & New York: Springer.

Kandel, D. B., & Davies, M. (1982). Epidemiology of depressive mood in adolescents. *Archives of General Psychiatry*, 39, 1205–1212.

Kanner, A. D., Coyne, J. C., Schaefer, C., & Lazarus, R. S. (1981). Comparison of two modes of stress measurement: Daily hassles and uplifts versus major life events. *Journal of Behavioral Medicine*, 4, 1–39.

Kanner, A. D., Feldman, S. S., Weinberger, D. A., & Ford, M. E. (1987). Uplifts, hassles, and adaptational outcomes in early adolescents. Journal of Early Adolescence, 7(4), 371–394.

Kaplan, H., Robbins, C., & Martin, S. (1983). Antecedents of psychological distress in young adults: Self-rejection, deprivation of social support, and life events. Journal of Health and Social Behavior, 24, 230–244.

Kelly, J. G. (1979). Exploratory behavior, socialization, and the high school environment. In J. G. Kelly (Ed.), Adolescent boys in high school: Coping and adaptation (pp. 245–256). Hillsdale, NJ: Lawrence Erlbaum Associates.

Keltikangas-Jarvinen, L., & Jokinen, J. (1989). Type A behavior, coping mechanisms and emotions related to somatic risk factors of coronary heart disease in adolescents. Journal of Psychosomatic Research, 33, 17–27.

Kessler, R. C., Price, R. H., & Wortman, C. B. (1985). Social factors in psychopathology: Stress, social support and coping processes. Annual Review of Psychology, 36, 531–572.

Kikuchi, J. (1977). An adolescent boy's adjustment to leukemia. Maternal Child Nursing Journal, 6, 37–49.

Kliewer, W. (1991). Coping in middle childhood: Relations to competence, Type A behavior, monitoring, blunting, and locus of control. Developmental Psychology, 27(4), 689–697.

Klingman, A., Goldstein, Z., & Lerner, P. (1991). Adolescents' responses to nuclear threat: Before and after the Chernobyl accident. Journal of Youth and Adolescence, 20, 519–530.

Kobasa, S. C. (1982). Commitment and coping in stress resistance among lawyers. Journal of Personality and Social Psychology, 42, 707–717.

Kobasa, S. C., Maddi, S. R., & Kahn, S. (1982). Hardiness and health: A prospective study. Journal of Personality and Social Psychology, 42, 168–177.

Koch, S. J. (1977). The interest and concerns of adolescents, grade seven through twelve, as expressed in their written composition. Dissertation Abstracts International, 37, 7729–7730.

Kossakowski, A. (1974). Social norms as determinants of adolescent behavior. Contributions to Human Development, 1, 80–89.

Kovacs, M. (1989). Affective disorders in children and adolescents. American Psychologist, 44, 209–215.

Krohne, H. W. (1990). Stress und Stressbewältigung [Stress and coping]. In R. Schwarzer (Ed.), Gesundheitspsychologie (pp. 263–277). Göttingen: Hogrefe.

Küppers, W. (1964). Mädchentagebücher der Nachkriegszeit. Ein kritischer Beitrag zum sogenannten Wandel der Jugend [Girls' diaries of the postwar time. A critical contribution on the so-called change of youth]. Stuttgart: Klett.

Kurdek, L. A. (1987). Gender differences in the psychological symptomatology and coping strategies of young adolescents. Journal of Early Adolescence, 7, 395–410.

Labouvie, E. W. (1986). The coping function of adolescent alcohol and drug use. In R. K. Silbereisen, K. Eyferth, & G. Rudinger (Eds.), Development as action in context (pp. 229–240). Berlin: Springer.

Lammert, M. (1988). Situational life changes: A model for coping with stress in adolescence. Child and Adolescent Social Work Journal, 5, 54–68.

Lamont, J., & Gottlieb, H. (1976). Convergent recall of parental behaviors in depressed students of different racial groups. Journal of Clinical Psychology, 32, 9–11.

Larsson, B., Melin, L., Breitholtz, E., & Andersson, G. (1991). Short-term stability of depressive symptoms and suicide attempts in Swedish adolescents. Acta Psychiatrica Scandinavica, 83, 385–390.

Laufer, R., & Wolfe, M. (1974). The concept of privacy in childhood and adolescence. In D. H. Larson (Ed.), Man–environment interactions (Proceedings of EDRA) (pp. 29–54). Washington, DC: Environmental Design Research Association.

Laursen, B. (1990). Contextual variations in adolescent conflict. Unpublished manuscript, University of Victoria, University of Maine.

Laursen, B. (Ed.). (1993). Close friendships in adolescence. New directions for child development (No. 60). San Francisco: Jossey-Bass.

Lazarus, R. S. (1966). *Psychological stress and the coping process.* New York: McGraw-Hill.

Lazarus, R. S. (1976). *Patterns of adjustment.* New York: McGraw-Hill.

Lazarus, R. S. (1981). Stress und Stressbewältigung - ein Paradigma [Stress and coping - a paradigm]. In S.-H. Filipp (ed.), *Kritische Lebensereignisse* (pp. 198–229). München: Urban & Schwarzenberg.

Lazarus, R. S. (1985). The trivialization of distress. In P. J. Ahmed & N. Ahmed (Eds.), *Coping with juvenile diabetes* (pp. 33–60). Springfield: Charles C. Thomas.

Lazarus, R. S. (1990). Theory-based stress measurement. *Psychological Inquiry, 1,* 3–13.

Lazarus, R. S., Averill, J., & Opton, E. (1974). The psychology of coping: Issues of research and assessment. In G. V. Coelho, D. A. Hamburg, & J. E. Adams (Eds.), *Coping and adaptation* (pp. 249–315). New York: Basic Books.

Lazarus, R. S., DeLongis, A., Folkman, S., & Gruen, R. (1985). Stress and adaptational outcomes: The problem of confounded measures. *American Psychologist, 40,* 770–779.

Lazarus, R. S., & Folkman, S. (1984). *Stress, appraisal and coping.* New York: Springer.

Lazarus, R. S., & Folkman, S. (1987). Transactional theory and research on emotions and coping. *European Journal of Personality, 1,* 141–169.

Lazarus, R. S., & Folkman, S. (1991). *Stress, appraisal, and coping.* New York: Springer.

Lazarus, R. S., & Launier, R. (1978). Stress-related transactions between person and environment. In L. Pervin & M. Lewis (Eds.), *Perspectives in interactional psychology* (pp. 287–327). New York: Plenum.

LePontois, J. (1975). Adolescents with sickle-cell anemia deal with life and death. *Social Work in Health Care, 1,* 71–80.

Lerner, R. M., & Busch-Rossnagel, N. A. (Eds.). (1981). *Individuals as producers of their own development: A life-span perspective.* New York: Academic Press.

Lewin, K. (1968). *Resolving social conflicts.* New York: Harper & Row.

Lewinsohn, P. M., & Rosenbaum, M. (1987). Recall of parental behavior by acute depressives, remitted depressives, and nondepressives. *Journal of Personality and Social Psychology, 52,* 611–619.

Lewinsohn, P. M., & Talkington, J. (1979). Studies on the measurement of unpleasant events and relations with depression. *Applied Psychological Measurement, 3,* 83–101.

Lewis, J. M. (1986). Family structure and stress. *Family Process, 25,* 235–247.

Lieberman, M. A. (1975). Adaptive processes in late life. In N. Datan & L. H. Ginsberg (Eds.), *Life-span developmental psychology: Normative life crises* (pp. 135–161). New York: Academic Press.

Lipets, M. S. (1984). The effect of juvenile diabetic camping on self-esteem and locus of control. *Dissertation Abstracts International, 45,* 676–677.

Lösel, F. (1983). Entwicklungsstörungen sozialen Verhaltens [Developmental disorders of social behavior]. In J. J. Kerner, H. Kury, & K. Sessar (Eds.), *Deutsche Forschungen zur Kriminalitätsentstehung und Kriminalitätskontrolle* (pp. 595–616). Köln: Heymanns.

Lösel, F., & Bliesener, T. (1990). Resilience in adolescence. In K. Hurrelmann & F. Lösel (Eds.), *Health hazards in adolescence* (pp. 299–320). Berlin: de Gruyter.

Lösel, F., Bliesener, T., & Köferl, P. (1991). Erlebens- und Verhaltensprobleme bei Jugendlichen: Deutsche Adaptation und kulturvergleichende Überprüfung der Youth Self-Report Form der CBCL [Adolescents' problems with perception of events and behavior: German adaptation and cross-cultural examination of the Youth Self-Report Form of the CBCL]. *Zeitschrift für Klinische Psychologie, 20,* 22–51.

Luborsky, L. (1977). Measuring a pervasive psychic structure in psychotherapy: The core conflictual relationship theme. In N. Friedman & S. Grant (Eds.), *Communicative structures and psychic structures* (pp. 367–395). New York: Plenum.

Lynch, D. J., & Arndt, C. (1973). Developmental changes in response to frustration among physically handicapped children. *Journal of Personality Assessment, 37,* 130–135.

Lynd, R. S., & Lynd, H. M. (1929). *Middletown.* New York: Harcourt Brace Jovanovich.

MacQueen, J. (1967). Some methods for classification and analysis of multivariate observations. *5th Berkeley Symp. Math., Stat. Prov., 1,* 281–292.

Magnusson, D. (1980). Personality in an interactional paradigm of research. *Zeitschrift für Differentielle und Diagnostische Psychologie, 1,* 17–34.

Magnusson, D. (1982). Situational determinants of stress: An interactional perspective. In L. Goldenberger & S. Breznitz (Eds.), *Handbook of stress, theoretical and clinical aspects* (pp. 231–253). New York: The Free Press.

Magnusson, D., & Olah, A. (1983). *Predictive control, action control, coping styles and state anxiety: An analysis of individuals and situations* (Rep. No. 613). Stockholm: Department of Psychology, University of Stockholm.

Malaviya, D. (1977). A study of reaction to frustration. *Indian Educational Review, 12,* 71–87.

Malless, G. C. (1978). Acquisition of social systems coping behavior: The effect of verbal instruction, behavior rehearsal, verbal warning, and the sex of subjects. *Dissertation Abstracts International, 38,* 3958–3959.

Malmquist, C. P. (1986). Children who witness parental murder: Posttraumatic aspects. *Journal of the American Academy of Child Psychiatry, 25,* 320–325.

Mar'i, S. K., & Levi, A. M. (1979). Modernization or minority status: The coping style of Israel's Arabs. *Journal of Cross-Cultural Psychology, 10*(3), 375–389.

Marotz-Baden, R., & Colvin, P. L. (1989). Adaptability, cohesion, and coping strategies of unemployed blue-collar families with adolescents. *Lifestyles, 10,* 44–60.

McCombie, E. L. (1976). Characteristics of rape victims seen in crisis intervention. *Smith College Studies in Social Work, 46,* 137–158.

McCrae, R. R. (1982). Age differences in the use of coping mechanisms. *Journal of Gerontology, 37,* 454–460.

McCrae, R. R. (1984). Situational determinants of coping responses: Loss, threat and challenge. *Journal of Personality and Social Psychology, 46,* 919–928.

McCune, N. (1988). Deaf in a hearing unit: Coping of staff and adolescents. *Journal of Adolescence, 11,* 21–28.

McKay, M. M. (1977). Adolescent problems: An examination of the rank comparison of the latent categories of problems as defined and ordered by high school students. *Dissertation Abstracts International, 38,* 3193.

Mechanic, D. (1962). *Students under stress.* New York: The Free Press.

Mehler, F. (1986). Zwischen Resignation, Verweigerung und Selbstausgrenzung. Subjektive Verarbeitungen von Jugendarbeitslosigkeit [Between resignation, denial, and self exclosure]. *Psychosozial, 14,* 130–145.

Mehler, J. F. (1979). Houseparents: A vignette. *Child Care Quarterly, 8,* 174–178.

Meichenbaum, D. (1977). *Cognitive behavior modification—an integrative approach.* New York: Plenum Press.

Meichenbaum, D., Henshaw, D., & Himel, N. (1982). Coping with stress as a problem-solving process. *Series in Clinical and Community Psychology: Stress and Anxiety, 8,* 127–142.

Meier, H. (1984). Persönlichkeitspsychologische Untersuchungen bei Diabetikern [Personality psychological research with diabetics]. In H. Schröder (Ed.), *Beiträge zur Pathopsychologie der Persönlichkeit* (pp. 102–120). Leipzig: Barth.

Merikangas, K., & Angst, J. (1992, November). *The challenge of depressive disorders in adolescence.* Paper presented at the conference "Youth in the Year 2000," Marbach Castle, Germany.

Merz, J. (1982). *Persönlichkeit und Copingstile* [Personality and coping style]. Diplomarbeit, Department of Psychology, University of Gießen, Germany.

Meyers, J., & Pitt, N. W. (1976). A consultation approach to help a school cope with the bereavement process. *Professional Psychology, 7,* 559–564.

Miller, P. H., Kessel, F. S., & Flavell, J. H. (1970). Thinking about people thinking about people thinking about . . . : A study of social cognitive development. *Child Development, 41,* 613–623.

Minde, K. K. (1978). Coping styles of 34 adolescents with cerebral palsy. *American Journal of Psychiatry, 135,* 1344–1349.

Mink, I. T., Nihira, K., & Meyers, C. E. (1983). Taxonomy of family life styles: I. Homes with TCR children. *American Journal of Mental Deficiency, 87*, 484–493.

Moffatt, J. E. (1975). A study of family stress during infancy as an independent cause of social adjustment and behavior problems at early adolescence. *Dissertation Abstracts International, 35*, 6168–6169.

Mönks, F. J. (1968). Future time perspective in adolescence. *Human Development, 11*, 107–123.

Monroe, S. M., & Simons, A. D. (1991). Diathesis-stress theories in the context of life stress research: Implications for depressive disorders. *Psychological Bulletin, 110*, 406–425.

Montemayor, R. (1982). The relationship between parent-adolescent conflict and the amount of time adolescents spend alone and with parents and peers. *Child Development, 53*, 1512–1519.

Montemayor, R. (1983). Parents and adolescents in conflict: All families some of the time and some families most of the time. *Journal of Early Adolescence, 3*, 83–103.

Montemayor, R. (1986). Family variation in parent-adolescent storm and stress. *Journal of Adolescent Research, 1*, 15–31.

Montemayor, R., & Hanson, E. (1985). A naturalistic view of conflict between adolescents and their parents and siblings. *Journal of Early Adolescence, 5*, 23–30.

Moore, D. (1987). Parent–adolescent separation: The construction of adulthood by late adolescents. *Developmental Psychology, 23*, 298–307.

Moore, S., & Rosenthal, D. (1993). *Sexuality in adolescence* (Adolescence and Society Series). London: Routledge.

Moos, R. H. (1974). *The human context: Environment determinations of behavior.* New York: Wiley.

Moos, R. H. (Ed.). (1976). *Human adaptation: Coping with life crises.* Lexington: Heath.

Moos, R. H., & Billings, A. G. (1982). Children of alcoholics during the recovery process: Alcoholic and matched control families. *Addictive Behaviors, 7*, 155–163.

Moos, R. H., Brennan, P., Fondacaro, M., & Moos, B. S. (1990). Approach and avoidance coping responses among older problem and nonproblem drinkers. *Psychology and Aging, 5*, 31–40.

Moos, R. H., & Moos, B. S. (1976). A typology of family social environments. *Family Process, 15*, 357–371.

Moos, R. H., & Moos, B. S. (1981). *Family Environment Scale Manual.* Palo Alto, CA: Consulting Psychologists Press.

Moran, P. B., & Eckenrode, J. (1991). Gender differences in costs and benefits of peer relations during adolescence. *Journal of Adolescent Research, 6*, 396–409.

Morawetz, A. (1982). The impact on adolescents of the death in war of an older sibling: A group experience. *Series in Clinical and Community Psychology: Stress and Anxiety, 8*, 267–274.

Moriarty, A. E., & Toussieng, P. W. (1975). Adolescence in a time of transition. *Bulletin of the Menninger Clinic, 39*, 391–408.

Moriarty, A. E., & Toussieng, P. W. (1976). *Adolescent coping.* New York: Grune & Stratton.

Morrison, D. M. (1985). Adolescent contraceptive behavior. A review. *Psychological Bulletin, 98*, 538–568.

Mullins, L., Siegel, L., & Hodges, K. (1985). Cognitive problem solving and life-event correlates of depressive symptoms in children. *Journal of Abnormal Child Psychology, 13*, 305–314.

Murch, R. L., & Cohen, L. H. (1989). Relationships among life stress, perceived family environment, and the psychological distress of spina bifida adolescents. *Journal of Pediatric Psychology, 14*(2), 193–214.

Murgatroyd, S. (1982). "Coping" and the crisis counsellor. *British Journal of Guidance and Counselling, 10*(2), 151–166.

Murphy, L. B., & Moriarty, A. E. (1976). *Vulnerability, coping and growth from infancy to adolescence.* New Haven, CT: Yale University Press.

Myers, W. A. (1976). Imaginary companions, fantasy twins, mirror dreams, and depersonalization. *Psychoanalytic Quarterly, 45*, 503–523.

Myers, W. A. (1979). Imaginary companions in childhood and adult creativity. *Psychoanalytic Quarterly, 48*, 292–307.

Neisser, U. (1976). Cognition and reality. Reading: Freeman.

Neugarten, B. L. (1979). Time, age, and the life cycle. American Journal of Psychiatry, 136, 887–894.

Newcomb, N. D., Huba, G. J., & Bentler, P. M. (1981). A multidimensional assessment of stressful life events among adolescents. Journal of Health and Social Behavior, 22, 400–415.

Newcomb, N. D., Huba, G. J., & Bentler, P. M. (1986). Desirability of various life change events among adolescents: Effects of exposure, sex, age and ethnicity. Journal of Research in Personality, 20, 207–227.

Newman, B. M., & Newman, P. R. (1975). Development through life. A psychosocial approach. Homewood, IL: Dorsey Press.

Nisbett, R. E., Caputo, C., Legant, P., & Marecek, J. (1973). Behavior as seen by the actor and seen by the observer. Journal of Personality and Social Psychology, 27, 154–164.

Nisbett, R. E., & Wilson, T. D. (1977). Telling more than we know: Verbal reports of mental processes. Psychological Review, 84, 231–259.

Nolen-Hoeksema, S. (1987). Sex differences in unipolar depression: Evidence and theory. Psychological Bulletin, 101, 259–282.

Nolen-Hoeksema, S. (1991). Responses to depression and their effects on the duration of depressive episodes. Journal of Abnormal Psychology, 100, 569–582.

Norell, J. E. (1984). Self-disclosure: Implications for the study of parent-adolescent interaction. Journal of Youth and Adolescence, 13, 163–177.

Nuckolls, K. B. (1972). Psychological assets, life crises, and the prognosis of pregnancy. American Journal of Epidemiology, 95, 431–441.

Oerter, R. (1977). Ein ökologisches Modell kognitiver Sozialisation [An ecological model of cognitive socialization]. Unterrichtswissenschaft, 6, 34–44.

Oerter, R. (1978). Zur Dynamik von Entwicklungsaufgaben im menschlichen Lebenslauf [On the dynamics of developmental tasks in human life-span development]. In R. Oerter (Ed.), Entwicklung als lebenslanger Prozeß (pp. 66–110). Hamburg: Hoffmann & Campe.

Oerter, R. (Ed.). (1985). Daseinsbewältigung im Jugendalter [Coping in adolescence]. Weinheim: VCH Edition Psychologie.

Offer, D. (1984). Das Selbstbild normaler Jugendlicher [The self-concept of normal adolescents]. In E. Olbrich & E. Todt (Eds.), Probleme des Jugendalters (pp. 111–131). Berlin: Springer.

Offer, D., & Offer, J. (1975). From teenage to young manhood. A psychological study. New York: Basic Books.

Offer, D., Ostrov, J. D., & Howard, K. I. (1989). Adolescence: What is normal? American Journal of Diseases of Children, 143, 731–736.

O'Hare, M. M., & Tamburri, E. (1986). Coping as a moderator of the relation between anxiety and career decision making. Journal of Counseling Psychology, 33(3), 255–264.

Olah, A., Törestad, B., & Magnusson, D. (1984). Coping behaviors in relation to frequency and intensity of anxiety provoking situations (Rep. No. 629). Department of Psychology, University of Stockholm.

Olbrich, E., & Todt, E. (Eds.). (1984). Probleme des Jugendalters: Neuere Ansätze [Problems of adolescence. New perspectives]. Berlin: Springer.

Palmonari, A., Pombeni, M. L., & Kirchler, E. (1990). Adolescents and their peer groups: A study on the significance of peers, social categorization processes and coping with developmental tasks. Social Behaviour, 5, 33–48.

Panzarine, S. (1985). Coping: Conceptual and methodological issues. Advances in Nursing Science, 7, 49–57.

Panzarine, S. (1986). Stressors, coping and social supports of adolescent mothers. Journal of Adolescent Health Care, 7, 153–161.

Parker, G. (1979). Parental characteristics related to depressive disorders. British Journal of Psychiatry, 134, 138–147.

Parker, J. G., & Asher, R. S. (1987). Peer relations and later personal adjustment: Are low-accepted children at risk? Psychological Bulletin, 102, 357–389.

Parker, J. G., & Gottman, J. M. (1989). Social and emotional development in a relational context. In T. J. Berndt & G. W. Ladd (Eds.), Peer relationships in child development (pp. 95–107). New York: Wiley.

Parkes, K. (1984). Cognition, cognitive appraisal and coping in stressful episodes. Journal of Personality and Social Psychology, 46, 655–668.

Parks, A. (1977). Children and youth of parents in divorce or without parents. Journal of Clinical Child Psychology, 6, 44–48.

Parry, G., Shapiro, D. A., & Davies, L. (1981). Reliability of life-event ratings: An independent replication. British Journal of Clinical Psychology, 20(2), 133–134.

Partington, J. T., & Grant, C. (1984). Imaginary playmates and other useful fantasies. In P. K. Smith (Ed.), Play in animals and humans (pp. 217–240). Oxford: Basil Blackwell.

Patterson, J. M., & McCubbin, H. I. (1987). Adolescent coping style and behaviors: Conceptualization and measurement. Journal of Adolescence, 10, 163–186.

Patton, A. C., Ventura, J. N., & Savedra, M. (1986). Stress and coping responses of adolescents with cystic fibrosis. Children's Health Care, 14, 153–156.

Payton, J. B., & Krocker-Tuskan, M. (1988). Children's reaction to loss of parent through violence. Journal of American Academy of Child and Adolescent Psychiatry, 27, 563–566.

Pearlin, L. J., & Schooler, C. (1978). The structure of coping. Journal of Health and Social Behavior, 19, 2–21.

Pervin, L. A. (1976). A free-response description approach to the analysis of person-situation-interaction. Journal of Personality and Social Psychology, 34, 465–474.

Petersen, A. C. (1988). Adolescent development. Annual Review of Psychology, 39, 583–607.

Petersen, A. C., & Crockett, L. J. (1985). Pubertal timing and grade effects on adjustment. Journal of Youth and Adolescence, 14, 191–206.

Petersen, A. C., & Ebata, A. T. (1987). Developmental transitions and adolescent problem behavior: Implications for prevention and intervention. In K. Hurrelmann, F. X. Kaufmann, & F. Lösel (Eds.), Social intervention: Potential and constraints (pp. 167–184). New York: Walter de Gruyter.

Petersen, A. C., Sarigiani, P. A., & Kennedy, R. E. (1991). Adolescent depression: Why more girls? Journal of Youth and Adolescence, 20, 247–271.

Petersen, A. C., & Spiga, R. (1982). Adolescence and stress. In L. Goldberger & S. Breznitz (Eds.), Handbook of stress. Theoretical and clinical aspects (pp. 515–528). New York & London: The Free Press.

Peterson, L., Mullins, L., & Ridley-Johnson, R. (1985). Childhood depression: Peer reactions to depression and life stress. Journal of Abnormal Child Psychology, 13, 597–610.

Petti, Th. A., & Wells, K. (1980). Crisis treatment of a preadolescent who accidentally killed his twin. American Journal of Psychotherapy, 34, 434–443.

Phares, V., Compas, B. E., & Howell, D. C. (1989). Perspectives on child behavior problems: Comparisons of children's self-reports with parent and teacher reports. Psychological Assessment: A Journal of Consulting and Clinical Psychology, 1, 68–71.

Piaget, J. (1951). Play, dreams, and imitation in childhood. New York: Norton.

Piaget, J. (1972). Intellectual evolution from adolescence to adulthood. Human Development, 15, 1–12.

Piers, E., Daniels, J., & Quakenbush, J. (1960). Identification of creativity in adolescents. Journal of Educational Psychology, 51, 346–351.

Raffaelli, M., & Duckett, E. (1989). "We were just talking . . .": Conversations in early adolescence. Journal of Youth and Adolescence, 18, 567–582.

Raskin, A., Boothe, H. H., Reatig, N. A., Schulterbrandt, J. G., & Odel, D. (1971). Factor analyses of normal and depressed patients' memories of parental behavior. Psychological Reports, 29, 871–879.

Rauste-von Wright, M., von Wright, J., & Frankenhaeuser, M. (1981). Relationships between sex-related psychological characteristics during adolescence and catecholamine excretion during achievement stress. Psychophysiology, 18(4), 362–370.

Reinhard, H. G. (1986). Depressive Herabgestimmtheit und Daseinsbewältigung im Jugendalter [Depressive mood and coping in adolescence]. Nervenarzt, 57, 354–359.

Reinhard, H. G. (1989). Defending and coping in psychically disturbed adolescents: I. Theory, results of factor analysis. Acta Paedopsychiatrica, 52, 232–240.

Reischl, T. M., & Hirsch, B. J. (1989). Identity commitment and coping with a difficult developmental transition. Journal of Youth and Adolescence, 18, 55–69.

Reiss, D. (1981). The family's construction of reality. Cambridge, MA: Harvard University Press.

Reiss, D., & Oliveri, M. E. (1980). Family paradigm and family coping: A proposal for linking the family's intrinsic adaptive capacities to its responses to stress. Family Relations, 29, 431–444.

Remmers, H. (1962). Cross-cultural studies of teenager problems. Journal of Educational Psychology, 53, 254–261.

Remmers, H., & Shimberg, B. (1954). SRA Youth Inventory (form S). Chicago: Science Research Associates.

Rice, K. G., Herman, M. A., & Petersen, A. C. (1993). Coping with challenge in adolescence: A conceptual model and psycho-educational intervention. Journal of Adolescence, 16, 235–252.

Richardson, R. A., Galambos, N. L., Schulenberg, J. E., & Petersen, A. C. (1984). Young adolescents' perceptions of the family environment. Journal of Early Adolescence, 4, 131–151.

Richman, J., & Flaherty, J. (1985). Coping and depression: The relative contribution of internal and external resources during a life cycle transition. Journal of Nervous and Mental Disease, 173, 590–595.

Rim, Y. (1985). Personality and values revisited. Personality and Individual Differences, 6(6), 779–780.

Rim, Y. (1986). Ways of coping, personality, age, sex and family structural variables. Personality and Individual Differences, 7(1), 113–116.

Ritchie, K. (1981). Research note: Interactions in the families of epileptic children. Journal of Child Psychology and Psychiatry and Allied Disciplines, 22, 65–71.

Rivenbark, W. H. (1971). Self-disclosure among adolescents. Psychological Reports, 28, 35–42.

Robertson, J. F., & Simons, R. L. (1989). Family factors, self-esteem, and adolescent depression. Journal of Marriage and the Family, 51, 125–138.

Rodin, J. (1980). Managing the stress of aging: The role of control and coping. In S. Levine & H. Ursin (Eds.), Coping and health (pp. 120–133). New York: Plenum Press.

Rogers, R. (1970). The "unmotivated" adolescent patient who wants psychotherapy. American Journal of Psychotherapy, 24, 411–418.

Roos, J. P. (1988). Behind the happiness barrier. Social Indicators Research, 20(2), 141–163.

Roosa, M. W., Beals, J., Sandler, I. N., & Pillow, D. R. (1990). The role of risk and protective factors in predicting symptomatology in adolescent self-identified children of alcoholic parents. American Journal of Community Psychology, 18, 725–741.

Roscoe, B., Krug, K., & Schmidt, J. (1985). Written forms of self-expression utilized by adolescents. Adolescence, 20, 841–844.

Roskies, E., & Lazarus, R. S. (1980). Coping theory and the teaching of coping skills. In P. O. Davidson & J. M. Davidson (Eds.), Behavioral medicine. Changing health lifestyles (pp. 38–69). New York: Brunner & Mazel.

Roth, S., & Cohen, L. J. (1986). Approach, avoidance, and coping with stress. American Psychologist, 41(7), 813–819.

Rouse, B. A., Waller, P. F., & Ewing, J. A. (1973). Adolescents' stress levels, coping activities and father's drinking behavior. Proceedings of the 81st Annual Convention of the American Psychological Association, 8, 683–684.

Rowlinson, R. T., & Felner, R. D. (1988). Major life events, hassles, and adaptation in adolescence: Confounding in the conceptualization and measurement of life stress and adjustment revisited. Journal of Personality and Social Psychology, 55, 432–444.

Russel, C. S., Olson, D. H., & Sprenkle, D. H. (1979). Circumplex model of marital and family systems. III. Empirical evaluation with families. Family Process, 18, 29–45.

Rutter, M. (1983). Stress, coping, and development. In N. Garmezy & M. Rutter (Eds.), *Stress, coping, and development in children* (pp. 1–43). New York: McGraw Hill.

Rutter, M. (1985a). Psychopathology and development. In M. Rutter & L. Hersov (Eds.), *Child and adolescent psychiatry* (pp. 720–739). Oxford: Blackwell Scientific Publications.

Rutter, M. (1985b). Resilience in the face of adversity. Protective factors and resistance to psychiatric disorders. *The British Journal of Psychiatry, 147,* 598–611.

Rutter, M. (1992, November). *Youth in the year 2000.* Paper presented at the conference "Youth in the Year 2000," Marbach Castle, Germany.

Rutter, M., Graham, P., Chadwick, O. F. D., & Yule, W. (1976). Adolescent turmoil: Fact or fiction? *Journal of Child Psychology and Psychiatry, 17,* 36–56.

Rutter, M., Quinton, D., & Yule, W. (1976). *Family pathology and disorder in the children.* London: Will.

Sachs, J. (1977). The relationships of ego strength, guilt, and moral attitudes in disturbed adolescents and their parents as a function of style of adolescents' coping behavior. *Dissertation Abstracts International, 37,* 4703.

Sanchez-Craig, B. M. (1976). Cognitive and behavioral coping strategies in the reappraisal of stressful social situations. *Journal of Counselling Psychology, 23,* 7–12.

Savin-Williams, R. C., & Berndt, T. J. (1990). Friendship and peer relations. In S. S. Feldman & G. R. Elliott (Eds.), *At the threshold: The developing adolescent* (pp. 277–307). Cambridge, MA: Harvard University Press.

Schaefer, C. E. (1969). Imaginary companions and creative adolescents. *Developmental Psychology, 1,* 747–749.

Schell, M. A. (1976). The effectiveness of modeling in altering unadaptive responses to failure in children. *Dissertation Abstracts International, 36,* 5282.

Schilhab, J. A. (1977). Influence of psycho-social factors in a newly integrated school. *Dissertation Abstracts International, 37,* 7650–7651.

Schinke, P., Schilling, R. F., & Snow, W. (1987). Stress management at the junior high transition: An outcome evaluation of coping skills intervention. *Journal of Human Stress, 13,* 16–22.

Schneewind, K. (1987). Familienentwicklung [Family development]. In R. Oerter & L. Montada (Eds.), *Entwicklungspsychologie* (pp. 971–1015). München: Psychologie Verlags Union.

Schulenberg, J., Goldstein, A., & Vondracek, F. W. (1991). Gender effects in adolescents' career interests: Beyond main effects. *Journal of Research in Adolescence, 1,* 37–62.

Seiffge-Krenke, I. (1974). *Probleme und Ergebnisse der Kreativitätsforschung* [Problems and results of research on creativity]. Bern: Huber.

Seiffge-Krenke, I. (1985). Die Funktion des Tagebuchs bei der Bewältigung alterstypischer Probleme im Jugendalter [The function of diaries for coping with age-dependent problems in adolescence]. In R. Oerter (Ed.), *Daseinsbewältigung im Jugendalter* (pp. 126–153). Weinheim: Edition Psychologie.

Seiffge-Krenke, I. (1986). Problembewältigung im Jugendalter: Übersichtsreferat [Coping in adolescence: A review]. *Zeitschrift für Entwicklungspsychologie und Pädagogische Psychologie, 18,* 122–252.

Seiffge-Krenke, I. (1987). Eine aktualisierte deutschsprachige Form des OFFER-Self-Concept-Questionnaires [A revised German version of the OFFER-Self-Concept-Questionnaire]. *Zeitschrift für Diagnostik und Differentielle Psychologie, 8,* 99–109.

Seiffge-Krenke, I. (1989). Testing the Bereiter model of writing: Cognitive and communicative aspects of diary writing during adolescence. In H. Mandl, E. de Corte, S. N. Bennett, & H. F. Friedrich (Eds.), *Learning and instruction. European Research in an international context* (pp. 385–396). Oxford: Pergamon.

Seiffge-Krenke, I. (1990a). Developmental processes in self-concept and coping behavior. In H. Bosma & S. Jackson (Eds.), *Self concept and coping in adolescence* (pp. 457–478). New York: Springer.

Seiffge-Krenke, I. (1990b). Coping and health-related behavior: A cross-cultural perspective. In K. Hurrelmann & F. Lösel (Eds.), *Health hazards in adolescence* (pp. 339–360). New York: de Gruyter.

Seiffge-Krenke, I. (1992). Coping behavior of Finnish adolescents: Remarks on a cross-cultural comparison. *Scandinavian Journal of Psychology, 33,* 301–314.

Seiffge-Krenke, I. (1993a). Coping behavior in normal and clinical samples: More similarities than differences? *Journal of Adolescence, 16,* 285–304.

Seiffge-Krenke, I. (1993b). Close friendships and imaginary companions in adolescence. In B. Laursen (Ed.), *Close friendship in adolescence* (pp. 73–88). San Francisco: Jossey Bass.

Seiffge-Krenke, I. (1994). *Close friendship in adolescent diaries.* Unpublished paper.

Seiffge-Krenke, I. (1995). *Health psychology in adolescence: Physical and psychological aspects.* Hillsdale, NJ: Lawrence Erlbaum Associates.

Seiffge-Krenke, I., & Shulman, S. (1990). Coping style in adolescence: A cross-cultural study. *Journal of Cross-Cultural Psychology, 21,* 351–377.

Selman, R. L. (1980). *The growth of interpersonal understanding.* New York: Academic Press.

Sharabany, R., Gershoni, R., & Hofman, J. E. (1981). Girlfriend, boyfriend: Age and sex differences in intimate friendship. *Developmental Psychology, 17,* 800–808.

Sharma, P., Sarawathi, T. S., & Gir, S. (1981). Role of parents and teachers in promoting social competence in children. *Child Psychiatry Quarterly, 14,* 134–137.

Shulman, S., & Klein, M. M. (1982). The family and adolescence: A conceptual and experimental approach. *Journal of Adolescence, 5,* 219–234.

Shulman, S., Seiffge-Krenke, I., & Samet, N. (1987). Adolescent coping style as a function of perceived family climate. *Journal of Adolescent Research, 2,* 367–381.

Siddique, C. M., & D'Arcy, C. (1984). Adolescence, stress, and psychological well-being. *Journal of Youth and Adolescence, 13,* 459–473.

Sigal, J. J., Silver, D., Rakoff, V., & Ellin, B. (1973). Some second-generation effects of survival of the Nazi persecution. *American Journal of Orthopsychiatry, 43,* 320–327.

Simonton, G. K. (1977). Cross-sectional time series experiments. *Psychological Bulletin, 84,* 489–502.

Slater, E. J., & Rubenstein, E. (1987). Family coping with trauma in adolescents. *Psychiatric Annals, 17,* 786–794.

Slavin, L. A., & Compas, B. E. (1989). The problem of confounding social support and depressive symptoms: A brief report on a college sample. *American Journal of Community Psychology, 17,* 57–65.

Smetana, J. G. (1988). Concepts of self and social convention: Adolescents and parents' reasoning about hypothetical and actual family conflicts. In M. R. Gunnar & W. A. Collins (Eds.), *Development during the transition to adolescence* (pp. 79–122). Hillsdale, NJ: Lawrence Erlbaum Associates.

Smetana, J. G., Yau, J., & Hanson, S. (1991). Conflict resolution in families with adolescents. *Journal of Research on Adolescence, 1,* 189–206.

Smith, R. E., Smoll, F. L., & Ptacek, J. T. (1990). Conjunctive moderator variables in vulnerability and resiliency research: Life stress, social support and coping skills, and adolescent sport injuries. *Journal of Personality and Social Psychology, 58,* 360–370.

Snyder, M. (1987). *Public appearances/Private realities: The psychology of self-monitoring.* New York: Freeman.

Sobel, N. J. (1979). A study in teaching frustration management to disruptive students. *Dissertation Abstracts International, 39,* 5452.

Spielberger, C. D. (Ed.). (1972). *Anxiety: Current trends in theory and research* (Vol. 1). New York: Academic Press.

Spirito, A., Overholser, J. C., & Stark, L. J. (1989). Common problems and coping strategies: II. Findings with adolescent suicide attempters. *Journal of Abnormal Child Psychology, 17,* 213–221.

Sroufe, L. A., & Fleeson, J. (1986). Attachment and the construction of relationships. In W. W. Hartup & Z. Rubin (Eds.), *Relationships and development* (pp. 51–72). Hillsdale, NJ: Lawrence Erlbaum Associates.

Sroufe, L. A., & Rutter, M. (1984). The domain of developmental psychopathology. *Child Development, 54*, 173–189.

Stark, L. J., Spirito, A., Williams, L. A., & Guevremont, D. C. (1989). Common problems and coping strategies: I. Findings with normal adolescents. *Journal of Abnormal Child Psychology, 17*, 203–212.

Statistisches Bundesamt (Ed.). (1990). *Statistisches Jahrbuch für die Bundesrepublik Deutschland* [Statistical Yearbook of the Federal Republic of Germany]. Stuttgart: Kohlhammer.

Steinberg, L. D. (1981). Transformations in family relations at puberty. *Developmental Psychology, 17*, 833–840.

Steinberg, L. D. (1989). Reciprocal relation between parent-child distance and pubertal maturation. *Developmental Psychology, 24*, 122–128.

Steinberg, M. A. (1974). Children's coping behaviors related to father absence. *Dissertation Abstracts International, 35*, 490.

Stern, M., & Zevon, M. A. (1990). Stress, coping, and family environment. *Journal of Adolescent Research, 5*, 290–305.

Stevens, M. S. (1988). Application of a stress and coping framework to one adolescent's experience with hospitalization. *Maternal-Child Nursing Journal, 17*, 51–61.

Stevens, M. S. (1989). Coping strategies of hospitalized adolescents. *Children's Health Care, 18*, 163–169.

Stoddard, F. J. (1982). Coping with pain: A developmental approach to treatment of burned children. *American Journal of Psychiatry, 139*, 736–740.

Stone, A. A., & Neale, J. M. (1984). New measure of daily coping: Development and preliminary results. *Journal of Personality and Social Psychology, 46*, 892–906.

Stuart, J. C., & Brown, B. M. (1981). The relationship of stress and coping ability of incidence of diseases and accidents. *Journal of Psychosomatic Research, 25*(4), 255–260.

Sullivan, H. S. (1953). *The interpersonal theory of psychiatry.* New York: Norton.

Swearingen, E. M., & Cohen, L. H. (1985). Life events and psychological distress: A prospective study of young adolescents. *Developmental Psychology, 21*, 1045–1054.

Temoshok, L., Riess, B. F., Rubin, R., & Leahy, R. (1978). Assessment and training in effective decision making for juveniles in trouble. *Corrective and Social Psychiatry and Journal of Behavior Technology, Methods and Therapy, 24*, 115–122.

Terr, L. C. (1979). Children of Chowchilla: A study of psychic trauma. *Psychoanalytic Study of the Child, 34*, 547–632.

Terr, L. C. (1983). Chowchilla revisited: The effects of psychic trauma four years after a school-bus kidnapping. *The American Journal of Psychiatry, 140*, 1543–1550.

Thearle, L., & Weinreich-Haste, H. (1986). Ways of dealing with the nuclear threat: Coping and defense among British adolescents. *International Journal of Mental Health, 15*, 126–142.

Thompson, C. P. (1982). Diary-keeping as a sex-role behavior. *Bulletin of the Psychonomic Society, 20*, 11–13.

Thomson, B., & Vaux, A. (1986). The importation, transmission, and moderation of stress in the family system. *American Journal of Community Psychology, 14*, 39–57.

Tobin-Richards, M. H., Boxer, A. M., & Petersen, A. C. (1983). The psychological significance of pubertal change. Sex differences in perceptions of self during early adolescence. In D. Brooks-Gunn & A. C. Petersen (Eds.), *Girls at puberty* (pp. 127–154). New York: Plenum Press.

Tolor, A., & Fehon, D. (1987). Coping with stress: A study of male adolescents' coping strategies as related to adjustment. *Journal of Adolescent Research, 2*(1), 33–42.

Torrance, P. E. (1962). Developing creative thinking through school experience. In S. J. Parnes & H. F. Harding (Eds.), *A source book for creative thinking* (pp. 31–48). New York: Charles Scribner's Sons.

Torrance, P. E. (1966). *Torrance Tests of Creative Thinking. Verbal Tests, Form A and B. Figural Tests, Form A and B.* Princeton, NJ: Personnel Press.

270

REFERENCES

Torrance, P. E. (1975). Assessing children, teachers, and parents against the ideal child criterion. *Gifted Child Quarterly, 19*(2), 130–139.

Tramontana, M. G. (1980). Critical review of research on psychotherapy outcome with adolescents. *Psychological Bulletin, 88*, 429–450.

Tyler, F. B. (1978). Individual psychosocial competence: A personality configuration. *Educational and Psychological Measurement, 38*, 309–323.

Tyszkowa, M. (1993). Adolescents' relationships with grandparents: Characteristics and developmental transformations. In S. Jackson & H. Rodriguez-Tomé (Eds.), *Adolescence and its social worlds* (pp. 121–144). Hillsdale, NJ: Lawrence Erlbaum Associates.

Vaillant, G. E. (1977). *Adaptation to life.* Boston: Little, Brown.

Vandewiele, M. (1980). On boredom of secondary school students in Senegal. *Journal of Genetic Psychology, 137*(2), 267–274.

Varni, J. W., Rubenfeld, L. A., Talbot, D., & Setoguchi, Y. (1989). Stress, social support, and depressive symptomatology in children with congenital/acquired limb deficiencies. *Journal of Pediatric Psychology, 14*, 515–530.

Vernberg, E. M. (1990). Psychological adjustment and experiences with peers during early adolescence: Reciprocal, incidental, or unidirectional relationships? *Journal of Abnormal Child Psychology, 18*, 187–198.

Vuchinich, S. (1987). Starting and stopping spontaneous family conflicts. *Journal of Marriage and the Family, 49*, 591–601.

Wagner, B. M., & Compas, B. E. (1990). Gender, instrumentality and expressivity: Moderators of the relation between stress and psychological symptoms during adolescence. *American Journal of Community Psychology, 18*, 383–406.

Wagner, B. M., Compas, B. E., & Howell, D. C. (1988). Daily and major life events: A test of an integrative model of psychosocial stress. *American Journal of Community Psychology, 16*, 189–205.

Walker, L. S., & Greene, J. W. (1987). Negative life events, psychological sources, and psychophysiological symptoms in adolescents. *Journal of Clinical Child Psychology, 16*, 29–36.

Wayment, H. A., & Zetlin, A. G. (1989). Coping responses of adolescents with and without mild learning handicaps. *Mental Retardation, 27*, 311–316.

Weight, J. A. (1979). Youth suicide: A study of common characteristics found among youths who committed suicide in four Utah counties 1970 through 1976. *Dissertation Abstracts International, 40*, 113.

Weinberg, S. (1968). Seminars in nursing care of the adolescent. *Nursing Outlook, 16*, 18–23.

Weinberger, G., & Reuter, M. (1980). The "life discussion" group as a means of facilitating personal growth and development in adolescence. *Journal of Clinical Child Psychology, 9*, 6–12.

Wellisch, D. K. (1979). Adolescent acting out when a parent has cancer. *International Journal of Family Therapy, 1*, 230–241.

Werner, E. E., & Smith, R. S. (Eds.). (1982). *Vulnerable but invincible. A study of resilient children.* New York: McGraw-Hill.

Wertlieb, D., Weigel, C., & Feldstein, M. (1987). Measuring children's coping. *American Journal of Orthopsychiatry, 57*, 548–560.

Westbrook, M. T. (1979). A classification of coping behavior based on multidimensional scaling of similarity ratings. *Journal of Clinical Psychology, 35*, 407–410.

Wills, T. A. (1986). Stress and coping in early adolescence: Relationships to substance use in urban school samples. *Health Psychology, 5*, 503–529.

Wohlwill, J (1977). Strategien entwicklungspsychologischer Forschung [Strategies of developmental psychological research]. Stuttgart: Klett-Cotta.

Wolchik, S. A., Braver, S. L., & Sandler, I. N. (1985). Maternal versus joint custody: Children's postseparation experiences and adjustment. *Journal of Clinical Child Psychology, 14*(1), 5–10.

Woodward, J. C., & Frank, B. D. (1988). Rural adolescent loneliness and coping strategies. *Adolescence, 23*, 559–565.

Wright, P. H. (1984). Self-referent motivation and the intrinsic quality of friendship. *Journal of Social and Personal Relationships, 1*, 115–130.

Wrubel, J., Brenner, P., & Lazarus, R. S. (1981). Social competence from the perspective of stress and coping. In J. D. Wine & M. D. Smye (Eds.), *Social competence* (pp. 61–99). New York: Guilford Press.

Young, D. M. (1980). A court-mandated workshop for adolescent children of divorcing parents: A program evaluation. *Adolescence, 15*, 763–774.

Youniss, J. (1980). *Parents and peers in social development.* Chicago: University of Chicago Press.

Youniss, J., & Smollar, J. (1985). *Adolescent relationships with mothers, fathers, and friends.* Chicago: University of Chicago Press.

Zlatich, D., Kenny, Th. J., Sila, U., & Huang, Sh. W. (1982). Parent-child life events: Relation to treatment in asthma. *Journal of Developmental and Behavioral Pediatrics, 3*, 69–72.

Author Index

Subject Index